AMERICAN MARTIAL ARTS ALLIANCE FOUNDATION

2ND Edition

AMAA LEGACY BOOK

A MARTIAL ARTS BIOGRAPHY ANTHOLOGY

10 YEARS ANNIVERSARY

EDITION

GRAND MASTER JESSIE BOWEN

Elite
PUBLICATIONS

AMAA Legacy Book 10th Anniversary Edition: A Martial Arts Biography Anthology 2nd Edition

by Grandmaster Jessie Bowen

Copyright © 2024 Elite Publications

Cover & interior design by Tiger Shark, Inc.

FIRST PRINTING: JULY 2024

SECOND EDITION: NOVEMBER 2024

PAPERBACK ISBN-13: 978-1-958037-25-6

HARDCOVER ISBN-13: 978-1-958037-26-3

KINDLE & EBOOK ISBN-13: 978-1-958037-27-0

Ordering Information: Special discounts are available on quantity purchases by corporations, associations, educators, and others. For details, contact the publisher at the below address. U.S. trade bookstores and wholesalers: please contact Jessie Bowen at (919) 618-8075 or via email to info@elitepublications.org.

Published by:

2120 E Firetower Rd, #107-58,

Greenville, NC 27858

Phone: (919) 618-8075

info@elitepublications.org

http://www.elitepublications.org/

LIBRARY OF CONGRESS CONTROL NO: 2024911862

PRINTED IN THE UNITED STATES OF AMERICA

MEET THE AMAA BOOK PROJECT TEAM

PUBLISHER:

Elite Publications

2120 E. Firetower Rd #107-58

Greenville, NC 27858

www.elitepublications.org

CONTENT EDITORS:

Jessica C. Phillips

Krystal Harvey

ASSOCIATE EDITOR:

Dr. Gwendolyn Bowen

DIRECTOR OF MARKETING:

Jessica C. Phillips

INTERIOR DESIGN & BOOK COVER:

Krystal Harvey

Tiger Shark, Inc.

www.tigersharkmediausa.com

CONTRIBUTOR:

Master Toby Milroy

TABLE OF
CONTENTS

TABLE OF
CONTENTS

WHO'S WHO IN THE MARTIAL ARTS
MARTIAL ARTS LEGACY
A Journey of a Thousand Miles...

ACKNOWLEDGEMENTS BY GRAND MASTER JESSIE BOWEN, PHD.

A Chinese proverb states, "A journey of a thousand miles begins with a single step." This proverb perfectly encapsulates the story behind the creation of the Who's Who Martial Arts Legacy book series. I want to express my heartfelt gratitude to those who have supported and inspired us over the past ten years, allowing us to transform a simple idea into an internationally acclaimed publishing company.

The inception of this series was inspired by the groundbreaking work of Dale Brooks and Jan Wellendorf, publishers of *Who's Who in American Karate* in the early 80s, and my martial arts instructors. Their invaluable contributions through their books *Essentials of American Karate, Ki, Kata, and Combat,* which are the foundation books of American Karate,

have played a pivotal role in shaping the martial arts community. As their student, I am truly privileged to have firsthand knowledge of the significance of legacy in the martial arts.

I would also like to extend my sincere appreciation to my wife, Dr. Gwendolyn Bowen, and my daughter, Jessica C. Phillips. Your unwavering support and countless hours dedicated to bringing this project to fruition have been instrumental. This project would not have been possible without you. Krystal Harvey, thank you for your hard work, commitment, and creative vision.

Furthermore, I would like to express a special thank you to Grandmasters Jan Wellendorf, Dale Brooks, Cynthia Rothrock, Bill Clark, Joe Corley, Jhoon Rhee, Jeff Smith, Bill "Superfoot" Wallace, Pat Johnson, Stephen K. Hayes, Chuck Norris, Ernie Reyes, Sr., Ron Van Clief, Toby Milroy, and the over 1,000 martial artists who have shared their martial arts journey in the Who's Who in the Martial Arts Biography Book Series. Your contributions have been invaluable, and it is our fervent desire that these individuals will forever live on through the pages of the Martial Arts Legacy book series.

Hanshi Jessie Bowen

Founder & President
American Martial Arts Alliance Foundation
Elite Publications
www.whoswhointhemartialarts.com
www.elitepublications.org

AMERICAN MARTIAL ARTS ALLIANCE FOUNDATION

WHO'S WHO IN THE MARTIAL ARTS
HONORING OUR MARTIAL ARTS HEROES

Shining the Spotlight...

FOREWORD BY MASTER TOBY MILROY

Dear Reader,

Whether you're deeply familiar with martial arts or not, I think you'll agree that you see martial arts everywhere! You likely even see martial arts schools in your local shopping center, in the movies, on television, and in major sporting events like the UFC and the Olympics.

Some of the biggest stars in the world are martial artists. Chuck Norris, Jason Statham, Bruce Lee, Joe Rogan, the Gracies, and more have become household names, but there is a huge community of dedicated, hardworking, honorable martial artists who seek neither fame nor fortune but rather simply to share their art with the world.

I see the results of martial arts every day. As a veteran

multi-school operator with thousands of students, former Chief Operating Officer of the National Association of Professional Martial Artists, the Executive Vice-President of Amerinational Management Services, and the Publisher for Martial Arts World News Magazine, I sit in the "crows' nest" of the industry, where I can see it from a bird's eye view. I've personally dedicated my life to helping students gain the benefits of high-quality martial arts and to providing school owners, instructors, masters, and grandmasters the systems, tools, and technology they need to grow their businesses and positively impact more people through martial arts.

These unsung heroes spend their days pouring their hearts out, teaching their students, young and old, helping them overcome obstacles in their daily lives, and almost magically transforming into better versions of themselves. Powerful personal transformations quietly happen every day in martial arts schools, dojos, dojangs, clubs, and academies all over the world.

So, when Grandmaster Jessie Bowen asked me to write this foreword to his new book, AMAA Foundation 10th Anniversary Martial Arts Legacy Biography Book, I not only considered it an honor but also a deep responsibility to help shed light on the powerful, life-changing work the esteemed martial artists profiled in this book are doing.

I've known and worked with Grandmaster Bowen for many years; he is an expert in life success, sports performance training, and international business coaching. He is a corporate educator for Duke Corporate Education and trains executives to break through barriers to achieve their next level of success. He is the former school owner of Karate International of Durham, Inc., and founder of Elite Publications, the American Martial Arts Alliance Foundation, the American Martial Arts Alliance Institute, and Elite Corporate Coaching.

His diverse educational background—holding a bachelor's degree in business, a Master's degree in Christian Counseling, a PhD in Humanities, and a Doctorate in martial science—arm him with the skills and strategies to help his fellow martial artists take their personal and professional lives to new levels.

He has served as a member of the physical education staff at Duke University for over 28 years, where he taught martial arts, mindfulness training, and bowling. His impact as a martial arts instructor is evident in the thousands of lives he has touched through his teaching.

Grandmaster Bowen is also a columnist and frequent contributor to *Martial Arts World News Magazine*, the industry trade journal for professional martial artists, sharing his knowledge, philosophy, and experience with thousands of martial arts school owners, instructors, masters, and grandmasters worldwide.

As part of Grandmaster Bowen's ongoing mission, his publishing company works with experienced martial artists and instructors to help them share their stories and wisdom with people who may otherwise not benefit from their lessons.

Grandmaster Bowen and his team hand-selected the dedicated martial artists featured in this anthology because of their dedication to excellence, commitment to their training and students, and contributions to their communities and our industry.

As you review each of the outstanding martial artists he's chosen for this honor, I think you'll begin to see why they are shining examples of excellence, peak performance, traditional values, honorable character, and dedication to the pursuit of the perfection of their personal character.

Each provides a profile in leadership and is a role model for anyone aspiring to improve their lives, relationships, professions, or families.

It's again my great honor to introduce to you Grandmaster Jessie Bowen and some of the most important martial artists in the world through the *AMAA Foundation 10th Anniversary Martial Arts Legacy Biography Book*.

Yours for success,

Master Toby Milroy

Executive Vice-President AMS

Executive Vice-President ATLAS Martial Arts Software

Publisher Martial Arts World News Magazine

1

WHO'S WHO IN THE MARTIAL ARTS
THE AMERICAN MARTIAL ARTS ALLIANCE

The Evolution...

The Genesis:

Grand Master Jessie Bowen established the American Martial Arts Alliance Foundation and Institute, previously known as the American Martial Arts Alliance Sport Karate Hall of Fame, Inc. His motivation stemmed from personal encounters with organizations that exploited individuals.

After achieving the rank of 8th-degree black belt, Hanshi Bowen stepped away from karate competition. He shifted his focus to his martial arts school, Karate International Durham Inc., and his tournament, the Durham Karate Open, which he hosted for nearly four decades. In 2001, an invitation to compete in the Karate Olympic trials in Honolulu, Hawaii, rekindled his competitive spirit. Despite being out of competition for over two years, he immediately began training for this seemingly once-in-a-lifetime chance.

Investing significantly in competition fees, travel, and accommodations, Bowen arrived in Hawaii with high hopes. However, the event turned out to be a scam. Participants gathered at the gym, waiting in vain for other countries to arrive. The tournament eventually started, but even local martial artists were absent. Many attendees fell victim to this deception,

highlighting the vulnerability of martial artists pursuing their dreams. This experience challenged the notion that all martial artists are inherently honest.

In response to this incident, Grandmaster Bowen launched the American Martial Arts Alliance and its Hall of Fame in 2001. Over the next 16 years, the organization united martial artists across the southeast, organizing tournaments and events. The success of the 2017 American Martial Arts Alliance Sport Karate League and Hall of Fame event inspired Grandmaster Bowen to expand his vision, leading to the establishment of the American Martial Arts Alliance Foundation and Institute.

The Foundation, a 501(c)(3) non-profit, focuses on education and scholarship funding for martial arts

athletes through its Future Leaders program. In 2023, it introduced the Future Leaders Scholarship Fund and the Cynthia Rothrock Scholarship Fund. The organization has also partnered with Elite Publications, becoming an official publisher for its clients. The Institute offers online classes and personal development training in marketing, coaching, and mentorship. The organization welcomes martial artists and schools seeking alignment with its mission and benefits.

The Biography Book Series: A Legacy in Print:

The organization's journey into publishing began in 2015 with a book honoring Grandmaster Bowen's teachers, Grandmasters Jan Wellendorf and Dale Brooks, founders of Karate International of North Carolina. This franchise organization impacted thousands of martial artists through schools across North Carolina.

Grandmaster Bowen, who owned a Karate International franchise from 1980 to 2018, drew inspiration from his teachers' earlier publication, "Who's Who in American Martial Arts" (1982-1984). This led to the creation of the Who's Who in the Martial Arts Biography Book series.

The series has evolved into a trilogy, with Martial Artists Changing Lives being the third installment. The first series was titled Who's Who in the Martial Arts, followed by Masters and Pioneers in the Martial Arts.

These publications serve as a testament to the rich history and ongoing evolution of martial arts, preserving the legacies of countless practitioners worldwide. They not only document the achievements of individual martial artists but also highlight the profound impact of martial arts on personal development and community building.

The success of these biography series underscores the martial arts community's desire for recognition and the preservation of its heritage. By featuring thousands of martial artists from around the globe, these books have become a valuable resource for inspiration, education, and historical documentation within the martial arts world.

The American Martial Arts Alliance Foundation continues to build on this literary legacy, using these publications as a platform to celebrate the diversity, dedication, and transformative power of martial arts. As the American Martial Arts Alliance moves forward, it remains committed to its core values of education, integrity, and community service, all while adapting to the changing landscape of martial arts in the 21st century.

The American Martial Arts Alliance is committed to the ongoing expansion and development of the martial arts community. It will continue to "Empower Martial Artists to Inspire the World."

WHO'S WHO IN THE MARTIAL ARTS SERIES TRIBUTE:

2015 - Jan Wellendorf and Dale Brooks

2016 - Cynthia Rothrock

2017 - Bill Clark, Joe Corley, Jhoon Rhee, Jeff Smith, Bill "Superfoot" Wallace

MARTIAL ARTS MASTERS AND PIONEERS SERIES TRIBUTE:

2018 - Pat Johnson

2019 - Stephen K. Hayes

2020 - Chuck Norris

MARTIAL ARTISTS CHANGING LIVES SERIES TRIBUTE:

2021 - Ernie Reyes, Sr

2022 - Bill "Superfoot" Wallace

2023 - Cynthia Rothrock

MARTIAL ARTS EXTRAORDINAIRE SERIES TRIBUTE:

2021 - Ron Van Clief

AMAA LEGACY SERIES TRIBUTE:

2024 - Featuring Past Tribute Honorees

SCAN TO OWN A PIECE OF
Martial Arts History...

GRAND MASTER BILL CLARK
MARTIAL ARTS INNOVATOR & VISIONARY
TOUCHING HUNDREDS OF THOUSANDS OF LIVES.

The new Grand Master Clark began his martial arts saga in 1966 in Omaha, Nebraska. He joined Eternal Grand Master H.U. Lee's first martial arts school in 1968 in the first steps of his life and industry changing voyage.

After achieving second degree black belt rank, with the urging and support of Master Lee, Bill Clark opened his first academy in Jacksonville, Florida in 1971. His work ethic, mixed with an exceptional fighter's heart, a quick wit and a sense of loyalty second-to-none, paved the path for success in his first school.

In an expedition that has included world class everything—point fighting, kickboxing, teaching, staff development, management, television commentary, judging, refereeing, seminars, organizing and so much more—Grand Master Clark has Walked the Talk of *EXCELLENCE.*

Grand Master Bill Clark became 9th Degree Grand Master William Clark in June, 2016, some five decades after his martial arts journey began. In a moving and spectacular presentation in Little Rock at the ATA World Championship, the organization and its leaders and members showed their appreciation for his lifetime of dedication with the highest rank bestowed on its Masters. In this nearly five-decade journey, Master Clark has touched hundreds of thousands of lives, from students to Chief Masters to friends and associates around the globe.

TRAINING INFORMATION

- Belt Rank/Titles: 9th Degree Black Belt (ATA), 9th Degree Black Belt (Warrior System), and 10th Degree Black Belt (PKA)

- Instructors/Influencers: Eternal Grand Master H.U. Lee

- Birthplace/Growing Up: Jacksonville, FL

- Yrs. In the Martial Arts: 56 years

FROM WHITE BELT TO GRANDMASTER

Grand Master Clark was born in Jacksonville, Florida where he grew up. He later moved to Omaha, NE to work with his uncle.

- 1966: He started his Martial Arts training in Omaha, Nebraska studying Aikido

- 1968: Trained with Eternal Grand Master HU Lee at Midwest Karate Federation (later known as ATA). During this time, he met and trained with lifelong friends Grand Master Richard Reed and Grand Master Robert Allimeir.

- 1970s: During this decade Master Clark was an integral part of the foundation of the ATA, helping organize & standardize ATA tournaments, helping write the original curriculum instructor's manual and the Scrolls of Songahm (describes the essence and tradition of the martial art). Ranked 8th in SEKA, KI, PKA

- 1971: After receiving the rank of 2nd Degree Black Belt Grand Master Clark headed back home to Jacksonville, Florida to open his first school. It consisted of 900 square feet, no bigger than a two- car garage.

- 1972: After only one year and testing 740 students, Master Clark had to relocate the facility to a stand-alone structure with two training floors, saunas, fitness equipment and offices.

- 1974: Master Clark was awarded ATA Instructor of the year. He also helped set up the ATA Top 10 structure for tournaments and new rules for competition.

- 1976: In addition to his many accomplishments with the ATA that year, Master Clark was an avid fighter in the PKA (Professional Karate Association) and was awarded the PKA fighter of the year award.

- 1978: He officially retired from the tournament circuit after winning the PKA Championships and the ATA Grand National Title

FROM WHITE BELT TO GRANDMASTER

- 1980s: While on the Founders Council of the ATA, helped Eternal Grand Master H.U. Lee create the new Songahm forms with Master Allimeir and Master G.H. Lee

- 1982: Master Clark opened his 2nd and 3rd schools in Jacksonville, to continue the growth of the ATA. Eternal Grand Master H.U. Lee awarded him the Presidential Achievement Award

- 1990s: Master Clark focused on program development for the ATA, helping to bring in weapons training and the Black Belt Club program. He designed and implemented sales procedures for the martial arts industry and became perhaps the most sought after speaker at yearly events such as the Martial Arts Industry Association Supershow, National Association of Professional Martial Artists (NAPMA) convention and others.

- 1997: Received Battle of Atlanta Centurion Award

- 2000s: Master Clark introduced a number of new martial arts styles to the ATA, creating programs that integrated Krav Maga, Kali and street self-defense into the current training.

- 2012: Master Clark was inducted into the International Martial Arts Hall of Fame.

- 2013: Received the Joe Lewis Eternal Warrior Award

- 2013: Received the Martial Arts Industry Association's Lifetime Achievement Award for his dedication to the martial arts.

- 2015: Earned the rank of Grand Master 9th degree Black Belt with the World Black Belt Association.

- 2016: Earns Grand Master Rank alongside lifelong friend Rob Allemeier.

- 2016: GM Clark wrote and filmed the first PERSONAL GROWTH program for Martial Artists. GM Clark continues to be focused on real-life Leadership Development, to ensure Eternal Grand Master H.U. Lee's vision is faithfully carried into the future.

- 2017: Featured on the cover of Who's Who Legends with lifelong friends Bill Wallace, Jeff Smith and Joe Corley.

- 2018-19: The introduction of the new global website TheEvolutionofKrav.com to augment the incredibly well organized Warrior Krav Maga System. Check it Out!

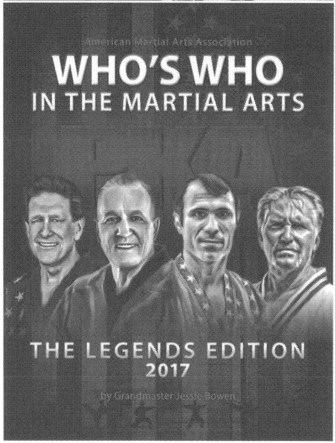

GRAND MASTER JOE CORLEY
PKA WORLDWIDE & THE BATTLE OF ATLANTA
MARTIAL ARTS INNOVATOR: THE SHOULDERS OF GREATNESS.

focus, personal discipline and integrity engendered by good martial arts training and competition. He has done that by promoting martial arts in his Atlanta chain of studios, his Battle of Atlanta World Karate Championship, and on television worldwide.

Corley began his karate classes at age 16, earned his black belt at 19, opened his first studio at 19, won three US titles in the next three years, founded the Battle of Atlanta at age 23, and has spread the word ever since. Joe has sought to share the most practical physical karate movements available and combine those real-life defensive techniques with modern American positive philosophy.

There are only a handful of men in martial arts anywhere in the world who have accomplished so much to further the martial arts philosophy and physical applications. As a fighter, Joe Corley won three United States Championships in point karate and retired as the number one ranked Middle Weight contender globally. Now a 10th-degree Black Belt in American Karate, Mr. Corley and his Black Belts have taught more than 50,000 men, women, and children in his chain of Atlanta studios.

As a Black Belt in Tang Soo Do, he opened Atlanta's first full-time karate studio in 1967 while he was still competing and expanded the studios to become the most well-known martial arts chain in the Southeast at that time.

In 1970, Joe Corley founded the BATTLE OF ATLANTA, one of the most prestigious open karate tournaments in the world. The Battle of Atlanta recently completed its 54th Anniversary. The Battle, now owned and produced by Truth Entertainment, again hosted competitors from all over the world.

A tlanta's Joe Corley is still a black belt and sports entrepreneur with a mission, most recently honored for Lifetime Achievement in 2019 Who's Who in Martial Arts and on the cover of the 2017 LEGENDS edition of the AMAA Who's Who in the Martial Arts 2017 edition. Now a Grand Master instructor with more than five decades of experience in the martial arts and the producer of PKA KARATE & KICKBOXING for television, Corley's life-long purpose for being has been to share with everyone the positive feelings of confidence, courage, intensity,

In the early '70s, Art Heller joined Joe Corley, Sam Chapman, Bill McDoanald, Larry Reinhardt, and Jack Motley ina meeting with Chuck Norris to kick off the South East Karate Association (SEKA) from which so any great Southeast Championsemerged.

In 1975, Joe Corley challenged Bill "Superfoot" Wallace for his PKA World Middleweight Title in what became a historic fight before 12,000 fans in Atlanta's Omni. Wallace won the first-of-its-kind 9-round bout. Master Corley would later be hired by CBS to cover Superfoot's future bouts because of his ability to articulate the inner workings of the sport and the techniques and strategies of the fighters.

Because of the great ratings at CBS, Master Corley also became the voice for American Karate and PKA KICKBOXING on other networks. He actually produced the programming and did commentary with long-term friends like Chuck Norris and the late Pat Morita (Mr. Miyagi) on NBC, CBS, ESPN, SHOWTIME, USA NETWORK, TURNER SPORTS, SPORTS CHANNEL AMERICA, PRIME NETWORK, SPORTSOUTH, and on international television syndication. As an expert analyst and host for PKA KARATE World Championships on the network, cable, and pay-per-view, Mr. Corley became synonymous with the sport to the millions of fans who followed the 1,000+ hours of coverage on television.

With events originating from such diverse locales as Canada, France, Belgium, South Africa, South America, and the United Arab Emirates, plus 50 cities in the United States, Joe Corley has educated 4 generations of sports fans.

Master Corley has been named Official Karate Magazine's Man of the Decade, was inducted into the prestigious Black Belt Magazine Hall of Fame and the International Tae Kwon Do Hall of Fame, and has received more awards than anyone can count.

But the thing that continues to drive Joe Corley is the knowledge that he and his accomplished associates can use all their experiences to share with everyone around the world on television the great feelings of confidence, courage, discipline, honor, and integrity that come from presenting the martial arts properly. His PKA WORLDWIDE KICKBOXING projects are the perfect vehicles to spread the messages of positive martial arts on a global scale.

"The unequaled success of the UFC, built on our previous successes, has set the stage for PKA Fighters to achieve the 'fame and fortune' the athletes of the UFC are now enjoying," he said.Joe is in regular meetings with astute sports entrepreneurs in order to kick off the new project for 2023 and beyond. "We have the UFC's own research to indicate the timing is perfect for us now," he said. At the same time, he is building the grassroots for PKA WORLDWIDE Associated Schools and Members with Don Willis— PKA Director of Membership–bringing together the best martial artists from around the globe.

Mr. Corley's bride–Christina– is his right arm and chief administrator in PKA WORLDWIDE. Mr. Corley's daughter, Christiana, 26, continues to be his lustrous link in this new millennium and his compelling force to make the martial arts world an even better place.

Master Corley's closest friends point to the PKA (& PKC) 10th Degree Grand Master certificate, saying the language of the certificate reflects the philosophy and humility they know to be the real Joe Corley.

Members, bringing together the best martial artists from around the globe.

Master Corley is consulting with several martial artists to share his experience and wisdom and has been recruited to consult on other projects outside of martial arts. One such project is the introduction of a generation system destined to change the worlds of Solar, Wind Generation, and later stage Electric Vehicles.

"Martial arts provided me with the opportunity to learn so many skills that apply to so many aspects of life," he said. "I look forward to this 'next half' of my time on the planet applying the skills learned. I also fiercely love being a student and look forward to learning as much as possible in this last half. Learning brings me joy", he smiled.

"After 19 years as a 9th Degree Black Belt, I was so proud to earn my 10th Degree from the PKC and Grand Master Glenn Keeney in 2016. I was honored to

have GM Pat Johnson, GM Allen Steen, and GM Pat Burleson approve the PKC promotion. It was doubly sweet because lifelong friend Jeff Smith earned his that same day. These 5 men have greatly influenced my martial arts career in so many ways, and it was so special to share the experience with all of them!"

Joe Corley has been named as Chief Executive Officer at PKA WORLDWIDE. Here he is working alongside PKA Vice Chairman Robert Gutkowski (former President of Madison Square Garden and Vice President of Programming at ESPN), PKA President Jeff Smith, PKA International Ambassador Bill Wallace, and PKA Global Director of Fighter Development Rick Roufus in the PKA HUNT FOR THE GREATEST STRIKERS ON THE PLANET IN 2023 and beyond.

At this printing, Joe and PKA WORLDWIDE had just completed 5 trials in New York, 2 in Texas, and in California and Washington State, where they identified 45 New Age Strikers to compete later in the Semifinals heading to the new PKA World Titles.

In a recent interview, Joe said, "The Combat Sports World, built on the shoulders of the PKA Movement dating back to 1974, is now ready for our new series. WE ARE ON THE HUNT FOR THE GREATEST STRIKERS ON THE PLANET!"

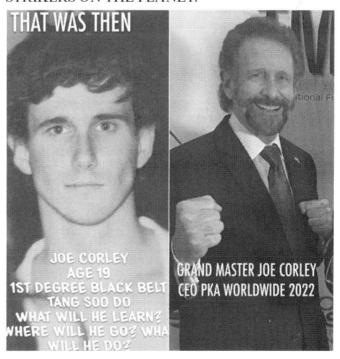

HUMILITY OF A GRANDMASTER
10TH DEGREE CERTIFICATE

One who has achieved the rank of GRAND MASTER in MARTIAL ARTS, in fact,

DOES NOT FEEL WORTHY…

Having BATTLED through the WARRIOR BLACK BELT RANKS OF 1ST, 2ND and 3RD DEGREE

And Having PROUDLY ADMINISTERED the TEACHER / INSTRUCTOR RANKS OF 4TH and 5th DEGREE

And Having SKILLFULLY & MASTERFULLY

EDUCATED THE INSTRUCTORS as a PROFESSOR 6th and 7th DEGREE and

Having CONSISTENTLY and DUTIFULLY GIVEN BACK TO THE MARTIAL ARTS COMMUNITY as 8TH and 9th DEGREE

The GRANDMASTER knows what he does not know; he knows how much there is left to learn.

At the same time, he embodies the sentiments in Master Educator Stephen R. Covey's 7 HABITS and his expression of HUMILITY: "Humility is the mother of all virtues. Courage is the father. Integrity the Child. Wisdom the Grandchild."

Having honorably carried out the BLACK BELT RESPONSIBILITIES above and having demonstrated exceptionally the virtues of

WISDOM, INTEGRITY, COURAGE and HUMILITY

THE PROFESSIONAL KARATE COMMISSION

DOES HEREBY BESTOW UPON

JOE CORLEY

THE GRAND MASTER RANK OF

10th DEGREE BLACK BELT

AN-SHU STEPHEN K. HAYES
LEGENDARY TEACHER, AUTHOR & SPEAKER
ONE OF THE MOST INFLUENTIAL MARTIAL ARTS MASTERS OF OUR TIME.

application to modern 21st century threats and pressures.

Stephen K. Hayes has spent his adult life in pursuit of perfection through Asian martial arts and spiritual traditions. He traveled throughout Japan, Tibet, Nepal, and India to find the best teachers.

A 1971 graduate of Miami University in Oxford, Ohio, he majored in speech and theater. Most notable to American audiences was his role, alongside Richard Chamberlain in the NBC mini-series Shogun.

Stephen K. Hayes began formal training in Asian martial arts as a teenager in the 1960s. By the autumn of 1985, he had earned a place in the prestigious Black Belt Hall of Fame, which honored him for his years of pioneering work introducing the Japanese ninja martial art of "accomplishment through invisible action" to the American public.

He is the founder of the martial art of To-Shin Do, a mind and body self-protection system based on the ancient ninja martial arts principles updated for

Stephen K. Hayes has taught and demonstrated effective self-protection skills to military and law-enforcement groups, including the U.S. Air Force Academy, the FBI Academy, and members of Britain's elite SAS. He has worked on special projects with the United States Defense Intelligence Agency. In 1991, Stephen K. Hayes took ordination to become a teacher of the Buddhist esoteric meditation tradition. He regularly served in the 1990s as a personal protection escort and security advisor for the Dalai Lama of Tibet during the Nobel Peace Prize laureate's North American travels.

Stephen and Rumiko, his wife of 42 years, born in Kumamoto, Japan, now travel the world as teachers. Their presentations inspire by translating their extensive backgrounds in martial and meditative arts into practical lessons for handling the pressures, uncertainties, and stresses of life.

For much of the year, he travels the world as a teacher, seminar leader, and lecturer. His informative and inspiring presentations translate his extensive martial and meditation arts background into practical lessons for handling the pressures, choices, uncertainties, and stresses of life in the modern Western world.

Stephen K. Hayes' interpretation of Japan's ancient warrior path of enlightenment creates a basis for understanding the power of directed intention as a tool for accomplishment. He emphasizes to audiences worldwide: "We must work to cultivate a state of fearlessness in recognition of the reality that there will be times when things do not go how we wish them to. We can learn to live positively and generate the results we need in life by creating a momentum of accomplishment. Our ninja martial arts training program shows us how to begin. It is then up to our own resourcefulness and commitment as to how far we take ourselves." - Stephen K. Hayes

Stephen K. Hayes is a husband, father of two daughters, and grandfather of five, he is a writer, teacher, and student of life. He is the author of over 20 books, which translate the timeless knowledge of the East into pragmatic lessons for contemporary Western life. His books have sold well over a million copies.

GRAND MASTER PAT JOHNSON
INSTRUCTOR & EPIC FIGHT CHOREOGRAPHER
A MENTOR EXTRAORDINAIRE TO MANY AND TO ALL.
1939 – 2023

with Chuck in developing one of the greatest teams of fighters the world has ever known. "Master Johnson set a standard in the Chuck Norris studios that became a model for instructors around the country", Joe Corley said. "When Master Norris invited me first to California to train, he introduced me to Master Johnson who became my mentor, instructor, Big Brother for life. I witnessed first-hand how he handled everyone from the little kids in his Sherman Oaks school to the top-rated instructors in the world to private students like Steve McQueen and the heads of major studios to visiting instructors from around the world. His patience and guidance are without peer, and every life he touched was improved. From where did this ability to guide and influence come?

Pat Johnson was born in Niagara Falls, New York. He was raised in a low-income area where he learned his scrappy fighting style and at the same time learned to appreciate the sincere love of a hard-working mom and nurturing family values. He also learned his strong work ethic, determination and drive here.

G rand Master Pat Johnson has made such an impact in so many lives that you can't even count them", said PKA President and Battle of Atlanta founder Joe Corley.

Most people will recognize first his genius for creating fight scenes in films grossing more than a billion dollars. It was Master Johnson who created the great action in Karate Kid I, II, III and IV, Ninja Turtles I, II and III, Mortal Kombat, Batman and Robin and so many more. Prior to that, he had been the chief instructor and general manager in Chuck Norris' chain of studios in the Los Angeles area where he worked

He began training in traditional Korean Tang Soo Do Moo Duk Kwan in 1963, while stationed in South Korea as a chaplain in the U.S. Army. While under the tutelage of a Korean master named Kang Lo Hee, Johnson earned his black belt in just thirteen months. After his army service ended, Johnson met and formed an association with Tang Soo Do instructor Chuck Norris. Johnson soon rose to the rank of chief instructor at Norris' school in Sherman Oaks, California in 1968. That same year, he formulated a penalty-point system still used by many karate tournaments.

In 1973, Norris founded the National Tang Soo Do Congress (NTC), and named Johnson as executive vice president and chief of instruction. In 1979, Norris disbanded the NTC and formed the United Fighting Arts Federation (UFAF), again naming Johnson as executive vice president.

In 1973, Pat Johnson also crafted the Tournament of Champions idea that Joe Corley implemented at the 1973 Battle of Atlanta, propelling the Battle of Atlanta into national prominence. Master Johnson brought Chuck Norris, Bob Wall, Mike Stone, and Tadashi Yamashita as officials with him, setting the stage for top-notch officiating at the Battle of Atlanta for many years to come.

In 1980, Johnson had a small supporting role in the feature film The Little Dragons (later known as The Karate Kids U.S.A.). In the film, Johnson played the karate instructor to a pair of young brothers (portrayed by Chris and Pat Petersen) who use their martial arts skills to foil a kidnapping plot.

In 1986, Johnson was promoted to ninth-degree black belt. Grand Master Johnson was a mentor, extraordinaire to all he encountered, and in high demand for seminars across the globe.

He is survived by his wife, Sue Johnson, of over 50 years; four sons, and two granddaughters, Lilly and Jolina Felix.

GRAND MASTER CHUCK NORRIS
ICONIC ACTOR AND HUMANITARIAN
LIGHTS. CAMERA. ACTION... AND GIVING BACK FOR A LIFETIME.

In the martial arts world, he is known by one name—Chuck.

In the film world, he is known as the nice guy who plays tough guys, and in real life is as tough as they come. And as nice.

And for those in the martial arts who have worked with him these past six decades, he is known to be a giving, inspirational leader who has positively affected many millions of lives, both directly and indirectly through his chosen fields of influence.

As the Who's Who Pioneers and Masters 2020 edition was being completed, Chuck and his wife Gena were at the Celebration of Life and Funeral Service for his friend of nearly six decades for two hours as he was being laid to rest. It was an assembly of the finest first and second generation American martial arts icons who had fought in the glory fighting era of Skipper Mullins and Chuck Norris.

Assigned the role of "honorary pallbearer" in the service program, the Mullins family said to Chuck "Sit here with Gena, and the young guys here will do the heavy lifting." Chuck's immediate response was, "No way. Skipper was my friend." These six words reflect the life attitude of Carlos Ray Norris, just two months after celebrating his 8th decade on the planet.

The American Martial Arts Alliance proudly dedicates this 2020 edition to the life and career of Grand Master Norris and his incomparable impact on American Martial Arts for these past six decades.

Born Carlos Ray Norris in Ryan, Oklahoma on March 10, 1940, Chuck was the eldest of his two brothers. Chuck's brother Wieland Norris, born July 12, 1943 was KIA in Vietnam in 1970.

Aaron Norris, the youngest of the three, has done everything with Chuck from producing and directing their film and television projects to serving as Chairman for United Fighting Arts Federation. The Norris family relocated to Torrance, California when Chuck was 12 years old, and he was enrolled in high school there until he graduated in the class of 1958.

Chuck Norris joined the Air Force after graduation from high school and was stationed in Korea where he was an MP (Military Police) while in the service. Chuck became a voracious martial artist. He trained every night in Tang Soo Do and spent all day Saturday and Sunday training in judo (yudo in Korea). He left Korea as Black Belt in Tang Soo Do and a brown belt in judo.

After returning to his home in California, he worked for Northrop Aviation and taught Tang Soo Do as a sideline. Just a couple of years later he had started teaching full time in his own martial arts school which not only flourished but also attracted a number of Hollywood's famous including Bob Barker from television and Steve McQueen from the movies.

Tournaments and Championships for a Decade...

Now an international film and television star, Chuck started out as a tournament fighter. That endeavor lasted for a decade from 1964 through 1974, and it was a spectacular time for him. By 1966 he dominated the tournament scene and was almost unstoppable in competition. Fast, agile, powerful and relentless, he was in the first era of the thinking man's fighters winning over the best known fighters of the time from coast to coast.

His first major tournament victories began in 1966 with wins at both the National Karate Championships and also the All-Star Championships.

In 1967 the Norris name became well known when he won the World Middleweight Karate Championship and the All-American Karate Championship.

He set records with victories in the Ed Parker Internationals, World Professional Middleweight Karate Championship, All-American Championship, National Tournament of Champions, American Tang Soo Championship, and the North American Karate Championship, all in 1968.

Determined, handsome and polite, Norris won the admiration of his peers the hard way. Privately he was esteemed as a man who was respected and envied in the ring, who loved "his Mom's apple pie" and who loved to fight. And he did it well. He compiled a fight record of 65-5 with victories over all other champions of the day, and retired as undefeated Professional Full-Contact Middleweight Champion in 1974.

In his own words, Chuck tells us, "Whatever luck I had, I made. I was never a natural athlete, but I paid my dues in sweat and concentration and took the time necessary to learn karate and become world champion."

Toward the end of his career as a fighter/competitor Chuck was a welcomed personality and friend to several of the country's major point and professional karate tournaments including one of the most prestigious events of the time, the Battle of Atlanta. Chuck attended many of the milestone events at the Battle of Atlanta, including the Professional Karate Association (PKA) events staged in Battle of Atlanta finals. Norris and company consisted of martial arts celebrities Pat Johnson, Bob Wall, Mike Stone, Tadashi Yamashita, and Chuck's star fighter students including Darnell Garcia, Howard Jackson, Chip Wright and John Natividad. And whether running a ring as Referee or Judge or merely watching a match, the fighters stepped up their game under Chuck's scrutiny.

ACTION IN FRONT OF THE CAMERAS…

Today we know that it was Steve McQueen, one of Norris' private students who became a close friend, who urged him to try acting, and he did. It began with an uncredited part in 1968 in The Wrecking Crew, an adventure movie starring Dean Martin, Elke Somer and Sharon Tate. But Norris wasn't alone in that film. Joe Lewis, Ed Parker, and Mike Stone were also very recognizable but uncredited as was Bruce Lee, a fight

and stunt advisor.

Now, over a half century later, the Chuck Norris filmography is overwhelmingly impressive. He has a star on the Hollywood walk of fame, well-deserved for leading roles in more than 30 motion pictures and five made-for-television movies. But even with these credits, he is likely best known to the viewing audience for his near 200 consecutive leading appearances in "Walker, Texas Ranger" as the show's hero, Cordell Walker.

But never really retired…

Retired but by no means inactive, Chuck is married to Gena O'Kelly, is a father and grand-father, and lives on a ranch in Navasota, Texas. He and his wife both serve on the board of the National Council of Bible Curriculum in Public Schools.

He and Gena are Spokespersons for the Total Gym Fitness infomercials.

Chuck and Gena, while digging for an additional water source for cattle, discovered a huge aquifer on the Norris property, and now distribute a healthy drinking

water, CForce Water. (CForce Bottling Co. is a certified woman-owned business founded in 2015 by Gena and Chuck Norris. Under CEO Gena Norris' leadership, CForce water is now available in dozens of states through thousands of retail locations. CForce is a full-service bottling facility that offers co-packing, raw bottle sales and branded product).

Chuck is also the author of five books.

He works for many charities, including the Funds for Kids, Veterans Administration National Salute to Hospitalized Veterans, the United Way, Make-a-Wish Foundation and KickStart, a nonprofit organization he created to help battle drugs and violence in schools.

He received "Veteran of the Year 2001" honor at the 6th Annual American Veteran Awards, visited US forces fighting in Iraq in November 2006, and he was made an honorary Marine in March 2007.

Chuck and his brother Aaron were made honorary Texas Rangers by Gov. Rick Perry on December 2, 2010 in Dallas, Texas.

He is a very vocal conservative Republican spokesperson and fundraiser, but has ruled out running for elected office himself, is a born again Christian, and an NRA member. In 2006 he won "The Jewish Humanitarian Man of the Year Award."

In and for the martial arts...

In 2005 he founded the World Combat League, a full-contact, team-based martial arts competition.

He has founded the Chuck Norris System which he evolved from Chun Kuk Do ("The Universal Way") and American Tang Soo Do.

He has a 10th degree Black Belt in the United Fighting Arts Federation Chuck Norris System, and also an 8th degree black belt in Tae Kwon Do.

He has a 3rd degree black belt in Brazilian Jiu Jitsu (UFAF B JJ) under the Machado Brothers.

He holds a black belt in UFAF Krav Maga Force (KMF).

And beyond ... Kickstart Kids

Thirty years ago as a martial artist and philanthropist Chuck stepped up to the line and took another fighting stance. It was in August of 1990 that he squared off and formed the Kick Drugs Out of America Foundation, and today it's known simply as Kickstart Kids. His goal was to provide a martial arts program that would instill in children all the character building traits that the martial arts could offer, and at no cost.

By 1992 Chuck, with the help of then-president George H.W. Bush, formally introduced the program to four schools in the Houston, Texas area. By 2003 and with the help of his wife Gena, the organization was formally renamed Kickstart Kids and is actively teaching character building through karate, empowering youth with core values including discipline and respect.

With the usual Norris tenacity, the program is a resounding success for Chuck and Gena. There are nearly 60 schools throughout Texas teaching almost 10,000 students, mostly in middle, junior and high schools. The not for profit organization is chaired by

Chuck and Gena, and there are now more than 90 people on staff.

and the United Fighting Arts Federation (UFAF)…

Chuck also put together the United Fighting Arts Federation (UFAF) in 1979 as the governing and sanctioning body for the Chuck Norris System. This is his personal development and fighting system evolved from Tang Soo Do and Chun Kuk Do. Since 2015, UFAF has provided technical standards for instruction and advancement in the system, and it also provides its students, instructors, and schools with Chuck Norris System rank certification, educational opportunities, special events, online community access, and other services.

Recently UFAF has expanded its scope to include other martial arts, specifically Brazilian Jiu Jitsu (USAF BJJ) and Krav Maga (KMF) in addition to the Chuck Norris System (CNS) and Chuck himself oversees UFAF's activities as Chairman, along with President Ken Gallacher and its board members, including brother Aaron, Reggie Cochran and others.

Chuck Norris is the most widely celebrated Martial Artist on the planet, and his legions of global fans raised their glasses in a collective toast as he has celebrated 8 glorious decades—Giving Back for a Lifetime.

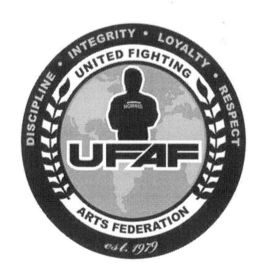

GREAT GRAND MASTER ERNIE REYES, SR.
WEST COAST WORLD MARTIAL ARTS
LIVING THE DREAM OF THE POWER OF TEAM AND FAMILY.

Thompson and myself, team and family have always been our top priority. Team has always been not just a vital part of our martial arts value system, but the heart and soul of our West Coast World Martial Arts Association (WCWMA) and West Coast Action Demo

Teams.

There is a saying:

Team — Together Everyone Accomplishes More!

My goal as a West Coast World Martial Arts teacher and leader is this saying:

Team - Together Everyone Accomplishes Mastery!

Team is good! But mastery of family is the ultimate!

It's the greatest!

During my lifetime, I have had the honor to have led and been a part of some amazing teams that have positively impacted and empowered the world over several decades. For both Great Grand Master Tony

But our WCWMA Teams became so much more than just a team. We always went deeper than that…we became a family. There are teams, and then there are great teams, so when you can create a team that becomes a family that loves each other, the feeling becomes magical and incredible. It becomes masterful! It's the greatest reward, one that your team will always cherish for the rest of their lives, and it's that bloodline that brings energy and life to future teams and generations to come.

I was born in the small agricultural town of Salinas, California on February 12, 1947. I was a kid who lived on the other side of the tracks, flunked kindergarten and first grade, and couldn't read or write. Who would have ever thought that I would one day become the purposeful leader and driving force behind a world-renowned team that would revolutionize the martial arts world in such a positive way?

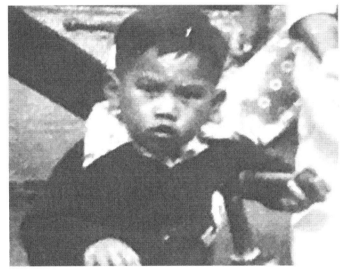

Through the creative, dynamic, and exciting performances of our Ernie Reyes' West Coast World Martial Arts Teams, we were able to educate, entertain, bring joy and laugher to the general public throughout the world about the positive benefits of martial arts as a way of life. We were able to impact and empower the world with this positive message for over four decades.

Because of the awe-inspiring performances of our Teams, and the incredible reach our WCWMA Teams had in delivering our positive message about the martial arts, I was honored on the national television TNT network as one of the greatest masters of the

20th Century. And as the leader of our WCWMA demo team, Karate Illustrated Magazine called me the Creator of Musical Forms.

The only thing that I created when I was a kid was havoc. I went to a catholic grammar school, where, back in the day, the nuns who were our teachers demanded discipline and ruled their classes with a ruler. This was the norm and everyone accepted it. But the nuns would constantly have to send me to the principal's office for fighting or disrupting their classes.

The only thing I loved about school was team sports. Maybe everyone made fun of me, being the dumb kid in class, but one thing the kids respected me for was that I was a very extraordinary athlete. The other kids and the coaches would always choose me to captain the team.

When my team wanted me to be the team captain, it made me feel that my life was finally worth something.

I definitely had an inferiority complex, and being a minority back in those days only amplified my insecurities. I was very shy and didn't talk very much, but when it came to team leadership, I had no problem rising up, taking charge, encouraging and giving direction to my teammates during our games. My teammates would either listen to me or I would beat them up. But overall everyone respected my leadership and friendship.

Little did I know as a kid that my experience being a team leader would be the seed planted within me which would eventually lead to me becoming a compassionate and devoted leader of our world-famous West Coast World Martial Arts Demo Teams.

During jr. high and my early years of high school the pattern was still happening. I was still getting bad grades and getting in trouble. But this time I was now being taught by Jesuit Brothers and they believed in strict old school discipline. They would straighten us up with the board of education. At the end of each day they would line us up for disobedient behavior and they would give us a swat on the rear. All of sudden I have a loss of memory but for some reason I would always be in that line up. I not only had a hard head. I had a hard butt.

But in eleventh grade, I became enlightened. I decided that I no longer wanted to be the dumb jock. So I teamed up with some of my athletic teammates who were smart, and I started to model their study habits and systems.

After practice we went straight to the library every night. But I was so far behind academically I would have to triple my study time, because I had a lot of catching up to do. I had to read and reread and yellow highlight each paragraph maybe three times, over and over again, to finally be able to comprehend the subject matter. I was fortunate to have teammates that cared for me in my educational development as I cared for them in their athletic development.

My love for team sports kept evolving and I became an all-star athlete. I achieved all-league honors and I was still being voted team captain in high school and in Jr. College.

Graduated from San Jose State University!

Learning to team up with a group of positive individuals at a young age made a major difference in my academic transformation. I even made it onto the honor roll. I kept that roll going right into college, and eventually graduated from San Jose State University with a BS Degree in Business Administration. The value of the team and family spirit was truly being integrated within me.

My passion to develop extraordinary teams with the family spirit is still going strong. I do my best to train, to teach, and to live martial arts to the highest level every day. I believe I have found my noble calling in life, and that is to make a positive difference in the world as a WCWMA Great Grand Master Instructor. Every morning before I get out of bed to start my day, I say to myself, "It's great to be alive!"

I say this because I had a traumatic experience in my life. In 2016, I found out that I had cancer and had to have my prostate removed. After the operation, I was fine for a couple of years, but in 2018, my PSA levels started to rise again. This caused great concern for my doctor, because I no longer had a prostate. My cancer had begun to recur.

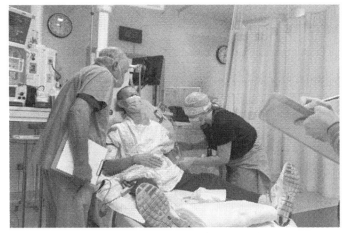

In 2021, I have been clinically diagnosed with stage-4 cancer. Each one of these stages that I had to go through during these past few years was extremely difficult for me to understand and comprehend, because I was continuing to train and teach every day and felt great.

But when the doctor came in and gave the news of my latest diagnosis to me Margie Reyes, my wife and soulmate for life, it was shocking and unbelievable to us. I didn't even know what stage I was in during this entire process, let alone what stage-4 cancer meant. So I asked the doctor to explain, and he said I am sorry to say it means it's incurable. As we left the Dr.'s office it brought tears of sorrow to our eyes, not knowing what to expect or what my future life would be.

Tremendous fear overcame me. I didn't know how long I was going to live. The side effects of the aggressive treatments that the doctor recommended and that I was going to have to go through would alter my way of life as a martial artist. I became depressed thinking that what I love most in life– my family, my WCWMA martial arts family, my noble calling in life to train, to teach, and to help empower people's lives– was all going to be taken away from me.

I knew it was time to do a reset. I immediately took a quiet moment to do some soul-searching and to refocus my state of mind, it being engulfed in negativity to a state of positivity that martial arts had taught me. Once I had refocused my own state of mind, I immediately gathered my personal family of Ernie Jr., Lee, Destiny, Espirit, Ki Reyes, and Great Grandmaster Tony Thompson, giving them the devastating news of my health condition. After talking with my kids and my lifelong friend, I then went to my martial arts school to be with my martial arts team and WCWMA family, to teach and train with my students and Black Belt instructors.

This type of response and action-step of gravitating towards my beloved teams and family brought some comfort and peace of mind to me after receiving the shocking life and death news from my doctor. It also uplifted my spirit, knowing that my teams' spirits and love would be with me as I go through my battle with cancer.

On February 13, 2021, the day after my 74th birthday, I was honored and awarded my 10th Degree Great Grand Master Black Belt by the Professional Karate Association (the "PKA"). Representing the PKA, Great Grand Masters Joe Corley, Jeff Smith, and Bill Wallace attended my awards ceremonies and made the presentation. It touched my heart deeply for these pioneers of martial arts in America, knowing about my medical condition, to take their time to be there for me during this time of my life. I felt they were like my martial arts family and brothers caring for me, as I care for them.

Although the martial arts industry presentation of my 10th Degree Great Grandmaster Black Belt was in February of this year, I actually tested for my belt in June of 2020 along with 560 of my Black Belt Candidates and Master Instructors. The test in itself was an amazing feat of doing the impossible from what seemed impossible to do, because it was just three months before our Mastery Test in June, then out of nowhere we were hit with the this lethal COVID-19 global pandemic crisis.

Never in our wildest dreams did we ever think that we would have to do a virtual Mastery and Black Belt Test via Zoom. We didn't even know how to use Zoom. This was one the most challenging experiences we have ever had to fight through together as one WCWMA team and family. But when all was said and done we created the greatest Black Belt Test and Mastery Test of our 43 associations' years history. Later I will explain how we as a WCWMA team and family pulled off this unbelievable Mastery Test of 2020.

I was presented my 10th degree and the highest rank of our WCWMA Association on February 13, 2021, in recognition of my contribution to the martial arts world because of our WCWMA teams and family's innovative and creative demonstrations that we have performed world-wide for decades.

This awards ceremony was one of my most treasured moments of my entire life. It was a celebration of life for me! I was celebrating my 10th degree black belt award and 74th birthday with our entire WCWMA Association family, friends, our invited special martial arts guests and PKA legends. But I was also celebrating what I love doing the most on that day, and that was training, teaching and doing a demo. I have done demos with our WCWMA Demo Teams for an incredible number of years, and so have my children, but we have never performed a demo with just our Reyes family only.

I am happy and grateful that all five of my children have trained in our WCWMA martial arts system. Our family has had some amazing memories that we will treasure forever, from when they were just babies being Little Dragons, to now being adult Big Dragons and having achieved their Master Instructor ranking. All my children– Ernie Jr., Lee, Destiny, Espirit, and Ki – are highly skilled and masterful in their execution of martial arts technique. They have all made a major contribution in making a difference in the world for generations, by all of them being on our WCWMA demo teams. Hmm… They must have had a great teacher that loved them and instilled our team and family spirit within them.

Our WCWMA Association has been known for its world-class WCWMA Demo Teams for over 40 years, so how could I receive my honorary 10th degree GM Black Belt without doing a demo? Not doing a demo was impossible for me! I was ready to perform by myself, but I volunteered my children at the last minute to do a demo with me. They had no idea that I was going to ask them to do a demo with me. At first when I asked them they were a little shocked, but quickly shouted "Yes Sir!" Then they rose up to the challenge. Everything was improv, no rehearsal. I told the audience that I was going to challenge them to see if this 74-year-old man still got it! My children are 20 years old to 40+ years old, and they are all world class level performers. For our demo at the awards ceremonies, I randomly chose different parts of our WCWMA curriculum and they did their best to compete against me.

I even asked Great Grand Masters Joe Corley, Bill Wallace, and Jeff Smith to be the judges of our competition as I battled my family. So when these legendary judges chose the best of the best after a few rounds of competition, I was fortunate to rise to the top and was declared the Grand Champion of the Reyes Family competition. I even had my kids take a break as I did the rest of the demo by myself showing my personal family and our WCWMA family that my heart and soul is still young.

Regardless of my cancer diagnosis, I still train every day to demonstrate The Master's Way, and to keep negative thoughts away. I believe it helps me heal spiritually. Doing a demo with my Reyes family and having all my children there to share my love and spirit with me on that special day was the most rewarding for me, not only as their instructor, but as their proud father and parent. If Marge, my wife, wasn't recovering from both knees being operated on, and one knee having full reconstructive knee surgery, she would have also definitely been out there as a proud mama with our Reyes fam! For my children it will be a lasting, one-of-a-kind memory in their martial arts life. They will never, ever forget that their father, the old man, still has a lot of kick left in his life. This Power of Team and Family was what they were brought up on, and what we all shared and demonstrated on this memorable day.

Your teams and family are only going to be great if you have a shining light to lead the way. You do this not just by telling your team or family what to do, but for you to keep doing it yourself! Remember this, age is not a factor! We may be getting old, but you don't have to act old, perform old, or be old!

GGM Joe Corley shared this saying with me: "Don't let the old man or old woman in!" I say, "Don't let old age catch you!" I believe you do this by thinking this: "I will not grow old in my mind! I will keep on moving, flowing, and glowing!" You must make this happen, "Impossible 2 Possible," no matter how old you get! This is how you create a supreme legacy for your team and family!

As a GGM martial arts teacher, here are three Life Skills that I do my best to teach our WCWMA students, Black Belts, Master Instructors to help them create their own positive supreme legacy for their lives:

1. Develop the Master's Mindset! This means to do the extraordinary. To go above and beyond the ordinary and to do it consistently during your lifetime.

2. Develop the Warrior Spirit! This means to have the indomitable spirit to never, ever quit or give up. To fight on until you overcome.

3. Develop the Power of Love! This means to be kind

© ERNIE REYES 2011

and give unconditional love to others in time of dire need, and to do it without expecting anything in return. Can you still bring love when people are dishonorable to you, disloyal to you or hate on you? If you can, that is a high level of Self-Mastery!

I not only try my best to teach these life skills to my students, but I do my best to live up to those life skills every day. Then I do my best to teach our WCWMA teams and family to live that same belief and value system. So why are we in pursuit of developing these three Powerful Forces to Mastery?

It's because we are trying our best to master our Mind, our Spirit, and our Heart! I believe if you can master those three impacting and empowering elements you will make a positive difference in the world during your lifetime.

Read Great Grand Master Ernie Reyes' full bio in the Who's Who in the Martial Arts *Changing Lives Series Vol. 6 Biography Book, Tribute to Ernie Reyes, Sr.*

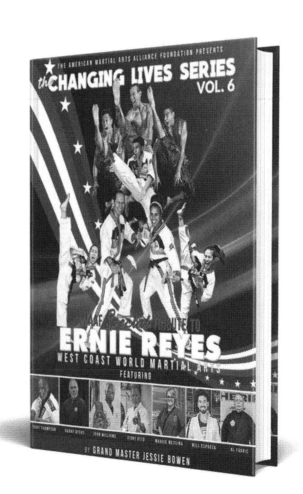

GRAND MASTER CYNTHIA ROTHROCK
THE QUEEN OF MARTIAL ARTS CINEMA
WORLD CHAMPION. MOVIE STAR. ROLE MODEL. ADVENTURE SEEKER.

When she was a 13-year-old growing up in Scranton, Pennsylvania, she started taking lessons at her parent's best friend's private gym. Little did she know then that this casual interest would lead to a full-time professional career. Her martial arts teachers quickly recognized her natural abilities and encouraged her to enter an open karate competition. By the time she had earned her first black belt, she was well on her way to becoming a martial arts champion. By 1982 Cynthia was one of the premier Kata (forms) and weapon competitors in the United States. Competing in divisions not segregated by male-female categories, she captured every title in open and closed karate competitions.

From 1981-1985 she was the undefeated World Karate Champion in both forms and weapon competition. She established a legacy of wins and accumulated hundreds of trophies for her martial arts prowess, an unparalleled feat even today! She is a consummate performer with Chinese weapons like the Chinese Double Broad Swords, Staff, Chinese Nine-section Steel Whip Chain, Chinese Iron Fan, and an assortment of Okinawan Kobudo and Japanese Bugei Weapons.

As a Forms and Weapon Champion, Cynthia Rothrock has traveled the world performing the intricacies of her martial arts arsenal. With precision flare and panache, she has demonstrated before hundreds of thousands of spectators across the globe. Her "action-packed" self-defense and fight scenario performances garnered her a reputation as a consummate professional in martial arts.

This international exposure soon propelled her to martial arts celebrity status, and within a mere period of less than two years, Cynthia became a household

Cynthia Rothrock is among the world's greatest martial arts/action film stars. Few other performers can match her presence and energy on the silver screen. She is the undisputed "Queen of Martial Arts Cinema." Cynthia Rothrock is an incredibly accomplished martial artist and action star. She holds five black belts in various Far Eastern martial arts disciplines. These arts include; Tang Soo Do (Korean), Tae Kwon Do (Korean), Eagle Claw (Chinese), Wu Shu (contemporary Chinese), and Northern Shaolin (classical Chinese).

name in martial arts circles. In addition to being featured on virtually every martial arts magazine cover worldwide, Cynthia appears in over 300 stories and articles in national and international publications. Some of these magazines include Black Belt Magazine (United States), Inside Kung-Fu (United States), Martial Arts Training (United States), Martial Arts Stars (United States), Inside Karate (United States), Sensei (Spanish Argentina), Australian Fighting Arts, China Sports (Beijing, China), Budo (Brazil), Combat Sport (Spanish-Brazil), Combat Magazine (England), Sushido (French), Kung-Fu Wu Shu (French), Karate Budo Journal (Germany), Australian Tae Kwon Do, The Fighters (England), Martial Arts Illustrated (England), Michael De Pasquale Jr.'s Karate International (United States), Budo Karate (Japan), Banzai International (Italy), Czarny Pas (Poland), Cinturon Negro (Spain), Ninja Weapons (United States), El Budoka (Spain), Kicksider (Germany), Impact Magazine (Germany), Karate Illustrated (United States), Ninja Weapons (United States), El Budoka (Spain), Kicksider (Germany), Impact Magazine (Germany), Karate Illustrated (United States), The Swedish Fighter's International (Sweden), Master (United States), Kung-Fu Illustrated (United States), The Fighter (Thailand), Masters Series (United States), The Martial Arts Gazette (United States), Karate Proþles (United States), Sport Karate International (United States), The World of Martial Arts (United States), The Dojo (United States), and hundreds of national and international newspapers.

Cynthia Rothrock is also one of the very select individuals inducted into the Black Belt Hall of Fame and Inside Kung-Fu Hall of Fame. Inclusions in renowned organizations include the Martial Arts Gallery of Fame, MARTIAL ARTS, Traditions, History, People, The Martial Arts Sourcebook, and dozens of other historical reference books of martial significance.

Cinematically, Cynthia burst onto the scene like a stick of dynamite after "starring" in a Kentucky Fried Chicken commercial in the early 1980s. Soon after, notable producers and directors like Fred Weintraub and Robert Clouse (Enter the Dragon) recognized her martial arts skills, and her career steadily climbed. Cynthia's first full-length motion picture was Yes Madam, where she co-starred with Michelle Yeoh. The movie turned out to be a hit and broke all box office records in Hong Kong. Cynthia and Michelle were on

Hong Kong's cinematic history! Cynthia Rothrock's movie career "shooting schedule" has taken her to some of the most exotic locations on the planet. Paradoxically, she has also endured some of the worse climatic conditions that anyone in the motion picture could ever anticipate — all in the name of making "action-adventure" motion pictures.

Publicity has followed Cynthia Rothrock through every stage of her illustrious career. She is the "media darling" of virtually every reporter, writer, and martial arts magazine worldwide. They know that she draws readers by the thousands to their publication. Her "image" and "career" is perhaps followed more closely (by martial arts enthusiast) than any other "martial arts" actors except Chuck Norris or Jackie Chan.

their way to becoming two of the world's most successful female action stars. When Cynthia was invited to Hong Kong to appear in motion pictures, she didn't know what to expect. Initially, she imagined they would do period pieces where she would wear tight pigtails and traditional Chinese costuming. Surprisingly, she soon discovered that she would star in Chinese action films set in modern times with contemporary themes. As a result, Cynthia Rothrock spent five years in Hong Kong, starring in Asian-produced motion pictures. She starred with Kung-fu greats Samo Hung and Yuen Biao during that time.

She was even offered a role opposite Jackie Chan in Armour of Gods, but Jackie got injured, so the company put her in Righting Wrongs with superstar Yuen Biao. During that Asian tenure, she, unbeknownst to her, has set a record of becoming the very first non-Chinese Westerner to carry an action movie single-handedly in Hong Kong. She left Hong Kong as one of the most celebrated action stars in

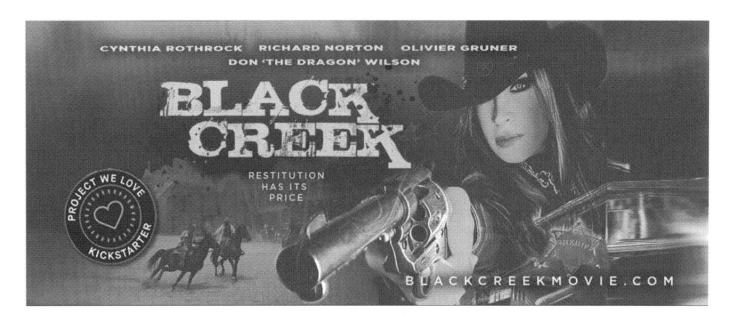

Rothrock on Film
THE QUEEN OF MARTIAL ARTS CINEMA

Cynthia Rothrock is a martial arts expert and athlete who became a film actress, starring in several highly successful action movies. She first made a name as an action actress in Hong Kong before going on to wow audiences on her home turf. At the time of her popularity, she was well-known as the "Queen of Martial Arts Films."

Upon completing her goal of being undefeated in competition, she began her martial arts acting career, starring in movies produced and filmed in Hong Kong. Her first movie, Yes, Madam, alongside Michelle Yeoh, broke box office records making her a massive star in Hong Kong. After three years of living in Hong Kong and finishing seven films, she returned to the United States to continue her acting career.

Today she has starred in over 60 movies and is, for the first time, developing and producing her very own action film titled Black Creek.

Black Creek is a dark, gritty, dystopian, western action martial arts film featuring a strong 'no-holds-barred' female protagonist portrayed by Cynthia. The plot centers around a sheriff's sister who seeks revenge against the terrifying leader of a group of outlaws after discovering he brutally murdered her brother, his wife, and other family members in a gritty southwestern town. Black Creek promises to deliver an adrenaline-packed ride from start to finish.

To learn more, visit BlackCreekMovie.com.

GRAND MASTER JEFF SMITH
WORLD KARATE CHAMPION & LEADER
OVER FOUR DECADES OF EXCELLENCE IN THE MARTIAL ARTS.

One of the most popular and highly respected martial artists in the world, Grandmaster Jeff Smith has influenced millions of Martial Artists around the world, both directly and indirectly.

Voted by his Top Ten peers as the Number One Point Fighter in the Nation in 1974 by Professional Karate Magazine, Jeff went on immediately to win the very first PKA World Light Heavyweight Kickboxing Championship title on ABC's Wide World of Entertainment.

All the while, he was training the next generation of International Champions, coaching them to World Titles, as he managed and taught the instructional staff of the Jhoon Rhee Institute schools in Washington DC. As articulate as he is dangerous, Grandmaster Smith has appeared before the camera as a multi-talented point fighter and PKA World Champion Kickboxer and as an expert analyst for the next generations.

Jeff Smith is one of the, if not THE MOST, multi-talented martial artists of all time. Champion, Innovator, Manager, Teacher, Coach, Mentor, Leader…and…and…and…

On June 17, 2016, Jeff Smith was awarded the rank of Grandmaster by the Professional Karate Commission with his 10th Degree Black Belt by Grand Masters Glenn Keeney and Allen Steen with the additional signatures and approval of Pat Johnson and J Pat Burleson.

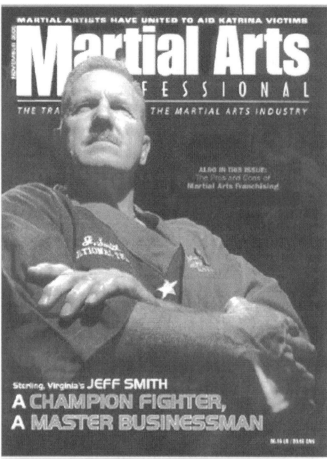

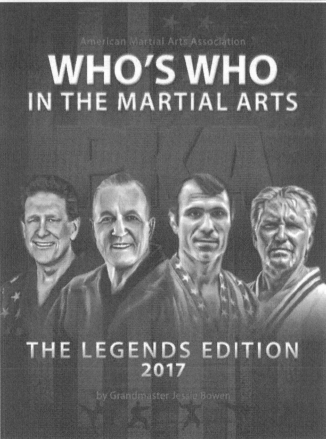

THE CURRICULUM VITAE OF GRAND MASTER JEFF SMITH

- 1964- Jeff enrolled in a Tae Kwon Do class at Texas A&I University in Kingsville, TX

- 1966—Jeff competes in his 1st Karate Tournament in Houston, Texas.

- 1966-Jeff receives his 1st Degree Black Belt from GM Jhoon Rhee in Kingsville, Texas.

- 1970-Jeff moves to Washington DC to Teach at the Jhoon Rhee Institute for Grand Master Rhee and enlists his top protégés to join him in DC, building the basis

- 1970-1985 Served as Senior VP for GM Jhoon Rhee's Institute of TAE KWON Do, training and managing all of the Managers and Instructors for his 12 locations.

- 1969-74 Jeff won many of the Top National Point Tournaments including Joe Corely's Battle of Atlanta, Ed Parker's International Karate , Allen Steen's US Championships, Mike Anderson's Top 10 Nationals Bob Maxwell's Ocean City United States Pro-Am, Jim Miller's Mardi Gras Nationals George Minshew's Houston Karate Olympics, The Pan Am Championships in Baltimore, Md. and the North American Tae Kwon Do Championships in Toronto, Canada to name a few.

- 1973-74 Jeff was ranked the number 1 point fighter in the USA by Professional Karate Magazine.

- 1973-2016 Jeff has been on the cover of every major martial arts publication and was selected by Washingtonian Magazine as one of Washington's top athletes.

- 1974- Jeff is the first recipient of the Bruce Lee Award (selected by Mrs. Bruce Lee and Professional Karate Magazine) and is listed in the first Who's Who of Martial Arts.

- 1974-80-Jeff is recognized worldwide as the seven-time PKA "World Light Heavy Weight Karate Champion."

- 1975- 50 million worldwide viewers observed Jeff's title defense against Don King's heavy weight fighter Kareem Allah as the co-main event of the Ali vs. Frazier III World Boxing Title Fight, known as the "Thrilla in Manila."

- 1980-90 Jeff was coach of the WAKO World Champion United States Karate Team winning consecutive World Titles in all those 10 years.

THE CURRICULUM VITAE OF
GRAND MASTER JEFF SMITH (CONTINUED)

- 1989-1993-Jeff performed at the White House for President Bush in the "Kick Drugs Out of Your Life" campaign and again with his students in California for President Bush in his "Drug Abuse is Life Abuse" program. Jeff conducted seminars in public schools all over the USA for the "Just Say No to Drugs" campaign.

- Jeff Smith has been named as Co-President of Sports and Operations at PKA WORLDWIDE. He is working alongside PKA CEO Joe Corley and Co-Presidents Rich Rose and Howard Dolgon in the PKA HUNT FOR THE GREATEST STRIKERS ON THE PLANET.

- Jeff and PKA WORLDWIDE completed their first trials in New York, where they identified 5 new Strikers to compete in Las Vegas in the Semifinals, heading to the new World Titles.

- 1974-1985 Jeff appears on ABC's "Wide World of Entertainment," "The Champions" TV series, and does Expert Commentary on Showtime, ESPN and Pay-Per-View events

- 1990-92 Jeff performed for Arnold Schwarzenegger on the White House lawn with his students for the "Great American Workout" for the President's Council on Physical Fitness.

- 2000-2016 Jeff is inducted into the Tae Kwon Do Hall of Fame, Black Belt Magazine Hall of Fame, NASKA Hall of Fame, Action Magazine's Martial Arts Hall of Fame, The Battle of Atlanta's Centurion Hall of Fame Award, and with Chuck Norris, is the first recipient of the Joe Lewis Eternal Warrior Award.

- 2005-Present Jeff is the National Director of Mile High Karate Franchises and Martial Arts Wealth Mastery Consultant with GM Stephen Oliver. Jeff owns and operates his own Mile High Karate School in Sterling, VA.

- He also travels globally, officiating at National and International tournaments. He conducts both Business and Training seminars for Martial Arts schools all over the world.

GRAND MASTER RON VAN CLIEF
PROLIFIC MARTIAL ARTS ICON
THE BLACK DRAGON

Duncan Leung, GM Ronald Taganashi, Frank Ruiz, Chaka Zulu, Harry Rosenstein, GM S. Henry Cho, George Cofield, GM Danny K. Pai, GM Ed Parker, GM Steve Muhammad, GM Bruce Lee (who named me The Black Dragon), GM Relson Gracie, Ronn Shiraki, and GM Al Dacascos.

Martial arts changed my entire life. It's become my way of life. It is my happy place. It is the best people builder, personal development, and character developer in my life. I am grateful to continue my journey and spread the knowledge and spirit of true martial arts.

I started martial arts with GM Moses Powell and GM Ronald Duncan at the St. John's Community Center in Brooklyn in 1959. As a teenager, I became a fan of martial arts movies. So, my brother Pete and I would hop on the train to Chinatown. In 1960, I met GM Peter Urban and became his student until I joined the U.S. Marine Corps (1960-1966). While in the Marine Corps, I studied karate -do in Okinawa and the Philippines. I was mentored by GM Presas, GM Leung Ting, GM Samuel Kwok, GM

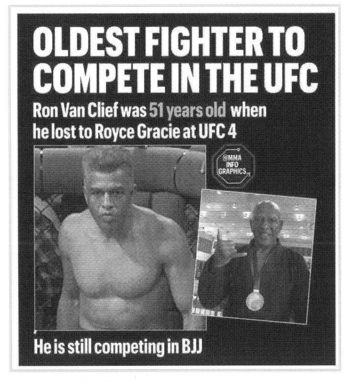

OLDEST FIGHTER TO COMPETE IN THE UFC

Ron Van Clief was **51 years old** when he lost to Royce Gracie at UFC 4

@MMA INFO GRAPHICS

He is still competing in BJJ

TRAINING INFORMATION

- Belt Rank/Titles: Sanuces- Black Belt, Shotokan Karate- 5th Dan, American (Urban) Goju-9th Dan, TKD-2nd Dan, Wing Chun- student, Wing Tsun-student, Modern Arnis-7th dan Lakan Pito, Relson Gracie Jiujitsu-Brown Belt

- Instructors/Influencers: GM Moses Powell, GM Ronald Duncan, GM Ron Taganashi, GM Frank Ruiz, GM Harry Rosenstein, GM George Cofield, GM S Henry Cho, GM Relson Gracie, Prof. Ronn Shiraki

- Birthplace/Growing Up: Brooklyn, NY

- Yrs. In the Martial Arts: 64 years

- School owner of Black Dragon Combatives/Black Dragon Dojo

PROFESSIONAL ORGANIZATIONS

- Screen Actor Guild (SAG) and AFTRA
- East Coast Stuntmen's Association
- Chung Wah Athletic Association
- Chinese Goju International
- International Sports Hall of Fame Advisory Board
- Negro Ensemble Company

PERSONAL ACHIEVEMENTS

- Martial Arts Champion
- Five-time World Karate Champion
- 15-Time All-American Karate Champion
- Black Belt Magazine Hall of Fame
- The first foreigner to headline Hong Kong Movies - 1974
- Senior Combatives Instructor for the United States
- Secret Service at NY World Trade Center - 1983-1993
- USMC Honorable Discharge - 1966

MAJOR ACHIEVEMENTS

- Author of the Manual of the Martial Arts, The Ron Van Clief Guidebooks White Belt to Black Belt, Black Heroes of the Martial Arts Vol 1, 2, and 3, The Hanged Man, Zentences, and Tao of the Black Dragon.

- Competed in over 900 tournaments in 57 years of International competition.

- Fought in UFC 4 at the age of 51 years old. Oldest Fighter to ever fight in UFC history and the first Commissioner of the UFC, 1995-1996.

- Trained over 500,000 students worldwide.

- Founded The Chinese Goju System and Black Dragon Aikijitsu in 1971.

- Started competing in Brazilian Jiujitsu competition at the age of 71 and still competing at 81 years old.

- Produced bio-pic The Hanged Man in 2020.

- Presently in post-production on the documentaries The Super Weapon 2 And Black Heroes of The Martial Arts.

- Worked as a stuntman and action director for over 40 years and was a member of the Stunt And Safety Committee for the Screen Actors Guild.

- Worked on over 100 films, television, and cable programs.

- Finishing "The Tao Of The Black Dragon," a 3D Animated feature film with Daetrix Master Art.

- Inducted into the International Sports Hall of Fame at the Arnold Classic by Dr. Robert Goldman, 2022.

BILL "SUPERFOOT" WALLACE
CREATOR OF THE SUPERFOOT SYSTEM
THE DEFINITION OF A LEGACY FULFILLED.

schoolteacher and his mom stayed home to raise him and his sister, Jackie, three years his senior.

Things changed at the age of ten when one day, Billy's dad came home to tell the family that they would be moving to Lafayette, Indiana, the town where he had grown up. While having a population of approximately 48,000 didn't qualify Lafayette as a major metropolis, it might as well have been New York City to young Billy.

During junior high, young Bill began to emerge as an athlete. Despite being a "little dinky kid," he played on the 7th and 8th-grade basketball teams.

As a freshman in high school, he went out for football and won the starting long-snapper position, snapping the ball back on punts and field goal/extra-point attempts. It wasn't his size or athletic prowess that won him the position, but rather he was the only one brave (or stupid) enough to put his head down to snap the ball as an angry nose tackle was breathing down his neck. Despite his diminutive size, he was perfect in getting the ball back to his teammates that season, giving him his first taste of athletic perfection.

After the football season ended, knowing that high school basketball was not in his future because of his small size, young Bill wandered the halls one day after school and saw these guys rolling around on the mats with each other. So, he asked the man who appeared to be in charge, Mr. Clausman, "What's that?"

"Wrestling," Mr. Clausman responded.

"Can guys my size do it?" young Bill asked.

"Yes!" Mr. Clausman responded, "In fact, a weight category of 95 pounds would fit you perfectly."

The Early Years

On December 1, 1945, William Louis Wallace, the man we would eventually learn to know and love as "Superfoot," was born to Harold Victor Wallace and Virginia Cop Wallace in Portland, Indiana.

Known as Billy as a youngster, his Portland days were grand, and he thoroughly enjoyed his life in idyllic midwestern America. Life was simple. He loved living in the small town, while his dad worked as a

Bill weighed only 89 pounds at the time and was so skinny that if he turned sideways and stuck out his tongue, he looked like a zipper, but he decided to try it. So, the person who would eventually grow up to become one of the all-time karate and kickboxing greats had found his first martial art, wrestling. Wallace would make the high school wrestling team that year as a freshman. He would go on to wrestling all four years in high school, beating the eventual state champion during his senior season.

Discovering His Left Hook

Most of us in high school have at least one person who plays the role of antagonist in our lives, that guy or gal who always seems to get under our skin, challenges us, and frequently bullies us. For Wallace, it was Don Gastineau.

While "Big Don" was a junior and Wallace a senior, Gastineau had a considerable height and size advantage as the starting middle linebacker on the football team. On the other hand, while Wallace had grown from his early days of freshman "zipper-hood," he still only tipped the scales at about 138 pounds.

After taking Gastineau's verbal abuse for the entire school year, Wallace finally had enough one day and asked "Big Don" to meet him after school to settle things.

Wallace nervously fretted about his scheduled after-school encounter for the next six hours in school that day. Finally, at the end of the school day, "Big Don"

brought his friends to the park, and Bill brought his. The first fight in Wallace's illustrious career was about to take place.

After much bantering and cajoling, Gastineau finally threw a right-hand punch that Wallace would later say "looked like it took a week to get there." This was when he used a move, he would utilize countless times in his kickboxing career. As the punch came towards him, Wallace instinctively leaned back, brought up his front shoulder, and delivered a devastating left hook over the top of the punch, knocking the bully to the ground and causing a bad gash over his right eye.

"Big Don" got back up and took another swing, and young Bill countered with the same technique, once again knocking down the bully. Wallace encouraged him to get up and go at it again, but with the blood streaming down Gastineau's face, they decided to call it a day.

When Wallace returned home, his father greeted him while sitting in his armchair and said, "Let's go."

"Go where?" young Bill questioned.

"To the hospital to visit your friend," the elder Wallace responded.

On the ride to the hospital, Bill's dad chastised him for beating up on a younger student.

"You don't understand, Dad..." Bill pleaded, but the elder Wallace would have none of it. That is, however, until they walked into the emergency room, and Mr. Wallace became slack-jawed as he saw a boy twice his son's size lying on the treatment bed after having had the gash over his right eye stitched up.

In his first and last street fight, the man who would become one of the most devastating fighters the martial arts world had ever known had not only found his power but learned he had a devastating left hook.

Many years later, Wallace was inducted into his alma mater's (Jefferson High School) Sports Hall of Fame in

Lafayette, Indiana. A young man approached him and said, "Mr. Wallace, my dad says he was a really good friend of yours."

"Oh really?" Wallace asked, "What's your dad's name?"

"Don Gastineau." the young man answered.

After a brief pause, Wallace responded,

"Well, you know, Don really helped me. He was a really good guy. I liked your dad. Tell him 'Thank you for everything he's done for me."

True champions always show respect to their opponents.

Off We Go, Into the Wild Blue Yonder (Or Not)

In May of 1963, young Bill Wallace was getting ready to graduate high school with no plans for what he wanted to do with his life. Then, one day, his best friend, Chip Mohlman, suggested that the two of them join the Air Force and learn how to fly planes.

"Sure, why not?" Bill responded, and they went down to the recruiting office to enlist. Since he was only 17 years old, Bill needed his parents' permission, and they provided their signatures.

Only weeks later, on June 10th, Bill and Chip found themselves flying down to Lackland Air Force Base in San Antonio, Texas, for basic training. There, Bill encountered not only one of his greatest nemeses but the only opponent to knock him out.

During his routine physical examination, a nurse drew blood from him. Seeing the needle enter his arm, he got queasy and fainted. His Air Force career is off to a stellar beginning. Needle 1, Bill Wallace 0.

What the Air Force recruiter had failed to share with young Bill and his friend is that to fly planes, they needed to be an officer and be accepted into flight school. As enlisted men, this was not an option for either of them. As a result, Bill would never pilot a plane but rather become a mechanic and, later, a combatives instructor during his four-year stint in the service.

After basic training, Bill was initially sent to Chennault Air Force Base in Illinois and later Wurtsmith Air Force Base in Michigan. Finally, Chip was sent to Texas. While they have spoken over the years on the telephone, this is the last time these enlisting best buddies would ever see one another.

Put On This Little White Jacket

While the Michigan summers near Lake Huron were beautiful, the winters were brutally cold. So, to keep from going crazy in the frigid temperatures, Airman 3rd Class Wallace looked for ways to spend his time off duty from the garage. Knowing that most guys go out drinking with their buddies each night (and he didn't drink), Bill looked for something else to occupy his time.

While in the base gymnasium one day, he inquired if the base had a wrestling team. Someone told him they were not sure about wrestling, but he should check out a "bunch of guys rolling around" in the back of the men's gymnasium.

Upon finding them, he noticed several men in white suits throwing each other all over the place. So, he asked the person who appeared to be in charge if there was a wrestling team he could join.

The man invited Bill to wrestle as he took off his white top (as well as his Black Belt), and the two began to grapple. Wallace had no problem taking his opponent down, even putting him on his back several times.

Then the man invited Bill to "put on this little white jacket" and said, "Now we're going to do this again."

Soon Wallace found himself bouncing off the walls and being thrown all over the mat like a ragdoll.

"What is this? I like this!" Wallace exclaimed.

"It's called Judo." the man replied.

And the rest is history...

Fast forward...

His most iconic exhibition, however, would be in 1990 against his good friend and fellow kickboxing legend, Joe Lewis, in Lake Tahoe, Nevada. While it was billed only as an exhibition, "Speed vs. Power" pitted two great champions who knew only one speed — "full" speed. They battled each other for seven rounds in a classic match of contrasting styles. Their heavy contact during the bout drew the ire of the Nevada Boxing Commission, who scolded them afterward for going too hard against each other.

"But that's how we fight!" the former champions told the commission as they both left the ring with black eyes.

Sharing His Wisdom with the World

While arguably being the most dominant and celebrated fighter the sport of kickboxing has ever known, it could be said that Bill Wallace has made an even greater impact through the teaching of his proven fighting system to literally millions of martial arts practitioners around the world. This has made him, some forty-plus years after his last title fight, still one of the most recognizable names in the martial arts industry.

Since 1972, he has traveled worldwide, sharing his unique fighting strategies with instructors and students through his Superfoot Seminars. Over five decades later, he is still gone almost every weekend of the month to some corner of the globe, connecting with aspiring martial artists and sharing his knowledge.

Some of the most prominent names in the martial arts,

including champions Don "The Dragon" Wilson, Rick "The Jet" Roufus, Dan "SuperDan" Anderson, and Keith Vitali, credit Bill "Superfoot" Wallace with positively influencing their fighting careers.

Not to be stopped by the recent pandemic, in 2020, he began his virtual class, the Superfoot Dojo, which is made available to instructors and students worldwide each week.

The Legacy

In addition to continuing to travel the world each month teaching seminars, Wallace has also focused his attention on sharing his vast array of knowledge with martial school owners and their students through the Superfoot System.

Official Superfoot Schools are certified to teach Wallace's unique fighting methods and provide Black Belt Testing opportunities for instructors and students. Each month, schools receive weekly drills and skills for the classroom, videos on business development and

staff leadership, as well as "Superfoot Stories" recounting the life, times, fighting strategies, and competition stories of Bill "Superfoot" Wallace himself. Individual memberships are also available.

When asked how long he wants to keep up his teaching schedule worldwide, he emphatically states, "I'll do this until the day I die. Then, when I can't do this anymore, you can just wheel me out in a chair, and I'll tell you what to do."

Today, Wallace continues to make his indelible mark on the martial arts world with the energy and enthusiasm of men and women half his age.

"I still have a blast teaching seminars," Wallace says with a huge smile and a twinkle in his eye. "What I teach is not the way of doing things, but a way. It works for me. Change it, modify it, play with it, and make it your own, and make sure to always have fun when you're doing it."

From his humble beginnings in small-town Indiana to the pinnacle of worldwide celebrity and fame, Bill Wallace will certainly go down as one of the most prolific figures the martial arts world has ever known.

Forever recognized, admired, and often imitated, there is only one Bill "Superfoot" Wallace.

About the Author: Chris Natzke is an 8th Degree Black Belt in the Superfoot System and serves as the organization's Director of Business Development and Black Belt Testing Coordinator. He resides in Denver, CO.

Read Bill "Superfoot" Wallace's full bio in the Who's Who in the Martial Arts Changing Lives Series Vol. 7 Biography Book, Tribute to Bill Wallace.

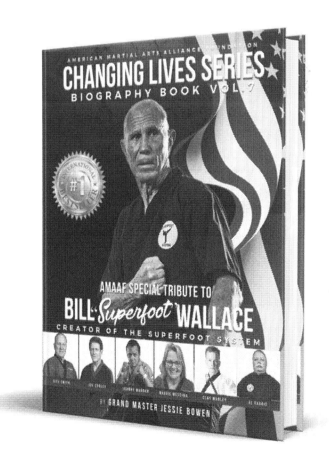

O'SENSEI JAN WELLENDORF
FOUNDER OF KARATE INTERNATIONAL
10TH DEGREE BLACK BELT. AUTHOR. BUSINESS & STYLE INNOVATOR.

Karate International, Terrydale Printing, and finally, developer and founder of Computer Dynamics, a nationally-known software estimating program for the printing industry. In addition, Mr. Brooks was the writer and editor of the Who's Who series of American Martial Arts Anthologies.

Jan Wellendorf was a founding partner of Karate International of North Carolina. Mr. Wellendorf and Mr. Brooks developed a brilliant marketing strategy for business management of door-to-door sales and home audio study courses. Mr. Brooks stepped down from Karate International to pursue his printing business in 1986.

Jan Wellendorf is a martial arts pioneer and the co-founder of Karate International of North Carolina. In 1974, he and his partner, Dale Brooks, founded Karate International, which was considered one of the early pioneers of American Karate. This style was used by martial artists who combined several martial arts systems into their teaching philosophy.

Karate International had its origin in 1957 in Cleveland, Ohio, and grew to 6 schools before moving to North Carolina in 1974. Their goal was to build one of the first martial arts franchise.

Dale Brooks, Nidan in Judo, is an exceptional entrepreneur of several successful businesses, including

The style of American Karate System was developed by Jan Wellendorf, a martial arts instructor, author, business manager, tournament competitor, and Black Belt. He began his martial arts study in 1963. He studied Japanese, Chinese, Korean, and Okinawan Karate. He is the retired president of the Karate International organization.

Out of his training grew the American Karate System. American Karate System utilizes the "three power society," the three powers of mind, body, and spirit. The American Karate System is an art that teaches a student balance of self. One should strive to develop the body so that it can do the bidding of the mind.

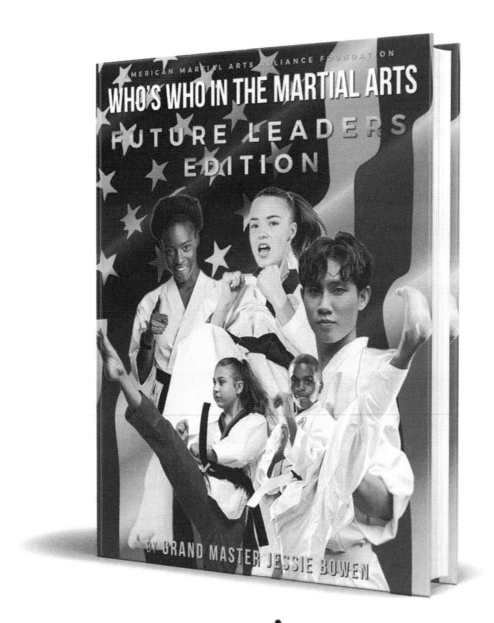

KATELYN MCMILLAN

" *Without martial arts, I'm not sure if I would have learned the skills to be determined, driven, and hard-working enough to get the grades I did to get accepted into the honors college...*

WHEN DID YOU BEGIN STUDYING MARTIAL ARTS & WHY?

I first started my martial arts training at six years old (13 years total of martial arts experience). I first became interested in martial arts when I was six years old and attended a block party in my town. I went over to the local Taekwondo Dojo's booth and broke a board. They offered me a free trial, so I showed up at their dojo for my free trial one day. Taekwondo was not a great fit for me, but my mom saw I had something for martial arts, maybe not that specific style.

My mom later did some research, and a few weeks later, I went for a free trial at my current dojo. Needless to say, I fell in love with Nick Cerio's Kenpo. I later started learning Shotokan from Sensei Steven Alleyne and Sensei Christian Tavares and immediately thought the use of power in Shotokan was amazing and best suited for competition.

HOW DOES STUDYING THE MARTIAL ARTS HELP YOU IN OTHER AREAS OF YOUR LIFE?

Martial arts practice has greatly improved an assortment of components in my life. My educational career has been greatly impacted. Many would think that the two are not correlated, but the determination and other traits that I have gained due to the practice of martial arts and competition have greatly impacted my work ethic, specifically in school and overall, in the best way possible. Without martial arts, I'm not sure if I would have learned the skills to be determined, driven, and hard-working enough to get the grades I did to get accepted into the honors college and pursue not one but two STEM majors: Biology and Neuroscience.

WHAT'S YOUR FAVORITE MARTIAL ARTS TECHNIQUE AND WHY?

My favorite martial arts technique is the hook-roundhouse kick. It is fast but effective, and you can hit both sides of the face instantly.

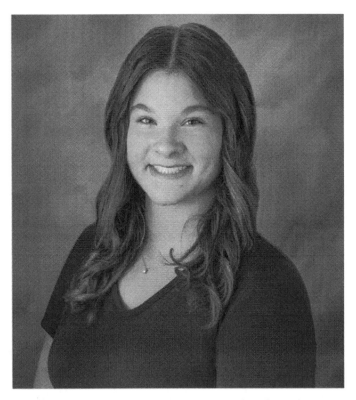

WHO HAS INFLUENCED YOU MOST IN YOUR MARTIAL ARTS STUDY?

Stephen Dwyer has influenced me the most in my martial arts studies. He has not only affected the style of my martial arts/competition forms, but he has also taught me the determination and skills needed to succeed. He taught me up to my 2nd-degree black belt rank and has laid a foundation for me to still be successful in competition and move up in the ranks since he has stepped away from the American art scene. He taught me how to bow in and present myself and to correct the most minor errors in my form the day before a World Circuit competition. All of the hours in the dojo and repetitions have given me the muscle memory that I need to perform at the highest level. I will forever be grateful for that.

WHAT DO YOU LOVE MOST ABOUT THE MARTIAL ARTS STUDY?

I love the aspect of comradery in martial arts study the most. The wins are great in all ways, but the friendships and coming together to cheer your friends on is the best feeling. I loved it so much that I joined one of the biggest open sport karate circuit teams. I would not change anything if I could!

TRAINING INFORMATION

- School Name: Nick Cerio's Kenpo
- Martial Arts Styles & Rank: Nick Cerio Kenpo (3rd Degree Black Belt) and some experience in Shotokan and American Kenpo
- Instructors/Influencers: Sensei Steven Alleyne, Sensei Christian Tavares
- Birthplace/Growing Up: Millbury, MA
- Year Started Training: 2011

PROFESSIONAL ORGANIZATIONS

- North American Sport Karate Association
- KRANE Ratings
- Sigma Sigma Sigma Sorority

PERSONAL ACHIEVEMENTS

- Acceptance into the University of Massachusetts Honors College
- Acceptance into a professional neuroscience research laboratory in the first semester of my freshman year of college

MAJOR ACHIEVEMENTS

- Multiple Martial Arts World Championships in North American Sport Karate Association and World Karate Commission
- National and State Title
- Diamond Ring Winner

ANY OTHER THOUGHTS?

Thank you for the opportunity. It is greatly appreciated.

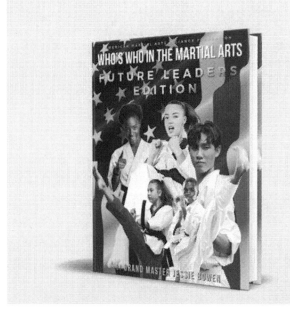

BRANDON
SINOPOLI

"

Be the martial artist who doesn't judge a book by its cover. Be the martial artist who strives to be better. Be the martial artist whom the next generation of fighters will look up to.

HOW DOES STUDYING THE MARTIAL ARTS HELP YOU IN OTHER AREAS OF YOUR LIFE?

Martial arts helps in other areas of my life because they teach you more than just how to kick and punch. They also teach you how to be a good person and have discipline. Martial arts create good, respectful people and have helped me become more mature and wiser than the average teenager.

WHAT'S YOUR FAVORITE MARTIAL ARTS TECHNIQUE AND WHY?

My favorite martial arts technique is the sidekick. I like it because it is effective, can sneak under a punch easily, and is satisfying to land on an opponent.

WHEN DID YOU BEGIN STUDYING MARTIAL ARTS & WHY?

I first started my martial arts study in the fall of 2015. Once COVID hit in 2020, I took a break for about a year and began pursuing martial arts again in 2021, and I continue to do it to this day. I have been studying martial arts for around 8-9 years now and hope to go for many more.

I began martial arts for two reasons. The first is that my father studies martial arts, and he is a huge inspiration to me. The second is that I was being bullied at school, and I was sick of it and wanted it to stop.

WHO HAS INFLUENCED YOU MOST IN YOUR MARTIAL ARTS STUDY?

The person who has influenced me the most in my martial arts studies is my father, David Sinopoli. My father is a role model in my life. He has accomplished many things in the martial arts world and positively impacted me. He is a large motivation to me to be a good martial artist and, most importantly, a good person.

WHAT DO YOU LOVE MOST ABOUT THE MARTIAL ARTS STUDY?

I love the amazing and talented people I meet and the life lessons and techniques I gain. The martial arts community is strong and full of good people, which I probably love the most in the martial arts study.

ANY OTHER THOUGHTS?

If you believe in yourself and your abilities, you will make it far. Many people look down on younger black belt martial artists and our abilities when they don't realize that we are the future. Don't let your ego and other people control your life. Be the martial artist who doesn't judge a book by its cover. Be the martial artist who strives to be better. Be the martial artist whom the next generation of fighters will look up to. Be you and only you.

TRAINING INFORMATION

- School Name: Cutting Edge Martial Arts
- Martial Arts Styles & Rank: Superfoot System- 1st Degree Black Belt, UFAF- 1st Degree Black Belt, Sento MMA- 1st Degree Black Belt, American Freestyle Karate- 1st Degree Black Belt, Joe Lewis Fighting Systems- Advanced Brown Belt, OSM Knife and Tomahawk Throwers Academy- Green Belt
- Instructors/Influencers: David Sinopoli, Walt Lysak Jr., Bill "Superfoot" Wallace, Phil Maldonato, Mykl Gross, Steve Giroux, Nelson Lebron, Terry Dow, Joe Foster
- Birthplace/Growing Up: North Adams, MA / Adams, MA
- Year Started Training: 2015

PROFESSIONAL ORGANIZATIONS

- Superfoot System, Joe Lewis Fighting Systems, UFAF, OSM Knife and Tomahawk Throwers Academy, American Freestyle Kaizen Association, Sento MMA, Sean Kelley Chinese Kenpo, PKA Professional Kickboxing Association

PERSONAL ACHIEVEMENTS

- I maintained high honors throughout middle school and obtained it in high school
- I was awarded the President's Physical Fitness Award
- I stood up to my bully, who bullied me through elementary school and middle school

MAJOR ACHIEVEMENTS

- I have obtained a few black belts in different systems
- I trained with many martial arts legends
- I was nominated twice for Junior Black Belt of the Year in the American Freestyle Kaizen Association Hall of Fame

WHO'S WHO IN THE MARTIAL ARTS

PKA WORLDWIDE

Honorees

JACK
BALLARD

> ❝
> *I learned daily from my students, so I'll always be a white belt. Never stop learning.*

WHY THE MARTIAL ARTS?

My life and journey with martial arts have been nothing but a way of life for me, and I have been involved with so many legends and instructors throughout my 50+ years. My years growing and going up the ranks go back to when it was just white, green, brown, and black belts in tournaments. My style was studied during my first adventures in Chinese Kenpo/Gung Fu with black belt Richard Alford and Grandmaster Joe Lewis in Fort Lauderdale, Florida, and Miami Beach, Florida. What a fantastic legend Joe Lewis was to meet.

Then I change to Yoshukai Chito Ryu through the late Bob Tait and U.S. GM Mike Foster. I studied with Bob Tait all the way to black belt. I learned so much from Bob's training to compete and be a great competitor. I placed in 55 out of 60 tournaments. Back in my day, we didn't have padded floors, just bare concrete floors.

After the tournament era, I got drafted by Grandmaster Harvey Hasting, the Bando Style and Former Heavyweight Kickboxing Champion. We all started back in the beginning with greats Don Wilson, Steve Shepard, Bill "Superfoot" Wallace, Benny "the Jet" Urqidez, Ted Pryor, and my training supports like Ron "Gator" Garlin, GM Joe Hess, and Joe Corley. Meeting Chuck Norris at one of the after-parties at Steve Shepard's event in Palm Beach, Florida, where he talked to Dan Wilson and me about the movie business.

I wouldn't trade any of the 50+ years of knowledge I've learned; teaching beginners to Black belts was the joy of my life. I learned daily from my students, so I'll always be a white belt. Never stop learning. There are so many great masters I've forgotten over the years. Tim Hautamaki was the best trainer in my corner. I talk to many of my brothers and sisters and still want to meet other martial arts legends.

Be strong in mind and body. God bless.

TRAINING INFORMATION

- Belt Ranks & Martial Arts Styles:
  Chito Ryu-10th degree

PERSONAL & MAJOR ACHIEVEMENTS

- 1971-72 Lotterman High School Football
- 1972 Graduated from Plantation High School
- 1976 Chito Ryu - Promoted to Shidan - Black Belt
- 1979 FBBA "Fighter of the Year"
- 1979-80 PKA Instructor of the Year and PKA Judge Certificate
- 2016 Who's Who AMAA Book Inductee
- 2018 AMAA Hall of Fame Inductee
- 2018 Who's Who Masters & Pioneers Inductee
- 2018 Eternal Joe Lewis Award and Ring
- 2019 Action Martial Arts Magazine "Esteemed Martial Artist" Award
- 2021 USHOF MAAI "Champions Distant" Award
- 2022 Living Legend Award AMAA
- 2022 Hall of Honor Inductee
- 2022 AMAA Achiever Award
- 2022 Zenith Warrior of Honor
- Top sensel taught under Bob Tait, Rex Lee, Harvey Hastings, John Scott, Dr. Joe Parish, Joe Hess, Joe Corley, and Steve Sheperd.

BOBBY S. BRIGGS

"
One of my favorite lessons is 'Success is never owned; it is rented. And the rent is due each and every day.'

WHY THE MARTIAL ARTS?

As a small, poor farm kid, I was always fascinated with martial arts, mainly because it was so mysterious to me. And I also loved anything physical for as long as I can remember (like football, boxing, martial arts, etc.).

I was a huge Bruce Lee and Chuck Norris fan at the same time. I played all kinds of sports throughout school. I had an elementary boxing coach recommend to me at one time that I should also take karate to help with my coordination. Little did he know that I had already gone to some karate classes as often as my family could afford to let me go. But when my

boxing mentor said this to me, I became more serious about martial arts. Since my family could not afford my karate classes, I worked harder to try and find ways to make money so I could attend karate classes as often as possible. Since I also loved sports so much, it soon became apparent that my karate was very helpful in my excelling in that also.

Karate greatly enhanced my athletic ability in the sports I played. But I soon discovered that as much as I loved sports, karate quickly became my life's love. I never gave up on sports. As a matter of fact, my karate and the sports that I played throughout school complemented each other very well. In the area where I was raised, there were very, very few places where I could go to find a martial arts school. Luckily for me, I did find some that had awesome instructors that led me in the right direction and became a very important figure in my life, and that's where and how my martial arts career began.

HOW HAS MARTIAL ARTS IMPACTED YOUR LIFE?

Martial arts has taught me a great deal. Most importantly, I believe it taught me to persevere and overcome any difficult obstacles I may face in my life. It's taught me that hard work ALWAYS pays off. It's taught me that where there's a will, there's a way.

Martial arts has always and continues to teach me valuable life lessons. One of my favorite lessons (quotes) is…" Success is never owned; it is rented. And the rent is due each and every day."

TRAINING INFORMATION

- Belt Ranks & Martial Arts Styles: Kidokime-ryu Karate-do-10th degree, JuDan; Okinawa-te-9th degree, KuDan; Kenpo Karate-5th degree, GoDan; Shotokan-1st degree, ShoDan; Shito-ryu-1st degree, ShoDan; American Gojo-ryu-1st degree, Shodan; Isshin-ryu Karate-1st degree; American Karate-1st degree, ShoDan; Hapkido-1st degree; Tae Kwon Do-1st degree

- Instructors/Influencers: Hanshi James White, Hanshi Bill Daniels, Kyoshi David Ray, Kyoshi Rick Sparks, Kyoshi Ken Herfurth, Sensei Chuck Taylor, Hanshi Hirokazu Kanazawa, O'Sensei Osamu Ozawa, Sensei Greg McMahan, Sensei Arvin Pearson, Sensei Ernest Watkins, Sensei Ronnie Delfino, Sensei Tony Simmons

- Birthplace/Growing Up: Spruce Pine, NC / Burnsville, NC

- Yrs. In the Martial Arts: 55+ years

- Yrs. Instructing: 46 years

- School owner, Manager & Instructor at Kidokime-ryu Karate-do Hombu Dojo,, Ranking Black Belt Instructor (Soke) for Kidokime-ryu Karate-do Worldwide

PROFESSIONAL ORGANIZATIONS

- National Universal Karate Association (N.U.K.A.) Lifetime Member
- American Martial Arts Association (AMAA) Lifetime Member
- Professional Karate Association Worldwide Lifetime Member (PKA)
- Kenpo Karate Institute Lifetime Member (KKI)
- Member of Numerous Civil, Military, Police, and Religious Organizations

PERSONAL ACHIEVEMENTS

- I have competed, won, and placed in hundreds of both sport karate (point fighting, Kata, weapons, and self-defense), as well as full-contact kickboxing all across the world, and have won numerous times. I am the defending Champion in many different categories.

MAJOR ACHIEVEMENTS

- Promoted to KuDan (9th Degree Black Belt) by the Okinawan Karate-do on Mar 22, 2014, in Okinawa-te Karate
- Promoted to JuDan (10th Degree Black Belt) by N.U.K.A. on Aug 4, 2018, in Kidokime-ryu Karate-do
- Inducted into the Martial Arts Legends Hall of Fame as the Karate Grandmaster of the Year
- Inducted into the Action Martial Arts Hall of Honors/Hall of Heroes for "Outstanding Achievements in the Martial Arts as a Grandmaster"
- Inducted into the Action Martial Arts Magazine World History Book, Action Martial Arts Magazine Hall of Honors, Official 20th Anniversary Issue
- Has been in multiple martial arts magazines, books, and newspaper articles
- Has been in multiple AMAA Changing Lives Martial Arts Biography Book Series
- AMAA Martial Arts Extraordinaire Bio book (for martial artists with more than 50 years of experience)
- Three "Who's Who in the Martial Arts" inductions
- Author of Kidokime-ryu Karate-do book
- AMAA Who's Who in the Martial Arts Hall of Honors

Become an
AMAA
MEMBER!

MAJOR ACHIEVEMENTS

- Inducted in the Action Martial Arts Hall of Honors 2022 for the "Platinum Lifetime Achievements"

- Action Martial Arts Hall of Honors as "Esteemed Martial Artist"

- Bushido Championship Instructor Award

- AMAA Changing Lives Legacy Award featuring GM Bill "Superfoot" Wallace, and inducted in the Who's Who in the Martial Arts Hall of Honors, 2022

- Inducted into the Cynthia Rothrock Premier Hall of Honors for "Platinum Lifetime Achievement," 2022

- Action Martial Arts Hall of Honors Inductee for 2023 for "Diamond Lifetime Contributions"

- Cynthia Rothrock Martial Artists Changing Lives

- Biography Book Edition and recipient of the AMAA Who's Who in the Martial Arts Legends Award for 2023

- Soke Briggs' Kidokime-ryu Karate-do received Style of the Year from the Action Martial Arts Hall of Honors 2024

- Soke Briggs' Dojo (Samurai Martial Arts) in Sparta, NC, received School of the Year from the Action Martial Arts Hall of Honors 2024

- Recipient of the Man of the Year Award in the Martial Arts from the Action Martial Arts Hall of Honors 2024

- Inducted in the Action Martial Arts Hall of Honors 2024 for Outstanding Achievements in the Martial Arts

- Has been interviewed and featured on numerous radio talk shows, as well as TV News stories featured on the Far East Network (FEN) for military personnel throughout Japan, Okinawa, and the Philippines

- Numerous Military (both Peacetime and Combat) Awards, Decorations, and Medals.

- Numerous Civilian Police Awards and Recognition

- Numerous Civic Awards and Recognitions

MARY
BRIGGS

❝
Martial arts has taught me perseverance — striving to reach your goal no matter how tough it gets.

WHY THE MARTIAL ARTS?

I started in martial arts late in life, more out of curiosity than anything else. I did not know anyone involved in martial arts; what little I saw of it was on TV or in the movies. Which means I didn't really know anything about it. I moved to Charlotte in 2000 to work for The Hartford Insurance Company and met Soke Bobby S. Briggs in 2008. Shortly after we met and got to know each other, I learned he was in martial arts. He talked to me quite a bit about martial arts, and I had a lot of questions. He told me about the style he practiced and that it was very disciplined. He explained some of the things he had learned, told me about his instructors, and all the places he had been able to practice and teach worldwide. And he told me about his current rank then and what other styles he had studied and held black belts in. He asked if I would be interested in taking martial arts classes, and I said I would like to try it.

Soon after, I took my first class with Soke Briggs as my instructor. I was in my forties at the time. I decided I wanted to see what it was really all about. It was tough in the beginning, and I wasn't sure about it at all. But I kept coming back to class. After a couple of months, I tested and earned my yellow belt. I wasn't sure if I wanted to continue, but something kept pulling me back to class. So, as the weeks and months passed, I trained and learned, tested, and passed belt tests. When I reached the intermediate level, all the different pieces of Kidokime-ryu Karate-do began to fit together slowly. And then it seemed that all of a sudden, I was training for my Shodan. After 4 ½ years, I faced the toughest test of my martial arts journey.

So, starting martial arts out of curiosity led to one of my greatest achievements: being the first female Shodan in Kidokime-ryu Karate-do.

HOW HAS MARTIAL ARTS IMPACTED YOUR LIFE?

Martial arts has made an impact on my life in multiple ways and in ways I never thought about. It has helped me gain and be more confident in my personal life and job, in my interactions with people I teach, and with people I work with. It has made me stronger, both mentally and physically. It has taught me how to defend myself. It has taught me the true meaning of character, of being disciplined in training, being more disciplined in everyday tasks, and again with my job.

Martial arts has taught me perseverance — striving to reach your goal no matter how tough it gets. It has taught me about self-control and what that means in the

TRAINING INFORMATION

- Belt Ranks & Martial Arts Styles: Kidokime-ryu Karate-do, YonDan (4th degree), Okinawa-te, Shodan (1st degree)
- Instructors/Influencers: Soke Bobby S. Briggs, Kyoshi Kenneth L. Herfurth
- Birthplace/Growing Up: Roanoke, VA / Bedford, VA
- Yrs. In the Martial Arts: 16 years
- Yrs. Instructing: 12 years
- School co-owner & Instructor at Kidokime-ryu Karate-do Hombu Dojo, PKA Worldwide Lifetime Member, AMAA Lifetime Member

PROFESSIONAL ORGANIZATIONS

- Professional Karate Association (PKA)
- American Martial Arts Alliance (AMAA)

PERSONAL ACHIEVEMENTS

- Numerous Employee of the Quarter Awards
- Numerous Employee of the Month Awards
- Numerous Civic Awards and Recognitions

MAJOR ACHIEVEMENTS

- Inducted into the Martial Arts Legends Hall of Fame as the 2019 Karate Instructor of the Year in Mt. Laurel, NJ, October 26, 2019
- Promoted to YonDan (4th deg Black Belt, August 8, 2020, by Kyoshi Kenneth L. Herfurth, endorsed by Soke Bobby S. Briggs, Hanshi James White, & Hanshi Bill Daniels)
- The first female to ever be promoted to Black Belt in Kidokime-ryu Karate-do
- Honored to be recognized as "The Ladies of PKA Worldwide"
- Has been in multiple Martial Arts Books/ Magazines
- Former Undefeated Kata (Forms) Champion and Grand Champion
- Received the Who's Who Legends Award AMAA Hall of Honors in Las Vegas, NV, 2021
- Inducted in the Action Martial Arts Hall of Honors 2022 for Outstanding Achievements in the Martial Arts
- AMAA Changing Lives Legacy Award featuring GM Bill "Superfoot" Wallace, and inducted in the Who's Who in the Martial Arts Hall of Honors, 2022

MAJOR ACHIEVEMENTS

- Inducted into the Cynthia Rothrock Premier Hall of Honors for "Instructor of the Year," 2022

- Action Martial Arts Hall of Honors Inductee for 2023 for "Esteemed Elite Warrior"

- Cynthia Rothrock Martial Artists Changing Lives Biography Book Edition and recipient of the AMAA Who's Who in the Martial Arts Legends Award for 2023

HOW HAS MARTIAL ARTS IMPACTED YOUR LIFE? (CONTINUED)

dojo, and I have found that it has also helped me maintain self-control in many different situations. Martial arts brought to the forefront the things that parents strive to teach their children — respect for themselves and others, discipline, integrity and what that means, humility, and honor in word and deed. It has taught me that true martial arts is a way of life. It has also impacted my life by showing me that I love and enjoy teaching karate. I love being able to teach others what I have learned and be able to watch them learn, grow, and succeed on their martial arts journey.

PAUL FULLER

"The ability to set goals, focus, and prioritize has been instrumental in helping me to achieve success in my own martial arts school.

WHY THE MARTIAL ARTS?

I started in 1981 at 11 years old after getting bullied every day in school. I began in Mu Duk Kwan Tang Soo Do and did that for about a year and a half until my buddy convinced me to go to his school, which taught Chang Hun Taekwondo. Those bullies eventually put me in a position where I had no choice but to deal with one of them, and I was never bothered again. I did Taekwondo until 1985, and at that point, I had to quit for financial reasons, and that turned into a 10-year hiatus.

These were the days of Jean Claude Van Damme, Steven Seagal, Jeff Speakman, and Adrian Paul, all of whom greatly influenced me to return to the arts. I had begun managing gyms at age 23 and thought that was what I would do with my life. Finally, I returned to my Taekwondo school in 2005 and got my black belt. I lived in the college town of Tuscaloosa, Alabama, and at the University, there were several clubs that taught various styles. During that time, I studied Yoseikan Budo, a hybrid of Kenjutsu, Aikijutsu, Judo, Shotokan, Jiujitsu, Kenpo, Kobudo, etc. I also took up Wing Chun, Bujinkan Taijutsu, Shinkendo, and Kenpo, trying to get as well-rounded as I could.

I had become an instructor at my Taekwondo school but knew I wouldn't have a full-time position there as many people were ahead of me to assume that role. I had decided I wanted to teach professionally, so I moved to Atlanta in 2005 and taught for Grandmaster Joe Corley of PKA Kickboxing and Battle of Atlanta fame at Joe Corley's American Karate, Taekwondo, and Kickboxing. Grandmaster Corley taught me how to be a good instructor and not just a drill sergeant. He also showed me the ropes of running a martial arts school professionally.

In 2006, I became certified to teach Kenpo in Arizona under Kyoshi Fred DePalma at DePalma's Team USA Martial Arts. Kyoshi DePalma helped me further refine my business skill set as well as my Kenpo skills. Life takes you to many unexpected places, and I wound up teaching in Colorado, Arizona, Alabama, Georgia, and briefly in North Carolina.

Kyoshi DePalma contacted me in 2019 to see if I wanted to purchase one of the schools in his franchise. I did so, and in 2023, I felt it was time to go my own way and rebrand my school as Zanshin American Karate and Kenpo.

HOW HAS MARTIAL ARTS IMPACTED YOUR LIFE?

Martial arts have given me the self-discipline to succeed in life. I confronted my bullies in high school and worked my way through college full-time. The ability to set goals, focus, and prioritize has been instrumental in helping me to achieve success in my own martial arts school. Martial arts have also given me the skill set needed to de-escalate potentially violent situations and "fight without fighting." Most importantly, I am privileged to pass this information on to future generations!

TRAINING INFORMATION

- Belt Ranks & Martial Arts Styles: 4th Degree Kenpo, 4th Degree Taekwondo, 3rd Degree Tiger Rock Martial Arts, also trained in Wing Chun, Combat Hapkido, Yoseikan Budo, Bujinkan Budo Taijitsu, and Shinkendo
- Instructors/Influencers: Grandmaster James Bailey, Grandmaster Joe Corley, Kyoshi Fred DePalma, Master Bill Wendel, Sensei Michael Fore, Sensei James Collier, Sensei Michael Philpott, Coach Martin Morthland, Shidoshi Robert Geyer, Grandmaster David Rivas
- Birthplace/Growing Up: Tuscaloosa, AL
- Yrs. In the Martial Arts: 34 years
- Yrs. Instructing: 26 years
- School owner, Manager & Instructor at Zanshin American Karate and Kenpo, PKA Worldwide Member

PROFESSIONAL ORGANIZATIONS

- PKA Worldwide
- American Martial Arts Association

PERSONAL ACHIEVEMENTS

- Bachelor's Degree in History with a minor in Anthropology from the University of Alabama
- Competed extensively in the 1990s on the USTA/ITA circuit and won many championships in forms and sparring
- Married the woman of my dreams, Christina Yi Ramirez, in 2022

MAJOR ACHIEVEMENTS

- Level 1 STX Instructor Filipino Martial Arts
- 2009 Battle of Atlanta Officials Hall of Fame
- 2023 inducted into the AMAA Who's Who in Martial Arts Hall of Honors
- 2023 Promoted to the title of Shihan by Kyoshi Fred DePalma

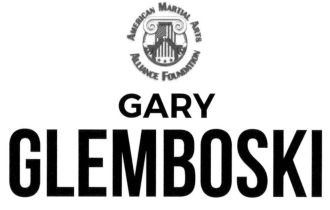

GARY
GLEMBOSKI

> "
> *My martial arts training held me in good stead in many altercations and at peaceful times, too, when there was time to reflect...*

southeast against talented fighters who were nationally rated. I stayed engaged in martial arts because of the structure and discipline, but a certain 'cool factor' was also involved. This was evident from the beginning.

When people found out I studied karate, there were always questions. This was especially evident in high school, where there were plenty of opportunities to defend myself verbally regarding my participation in karate.

With time comes promotions, and I was eventually promoted to my current rank. It was totally unexpected, but I am grateful for the faith my instructor has put in me and humbled by it.

HOW HAS MARTIAL ARTS IMPACTED YOUR LIFE?

I have said many times that if it wasn't for martial arts, I would either be dead or in prison. I was not a bad kid but easily bored, and martial arts gave me structure and focus. Probably too much - It was all I did throughout high school and before enlisting in the Marine Corps. Over the years, my mindset has shifted

WHY THE MARTIAL ARTS?

I had a friend in 7th grade who went to class with his two brothers and father. I initially asked my parents; my mom was supportive, but my dad was against it—at first. It took about a year before I finally wore them down and could attend classes. After a few months, we moved from New Mexico, where I first started, to Savannah, Georgia, where I have been since.

I found a karate class at the local YMCA and began training again. Subsequently, we opened the first karate dojo in the city, and I was eventually promoted to black belt in late 1970. After joining the Marine Corps, I could continue training with my instructor as I was stationed about an hour away. After leaving the Marine Corps, I had several schools and continued training, eventually earning some notoriety in the

HOW HAS MARTIAL ARTS IMPACTED YOUR LIFE? (CONTINUED)

somewhat, but I still focus on my training at the expense of many other pursuits. Fortunately, I initially had a great support unit from my parents (although my father would have rather had me play football or baseball) and my friends and training partners. This went on until the early '80s, when I stopped competing due to lack of time and interest. The discipline it took to continue training manifested itself through my school studies, several major operations over the years, and many nights on the streets dealing with the less-than-savory elements of our society.

My martial arts training held me in good stead in many altercations and at peaceful times, too, when there was time to reflect and remember the amazing journey I have been able to take because of martial arts.

TRAINING INFORMATION

- Belt Ranks & Martial Arts Styles: 9th Dan-Shorinken Karate, 3rd Dan-Hakko Ryu Jiu Jitsu, 3rd Dan,-Hojutsu Ryu, 1st Dan-Shotokan Karate, Defender: Police Judo Level 10 Black Belt Instructor, Force Necessary: Gun Level 10 Black Belt Instructor, Police Tactics Instructors of America Regional Director-Level 4 Instructor, Raven Master Combatives Instructor
- Instructors/Influencers: Fred Absher, Don Ogle, James L. Semmes, Jr. (current)
- Birthplace/Growing Up: Hicksville, NY / Las Cruces, NM / Savannah, GA
- Yrs. In the Martial Arts: 56 years
- Yrs. Instructing: 54 years
- School owner & Instructor at Southern Black Belt Academy, PKA Worldwide Member

PROFESSIONAL ORGANIZATIONS

- Professional Karate Association Worldwide Member
- Police Tactics Instructors of America
- United Fighting Arts Federation (UFAF)
- ASIS (American Society of Industrial Security)
- FBINAA (FBI National Academy Alumni Association)
- Georgia Association of Law Enforcement Firearms Instructors (GALEFI)
- National Law Enforcement Firearms Instructor Association (NLEFIA)
- International Association of Law Enforcement Firearms Instructors (IALEFI)

PERSONAL ACHIEVEMENTS

- Published Author - Tao - Way of the Gun
- Staff Writer for Armed Lifestyle Magazine
◊ Studying/teaching martial arts for 56 years
◊ Over 100+ tournament awards for fighting, forms, and weapons
◊ Three Grand Championships
◊ Two-time Light-Heavyweight Fighter of the Year (Southeast Karate Association)
◊ Two-time fighter of the year (South Georgia Karate Circuit)
◊ #3 Fighter in Southeast Region (Karate Illustrated Magazine)

PERSONAL ACHIEVEMENTS (CONTINUED)

◊ The only fighter to ever knock down Jeff Smith, former Light Heavyweight World Champion

- Joe Lewis Dragon Image Fighting Award
- Museum of Sport Karate History General
- Inductee - United States Martial Arts Hall of Fame
- Graduate degree in Public Administration
- Married to my wife, Darlene, 43 years

MAJOR ACHIEVEMENTS

US Marine - 1971-1975

- Meritorious Mast for outstanding performance
- US Army Reserve - 11th Special Forces Group
- Awarded the Medal of Valor and Silver Star for performance during SWAT operations
- SWAT Team member for 25 years and commanded the unit for 13 years
- Was responsible for security during the 1996 Olympics in Savannah, GA
- Retired LEO - 43 years

Become an
AMAA
MEMBER!

WILLIAM DAVID
GRADY

"
As I enter the "winter" of my life, I hope to continue training and learning and seeing how the arts continue to change and adapt.

WHY THE MARTIAL ARTS?

My martial arts journey started at the Karate School of Asheville when I was ten years old, with Larry Hodges & Jerry Dula. My parents and grandfather got me started to overcome an overweight issue and some bullying issues at school. Thus began my journey into the world of martial arts that I continue to this day - 44 years later.

HOW HAS MARTIAL ARTS IMPACTED YOUR LIFE?

It has been a lifelong journey through each season of my life. As I enter the "winter" of my life, I hope to continue training and learning and seeing how the arts continue to change and adapt. It has also continued forward with most of my children being involved in the Arts to differing degrees.

TRAINING INFORMATION

- Belt Ranks & Martial Arts Styles: 8th Degree - American Freestyle Karate/Legends of The Carolinas, minor rankings in Judo, BJJ, Aikido, and Kenpo
- Instructors/Influencers: Larry Hodges; Current: Patrick Dodd, Shaun Dillon, Steven Montgomery, Ryan Deleo, and Bob Deluca; Past: Jerry Dula, Butch Marks, Trent Codd, Josh Learner, Shannon Dehart, Sifu Larry Rice, Johnny Huskey, Bryan Weatherman and others
- Birthplace/Growing Up: Asheville, NC
- Yrs. In the Martial Arts: 44 years
- Yrs. Instructing: 20+ years
- PKA Worldwide Member

PROFESSIONAL ORGANIZATIONS

- PKA Worldwide

PERSONAL ACHIEVEMENTS

- Seven wonderful children
- Married over 30 years

MAJOR ACHIEVEMENTS

- Black Belt at the age of 13 (youngest at the time for the Karate School of Asheville)
- 2nd Degree earned by age 15 (youngest at the time for the Karate School of Asheville)
- 1988-89 DOJO Light Heavyweight Fighter of the Year
- 1989-90 AAU NC State Games Gold Medalist Light Heavyweight
- 1988 Winner Bad Man Full Contact Contest
- 1989 Defended Bad Man Full Contact Title
- 1989-1993 UNC Chapel Hill 3X Varsity Letterman
- 1990-91 AAU NC State Games Gold Medalist Light Heavyweight
- Amateur Full Contact Record: 18-1-0
- 1995-2002 Co-owner (Head Instructor) with Larry Hodges (Director of Education) for Four Seasons Martial Arts - One of the largest studios in the WNC area at the time. Multi-discipline art & philosophy: Karate, Kobudo, Judo, Jujitsu, Jeet Kune Do, Filipino Martial Arts, Muay Thai, and Cardio Kickboxing.
- 1999 Sport Jujitsu Nationals Double Silver Medalist (Grappling & Striking)

DAVID
HOGAN

“

Martial arts made me a better partner, better leader, and better parent. My journey continues.

dojo, and my son is now an instructor in Jujitsu, training law enforcement officers.

HOW HAS MARTIAL ARTS IMPACTED YOUR LIFE?

To this day, martial arts make me a better man. I am more focused on everyday tasks and continue to grow and be more positive in my actions. Martial arts made me a better partner, better leader, and better parent. My journey continues.

WHY THE MARTIAL ARTS?

I started martial arts in 1996 because of an invitation from then my 5-year-old son, Joe Sam. He was a student at Masters Studios of Self Defense in Charleston, South Carolina. My first sensei was Reggie Westbrook at the James Island location. He continues to teach and is a 7th-degree black belt in Kempo. The school continues with multiple locations in the Charleston area. They continue to encourage family participation. This was a healthy and fun way to work out and, most importantly, an opportunity to spend quality time and share with my son. We both continue our training, myself through Bill "Superfoot " Wallace's weekly

TRAINING INFORMATION

- Belt Ranks & Martial Arts Styles: Kickboxing, Black Belt 1st Dan-Superfoot System, Sport Karate-Brown Belt Advanced, American Kenpo-Blue Belt
- Instructors/Influencers: GM Bill "Superfoot" Wallace, Master Jim Ginter, Master Chris Natzke, Master Terry Dow, Sensei Crystal Myers
- Birthplace/Growing Up: Charleston, SC
- Yrs. In the Martial Arts: 30 years
- Yrs. Instructing: 5 years
- PKA Worldwide Member

PROFESSIONAL ORGANIZATIONS

- PKA Worldwide

PERSONAL ACHIEVEMENTS

- I am a devoted husband and partner and a proud parent
- I rose to the top of my profession and contributed to its growth and advancement
- I modeled a strong work ethic; my son is and continues to be self-reliant

MAJOR ACHIEVEMENTS

- Winning 14 major national and world tournaments
- 2-time U.S. Open champion - 35+ Men's Sparring (1996) and 40+ Advanced Forms (2000)
- 2-time Battle of Atlanta champion - Advanced Belts 40+ Forms and Weapons
- 2-time Boston International champion - 40+ Fighting (1998) and Advanced Belts Forms (1999)
- Ocean State Grand Nationals - Advanced Forms (1999)
- New England Open - Advanced Forms (1999)
- 2-time Bermuda World Open Men's, Forms and Weapons (1998)
- New Jersey Open - Senior Forms champion (1997)
- 2-time All-Star Nationals - Fighting and Forms (1997)
- Diamond Nationals - Advanced Sparring (1999)
- 3-time NASKA National Champion - Senior Fighting (1996), Senior Fighting (1997), Senior Forms (1999)
- KRANE (Krane Referees Assn., of New England) World Champion - 3 Divisions, 40+ Intermediate Forms, Fighting, and Weapons (1998)
- KRANE - Triple Crown Winner, 40+ Adv. Men's Forms (1999)
- WKU (World Karate Union Hall of Fame Ratings System) Executive Men's Fighting, Rated #1 (1998)
- Executive Men's Forms, Rated #1 (1999)

ARTURO MESSINA

"

Martial arts are a point of reference, a refuge for me...

WHY THE MARTIAL ARTS?

I started martial arts in 1980 because I was fascinated by the world I saw in films inspired by actors like Chuck Norris, his strength and determination inspired me; Bruce Lee, his speed and strength; Bill Wallace, his incredible kicks; and then Van Damme. I wanted to imitate them; they were myths for me.

Often in those years, I fought with other boys, but they were the ones who took the beatings; I couldn't lose, so I fought and won. I was a shy, introverted boy, but I absolutely did not want the other boys to beat me and my brothers. I often got into fights in the street to defend them. I was alone; I didn't have a team of friends behind me. One day, I got into a fight with a group of boys. It was me and my brother. They were beating us, and then I got angry; I turned around and fought with their boss. I won, and they let me go.

From that day, I understood that I wanted to learn more about the world of fighting, not from fights, but I was fascinated by one-on-one combat.

One day, a karate school arrived in my town. I signed up, and it was love at first sight. I was fascinated by Kata; I practiced them constantly. I was ten years old, and they were an obsession. I practiced them physically and repeated them mentally. And then the fight. I trained six days a week in two different gyms with my teacher. I saw the older boys give incredible and very fast blows. In those days, the protections were minimal. We hurt ourselves a lot, but we tolerated the pain. It was full contact for kids in those days, and then, one day, I had to get braces. Imagine iron in your mouth; mouthguards existed but were used very little, almost not at all, only in real full contact for kids of age. With my teacher, I decided not to fight until I removed the braces. Useless after a week, I was already on the tatami fighting. When I was outside the tatami, I was in pain. I had to be in there to fight. It was like a call; even today, I no longer fight if I'm not inside the ring. I feel like a call that pushes me to participate.

Our competitions back then were incredible and violent, with minimal protection. We hurt ourselves a lot, but I kept returning to continuously fight to improve. When I came across a stronger teammate, it

The fighters were something extraordinary, and the crowd of fans shouting and cheering for you are memories that remain in my mind. It must be said that the '80s/'90s were the golden era of martial arts. The epic films at the cinema were something incredible. You could breathe martial arts everywhere at school and on the street. You heard about them all the time. The turnout in the dojos was at the highest levels. Everyone wanted to excel in that art in which their myths fought in the films; the number of black belts was very high, and the technical level at the highest levels was all super incredible.

Full contact karate was like a challenge for you, and just as a child, you wanted to know who was the strongest in the neighborhood. As a boy, my curiosity was who was the strongest in the gym, the strongest in the nation, or the world. Even today, I ask myself this question: who is the strongest?

I think there is a star that guides us on our path that we try to rebel against like I did. I often wanted to leave this sport, martial arts because friends played other sports such as football, tennis, etc. I felt like I was excluded from them, but every time I returned like a rubber band, the more I moved away, the more I returned to martial arts. Then, one day, I understood this was my art, and I abandoned the idea of doing other sports.

TRAINING INFORMATION

- Belt Ranks & Martial Arts Styles: Kickboxing, Point Fighting, Light Contact, Full Contact - 5th Dan, Karate Style Shotokan - 6th Dan, Ninjutsu Jujutsu — MMA, Chishin Ryu — Japan, Esperto Difesa Personale Armata

- Instructors/Influencers: Master Marchese Giuseppe

- Birthplace/Growing Up: Rosarno, RC

- Yrs. In the Martial Arts: 39years

- Yrs. Instructing: 15 years

- School owner at A.S.D. Fitness Club Scorpion Kai, PKA Worldwide Member, Maestro

PROFESSIONAL ORGANIZATIONS

- IAKSA
- WMMA
- WMKF

PERSONAL ACHIEVEMENTS

- 8-Time Italian National Kickboxing Point Fighting
- Champion
- 3-Time Italian national Full Contact
- Kickboxing Champion
- 3-Time Italian Shotokan Style Kata Champion
- 2-Time European Kickboxing Champion

MAJOR ACHIEVEMENTS

- World Cup Champions 2018 IAKSA, San Marino

HOW HAS MARTIAL ARTS IMPACTED YOUR LIFE?

Martial arts are a point of reference, a refuge for me. You feel good, all anxieties and fears pass, and only practice and training exist. I feel in my calm, serene world no matter how much I fight; this serenity is also reflected in daily life. However, it had to be fed like a fire that must be fed in order to stay lit. This tranquility is reflected in daily life; I feel calmer and relaxed, but not always; life is hard.

In my relationship with others, I feel more confident, more strength, and determination not to give up and continue until I reach my goals. I know that without sacrifices, you cannot achieve certain goals. The discipline, respect, and punctuality learned in the dojo are reflected in behavior with others, although not always reciprocated. As a teacher, I strive to instill these values in my athletes. However, it is challenging due to the evolving nature of today's youth. The ultimate obstacle lies with the parents, making it imperative for me to begin my journey of teaching and discipline with them.

There was a period in my life in which I suffered for love. I was on the ground, destroyed, anxious, and with very high blood pressure. My body was out of control, and I had no peace. I left martial arts in that period to study at a university. It was hard. I felt like not making it, and then I thought I had to return to martial arts; I told my teacher I wanted to return. He told me it would be hard. The body relaxes the mind when you don't practice. I succeeded, and I returned to martial arts. They were difficult years, but perseverance paid off at the end of the year; martial arts were my lifeline in that period, and I then managed to finish my studies and achieve all my goals.

TIMMY PICKENS

"

True martial arts is so much more than learning to fight. True martial arts teaches lifestyle change and a true way of life.

Styles, and Inside Kung Fu, to name a few. I have two students, Tim Roy and Master Amber Crabtree, who also wrote books on our style.

I love teaching and continue to teach women's self-defense, police, and our military free of charge. As my teacher has always said, "Be humble, be pure of heart, and be a better person than you were yesterday."

HOW HAS MARTIAL ARTS IMPACTED YOUR LIFE?

Martial arts has helped me have the confidence to achieve goals and exceed them. My martial arts encompasses everything I do in life, whether it be my education, ministry, personal relationships, job, or teaching. I train my body to be healthy, my mind to be calm, and my spirit at peace. I love teaching others not only how to protect themselves in these difficult times but also how to succeed in life. True martial arts is so much more than learning to fight. True martial arts teaches lifestyle change and a true way of life.

WHY THE MARTIAL ARTS?

I began training under Dr. Ng at the age of 12. I was raised poor and bullied in school. I started competing in regional, state, and national tournaments in the 1980s and was rated top five by the Professional Karate League of America. In 1986, I won 1st place in forms and 2nd in weapons black belt division at the Battle of Atlanta. I received my grandmaster rank in Six Harmonies Eight Methods Boxing in 2005. Dr. Ng honored me by publicly passing me his successorship over his family styles in 2017. I have taught over 2000 students and have 17 state, national, and international champions. I have written four books on Dr. Ng's family style and have written and appeared in numerous articles for Karate Illustrated, Black Belt Magazine, Masters and

TRAINING INFORMATION

- Belt Ranks & Martial Arts Styles: Grand Masters Six Harmonies Eight Methods Boxing, Grand Masters in Six Harmonies Drunken Boxing, Grand Masters Poison Hand Style, and Masters in the following: Southern Golden Monkey, Bat Style, and Golden Snake Fist. Listed in the Chinese Liu He Quan Chinese lineage.

- Instructors/Influencers: Great Grandmaster Dr. John Winglock Ng, the late Professor David Ng

- Birthplace/Growing Up: Albany, KY

- Yrs. In the Martial Arts: 45 years

- Yrs. Instructing: 36 years

- School owner, Manager & Instructor at Ng Family Elite Guard, PKA Worldwide Member

PROFESSIONAL ORGANIZATIONS

- PKA Worldwide Member
- PKL

PERSONAL ACHIEVEMENTS

- Rated top five region seven by PKL in the 1980's
- Author
- Midwest Regional Director World Stunt Organization
- Producer/Director Stunt Choreographer

MAJOR ACHIEVEMENTS

- Masters in Nursing
- PhD Nursing
- Grandmasters Chinese Kung Fu
- Published Author
- Stunt actor/Choreographer
- Minister

JERRY
PIDDINGTON

> *Martial Arts has guided my life and helped me meet some of the most incredible people in the world.*

invited him to create his own style. On May 2, 1972, Mr. Piddington was declared the Headmaster and Founder of American Open Style Karate under the USKA sanctified charter, established by O'Sensei Trias, which was internationally ratified on May 30, 1975. In February 2000, Mr. Piddington was declared Headmaster of American Shorei/Shorin Karate by Hanshi John Pachivas, Grandmaster of Shuri-ryu Karatedo, and was awarded his 10th degree black belt.

WHY THE MARTIAL ARTS?

O'Shihan Piddington has a martial arts career that spans decades, and he has studied with some of the most famous martial artists in the world. His first teacher was Caylor Atkins in Shotokan. Continuing his career, Mr. Piddington trained in Shorin-ryu with Tom Crites and Tadashi Yamashita, Hawaiian Kenpo with Michael Stone, Japanese Goju-ryu with Chris Armstrong, and Kempo with Ed Parker. Mr. Piddington was also a student and friend of O'Sensei Robert Trias, Father of American Karate.

O'Sensei Trias took notice of Mr. Piddington and

HOW HAS MARTIAL ARTS IMPACTED YOUR LIFE?

Martial Arts has guided Mr. Piddinton's life and helped him meet some of the most incredible people in the world.

In the 1970s, Mr. Piddington was one of the four promoters of Mike Stone's Four Seasons National Tournaments, along with Algene Caraulia, Pat Burleson, and Mike Stone. Mr. Piddington pioneered kickboxing on the East Coast by promoting five major kickboxing title fights in Charlotte, North Carolina. He was a co-writer with Joe Corley, establishing the rules for the Professional Karate Association (PKA), which is documented in the 1974 issue of Sports Illustrated. As founder of the National Karate Association (NKA),

TRAINING INFORMATION

- Belt Ranks & Martial Arts Styles: Shorin Ryu -10th Dan, Shorei Ryu-10th Dan, American Open Karate-10th Dan, Okinawan Kobudo-10th Dan
- Instructors/Influencers: Robert Trias, Caylor Atkins, Tom Crites, Tadashi Yamashita, Michael Stone, Chris Armstrong, Ed Parker
- Birthplace/Growing Up: CA
- Yrs. In the Martial Arts: 62 years
- Yrs. Instructing: 62 years
- Instructor & PKA Worldwide Member

PROFESSIONAL ORGANIZATIONS

- American Karate Academies National Association
- PKA Worldwide

PERSONAL & MAJOR ACHIEVEMENTS

- Founder of American Karate Academies National Association
- Founding member of PKA Worldwide
- Founding member of Kaizen Invitational Martial Arts Tournament League

HOW HAS MARTIAL ARTS IMPACTED YOUR LIFE? (CONTINUED)

Mr. Piddington promoted the first eleven-round world title kickboxing match, with Jeff Smith winning a decision over Keith Haflick for the 1977 Light Heavy Weight Championship of the World.

Also, under the NKA sanction, Mr. Piddington promoted the first World Tag Team Kickboxing Championships with the Gold Dust Twins, Ricky and Randy Smith, defeating Dale Cook's double pro team from Tulsa, Oklahoma, considered by many as some of the best kickboxing action to this date. Mr. Piddington founded The Charlotte Warhawks, an undefeated five-man kickboxing team that included some of his most notable fighters — Danny McCall, Keith Haflick, Jimmy Horsley, Ricky Smith, and Randy Smith. The team was coached by Danny Wilson and managed by Gene Smith.

TED
PRYOR

"
From World Kickboxing Champion to a Martial Arts Master and a Master Business Entrepreneur

Police Department, as well as for the DEA, FBI, and Secret Service. Additionally, he provided high-level bodyguard services for prominent personalities such as Elvis Presley and Don Johnson.

As he transitioned into the business world, Ted Pryor drew on his dedication to martial arts and strong work ethic. He established and managed a chain of 15 self-service car washes called One Stop Car Wash. In 1990, he entered the childcare industry with Tutor Time Learning Systems, Inc., where he held multiple key positions. He served as Senior Vice President of Planning, Development, and Marketing. Additionally, he played a crucial role as an equity partner in expanding the franchise into a 250-unit network spanning 24 states and 10 countries.

In 1999, Pryor founded Children of America (COA), a company dedicated to providing high-quality childcare and educational centers. With over 35 years of experience in the childcare industry, Pryor's expertise has been crucial in establishing COA as one of the largest educational childcare providers in the United States, with more than 70 schools.

In addition to his brick-and-mortar professional endeavors, Pryor has also been involved in the film industry. He collaborated with iconic action star Chuck Norris in several films. Pryor also founded

T ed Pryor is a multi-talented world kickboxing champion with a diverse post-ring career that spans multiple industries and continents. From his impressive kickboxing achievements to his successful business ventures, Pryor has made a lasting impact in combat sports and child education and care.

Pryor began his martial arts journey at the age of 13. He went on to become a professional kickboxer during the full-contact karate era and held the title of WKA Super Middleweight World Champion from 1982 to 1987. Pryor remained undefeated in various high-profile competitions, including the 1990 USA vs. Russia event, which cemented his reputation as a kickboxing powerhouse. Recognized as "Best of Breed" in martial arts, Pryor's exceptional skills and contributions to the sport were widely acknowledged as he competed and excelled across Asia, Europe, and the United States.

Ted was also a skilled martial artist outside the ring. He worked as a tactical instructor for the Palm Beach

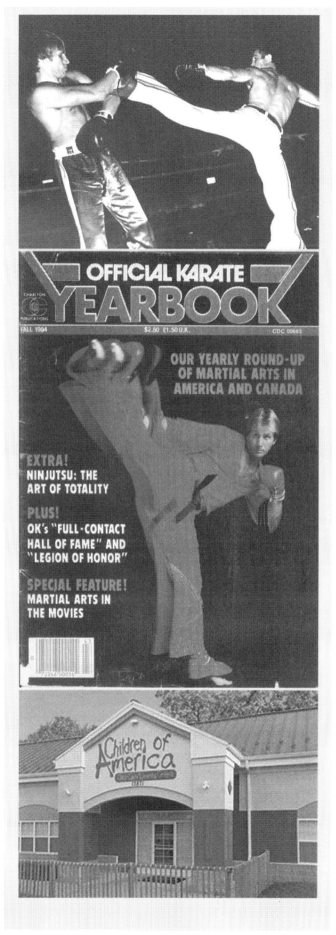

World Films and served as the executive producer for acclaimed movies such as *The Butcher, The Last Sentinel,* and *Soft Target.* These movies garnered international recognition upon release on major networks like NBC, Universal, and HBO.

Today, Ted Pryor enjoys retirement with his wife, Shien-Lin, and their five children. Despite stepping back from the daily operations of COA, Pryor remains actively involved as the founder, continuing to provide unwavering support to those in need. His dedication to giving back to the community led to the establishment of the Pryor Family Foundation, further solidifying his legacy of philanthropy and impact.

Ted Pryor's autobiography, *Three-Time World Champ: The Death-Defying True Story of a Multiple Title Kickboxer, Turned Smuggler…Turned Multi-Talented Business Icon* is set to release on December 4, 2024.

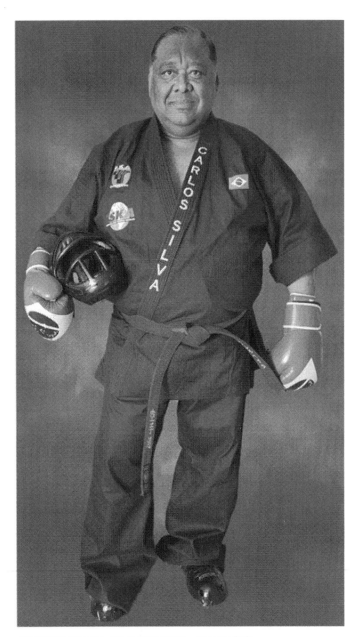

CARLOS SILVA

"
Martial arts is part of my life. There is no me without martial arts. My whole life is dedicated to it.

After receiving a black belt in kickboxing from Master Alfredo Apicella of the World Association of Kickboxing Organizations (WAKO), he assumed the Chairmanship of the Hammerhilt Kickboxing Association of Paraíba and later, with advanced graduation and a member of the Brazilian Kickboxing Confederation. Master Silva created the Federation of Kickboxing of the State of Paraíba, making this federation one of the first of the sport in the country, that later changed its name to Federation of Kickboxing Full Contact of the State of Paraíba.

In 1990 he founded the Brazilian Confederation of Traditional Kickboxing (CBKBT). Since then, CBKBT's mission has been to teach American kickboxing, known as "traditional," because it diverges from these chains that do not follow the line adopted in the United States of America to teach this modality.

Grandmaster Carlos Silva holds the title of 10th Dan in Kickboxing, 9th Dan in Karate Shorei Ryu, Kru in Muaythai, 1st Dan in Taekwondo Kukiwon, 5th Dan in Hapkido, 1st Dan in Shotokan Karate, and has also dedicated time to the study of Ninjutsu. Silva has been a cover of Fight Magazine in Brazil, and Kumite Magazine, Greece, has also published his work.

WHY THE MARTIAL ARTS?

Grandmaster Carlos Roberto Silva (João Pessoa, December 4, 1961) is a Brazilian kickboxer. At the present time, he holds the Brazilian Confederation of Traditional Kickboxing Presidency.

At age 12, he began his studies in martial arts, practicing Judo and Shotokan karate. Later, he was introduced to Muay Thai by Professor Carlos Nunes. After that, he met Shihan Pericles Daiski Veiga and started in the Shorei Ryu style of then Master Moritoshi Nakaema and at the same time went on to promote events and the development of kickboxing.

TRAINING INFORMATION

- Belt Ranks & Martial Arts Styles: Kickboxing -10th Degree Black Belt, Shorei Ryu Karate-9th Degree Black Belt, Hapkido-5th Degree Black Belt, Taekwondo WTF-3rd Degree Black Belt, Ninjutsu Togakure Ryu-1st Degree Black Belt, Kru Muaythai

- Instructors/Influencers: Bill Wallace, Joe Corley, Morotoshi Nakaema, Yoshizo Machida, Yasuiuki Sasaki, John Pelegrini, Jack Stearn Papasan

- Birthplace/Growing Up: Joao Pessoa + Paraiba State, Brazil

- Yrs. In the Martial Arts: 43 years

- Yrs. Instructing: 38 years

- School Owner, Manager, Instructor at CBKBT USA, PKA Worldwide Member

PROFESSIONAL ORGANIZATIONS

- AMAA
- PKA
- ISKA
- IHC
- CBKBT
- WUKO
- WAKO
- WTKA
- USMA
- USKF
- NKKF
- DKI
- COME ON IN

PERSONAL & MAJOR ACHIEVEMENTS

- AMAA Hall Of Fame
- ISKA Man Of The Year
- Hall Of Honors Hall Of Fame
- USMAA Hall Of Fame

In 2019 Grandmaster Silva introduced PKA WORLDWIDE to South America. PKA is the organization that created professional martial arts for television in the United States in 1974, naming the first World Champions of Bill "Superfoot" Wallace, Jeff Smith, Joe Lewis (RIP), and Isaias Duenas. Grandmasters Bill Wallace and Joe Corley joined Grandmaster Silva in Brazil in 2019 for a series of PKA Seminars and Certifications.

HOW HAS MARTIAL ARTS IMPACTED YOUR LIFE?

Martial arts is part of my life. There is no me without martial arts. I have been practicing martial arts for 43 years. My whole life is dedicated to it. I am an Ambassador of Martial Arts for the world.

JIM
SNOWBERGER

"

I feel that my success in life is that I have given kids and adults a chance to learn not only self-defense but life lessons.

WHY THE MARTIAL ARTS?

Growing up in rural Indiana in the 1950s and 1960s, there was no martial arts, and we heard almost nothing about it. After I joined the United States Marine Corps in 1968, I had my first class in what at that time was called hand-to-hand combat training; my first thought was, how cool is this? I fell in love with it, and after my service in Vietnam in 1969-1970 and I finished my enlistment, I needed something to work out my feelings. A little training and a heavy bag helped a lot. The more I trained, the more I wanted to learn.

To answer the question simply, why did I get started in martial arts? I feel it was my destiny.

HOW HAS MARTIAL ARTS IMPACTED YOUR LIFE?

After serving in Vietnam as a squad leader from 1969-1970, I was stationed at Camp Lejeune, North Carolina, for the remainder of my enlistment. I was swamped raising my family and working to pay the bills like everyone else. When I realized how much I enjoyed Hand-to-hand combat in the Marine Corps, I started looking for places to train. In rural Indiana, there was not very much to choose from; my first training was in Judo with a guy who had learned some in the Army while stationed overseas. That was fun to learn, but I wanted something else. I then started to look for other things when I had time with the kids. I tried several different martial arts systems and instructors but still wasn't satisfied.

In 1988, I found Soke Thomas Burdine and Tae Kwon Do and Karate Do; this was what I was looking for (back then, I could still kick people in the head). Two things set me on the path I'm on now: one was martial arts, and the other was meeting my wife, Kelli, through martial arts. In 1998, we opened our school called Snow's Martial Arts Federation. I never knew I would enjoy teaching so much; as I said, I live in rural Indiana and never meant the school to be my livelihood.

I worked at a factory and ran the school in the evenings. I knew that if I charged too much for classes, I would have very few students, and many people who would benefit from learning martial arts would not be able to do it.

TRAINING INFORMATION

- Belt Ranks & Martial Arts Styles: Tae Kwon Do - 9th Dan, Karate Do - 9th Dan
- Instructors/Influencers: Soke Thomas Burdine, Grandmaster Larry Goris
- Birthplace/Growing Up: Williamsport, IN / Delphi, IN
- Yrs. In the Martial Arts: 54 years
- Yrs. Instructing: 30 years
- School owner & Instructor at Snow's Martial Arts Federation, PKA Worldwide Member

PROFESSIONAL ORGANIZATIONS

- PKA
- Kokon Ryu Renmei Bujustu - Soke Thomas Burdine
- USA Martial Arts -Dr. Jim Thomas
- United States Martial Arts - Professor Marty Cale

PERSONAL ACHIEVEMENTS

- Having the chance to work with and teach kids. I enjoy helping them learn martial arts and life skills, such as not taking the easy way out and quitting when things get hard. I also work with Marine Corps veterans as the Commandant of the Marine Corps League Detachment 1411. We do not only help Veterans but also do a great deal of community service.

MAJOR ACHIEVEMENTS

- World Karate Hall of Fame - Master of the Year - Professor Frank Tasetano
- World Martial Arts Hall of Fame - Lifetime Achieve Award - Professor Ed McLauchlan
- United States Martial arts Hall of fame - Silver Life Award - Professor Marty Cale
- United States Martial Arts International Hall of Fame -Master instructor of the year and Outstanding Martial Artist of the year - O'Sensei Phillip Porter

HOW HAS MARTIAL ARTS IMPACTED YOUR LIFE? (CONTINUED)

I feel that my success in life is that I have given kids and adults a chance to learn not only self-defense but life lessons. I always thought that if something I have done or said could only help one person become a better person, then I would have success. I have helped several, and my wife and I are so blessed to have had the opportunity. I tell people that I can't believe that a kid from Delphi, Indiana, would get to travel the world and get to meet so many fascinating people.

RICK
SPARKS

“

I have won several tournaments and Grand Championships, but I found it much more satisfying to see your students winning than winning yourself.

WHY THE MARTIAL ARTS?

I grew up in a small rural Western North Carolina Community. I have always been into sports; however, the selection of sports was very limited here. I played football from Little League through high school and always as a quarterback. Growing up, I had always watched martial arts movies and found that they captivated me, but there was nowhere around this community to take lessons.

In 1974, I enlisted in the United States Army, and while I was stationed in Germany, I met a gentleman who was a black belt in Judo. I took some lessons from him and became very interested when the gentleman was transferred out. After my tour with the Army, I returned to my small hometown and opened a Sporting Goods Store. Not long after opening, a gentleman stopped in one day and inquired

if I could order karate gear. Long story short, I started studying Shito-Ryu with Hanshi Bill Daniels.

Hanshi Daniels was an East Coast Full Contact Champion for eight years. I was in his corner during most of his fights. So, I came through the ranks of old-school "hard style." Hanshi Daniels moved away from the community around 1980. After receiving my Nidan Degree, I opened my own school, where I taught for several years. There was nowhere in this area for advancement.

I eventually met Master Louis Shaw out of Charleston, South Carolina. The late Master Shaw had moved up here in the mountains, came to my dojo, and started training me in Kenpo. After many private lessons and several years, I advanced to 7th degree in Kenpo. Mr. Shaw turned over his Kenpo Karate Institute to me shortly before his passing.

I then reconnected with Hanshi Daniels and received my 5th degree in Shito-Ryu. I started studying with Soke Bobby Briggs somewhere around 2016 and 2017 and was promoted to Hachidan by Soke Briggs.

HOW HAS MARTIAL ARTS IMPACTED YOUR LIFE?

Martial arts has been my complete lifestyle for the past 50 years. I always have something going on in martial arts. At 69 years old, I still teach two nights a week. We hold two tournaments of our own every year, The Appalachian Japanese Invitational, and lots of time and effort goes into these events. I take my students to several tournaments every year. I spend a lot of my weekends at tournaments, judging and refereeing. I have total support from my wife and family.

I have a small construction company that I still run daily. All my non-working time has been devoted to martial arts. I have traveled thousands of miles related to martial arts, all the tournaments, seminars, and parties. I participated in the competition trail for several years before setting into just teaching and coaching. I have won several tournaments and Grand Championships, but I found it much more satisfying to see your students winning than winning yourself.

TRAINING INFORMATION

- Belt Ranks & Martial Arts Styles: Shito-Ryu - 5th Degree, Kenpo - 7th Degree, Kidokimi-Ryu - 8th Degree, Shodan Black Belt from Cancer Warriors
- Instructors/Influencers: Hanshi Bill Daniels, The late Master Louis Shaw, Soke Bobby Briggs
- Birthplace/Growing Up: Mitchell County, NC
- Yrs. In the Martial Arts: 49 years
- Yrs. Instructing: 44 years
- School owner & Instructor at Blue Ridge Martial Arts, PKA Worldwide Member

PROFESSIONAL ORGANIZATIONS

- Master Mason
- Lifetime PKA Member
- AKANA Member

PERSONAL ACHIEVEMENTS

- MVP Awards High School Football
- Pinnacle Tomoe Award From AKANA - Hanshi Jerry Piddington & Hanshi Danny McCall
- Inducted into The Legends of the Carolinas Martial Arts 2018
- Appointment to Kyoshi 2018

MAJOR ACHIEVEMENTS

- Induction into The Legends of the Carolinas Martial Arts
- Pinnacle Tomoe Award from AKANA
- Black Belt from Cancer Warrior Survivor

HOW HAS MARTIAL ARTS IMPACTED YOUR LIFE? (CONT.)

My first black belt, which I promoted in the early 1980s, is now a Soke. I'm proud of him. One student has won the World Championship in Orlando, Florida, in Kumite. I'm a very proud instructor. The most satisfying of all is when someone comes up to you and tells you of the impact you have made on their life. Now, that is rewarding. So, martial arts has impacted my life on every level.

MATTHEW
STEPHAN

"
Martial Arts have impacted me by achieving good health, a body that is physically sound and, of course, a mind that is focused and has great awareness and determination.

HOW HAS MARTIAL ARTS IMPACTED YOUR LIFE?

Martial arts started impacting my life by taking me to places for the first time. When I went to Okinawa and Japan, it was my first time on an airplane, my first time in the ocean, and my first time outside of the United States. Traveling around to tournaments, I have met many martial arts students, instructors, masters, and grandmasters. There are many great competitors out there, and I have competed with them. To be your "very best" is tough to do, but to be "the best of the best" is even tougher.

I have taught many Tournament Champions at my school (Shogun Self Defense). I have also taught my daughter (Trinity) and my son (Joshua). Joshua recently earned his black belt from me. He is also a Tournament Champion.

Martial Arts have impacted me by achieving good health, a body that is physically sound and, of course, a mind that is focused and has great awareness and determination.

I have always stood by my personal koan: "Through Jesus Christ and my martial arts training, I will stand firmly on the summit of existence."

WHY THE MARTIAL ARTS?

I started martial arts to learn how to fight, but with martial arts, I also learned how to live.

Matthew Stephan

TRAINING INFORMATION

- Belt Ranks & Martial Arts Styles: Karate: Shuri Ryu - 6th Dan Black Belt, Ju Jitsu; Yoshin Ryu - 5th Dan Black Belt
- Instructors/Influencers: Shuri Ryu: Grand Master Robert Bowles, Grand Master Woodrow Fairbanks; Yoshin Ryu: Master Jeffery Moore, Master Parker Shelton-Judo
- Birthplace/Growing Up: Fort Wayne, IN
- Yrs. In the Martial Arts: 34 years
- Yrs. Instructing: 26 years
- School owner & Instructor at Shogun Self Defense, PKA Worldwide Member

PROFESSIONAL ORGANIZATIONS
Lifetime Member
- PKA
- USKA
- PKC
- UPMAC
- CBBA
- USMA

PERSONAL ACHIEVEMENTS
- Bachelor of Science in Business
- Alpha Chi Fraternity
- Summa Cum Laude
- Outstanding Graduate at Indiana Institute of Technology
- Top 25 Sales at ADT for 16 years
- Shogun Self Defense LLC
- Co-owners with my wife (Misty) at Paws-n-Claws Pet Care Palace

MAJOR ACHIEVEMENTS
- PKC Indiana State Karate Champion 1996
- PKC Indiana State Karate Champion 1997
- PKC Indiana State Karate Champion 1998
- PKC Indiana State Karate Champion 2000
- PKC Indiana State Karate Champion 2003
- PKC Indiana State Karate Champion 2017
- PKC Indiana State Karate Champion 2019
- PKC National Champion 1997-1998
- PKC National Champion 1999-2000
- USMA Alliance Tournament Champion 2008 - 2018
- UPMAC Circuit Champion 2017, 2018, 2019
- CBBA Circuit Champion 2002
- USKA World Champion 1998
- USKA World Champion 2019
- Cleveland Martial Arts Hall Of Fame 2021
- USMA Alliance Hall of Fame 2008
- Illinios Karate Team 2009
- USMA Alliance Budo Society Member 2008
- Fairbanks Budo Society Member 2023

GREG
SUTHER

" *Continued study of martial arts has given me a broadened sense of community with friends and associates from around the world.*

WHY THE MARTIAL ARTS?

Being shy and somewhat socially awkward as a boy, I was a perfect target for bullies. I had seen Bruce Lee on The Green Hornet TV show and was intrigued, thinking, "This could save me." Then, I watched a girl at school doing Tae Kwon Do at the school talent show. I was impressed by the transformation when she performed. I began to ask for lessons, but my dad said, "You have a saxophone and play in the band. If you have any spare time, you'll be practicing on the saxophone." This was in my mid-teens.

At 23, my girlfriend began classes at Sam Chapman's American Karate in Greenville, SC. As we talked about her classes, I was excited again. For my 24th birthday, she gave me an introduction to karate course that consisted of three private lessons on the basic punches, blocks, kicks, and stances. I was hooked and enrolled immediately. She quit the day I started, but I never looked back.

At 24, I was still so shy that I was reluctant even to call in a pizza order for fear of what the kid at the pizza store would think of my voice. Sam Chapman was larger-than-life, an imposing giant who scared me just being around him. But he inspired me and fueled me to be better than I thought I could be. As we wrapped up my first test (for gold belt), he said something that challenged me. "There are 20 of you here," he said. "Most of you will drop out within six months. A couple of you will get to green belt. One of you, maybe one, will get to brown belt. And, hopefully, that person will push through to be a black belt." I was determined that the one would be me. From then on, I was relentless in my training, focused on not disappointing Mr. Chapman. I knew that someone would always be faster, someone would always be stronger, and someone would always have better technique, but no one would ever try harder than me.

HOW HAS MARTIAL ARTS IMPACTED YOUR LIFE?

My study of martial arts facilitated my development from a shy, reticent young man with no direction and no confidence to a confident, encouraging, and supportive teacher and trainer. Studying martial arts helped me to be analytical and gave me the ability to deconstruct an idea of its basic parts in order to determine which parts are valid and which parts could/ should be altered.

Martial arts study showed me the differences in learning abilities, leading to an empathetic teaching style. Continued study of martial arts has given me a broadened sense of community with friends and associates from around the world.

TRAINING INFORMATION

- Belt Ranks & Martial Arts Styles: Sam Chapman's American Karate - 9th Degree Black Belt, Joe Corley American Karate - 5th Degree Black Belt, Jay T. Will Kenpo - Orange Belt
- Instructors/Influencers: Sam Chapman, Bobby Tucker, Joe Corley, Asa Gordon, Jay T. Will
- Birthplace/Growing Up: Greenville, SC
- Yrs. In the Martial Arts: 47 years
- Yrs. Instructing: 44 years
- School owner, Manager & Instructor at Zanshin American Karate and Kenpo, PKA Worldwide Member

PROFESSIONAL ORGANIZATIONS

- SEKA
- PKA

PERSONAL ACHIEVEMENTS

- BA in English
- Certified Luthier

MAJOR ACHIEVEMENTS

- 1980 SEKA Brown Belt Heavyweight Fighter of the Year
- 1981 SEKA Black Belt Middleweight Fighter of the Year
- 1982 Certified Kickboxing Official for the PKA, ISKA, and the PKC
- 2018 Joe Lewis Eternal Warrior Award Recipient
- 2019 Carolina Legends of the Martial Arts Inductee
- 2023 South Carolina Black Belt Hall of Fame "Bobby Tucker Courage Award" Recipient
- 2024 Named Director of PKA Associated Schools

DALIA VITKUS

"Though I am a work in progress, I continue to attract those in need of what I can offer as a martial artist and all that comes with that...

WHY THE MARTIAL ARTS?

Martial arts have always fascinated me, as I watched Bruce Lee movies growing up in Chicago. I often thought that if I knew how to protect myself and others using martial arts skills, my family and neighborhood would be a safer place. I took a women's self-defense karate class in my first year of college and loved it! But back then, it was such a man's martial art, and I was very shy, so I did not pursue my passion until much later.

In 2006, I had an epiphany. I pursued my academic goals in Criminal Justice and found a local martial arts school near me. I was the only female in the adult class with male color belts; I was the only student to achieve a black belt in that class. Later, I worked with at-risk youth at a Taekwondo Academy in Benton Harbor, MI. That was when Bill Wallace saw how I was being taken advantage of and helped me overcome that and begin my own martial arts school in St. Joseph, MI. It was amazing!

Along with my Master's Degree in Criminal Justice, I have achieved a 3rd Degree Black Belt in Taekwondo; I am certified with the World Taekwondo Federation, am an instructor, and recently earned a 4th Degree Black Belt in Superfoot System. I have trained with world-renowned martial artists, including Bill "Superfoot" Wallace, Senior Grandmaster Edward B. Sell, and Senior Grandmaster Brenda Sell of the U.S. Chung Do Kwan, Assoc. In 2016, I was inducted into the U.S.A. Martial Arts Hall of Fame and received an award as Leading Female Black Belt of the Year in recognition of my accomplishments as a dedicated martial artist and bullying prevention program.

My instruction focuses on self-defense for life: strength, encouragement, learning, and fitness. This incorporates strengthening balance, coordination, and fitness for a healthy mind, body, and spirit, thereby reducing stress, promoting inner peace, and empowering one to succeed in life.

I bring the unique and exciting Superfoot System of martial arts instruction, which includes traditional Taekwondo and Kickboxing, to my New Wave Kicks private lessons and seminars in St. Joseph, MI. These well-developed disciplines provide positive skills for students of all ages. Children benefit from the discipline. This martial art is beneficial to them both physically and in their lives as grades and behavior improve! Adults acquire skills in physical balance and coordination while reducing stress and learning the art of self-defense of oneself and others.

My passions include self-defense for women and senior citizens, working with children of all ages, and family Taekwondo and Kickboxing. I am dedicated to bullying prevention, building self-esteem and positive growth, and suicide prevention with today's youth and adults, which is also part of the New Wave Kicks Martial Arts program.

I bring a positive, outgoing, fun, and energetic spirit to my classes and feel that it opens one to a world of fantastic opportunities for fitness, health, self-confidence, and self-defense. Come join me in this NEW WAVE of fitness and self-defense for life!

TRAINING INFORMATION

- Belt Ranks & Martial Arts Styles: 3rd Degree Black Belt — Taekwondo, 4th Degree Black Belt - Superfoot System
- Instructors/Influencers: Bill "Superfoot" Wallace, Grandmaster Brenda Sell
- Birthplace/Growing Up: Chicago, IL
- Yrs. In the Martial Arts: 18 years
- Yrs. Instructing: 14 years
- School owner, Manager & Instructor at New Wave Kicks LLC, PKA Worldwide Member, Member and Charter school of the U.S. Chung Do Kwan Association

PROFESSIONAL ORGANIZATIONS

- Member U.S. Chung Do Kwan Association
- Member PKA Worldwide
- Student/Member Superfoot System Dojo
- National Sport Karate Museum Ambassador

PERSONAL ACHIEVEMENTS

- Achieved 3rd Degree Black Belt in Taekwondo
- Achieved 4th Degree Black Belt in Superfoot System
- Adjunct Professor at Colorado Technical University Online
- Case Manager at the Berrien County Juvenile Center
- Lithuanian Sea Scout Organization Counselor/Officer
- Gave birth to and raised two sons and a daughter

MAJOR ACHIEVEMENTS

- Achieved Officer rank in the Lithuanian Sea Scout Organization
- Achieved 3rd Degree Black Belt in Taekwondo
- Achieved 4th Degree Black Belt in Superfoot System
- Own and operate the New Wave Kicks Martial Arts and Kickboxing School
- Inducted into the Alliance Black Belt Hall of Fame
- Master's Degree in Criminal Justice

HOW HAS MARTIAL ARTS IMPACTED YOUR LIFE?

My practice in Taekwondo and the Superfoot System has helped me become a much better, positive, stronger version of myself. Being an empath and natural healer attracts many individuals needing help. Building up my self-confidence and self-esteem has helped me to help others better. Though I am a work in progress, I continue to attract those in need of what I can offer as a martial artist and all that comes with that, such as integrity, courtesy, perseverance, self-control, and especially, indomitable spirit!

TIMOTHY WHITE

"

My life as a martial artist has evolved through communication, learning, and caring for those who think like you.

I started studying Kung Fu systems with the late GM Tak Cheung Wong. GM Wong became my greatest mentor in martial arts. I started working for the Indiana State Capitol Police in 1977 and met GM Dan Onan. I started training police tactics with him since he was a lead instructor for the State Department of Corrections, which kept my interest in police tactics. After several years of teaching officers from different agencies, I realized something was missing from the training, and that was a true martial arts concept.

Martial arts led me to Active/Passive Countermeasures, PPCT, the Risk Management System, and others. I then became an ASP and OC instructor, and then I became an Indiana Law Enforcement Training Board Certified Instructor so that I could teach officers in the state of Indiana. I have continued that mission as of today.

Martial arts have allowed me to be more than I had intended. Since I began practicing martial arts, I have achieved many things, motivating me to continue training.

WHY THE MARTIAL ARTS?

I started martial arts in the Army stationed in Darmstadt, Germany. I began this journey to enhance my self-defense skills and physical fitness levels. I met Mr. Wes Ruiz, who was teaching in the racquetball court at the post gym. It was sort of funny since most of the class was Puerto Rican, and I was the only white guy in the class. They accepted me as one of them. I continued studying with this group and the origin of Kiru-Do Karate.

I was growing spiritually and physically, which motivated me to continue studying martial arts. After two years of studying with Mr. Ruiz, Mr. Ruiz transferred back to the United States, and I started studying Tae Kwon Do with Mr. Jay Park. I made it to 3 Kup in TKD. I then transferred back to the USA and got involved in police and security work.

HOW HAS MARTIAL ARTS IMPACTED YOUR LIFE?

When I first started in martial arts, I didn't know where it would take me. I was seventeen years old and in the US Army. However, over the years, I have made strides to keep the martial arts close to my heart and soul. It has helped me in my law enforcement career as a Defensive Tactic and Physical Force Instructor. It has brought me in contact with many well-known trainers and opened my eyes to many different aspects of martial arts. I have met and trained with some of the best in the business. This in itself has enabled me to survive during the Covid-19 Pandemic.

My life as a martial artist has evolved through communication, learning, and caring for those who think like you. Martial arts has taught me that I can compete on any level and still enjoy the competition and the winning. In 2021, I won two state titles in weapons and forms in the Tournament Karate Association tournament season. This had a great impact on how I grew in the future.

At one point, I thought I might have to close my martial arts club, but my black belts came in and helped teach, make donations to the club, pay rent, etc. They made sure they had a place to train and learn. I am honored to have such students in my martial arts club.

TRAINING INFORMATION

- Belt Ranks & Martial Arts Styles: Molum Pai Kung Fu-Grand Master/System Inheritor, Kiru-Do Karate-8th Dan, Okkuy-Ryu Jujutsu-7th Dan
- Instructors/Influencers: The late GM Tak Cheung (Felix) Wong, GM Wes Ruiz, the late GM Dan Onan
- Birthplace/Growing Up: Greenville, SC
- Yrs. In the Martial Arts: 52 years
- Yrs. Instructing: 49 years
- School owner, Manager & Instructor at PSI/Molum Combat Arts, PKA Worldwide Member

PROFESSIONAL ORGANIZATIONS

- Fraternal Order of Police
- Professional Karate Association
- Professional Karate Commission
- American Martial Arts Alliance
- Tournament Karate Association
- Military Police Regimental Association
- Health Safety Institute
- United States Martial Arts Association
- Eastern USA Karate Association

PERSONAL ACHIEVEMENTS

- Keeping my martial arts studio open during Covid-19
- Winning TKA State Titles for Weapons and Forms
- Being inducted into the Sport Karate Museum
- Being inducted into the Warrior Society Hall of Fame
- Retiring from the US Army in 1995
- Top Ten Competitor in the PKC 2002 to 2010

MAJOR ACHIEVEMENTS

- Co-Authored Cell Extractions for Prisons and Jails
- Being inducted in the Who's Who in the Martial Arts biography books 2017 to 2023
- Being appointed an Ambassador for AMAA
- Being honored by Action Martial Arts Magazine 2015 to 2019
- Surviving Covid-19

DR. JOHN
WILLIAMS

"

Studying the arts has had an impact on my life by making me learn more about myself and my abilities.

WHY THE MARTIAL ARTS?

It all started with Dr. John Williams' brother, GM Jesse Mack Williams, a champion in kickboxing. He called Jesse his hero when he was growing up. He soon found himself using Jesse as a shield, and never knowing how to defend himself, his brother would train them as his children with every chance he had. Dr. John Williams stated, "I must say that until I started taking martial arts, I never fought back." One day, he got tired of getting beaten down and took classes at the Roy Walker gym in Clovis, New Mexico, where his instructor was Master Westly Scott. After a few fights under his belt and winning becoming easier and easier, he defended himself from the bullies and those around him. He remembered he only had one fight in high school, and it ended with him kicking a boy through a window, then dragging him out, mounting him for the finish before the

teachers pulled him from the boy. He added, "Martial arts have taught me much-needed discipline. I learned to use it as a very last resort!

Dr. John Williams is the youngest of fourteen children. His mentor, Etter Mae Houston, told him that he was smart and could be anything in life that he wanted to be. That's when Dr. Williams made a tremendous change in his life. With the improvement of his self-confidence and self-worth, he graduated high school in 1986 after failing seventh grade three times. He was the first of fourteen children to finish high school and go to college; he joined the US Army in December of 1988 and was medically retired after 11 years of service.

He has received numerous awards for volunteering his time and service to the community, no matter where his family was stationed. His list of awards, educational certifications, and degrees is extensive and distinguished. Some of his accolades include the Extraordinary People Award, the US Army Dr. Mary E. Walker Award, a Doctorate in Humanity, a Doctorate of Christian Counseling & Communication, recognition in the Cambridge Who's Who 15th Edition, the Lifetime Volunteer Achievement Award from former President Trump and President Biden, the Top 40 under 40 Award, a Doctorate of Youth Work, a

TRAINING INFORMATION

- Belt Ranks & Martial Arts Styles: 7th Degree Black Belt — American & Korean TaeKwonDo, 5th Degree Black belt — Shotokan System, 5th Degree Black belt — Sugar Ryu Jiu-jitsu, 5th Degree Black belt — International Bushite Kenpo Karate Federation, Brown Belt — Combative Aikido, Black Belt — International Martial Arts Council of America

- Yrs. In the Martial Arts: 40 years

- Yrs. Instructing: 9 years

- School owner, Manager & Instructor at Williams Elite Martial Arts Colorado, Midwest Martial Arts Southern Conference (MMASC), Grand Master Anthony's Martial Arts School, Fighting Tiger Karate School, Williams Elite Martial Arts School

PROFESSIONAL ORGANIZATIONS

- Lifetime Member, Board Member American Martial Arts Alliance (AMAA) Foundation

- Lifetime Member, PKA Worldwide

- Lifetime Member, World Organization of Mixed Martial Arts (WOMA)

- Ambassador, Midwest Martial Arts Southern Conference (MMASC)

- Ambassador, Global Network for Peace, April 2024, Argentina

- Lifetime Achievement Award, International Bushite Kenpo Karate Federation

- Kappa Alpha Psi Fraternity

- Awards Director, Extraordinary People Award

- Mr. International, Today's International Men

- Come On In Inc. CEO/Founder

- President, C.O.IN Community Academy

PERSONAL ACHIEVEMENTS

- Chief Executive Officer and Founder, 2024 Williams Elite Hall of Honor

- 2023 Innovative Leader and Promoter of I.S.K.A. Organization

- 2023 Special Congressional Recognition Award

- 2023 Award of Excellence, C.B.K.B.T. USA

- 2023 Leadership Award, Kuntaw Legacy International Martial Arts (KLIMA), Filipino Martial Arts (FMA)

Master of Youth Work, recognition as an Executive Patron of Nigeria, Africa, and as an African High Chief, Indian Councilman of the Cherokee Indian Tribe, and Master Mason of the Year as 32nd Degree & Shriner of the Year.

Dr. John Williams is the Founder of the Come On In Elite Incorporation and the Founder of C.O.IN Community Academy and the Elite Brand. He has received a Humanitarian Leadership Award, Joe Lewis Memorial Natural Fighter Award, Jim Harrison Memorial Fighter Award, Blytheville, Arkansas Key to the City Award and Fountain, Colorado Key to the City Award. He is also a member of several distinguished organizations. Dr. Williams authored the international bestselling book *Dr. John Williams More Than A Martial Artist.*

HOW HAS MARTIAL ARTS IMPACTED YOUR LIFE?

Over his relatively short career as a martial artist, Dr. John Williams was honored to meet some of the most incredible people. He has traveled and competed with some of the best of the best. Studying the arts has had an impact on his life by making him learn more about himself and his abilities; it has taught him how to always push beyond what he thinks is his stopping point.

To take a child who has never had the privilege to step into a dojo, then to have them progress from white belt to black belt, the fight for a championship is what Dr. Williams, as a leader, looks forward to each time he trains a new student. The greatest influence on his life has been having his students' parents believe in him and what he's doing, inspiring them to express that they want their children to be like him … Priceless!

PERSONAL ACHIEVEMENTS (CONTINUED)

- 2023 Graduated with a Doctor of Philosophy in Martial Arts Science, PhD - M.A.S.
- 2022 Great Masters of the Martial Arts
- 2022 Elite Publications Author Award
- 2021 Certified Life Purpose Life Coach
- 2021 Certified Professional Life Coach
- 2021 Certified Emotional Intelligence Life Coach
- 2021 Certified Happiness Life Coach
- 2021 Grand Master, Grandes Mestres Das Artes Marciais, Sao Paulo, Brazil
- 2021 International Impact Book Awards Winner (More Than A Martial Artist Paperback)
- 2019 and 2021 Lifetime Achievement Presidential Award
- 2018 and 2021 Presidential Volunteer Award (Gold)
- 2020 MMASC Co-King of the Midwest
- Dr. James Von Debrow III Leadership Award
- Dr. James Von Debrow III Humanitarian Leadership Award
- MMASC 1st Place Super Senior Division Black Belt Forms
- MMASC 1st Place Light Heavyweight Sparring
- MMASC 2nd Place Senior Black Belt Sparring

PERSONAL ACHIEVEMENTS (CONTINUED)

- 2017-2018, 2020 MMASC Triple Crown Winner
- 2017, 2019-2020 MMASC Men's Black Belt Competitor of the Year
- 2019 Team Council & Coach Combative Martial Arts Team USA
- 2020 MMASC National Hall of Fame
- 2019 Ozzie Crew Hall of Fame
- 2016 Iron Fist 424 Black Belt Fighting Club
- Founder of Come On In, Inc.
- Founder of C.O.IN Community Academy
- 2018 Come On In Day Proclamation, Columbus, Georgia
- Director of Presidential Volunteer Awards
- Executive Director of Who's Who Black Globe Awards
- Licensed Christian Chaplain
- Graduated as Doctor of Philosophy in Christian Counseling
- Certified Diesel Mechanic, Penn Foster Career School
- Graduated in Automotive Mechanics, International Correspondence School

MAJOR ACHIEVEMENTS

- 2024 ISKA Bronze Medalist, 50 & Over Class AA Blackbelt Men LW Point Sparring
- 2024 ISKA Bronze Medalist, 50 & Over Class AA Blackbelt Men Creative Forms
- Master Hall of Honor and Fame IAKSA
- 2024 Hall of Fame of Martial Artists, ASAMCO Martial Arts, Brazil
- United States Martial Arts Hall of Fame Inductee
- United States of America Martial Arts Hall of Fame Inductee
- Midwest Martial Arts Hall of Fame Inductee
- 2023 Universal Martial Arts Hall of Fame Inductee
- 2023 Black Martial Arts Masters Virtual Museum & Hall of Fame-Hall of Heroes
- 2023 AMAA Tribute to Cynthia Rothrock Hall of Honor Inductee
- 2022 AMAA Tribute to Bill Super Foot Wallace Hall of Honor Inductee
- 2021 AMAA Tribute to Ernie Reyes, Sr. Hall of Honor Inductee
- 2020 MMASC National Hall of Fame
- 2019 Ozzie Crew Hall of Fame
- 2016 Iron Fist 424 Black Belt Fighting Club
- 2019 and 2021 Lifetime Achievement Presidential Award
- 2018 and 2021 Presidential Volunteer Award (Gold)
- 2017-2018, 2020 MMASC Triple Crown Winner
- 2017, 2019-2020 MMASC Men's Black Belt Competitor of the Year
- Twenty-three (23) Times Grand Champion
- Twenty-seven (27) Times Grand Champion Runner-Up
- Seven (7) Times Tiger Rock Martial Arts National Champion
- Three (3) Times Tiger Rock Martial Arts World Champion, Board Breaking Champion
- Seven (7) Times Tiger Rock Martial Arts District Champion

DON
WILLIS

"

Martial arts have enabled me to achieve many good things in my life and overcome many obstacles.

TRAINING INFORMATION

- Belt Ranks & Martial Arts Styles: 9th Dan-American Karate, 9th Dan-World Kobudo Federation

- Instructors/Influencers: I.J. Kim, Curtis Herrington, Andy Horne, Chuck Norris, Glenn Keeney, Joe Corley, Bill Wallace, Jeff Smith, Joe Lewis, John Therien

- Birthplace/Growing Up: Canton, OH

- Yrs. In the Martial Arts: 64 years

- Yrs. Instructing: 40+ years

- Instructor & Co-founder of PKA Worldwide, PKA Worldwide Director of Associated School and Members, Chairman, PKA Worldwide Rank Committee

PROFESSIONAL ORGANIZATIONS

- PKA Worldwide
- PKC Professional Karate Commission

WHY THE MARTIAL ARTS?

Don was a more petite boy when he was young, making him an easy target for bullies. He was picked on quite a bit, and he did not have a lot of self-esteem. Don joined the military in 1960 when he was just 17 and loved the hand-to-hand combat. He worked out with anyone he could for his three years in the service. When he was discharged in 1963, it was impossible to find a school, but he found a few guys who knew "a little" to work out with. He finally joined a Tae Kwon Do school in 1965 and attained a black belt in 1969.

Martial arts have enabled Don to achieve many good things in his life and overcome many obstacles. He believes that this is due to the never-quit mindset prevalent in martial arts. He has emphysema and attributes his breath control training and never-quit attitude to his ability to keep going.

Don competed in all divisions from the 1960s "Blood and Guts" era until 1975 and has amassed over 100 trophies and awards.

PERSONAL ACHIEVEMENTS

- Police Training Sergeant - Canal Fulton, OH
- Nominated for Ohio Governor's Cup - National Competitor all divisions
- Presidential Sports Award from Richard Nixon
- Founder of the Don Willis American Karate System
- Opened the first Martial Arts school in Ft. Lauderdale, FL 1970
- Operated Martial Arts schools in Florida and Ohio
- Founded Don Willis International

MAJOR ACHIEVEMENTS

- Member of the Professional Karate Association Executive Committee
- As Chairman of the Professional Karate Association's Reps and Officials Committee, Don personally trained well over 1000 PKA Officials worldwide.
- In 1983, he was the only person ever to be awarded both Professional Karate Association Man of the Year and Professional Karate Association Official of the Year.
- On behalf of the PKA, Don traveled as far from home as Nice, France, and Anchorage, Alaska, and he has represented the association in almost all of our CONUS states.
- Don was also the original United States Director of Operations for the Professional Karate Commission and he had worked alongside GM Glenn Keeney in building that organization's recognition in the Martial Arts.
- Don was presented with the Joe Lewis Eternal Warrior Award, which has been the highlight of his martial arts career.
- Most importantly, Don teamed with GM Joe Corley to grow PKA WORLDWIDE. He says, "I consider my long-time friendships with GM Glenn Keeney and GM Joe Corley as a major achievement. These two have done more than I can say to build martial arts."
- Don is retired and now lives on what he calls his Florida "5-acre zoo." He enjoys spending time with nature, animals, and bass fishing with his best friend and retired Air Force Captain Bucky Miller, his fishing partner of nearly 18 years.

ORGANIZATION
Of the Year

GREAT GRAND MASTER ROB CASTRO
ROB CASTRO'S SHAOLIN KENPO

Roy Robert Castro (aka Rob Castro) was born into a family of martial artists. He was the third of seven children raised by San Francisco Martial Arts Legend Ralph Castro. He has been punching and kicking since he was born. Today, Rob Castro is the head of the Shaolin Kenpo Family and holds the rank of Great Grandmaster.

GGM Castro was born into the martial arts and has practiced his father's art daily or weekly over his entire life. He says, "Martial arts are just a part of who I am. I've had the opportunity to share that with my family, have had many great experiences throughout my life, and teach many great people this great art."

The International Shaolin Kenpo Association

To understand the journey of the International Shaolin Kenpo Association, we look to the roots of its founder—Rafael Pablo Castro Jr., aka Ralph Castro, who was born and raised in Hawaii.

Like other children, he enjoyed sports and playing with family and friends in the sunshine and the ocean. His family was poor but happy and loving; he received his first pair of shoes at ten. His first experience with Martial Arts was when he began training in Boxing with his father, Rafael BOSS Castro, a well-known Boxer in Hawaii. As a young man, he met and trained with Professor William K.S. Chow, a local karate instructor of Chinese and Hawaiian descent. Professor Chow is credited for teaching students who started many of the world's leading Hawaiian martial arts. Among the students who made their way to the US mainland were Kenpo Karate founders Edmund Parker Sr. and Ralph Castro. Joseph and Adriano Emperado founded the Kajukenbo system, and Professor Chow is credited with ties to the Tracy Brothers Kenpo Karate lineage.

In the 1950s, Ralph Castro began teaching karate lessons in his home until the class outgrew the space. San Francisco 1958 was the first year Ralph Castro went public, opened a school, and began teaching karate publicly. He would teach karate for the remainder of his life. His business sign read Ralph Castros Kenpo Karate from 1958 to 1981 when the name was changed at the suggestion of his teacher, Professor William K.S. Chow. Professor Chow loved what his student Ralph Castro had created, and because his creation stood out differently from other Kenpo Karate systems at that time and because it resembled what he had experienced with his Chinese grandfather's practice, he wanted the name of the art to reflect its graceful and fluid motions akin to Chinese Kung-fu of the Shaolin Temple.

In 1981, his art became known as Ralph Castros Shaolin Kenpo, and in the same year, Ralph Castro's International Shaolin Kenpo Association was founded.

Ralph Castro's personal life was deeply intertwined with his martial arts journey. With his wife, Pat Castro, they raised seven children, all of whom were introduced to their father's martial arts at a young age. The family's commitment to karate, with the children becoming known as Ralph Castro's Magnificent Seven, is a testament to Castro's dedication and the success of his family business.

The 1960s and 1970s were the beginning of many good years for the Castro family. Traveling with his Magnificent Seven and doing demonstrations helped promote the family business. Through this and his several schools now running in the Bay area, he was able to branch out and host his own tournament, the California Karate Championships, aka the CKC.

The California Karate Championships helped create legends, including Chuck Norris, Joe Lewis, and Bruce Lee. There were many great martial artists worldwide who attended as competitors or special guests. The CKC was the largest tournament held annually in northern California. The CKC began in 1967 and ended in 2000, but plans are underway for the rebirth of this historic martial arts event. The greater martial arts community eagerly anticipates its comeback, with plans to launch in 2025.

Edmund Parker Sr., the founder of American Kenpo, held the Long Beach Internationals in southern

California. It was there in 1964 that a relatively unknown martial artist from Hong Kong named Bruce Lee made his debut, and on the very same day, "an 8-year-old named Rob Castro did a performance that brought the crowd to its feet in resounding applaud" paraphrase from his book Unsettled Matters, courtesy of Mr. Tom Bleeker, Co-author of DRAGON, The Bruce Lee Story.

Ralph Castro's contributions to martial arts did not go unnoticed. His achievements were recognized in various publications, with his photo gracing the covers of Inside Kung Fu Yearbook in 1982, Official Karate in 1985, Karate Kung Fu in 1987, and Black Belt Magazine in 1988. His induction into the Black Belt Hall of Fame in 1988 and feature in Black Belt Magazine's yearbook in 1989 further solidified his status as a martial arts legend. Besides these awards, his karate uniform is publicly displayed at the Martial Arts History Museum in Los Angeles, CA.

Great Grandmaster Ralph Castro's organizational involvement is also impressive. He was an AAU Vice President as early as 1971-1972 and maintained active membership in the International Kenpo Karate Association from 1958-1982. He was also active within ATAMA since 1984, serving as the National Board's Vice President in 1985 and President in 1986-1988.

His children are equally impressive, having spent an entire lifetime dedicated to the art their father created. Many highly skilled practitioners have been loyal to their instructor, Ralph Castro, some of whom began their journey with him in the 1960s.

The Shaolin Kenpo Family Tree has branches that list scores of masters and grandmasters who have dedicated their lives to this art, spending decades teaching Ralph Castro's Shaolin Kenpo and providing a living to their families by teaching the art created upon Ralph Castro's dreams.

Upon his passing in 2019, the mantle was given to his son, Great Grandmaster Rob Castro. He has accepted his father's wishes to carry on the legacy, doing so circumspectly, one day at a time.

With the help of family and friends, the support of all Shaolin Kenpo Association Schools, and our sisters and brothers in many diverse martial arts communities, the future of the International Shaolin Kenpo Association looks bright.

We wish to acknowledge those who have contributed to our recent success: GM Samuel Lee Ellis and the Unified Grand Masters Association of America in Salt Lake City, Ut; Soke Paul Cervizzi and his outstanding organization in Boston, Mass; GM Paul Casey, the Kenpo Karate Hall of Fame; the American Kenpo family; Senior Grandmaster Sifu Al Dacascos and the International Kajukenbo Association, Honolulu, Hawaii; his students Master Sean Harflinger, Honolulu, Hawaii; and a loyal friend of Shaolin Kenpo, Master Sonny Pabuaya, Winnipeg, Canada. A special thank you to GM Jessie Bowen and the American Martial Arts Alliance Foundation team for all of your expertise and skills as we work together to build a better world.

May God Bless us all in 2024 and the years to come.

TRAINING INFORMATION

- Belt Rank/Titles: Ralph Castro's Shaolin Kenpo-13th Degree
- Instructors/Influencers: Ralph Castro
- Birthplace/Growing Up: Honolulu, HI / San Francisco, CA
- Yrs. In the Martial Arts: 63 years
- Yrs. Instructing: 55+ years
- School owner, Manager & Instructor at Ralph Castro's Shaolin Kenpo, Head of the International Shaolin Kenpo Association

PROFESSIONAL ORGANIZATIONS

- International Shaolin Kenpo Association

PERSONAL ACHIEVEMENTS

- Great Grandmaster Rob Castro has achieved many things over the years. Of these, his main achievement is being the son of two amazing parents and the brother of six siblings who have all excelled in life while in martial arts circles and outside of it in everyday living. As a small child, he remembers learning from his father and observing his father as he visited with his friends in the basements in San Francisco's Chinatown in the early 1960s. These men were Wally Jay, Bruce Lee, Ed Parker, Jimmy Lee, and men of that generation. But, he feels his greatest achievements are teaching those the art his father developed and sharing this with them.

MAJOR ACHIEVEMENTS

- GGM Castro is very proud that his family tells him he's a respected husband, father, son, and brother. He's grateful to have people in and outside his organization who say he's a leader who works honestly for the good of the entire family and martial arts community.

Top Martial Arts Schools

PRESENTED BY

MARTIAL ARTS EXTRAORDINAIRE
MAGAZINE

HOW DID YOU GET STARTED IN THE MARTIAL ARTS?

In 2006, I was stationed in Landstuhl, Germany. I was stressed because of so many service members coming back injured from Iraqi Enduring Freedom (Iraq). Those service members were under my command at Landstuhl Regional Medical Center before transferring to Walter Reed Army Medical Center for treatment. My son was already in martial arts and wanted to quit to play basketball. I made a deal with him. I asked him, "If I joined, will you stay in?" And he agreed. His martial arts instructor allowed us to train together, which was

MURIEL
BROWN

JAGUAR DOJO
SAN ANTONIO, TX

"
Due to my martial arts experience and military training, I will always be a mentor and share my knowledge with others.

SCHOOL & TRAINING INFORMATION
Years in business: 3 1/2 years
Style of Martial Arts: GoJuRyu
School website: www.jaguardojo.com
Belt Rank/Titles: 4th Degree
Yrs. In the Martial Arts: 18 years

ORGANIZATIONS & AFFILIATIONS
Black Knight Karate Association, Lifetime Member
United States Martial Arts Hall of Fame, Member

HOW HAS YOUR MARTIAL ARTS SCHOOL IMPACTED YOUR COMMUNITY?

The Jaguar Dojo family has participated in serving food to underprivileged kids; approximately 300 families were served. We partnered with a community church group to serve food to senior citizens. The Jaguar Dojo family also participated in the Children for Hunger Fund. During this event, more than 500 food boxes were packed and distributed to families in San Antonio. This has become a quarterly event for our dojo. Lastly, we assisted with distributing toys to qualified families prior to the Christmas holiday.

so rewarding. I used the martial arts techniques of GoJuRyu for focus, discipline, time management, and stress relief. More importantly, I wanted to keep that bond with my son, which was so important to me.

HOW HAS MARTIAL ARTS INFLUENCED YOUR LIFE?

Training in martial arts has changed my life in so many ways. Since I started, I always wanted to perform well and give my best. It has allowed me to gain critical knowledge to protect myself and my family. I've overcome adversity and completed 27 years of military service. Becoming a martial artist has taught me to be humble, patient, and mentally and physically strong. It has allowed me to reach goals that I had never imagined. I have traveled all over the world, competing on world and national teams. I have met wonderful martial artists who have groomed me to be the best I can be. Due to my martial arts experience and military training, I will always be a mentor and share my knowledge with others.

Become an
AMAA
MEMBER!

JOHN
CHUNG

JOHN CHUNG
TAE KWON DO
LEESBURG, VA

"

The passion of Martial Arts has given me the opportunity to pay it forward by teaching since 1972.

SCHOOL & TRAINING INFORMATION
Years in business: 40 years
Style of Martial Arts: Tae Kwon Do
School website: www.johnchung.com
Belt Rank/Titles: 9th Dan
Yrs. In the Martial Arts: 54 years

ORGANIZATIONS & AFFILIATIONS
World Cup Martial Arts Organization
PKA Wordwide

HOW DID YOU GET STARTED IN THE MARTIAL ARTS?

At a young age, I was interested in martial arts. In Korea, I took Judo at my middle school. In 1970, at the age of 12, I came to Washington, D.C., and began training in Tae Kwon Do with my uncle and Founding Father of American Tae Kwon Do, Grand Master Jhoon Rhee. Martial arts has taught me to be a student for and of life. It has taught me the benefits of being a competitor and the joy of being the best individual I choose to be. My passion for martial arts has given me the opportunity to pay it forward by teaching since 1972.

I have also been blessed as a competitor, to be the Champion of the World, and to have traveled and enjoyed many martial artists and their cultures from various countries.

My philosophy: Learn Something, Get a Good workout, and Have Fun! This has been my school motto and theme where students of all ages benefit.

Martial arts has taught me to see, experience, and live life positively and gratefully. I believe the president of the first grade is just as important as a person as the president of a company. Everyone is treated with respect.

Always try your best; effort is the most important quality, and seek joy in your goals and achievements.

Seminars and training camps for martial artists of all styles and levels have given me great opportunities to continually share my experiences as a student, competitor, instructor, and business owner. Hosting

PERSONAL TIMELINE

- 1970: No Belt
- 1974: Black Belt
- 1977: PKA National Champion
- 1979: US Champion
- 1981: World Champion
- 1982: Black Belt Hall of Fame
- 1982: PKA Tournament Competitor of the Year
- 1983: World Champion
- 1984: Inductee Karate Hall of Fame
- 1985: World Champion
- 1989: Diamond Nationals Hall of Fame
- 1990: NASKA Hall of Fame
- 1990: Fighter International Hall of Fame
- 1993: World Martial Arts Hall of Fame
- 1996: Bluegrass Nationals Hall of Fame
- 1997: Founder of Sidekick International Competition Team
- 1998: Promoter of the Sidekick International Martial Arts Championship
- 1999: Promoter of the World Cup Finals Open Martial Arts Championship
- 2000: President of the World Cup Martial Arts Organization
- 2005: Ocean State Grand Nationals Hall of Fame
- 2006: World Mundo Federation Hall of Fame
- 2009: Universal Martial Arts Association International Hall of Fame
- 2012: All Pro Tae Kwon Do Martial Arts Hall of Fame
- 2013: New York Tournaments Martial Arts Hall of Fame

tournaments and motivational speeches has been well received and appreciated by both martial artists and non-martial artists.

In the years 1970-1987, I was fortunate to have competed in all major tournaments, nationally and internationally,

winning world championship titles since 1981. Some awards include the 2014 Masters Hall of Fame, the 2014 World Wide Tae Kwon Do Award, the 2015 AmeriKick Internationals Hall of Fame, the 2016 Joe Lewis Eternal Warrior Award, and 30 years of Teaching Boot Camp for Martial Artists. Students worldwide come to train together to improve, learn, and experience world-class training.

HIGHLIGHTS:

"People go to camps to meet a champion. We come to John Chung's camp to become a champion!"

"The best in the world! "King of Kata!" "World Forms & Fighting champion!" Any describe only one person.

Student of Grandmaster Jhoon Rhee, father of American Tae Kwon Do, John Chung.

John Chung, with his famous perfect side kick and techniques, has revolutionized the level of competition. Pioneer of musical forms and perfectionist of traditional forms, the King of Kata, John Chung, has brought the standard of excellence to the forefront.

World forms and fighting John Chung is passing down his experience and spreading his martial arts knowledge to students of Karate, Kung Fu, and Tae Kwon Do. The best in the world, John Chung, excels as an instructor. The knowledge to understand and improve technically, along with the edge to win in competition, is currently given in worldwide seminars.

All seminars vary from Tae Kwon Do history, traditional forms, musical forms, and self-defense (applications of techniques) to the necessary basics in stretching, strengthening, tournament and continuous sparring, and open competition.

HOW HAS MARTIAL ARTS INFLUENCED YOUR LIFE?

Martial Arts, Tae Kwon Do, has been part of my life for the past 54 years. Every aspect of my life is influenced by martial arts, family, friends, and colleagues.

HOW HAS YOUR MARTIAL ARTS SCHOOL IMPACTED YOUR COMMUNITY?

My martial arts program continues to impact my community positively.

Become an
AMAA MEMBER!

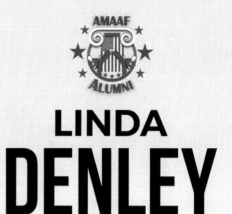

LINDA
DENLEY

TEXAS BLACK BELT ACADEMY
SPRING, TX

> ❝
> *My life has been enhanced as a result of being in martial arts. I have had the opportunity to make history.*

HOW DID YOU GET STARTED IN THE MARTIAL ARTS?

I had never considered taking martial arts classes before the day it entered my mind. One day, I thought about karate, and I enrolled in classes the next day. I never thought I would stay with it or become a 17-time World Champion.

I had no goals initially except to be the best I could be. I started karate only as an extracurricular activity. I was very fortunate to have an instructor who saw early on that I had the athletic ability to become great at the arts. It was truly a gift from GOD.

SCHOOL & TRAINING INFORMATION
Years in business: 45 years

Style of Martial Arts: Tang Soo Do, Tae Kwon Do, SHOTOKAN and Bushido Kai

Belt Rank/Titles: 10th Dan Grand Master

Yrs. In the Martial Arts: 51 years

ORGANIZATIONS & AFFILIATIONS
AKBBA (American Karate Black Belt Association)

Bushi Ban International

ISKF (International Sports Karate Federation)

My life has been enhanced as a result of being in martial arts. I have had the opportunity to make history. I am recognized as the greatest woman fighter of all time. I was also the first woman to appear in The Black Balt Hall of Fame in 1980. I have the opportunity to speak about my success to others. I am a role model in my community, marital arts studio, and church.

My philosophy toward martial arts and anything else you do in life is: "Give It Your All, and Your Best Will Come Out of It." Be enthusiastic about everything.

I influence my students, instructors, competitors, parents, or anyone else who passes through my life, and you will never know what you are good at until you try it. Karate was not my first love. I just had the ability to be a world champion in martial arts. I also qualified to compete in the track and field Olympics in 1976; however, my professional career in martial arts made me ineligible. I also have had an opportunity to play with the WNBA, but, at that time, there was no career in it for women.

Martial arts has taught me to be more patient, disciplined, and, most of all, confident. Before I studied karate, I was the shyest person in the world. Now, I can stand before hundreds of people to speak or give a seminar. As of now, I still frequently travel the world, giving seminars, workshops, and classes.

HOW HAS MARTIAL ARTS INFLUENCED YOUR LIFE?

Martial arts have had a big influence on my life. Martial arts helped me develop character, confidence, belief, courage, and many other attributes. I have had the opportunity to appear on the cover of countless martial arts magazines, appear in several motion pictures, be inducted into 35-plus halls of fame, travel the world teaching workshops, become a 17-time World Champion, and meet many wonderful people. Without the martial arts, some of these things would not have happened. Only God knew.

HOW HAS YOUR MARTIAL ARTS SCHOOL IMPACTED YOUR COMMUNITY?

Texas Black Belt Academy has impacted our community in so many positive ways. With the training in martial arts, we have helped many to develop self-esteem, confidence, motivation, a positive lifestyle, and a sense of awareness; we have helped so many disenfranchised children to become champions.

STEVEN DEVERS

LEE'S TAEKWONDO
CLASS & MARTIAL ART
CRAMERTON, NC

"

As an instructor, I do my best to demonstrate the character qualities that I teach my students...

SCHOOL & TRAINING INFORMATION

Years in business: 47 years
Style of Martial Arts: Taekwondo
School website: www.leestkdclass.com
Belt Rank/Titles: 4th Dan
Yrs. In the Martial Arts: 16 years

ORGANIZATIONS & AFFILIATIONS

World Taekwondo
AAU Taekwondo

HOW DID YOU GET STARTED IN THE MARTIAL ARTS?

My journey in martial arts began at the U.S. Taekwondo College in Chester, VA, under the guidance of Master Kim. I was 13 at the time. After a year of training, I took a break to pursue soccer. It wasn't until I was 26 that I rediscovered my passion for Taekwondo, this time under the tutelage of Grandmaster Nam Hi Lee at Lee's Taekwondo Class & Martial Art in Colonial Heights, VA. I continued my training under him until December 2018, when he retired and passed on his school to me.

HOW HAS MARTIAL ARTS INFLUENCED YOUR LIFE?

Martial arts has greatly influenced my life for the better. As an instructor, I do my best to demonstrate the character qualities that I teach my students, which are Courtesy, Integrity, Perseverance, Self-control, and Indomitable Spirit. I also teach my own children and do my best to cultivate the Five Tenets of Taekwondo within them.

HOW HAS YOUR MARTIAL ARTS SCHOOL IMPACTED YOUR COMMUNITY?

I teach at a Taekwondo Club for eight weeks each semester at a local middle school. This allows students to be exposed to martial arts with no monetary commitment. It also shows the students how much commitment is required to truly study a martial art.

Become an
AMAA MEMBER!

NICK
DONATO

THE PIT MARTIAL
ARTS HEALTH& FITNESS
NSW, AUSTRALIA

"
Our primary goal is to empower all
who walk through the door.

SCHOOL & TRAINING INFORMATION

Years in business: 40 years

Style of Martial Arts: Kwonbopdo TKD, Benkanryu Ju-Jitsu & Kobujutsu + Tai Chi, Boxing & Kickboxing

School website: www.thepitmartialarts.com/au

Belt Rank/Titles: 8th Degree

Yrs. In the Martial Arts: 56 years

ORGANIZATIONS & AFFILIATIONS

WHFSC - World Head of Family Sokeship Council

WTO - World TKD Organization

Museum of Sports Karate

ITC - International TKD Confederation

WMARA - World Martial Arts Ranking Association

IMACA - International Martial Arts Council of America

HOW DID YOU GET STARTED IN THE MARTIAL ARTS?

I started boxing with my uncles as a kid and was introduced to martial arts as a teen. It was the realistic self-defence aspects that drew me initially. Over the years, the underlying lessons we learn about ourselves through the vehicle of kick, punch, etc., have continuously driven me to learn, search, and study all martial arts techniques, science and history. Boxing and kickboxing are always their rawest forms of strike work and defense.

Combative Tae Kwon Do has always made sense to me with its combination of hand skills coupled with

Over the years, we have enjoyed outgrowing two full-time HQ dojos that have always supported many regional schools. We currently are based at our biggest full-time dojo, 'The PIT Martial Arts Self Defence & Fitness Centre' in Smeaton Grange. We support five well-established regional schools in NSW, with a new one on the way in Queensland later this year. Our diversity of study and understanding of the life cycle have enabled us to share the best that martial arts have to offer, regardless of age.

HOW HAS MARTIAL ARTS INFLUENCED YOUR LIFE?

Martial Arts, the study, the community, and the colleagues that I have trained with and alongside have made our school and all the instructors in it who we are today. We share, learn, and evolve always. Our primary goal is to empower all who walk through the door to strive to be the best they can be in all they do and to use "no way as a way." We encourage them to.' face life front on, make the most of every situation and opportunity that comes their way, learn about themselves, and be solid in that understanding, yet flexible enough to adapt and pivot when needed. We emphasize the importance of a balanced life filled with goals and dreams.

HOW HAS YOUR MARTIAL ARTS SCHOOL IMPACTED YOUR COMMUNITY?

As we celebrate our 40th anniversary of teaching, training, coaching, and educating our local communities, we take pride in the numerous achievements we've made. We've educated countless school children in martial arts, stranger danger, and self-defence. We've assisted and inspired struggling teens to tackle life differently. We've also helped local businesses and corporate companies.

advanced kicking techniques. Japanese Jujitsu is imperative for its in-depth study of upright-to-ground defense maneuvering. Kobujutsu is for the inclusion of weaponry and its transitions and blended science of many weapons. Tai Chi for the internal self, plus lethal techniques, hides in plain sight. It certainly does take a lifetime and more to understand the intricacies of martial arts worldwide. I started out teaching to assist with classes and share some knowledge with a few mates, which then evolved into part-time teaching. My love of martial arts and all it had done for me eventually pushed me across the line, turning it into a full-time profession. It hasn't been an easy road, but it has been extremely rewarding and always evolving.

KYLE FORREST

KYLE'S ISSHINRYU ACADEMY
LEXINGTON, NC

"

This journey has been so life-changing that the qualities I have instilled in my soul are unexplainable...

HOW DID YOU GET STARTED IN THE MARTIAL ARTS?

I, Kyle Forrest, was a very competitive person as a child and adolescent, participating in baseball, soccer, basketball, and boxing. When I graduated high school, I was eager to find something competitive that I could be a part of. There was a local karate school in the area. At that entrance of that dojo, my life changed, and I found my destination. After diligent time and training, I found myself training every day versus the two days a week the dojo offered. Yes, I was obsessed with this new kind of life and knew I wanted to pursue this lifestyle extensively.

SCHOOL & TRAINING INFORMATION
Years in business: 25 years
Style of Martial Arts: Isshinryu Karate
Belt Rank/Titles: Hachi-Dan 8th Degree
Yrs. In the Martial Arts: 35 years

ORGANIZATIONS & AFFILIATIONS
United States Isshinryu Karate Association (U.S.I.K.A.) N.C., Board Representative
United States Isshinryu Karate Association (U.S.I.K.A.) N.C. Board Representative
Owner and President of the IKC Isshinryu Karate Council

With constant training inside and outside the dojo, I acquired some attributes and noticed many changes in myself. These changes were things that others took notice of as well. Not limited to physical strength and endurance, the changes I'm proposing are deeper than you can imagine. I was developing skills that I needed to challenge to the fullest, and that was my approach to situations and goal setting. These challenges were difficult because I had never faced life obstacles on this level. I knew I had to make a change.

At a tournament, I was fighting in the championships at a high level of public notification. The sponsor I had on my back went against my testimony, especially when I saw a child with the sponsor's name on the front and my name on the back. That's when my life changed. I ask myself what testimony I am leading and what direction I am leading in the future. At this moment, I chose to drop the sponsor and create my own school to set and promote positive direction for others and provide an outlet to help others with their life journey. This is why I decided to open my own dojo/training center with the help of my sensei, Hanshi Phil Little. With his direction, Kyles Isshinryu Academy was formed and developed.

With a life standard at my school, we will promote our Lord and Savior first and protect and preserve the lineage and heritage in which we were developed. With our program in existence, now it's time to begin our journey, and we did. Thirty-five years later, here we are. All I can say is thank you to my instructor, my students, and most importantly, My Lord and Savior, Jesus Christ.

HOW HAS MARTIAL ARTS INFLUENCED YOUR LIFE?

Martial Arts has created a platform for my life that has been a direction of travel that I could never have imagined. The direction this road lead me was understanding the true elements of the treasures of life. This journey has been so life-changing that the qualities I have instilled in my soul are unexplainable, but I'll try. Some qualities I obtained that should be exposed are but are not limited to the art of being honest. Be honest in all areas. To be honest, we must possess the art of being humble. Being humble is the art of being able to accept criticism from others with the understanding of learning. The art of integrity. Doing the right action or taking the path even if no one notices or recognizes the action. Another possession of the art is loyalty. Be loyal to yourself, be honest with yourself, and be humble when you do wrong. Be loyal to these qualities, and people will be loyal to you. The influence of martial arts in my life has been tremendous and has taught me that others are more important than myself; this creates progression and not degression in lifestyles. What is an art to some has become a lifestyle to me.

HOW HAS YOUR MARTIAL ARTS SCHOOL IMPACTED YOUR COMMUNITY?

Kyles's Isshinryu Academy has made a statement in our community by creating free programs to include our community leaders. We currently offer programs for leadership and self-defense programs free to all military police departments, Firefighters, and EMS or all medical staff. Their safety is our target goal. Community programs like the Second Chance Program were developed to help troubled teens or criminals with first-time offenses with direction. Another program developed at our school is the Seals Program, which is self-defense for armed leaders and service members. We have a Thanksgiving fire-cooked chicken dinner every year to feed unfortunate families. We offer free self-defense classes at our lady's battered women's shelter. We currently are a proud sponsor of the epilepsy foundation, doing a fundraiser and free public displays for this event annually. At Christmas time, we have rebuild-a-bike for kids, where we have donated broken bicycles to be reworked and made new ones to give a kid a bike for the Christmas Program.

Our community is our home, and we need to help it grow. But our community is not limited to our location; it spreads on a broader scale, wherever we are. That's why we travel to different areas to spread our testimony. This year, Team KIA has already visited nine states, spreading our training, sharing our knowledge, and promoting Jesus Christ wherever we land. Thank You, and God Bless.

Become an
AMAA MEMBER!

TIM
HARRISON

TM MARTIAL ARTS
JOLIET, IL

As we continue to grow, we remain dedicated to our mission of empowering and uplifting our community...

SCHOOL & TRAINING INFORMATION

Years in business: 21 1/2 years

Style of Martial Arts: TKD, Combat Hapkido, Kickboxing

School website: www.tmmartialarts.com

Belt Rank/Titles: 8th Dan

Yrs. In the Martial Arts: 50 years

ORGANIZATIONS & AFFILIATIONS

International Combat Hapkido Federation

Independent TKD Association

PKA

Superfoot Systems

Stephen Oliver's Martial Arts Wealth Mastery

HOW DID YOU GET STARTED IN THE MARTIAL ARTS?

Grandmaster Timothy S. Harrison is an 8th-degree black belt in Tae Kwon Do, a 7th-degree black belt in Combat Hapkido, a 1st-degree black belt in Joe Lewis Fighting System, and a 1st-degree black belt in Superfoot Fighting Systems. He is a certified instructor with the International Police Defensive Tactics Institute, the Military Combatives Association, and C.O.B.R.A self-defense.

Grandmaster Harrison is also an instructor certified by the International Combat Hapkido Federation in

Ground Survival and Anatomical Targeting Strategies, and Tactical Jeet Kune Do Principles by Grandmaster Joe Lewis.

He has been awarded many honors over the years: being inducted into the Action Martial Arts Hall of Fame in 2007 and 2011, Budo International Magazine Outstanding Achievement Award; Combat Hapkido 2006 Hapkido Instructor of the Year by the USA Martial Arts Hall of Fame and by the World Head of Family Sokeship Council, Master of the year Combat Hapkido 2019; American Martial Arts Alliance Who's Who Legends Award 2020 & 2022; International Combat Hapkido Federation Founder's Hall of Honors Award 2022; and induction into the International Spartan Hall of Warriors Society 2024. Grandmaster Timothy Harrison was knighted into the illustrious Order of the Redeemer in May of 2024 in a ceremony filled with tradition and prestige.

In addition to his esteemed accomplishments within the martial arts industry, Grandmaster Harrison also became a published author. He released his first book, 7 Sure Ways to Build Strong and Successful Children, in 2023.

Grandmaster Harrison started studying martial arts in 1972 at Tracy's Kenpo Karate in Downer Grove, Illinois. He studied there until approximately 1976. In the mid- to late 1980s, he started in Tae Kwon Do and traditional Hapkido. In 1997, he attended Karate College in Radford, Virginia. While there, he was introduced to Grandmaster Joe Lewis, Grandmaster Bill "Superfoot" Wallace, and many other well-known martial artists. Grandmaster Harrison received his black belt from Grandmaster Joe Lewis in 2008.

Grandmaster Harrison opened his school, TM Martial Arts Academy, on February 3rd, 2003. The academy teaches Tae Kwon Do and Grandmaster Pellegrini's Combat Hapkido, as well as various kickboxing and self-defense programs and seminars. It focuses on character development, self-defense skills, and strong leadership—even among the youngest students.

Grandmaster Harrison has two sons. Timothy is a small business owner, and Marc is a police officer and a United States Marine. They all reside in the Chicagoland area.

HOW HAS MARTIAL ARTS INFLUENCED YOUR LIFE?

Martial arts has shaped me into the person that I am today. Through years of training and experience, I have learned confidence, leadership, fairness, and, of course, self-defense.

Little did I know that when I was fortunate enough to start my martial arts training at age 6, it would turn into my career and livelihood 30 years later.

I have met many great and interesting people, some of whom have had a major impact on shaping my life as I know it so far. I have built lifelong relationships and look forward to building more.

Through my martial arts school, I have had the pleasure of being a part of and impacting thousands of students' lives. This, in and of itself, I consider to be the greatest honor that I could incur.

Become an
AMAA MEMBER!

HOW HAS YOUR MARTIAL ARTS SCHOOL IMPACTED YOUR COMMUNITY?

TM Martial Arts Academy's impact on the community is multifaceted, encompassing personal development, family unity, leadership cultivation, healthy living, community support, and safety. Our commitment to excellence in martial arts training and holistic development ensures that our students are not only skilled martial artists but also well-rounded individuals who positively contribute to society. As we continue to grow, we remain dedicated to our mission of empowering and uplifting our community through the transformative power of martial arts.

Our structured programs, from the "Little Ninjas" class to adult martial arts training, instill discipline, confidence, and resilience. We encourage family participation through events and classes that allow parents and children to train together. This shared experience creates a unique bonding opportunity, fostering mutual respect and understanding. Our leadership development program is a cornerstone of our impact. Through structured training, mentorship, and community service projects, graduates of our program often emerge as confident leaders in their schools and communities, taking on roles that allow them to inspire and guide others.

Community building is at the heart of what we do. TM Martial Arts Academy is a place where students, instructors, and families come together to support each other. The friendships and support networks formed here extend outside the dojand, creating a close-knit community that stands together in both challenges and celebrations.

JARROD
KEESLING

AMERICAN ELITE
MARTIAL ARTS
ROCK HILL, SC

"

Being a student, competitor, instructor, and school owner has been with me since a young age and has never left me.

SCHOOL & TRAINING INFORMATION

Years in business: 13 years
Style of Martial Arts: American Freestyle Karate
School website: www.americanelitemartialarts.com
Belt Rank/Titles: Godan-5th Degree Black
Yrs. In the Martial Arts: 30+ years

ORGANIZATIONS & AFFILIATIONS

Community Martial Arts Foundation
Independent Martial Arts Federation

HOW DID YOU GET STARTED IN THE MARTIAL ARTS?

I began my journey in martial arts as a kid in the early 90s when my parents signed me up for a karate class at my local recreation center in Cary, North Carolina, taught by Mr. Jerome Nojima. He was a wonderful instructor who kept classes lighthearted and made karate as fun as it was challenging, which sparked the love of martial arts that I carry to this day.

I earned my black belt in 1999, just before moving away to college. I continued training with the karate club at Appalachian State University. After graduating with a degree in mathematics, I was offered a job teaching karate in Charlotte, NC. I moved to Charlotte and taught for a few years, which I loved, and that affirmed my desire to make karate my life's profession. In 2010, I left my instructor position to pursue my dream of starting my very own karate program. I called it American Elite Martial Arts, and it has been a tremendous labor of love.

Giving up a steady paycheck and risking everything to start my own program has been one of the most difficult experiences of my life but also one of the most rewarding. I have no regrets about my decision. I was fortunate to have incredible support from both family and friends as I took on an incredible workload to build an organization. Today, I bring my passion for martial arts to hundreds of students each week, and I can't imagine anything else I'd rather be doing.

I keep in regular contact with incredible mentors for myself and our program. The founder of American Freestyle Karate, Professor Dan Anderson, has made the trip from Portland, Oregon, several times to visit our school. Even my original karate teacher, Sensei Jerome Nojima, has been a regular guest instructor for us. In 2023, when I was conducting an awards ceremony for a group of our graduating black belts, Sensei Nojima presented me with my Godan (fifth-degree black belt) promotion.

HOW HAS MARTIAL ARTS INFLUENCED YOUR LIFE?

Martial arts has been such a huge part of my life that it's difficult to even know where to begin this answer. Being a student, competitor, instructor, and school owner has been with me since a young age and has never left me. I've found that the student hat is the one that I never take off. I try to approach every new experience in both martial arts and life in general with a "white-belt mind," always seeking to learn and be receptive to different ideas.

As I have moved through different phases of life and moved to different geographical locations, I have often had to shift my training. I have been incredibly blessed

HOW HAS MARTIAL ARTS INFLUENCED YOUR LIFE? (CONT.)

to have known many incredible instructors in my journey, and I am grateful to all of them for what they have given me. The qualities I admire most about my instructors are not so much their skill and knowledge of martial arts but how they carry themselves as a person. I've been fortunate to have instructors who, despite having great skill and knowledge, still conduct themselves with incredible humility and patience toward their students and freely show respect and courtesy to everyone around them. I feel like those are the greatest qualities of a martial arts instructor, qualities that I try my best to instill in myself every day, both in and out of the dojo.

HOW HAS YOUR MARTIAL ARTS SCHOOL IMPACTED YOUR COMMUNITY?

Since its humble beginnings in 2011, American Elite Martial Arts (AEMA) has grown to be known as one of the best martial arts programs in Charlotte, North Carolina, and surrounding areas. AEMA has greatly impacted the Charlotte area by being one of the only martial arts schools that offer our low-cost membership option and flexibility to attend any of our locations. We also integrate ourselves with our community, as all of our class locations are held in local schools, churches, and recreation centers. We believe martial arts has incredible benefits for kids and should be available to all kids, regardless of their family's income.

American Elite Martial Arts has grown by leaps and bounds over the past decade, serving hundreds of students and watching them grow from beginner white belts and many mature to black belts. By having an affordable and accessible program, we have been able to serve our community with our popular kid's karate program. We start as young as

HOW HAS YOUR MARTIAL ARTS SCHOOL IMPACTED YOUR COMMUNITY? (CONTINUED)

age five and serve all ages up through adulthood. We practice the style of American Freestyle Karate, a hybrid martial art that combines a solid foundation in traditional Japanese/Okinawan style karate with elements from other martial arts, including Taekwondo, Kung Fu, Jujutsu, Muay Thai, boxing, weapons training, and others. This martial arts style was born from competition, where practitioners adopted techniques from other styles to keep an edge on their opponents. Our classes display a fusion of both Japanese and American cultures to pay respects to the traditional Japanese roots of our art as well as acknowledge its evolution into what is now a truly American form of karate. American freestyle karate is a living art that is constantly growing and evolving to meet the challenges of the modern world. It is a powerful tool for self-defense and complete exercise for the mind, body, and spirit of students of any age.

We are incredibly thankful for the love our community has shown American Elite Martial Arts as we were awarded the Gold Level for Charlotte's Best Martial Arts Studio in 2023 via The Charlotte Observer. We pride ourselves on helping students become physically strong and also developing within them an inner purpose and reason for joining martial arts. At the end of our program, we envision that not only will our students acquire martial arts and self-defense techniques that will get them ready for anything, but they will be both mentally and physically strong individuals of character and purpose. All of this is made possible through the ability to offer our low-cost and flexible program so anyone who has a desire to practice martial arts can.

JOHN
KRAFT

PACIFIC SHAOLIN
KENPO
SHELTON, WA

"

For me, martial arts is a home and a lifestyle, and it is at the forefront of my thoughts as much as God...

SCHOOL & TRAINING INFORMATION

Years in business: 31 years
Style of Martial Arts: Kenpo
School website: www.nwsholinkenpo.com
Belt Rank/Titles: 4th Degree
Yrs. In the Martial Arts: 53 years

ORGANIZATIONS & AFFILIATIONS

Northwest Shaolin Kenpo Association

HOW DID YOU GET STARTED IN THE MARTIAL ARTS?

1970-71, a friend invited me to join him in Tae Kwon Do. We were both juniors in high school. It was fun, and I did it throughout the school year. I had some self-defense basics in Boot Camp in the U.S. Navy in 1972. Then, in 1978, I began to learn Ralph Castro's Shaolin Kenpo on a more serious level; I needed self-defense - having my life threatened by being told I would be killed. My training was survival. I was raising a family in those years, and family came first, so training was hit and miss as we had the money. It took me 14 years to earn a black belt.

In the late '80s, I began teaching children and then adults and competing in local tournaments, doing well in fighting. In 1993-94, I opened a school with my family and long-time training partner Sue Messenger and her family. Our school, Pacific Shaolin Kenpo, opened to the public in Aberdeen, WA, and became a thriving school for many years. A series of unexpected things happened at the end of the 90s, and the school closed its doors. I had to quit teaching and training. I returned from retirement in 2014.

I was welcomed with open arms by my instructor, Ralph Castro, and the martial arts community. Having been away for 14 years allowed me a new perspective, and I began to notice my peers were struggling, having stayed day after day, year after year. As a result of what I saw happening, I've been trying to unite martial arts, making them stronger and healthier, in hopes of helping Grandmasters in their retirement years.

Now, I teach self-defense as a community service. I'm very grateful to be recognized as an instructor on a national level for my past accomplishments in the ring, notably competing at a world championship level when I retired, and for the many students who were instrumental in my success as an instructor.

Become an
AMAA MEMBER!

HOW HAS MARTIAL ARTS INFLUENCED YOUR LIFE?

For me, martial arts is a home and a lifestyle, and it is at the forefront of my thoughts as much as God, family, and country. I was once so shy that I wouldn't talk to anyone, but thanks to martial arts training, I have overcome that obstacle and have also conquered many other fears.

Martial arts, even with its ups and downs, is a special place. For some, it will be the only home that will ever fill the void when we are absent from it and those we love.

HOW HAS YOUR MARTIAL ARTS SCHOOL IMPACTED YOUR COMMUNITY?

An accurate description of our martial arts school would be that we made positive contributions as a business in our local community.

Every business owner's goal is to be successful. We achieved that through those we touched who allowed us to be a part of their daily lives, some for months and some for years.

Many former students share stories of how our school, instructors, and classmates helped them become more focused and involved, finding a path to personal success. Students of our school felt, then and still today, a close family bond. This caring attitude has been a positive driver in the student's lives as they raised families and became contributors to society and the local community.

Two success stories stand out: one is a young man raised in a family in crisis. He wrote a letter several years after leaving our school thanking me for what I had done to help him find a direction and a career. I didn't know his home life was so hard because he didn't discuss it. It was a surprise to find out that I had helped him beyond the doors of the classroom. I was only being a friend, and I gave him a ride to or

HOW HAS YOUR MARTIAL ARTS SCHOOL IMPACTED YOUR COMMUNITY? (CONTINUED)

from class occasionally, and we chatted. Later, he joined the Army, found a career, wrote a nice letter, and thanked me. He said I was a huge positive influence; I had turned his life around and encouraged him to believe in himself.

A second story is about a local school teacher who brought his son to us for lessons. He said his son was quite often bullied on the playground by three boys who would beat him up, and he would look out of his classroom window and see his son on the ground with these boys over him, laughing and ridiculing him. He asked for my help. After about a year, I asked the father about the problem with the three boys who bullied his son. He said, smiling, "Oh, one day, I looked out of the classroom window, and the three boys were on the ground." He continued, "My son wasn't angry; he was having fun."

At the height of our success, our school, Pacific Shaolin Kenpo, was fully engaged with classes six days a week and alternate Yoga classes offered on Sunday afternoons. Today, Pacific Shaolin Kenpo doesn't operate out of a brick-and-mortar but continues through workshops, seminars, and community involvement locally and nationally.

HOW DID YOU GET STARTED IN THE MARTIAL ARTS?

One sunny day, Maggie found herself in the park, accompanied by her sister-in-law, Ewilda. Little did she know that this outing would mark the beginning of an incredible journey. Ewilda, a skilled martial artist in Shotokan Karate, decided to share her knowledge with Maggie, starting with the basics of kicks and punches.

To Maggie's surprise, she quickly caught on and discovered a newfound passion within her. The combination of freedom and control that martial arts provided resonated deeply with her, transporting her to

MAGGIE MESSINA

TAECOLE
TAE KWON DO
AND FITNESS, INC.
ALBERTSON, NY

"

Martial arts not only gave me a new lease on life, but it also saved me.

SCHOOL & TRAINING INFORMATION

Years in business: 28 years

Style of Martial Arts: TaeKwonDo, Shotokan Karate, TaiChi

School website: www.taecoletkd.com

Belt Rank/Titles: 8th Dan Black Belt

Yrs. In the Martial Arts: 39 years

ORGANIZATIONS & AFFILIATIONS

AMAA, ITF, KMK, ITBA, UITF, NAEYC, NASKA, WKC

a more serene state of being. In her late teens, Maggie embarked on a personal training journey with Grandmaster Sir Henry Cho, a renowned black belt holder. Under one of his black belt instructors (Tibor Szalai), she progressed to the green belt rank.

Maggie's love for martial arts grew, and she yearned to expand her training by learning from other talented artists. However, being a woman in the male-dominated martial arts scene of the 1980s presented its challenges. She tirelessly searched for a suitable school, eventually hearing rumors about a hardcore training center (Kang System) in Brooklyn, NY, known for its no-nonsense approach.

Although hesitant, Maggie's curiosity got the better of her, and she mustered the courage to visit the school. The sight and sounds of intense training and the scent of sweat filled the air, both intimidating and exhilarating her. This environment was a far cry from the basement where she had been training before.

As Maggie progressed through her martial arts journey, her vision of opening her own school began to take shape, fueled by her determination and the rank of brown belt she had achieved. She was well aware of the hurdles she would have to overcome, but those early days of struggle molded her into the resilient woman she is today. She remains true to her core values, never forgetting the transformative power of Tae Kwon Do in shaping individuals, including herself.

HOW HAS MARTIAL ARTS INFLUENCED YOUR LIFE?

People often wonder about the impact martial arts has had on Maggie's life. Martial arts have been her saving grace. It has provided her with a clear sense of purpose and instilled a strong belief in herself. Through martial arts, she has embraced valuable core values and stayed away from the dangers of the streets. It has kept her focused and taught her the importance of finding happiness within herself. Martial arts has opened doors for Maggie, revealing her true calling to help others grow and believe in themselves, regardless of their background. Unlike other influences, martial arts promotes a clean and healthy lifestyle, free from the temptations of drugs and alcohol. It emphasizes self-improvement from within, strengthening the core of who you are. Maggie is immensely grateful for the role martial arts has played in her life, especially considering how easy it is to get distracted and led astray. It has also empowered her, regardless of her gender, to realize that she possesses the same strength as anyone else. With martial arts, Maggie can achieve anything that she sets her mind to, as long as she is willing to put in the work, refuse to accept failure, and stay on the right path. So, when someone asks Maggie how martial arts has influenced her life, Maggie's answer is simple: "It not only gave me a new lease on life, but it also saved me."

Become an
AMAA MEMBER!

HOW HAS YOUR MARTIAL ARTS SCHOOL IMPACTED YOUR COMMUNITY?

TaeCole is a remarkable woman-owned martial arts school that has significantly impacted its community and the world for many years. TaeCole possesses an unwavering determination to help others believe in themselves and achieve their goals. TaeCole is deeply involved in various community initiatives, such as planting trees, providing college scholarships, and offering tuition assistance to those in need. TaeCole is also actively engaged in organizing toy drives, clothing drives, and food drives, consistently striving to be a positive force for change wherever needed. Additionally, TaeCole has dedicated its time to mentoring children from a young age, fostering a system where the children become mentors by the time they leave for college. As a result, these young individuals are well-prepared, compassionate, and intelligent, ready to embark on their next chapter in life.

HOW HAS YOUR MARTIAL ARTS SCHOOL IMPACTED YOUR COMMUNITY? (CONTINUED)

Furthermore, TaeCole's Maggie Messina is the founder of Swerv4change.com/Female Fighters Matter Too, an organization that aims to level the playing field for female athletes worldwide. This organization works tirelessly to bring about change, whether it is through promoting diversity, providing education, or supporting those who are economically disadvantaged. TaeCole believes in equipping individuals with the necessary tools to achieve their aspirations, regardless of their background or educational level. Through her efforts, she has positively impacted the lives of thousands of people. Its journey is dedicated to continuing this mission, changing lives, and empowering individuals to make a difference in their own communities.

TaeCole also advocates for values such as courtesy, integrity, perseverance, and a can-do spirit. These values are not just preached but practiced every day. Together, we can join forces and change the world, creating a safer and happier place for all. TaeCole remains dedicated to being an agent of change, inspiring others to do the same.

Perseverance is another value that Maggie embodies and instills in TaeCole. She faces challenges head-on and never gives up, always striving to overcome obstacles and achieve her goals. Her can-do spirit is evident in her positive attitude and belief that anything is possible with determination and hard work.

These values are important to Maggie personally and are also ingrained in the organizations and initiatives she leads. By practicing these values every day, TaeCole sets an example for others and encourages them to embrace these principles in their own lives, positively affecting communities near and far.

HOW DID YOU GET STARTED IN THE MARTIAL ARTS?

EARLY YEARS

Grandmaster Jerry Otto, a distinguished figure in the martial arts community, has dedicated his life to pursuing and teaching martial arts. His journey began in the mid-1960s in Taiwan, where he studied local Chinese Kung Fu in a small village on Yamingshan Mountain. Returning to the United States in 1973, he continued his training in Okinawan Shorin-Ryu and Chinese Kempo, earning his first-degree black belt in 1978. In 1981, he established the legendary Shen Dragon Karate

JERRY
OTTO

SHEN DRAGON
KARATE DOJO
ST. THOMAS, VI

" Throughout my life since my early 20s, martial arts have always been my compass...

SCHOOL & TRAINING INFORMATION
Years in business: 43 years
Style of Martial Arts: Okinawa Shorin-Ryu Karate, Krav Maga
School website: www.shendragonvi.com
Belt Rank/Titles: Hanshi-Dan
Yrs. In the Martial Arts: 52 years

ORGANIZATIONS & AFFILIATIONS
Martial Arts Association (Gary Alexander, Founder)
United Karate Kung Fu Association (Lou Cassamassa, Founder)
Oriental Defensive Arts Association (Master Condi)

COMPETITIVE ACHIEVEMENTS

Otto's prowess in martial arts is evident in his remarkable competitive record. He debuted in national tournaments in 1987, defeating the top competitor in his division and securing six first-place finishes in national championships. His undefeated season in Kata and Weapons in 1989 led to his recognition as the greatest senior competitor in these categories in the history of the national circuit. In 1988, he was inducted into the Professional Karate League Hall of Fame as Senior Competitor of the Year.

COMMUNITY IMPACT AND INITIATIVES

Beyond his competitive and instructional achievements, Otto has significantly impacted his community. The Shen Dragon Karate Dojo in St. Thomas, Virgin Islands, offers a comprehensive curriculum that includes Okinawa Shorin-Ryu Karate, Krav Maga, and self-defense classes for all ages. The dojo emphasizes character development, confidence, respect, and positivity.

In 2017, Otto, his wife Celine, and his son Bryan established the current Shen Dragon Dojo on the Antilles School campus in St. Thomas. Despite setbacks from hurricanes Irma and Maria, they reopened in January 2018 and quickly outgrew their initial space, moving to Buccaneer Mall by the end of the year. The dojo now serves approximately 130 students and was named the 2019 Martial Arts School of the Year by the American Martial Arts Alliance.

LEGACY AND PHILOSOPHY

Grand Master Otto's teaching philosophy emphasizes turning negativity into positive energy and fostering a culture of respect and compassion. His approach is encapsulated in the Shen Dragon Menkyo-Bushido Tea Ceremony, a profound Black Belt ceremony that highlights the essence of humility, honor, tradition, and warriorship.

Jerry Otto's legacy is one of excellence in martial arts, community service, and positive social impact. Through his continued dedication and innovative initiatives, he remains a pillar of strength and inspiration in the martial arts world.

ORGANIZATIONS & AFFILIATIONS (CONT.)

- West Virginia Chinese Martial Arts Association (Master Denis Decker)
- East Coast International Kosho-Shorie Association (Master Nimr Hassan)
- U.S. Tang Sho Dau Chinese Martial Arts Federation (Master Steve L. Martin)
- Yamashita International Martial Arts Association (Hanshi Tadashi Yamashita)
- Okinawa Kenpo Karate Kobudo Dharma-Ryu Dojo (Grand Master Paul Ortino)
- Kenpo Jujutsu Ryu Kosho Kenpo Ryu Schools and Temples (Grand Master Edward Hartzell)
- Victory Martial Arts International Council — Lifetime Member (Grand Master Jason Victory)
- American Martial Art Alliance — Charter Member (Grandmaster Jessie Bowen)
- World Head of Family Sokeship Council

AWARDS & RECOGNITIONS

- American Martial Arts Alliance Foundation world history books
- Action Martial Arts Magazine Hall of Honors Golden Lifetime Achievement Award (2018)
- Joe Lewis Eternal Warrior Award at the Battle of Atlanta (2018)
- AMAA "Eagle Alumni Award" and Who's Who in the Martial Arts Award (2018)
- Featured in "The World's Greatest Martial Artists, Volume 9" by Ted Gambordella
- AMAA "Martial Arts School of the Year" for Shen Dragon Karate Dojo (2019)
- Inducted into the Martial Arts Hall of Honors by Action Martial Arts Magazine (2020)
- Presidential Lifetime Achievement Award by President Biden (2023)
- Nominated into the World Head of Family Sokeship Council (2017)
- Received the "International Grandmaster of the Year" Award from the World Head of Family Sokeship Council - 2023.
- Featured on the YouTube channel "52 MASTERS" hosted by Karate Kid III star Master William Christopher Ford

HOW HAS MARTIAL ARTS INFLUENCED YOUR LIFE?

Life has many obstacles and diversions that tend to set one off course of your intended path. Life lessons aren't always the teacher of all things. However, throughout Otto's life since his early 20s, martial arts have always been his compass to reset his direction.

Kata is mainly seen as a physical set of non-consensual combative movements that teaches one how to survive and attack. But to Otto, Kata is so much more. Kata has embedded the inexhaustible mindset of never giving up. It causes him to have a higher standard and to persist in achieving perfection. (This drives his wife crazy.)

As a senior construction project manager, he has worked with several top U.S. development and construction companies. Without consciously trying to do his best, he inevitably exceeded his superiors' expectations.

HOW HAS MARTIAL ARTS INFLUENCED YOUR LIFE? (CONT.)

The profound accomplishments by simply trying, based on his mental, physical, psychological, and spiritual everyday life, have elevated him to be the best in his endeavors.

Happily, at 73, Otto is still in the mental and physical state of a man 20 years younger. Martial arts is so embedded; it is his life.

HOW HAS YOUR MARTIAL ARTS SCHOOL IMPACTED YOUR COMMUNITY?

NONPROFIT AND FILM CONTRIBUTIONS

Otto's influence extends into the realm of nonprofit work and film. He founded the Virgin Islands Martial Arts Development Association, Inc. 501(c)3 (VIMADA) to provide educational and scholarship opportunities for children who otherwise might not have access to martial arts training. VIMADA also works to integrate martial arts programs into local elementary schools and offers training to Virgin Islands Police, Federal Law Enforcement and women's groups.

In 2021, Otto produced and choreographed "Black Feather," a short-action film that won seven awards at the Action on Film Festival in Las Vegas.

His current feature film project (2024) will be filmed in the US Virgin Islands and aimed at raising awareness about human trafficking through the lens of martial arts

NATHAN
PORTER

RISING STORM
TRAINING ACADEMY
WOBURN, MA

"
I never realized how a teaching opportunity would help my own skillset. When you teach, you learn twice.

SCHOOL & TRAINING INFORMATION

Years in business: 22 years
Style of Martial Arts: Rising Storm Kempo
School website: www.risingstormacademy.com
Belt Rank/Titles: 7th Dan
Yrs. In the Martial Arts: 27 years

ORGANIZATIONS & AFFILIATIONS

World Martial Arts Federation
Martial Arts Research Institute
US Black Belt Society
Action Martial Arts Hall of Honors

HOW DID YOU GET STARTED IN THE MARTIAL ARTS?

Growing up in the 80s, my childhood was heavily influenced by Teenage Mutant Ninja Turtles, GI Joe, and martial arts movies. However, martial arts training was never in the budget. My training back then consisted of self-taught flips and kicks while acting out things I saw on TV. When wrestling in high school and holding my own job, some friends invited me to kickboxing. On my first day doing kickboxing, I broke their heavy bag with a roundhouse kick. The kickboxing instructor told me I should do karate. The next day, I did karate and fell in love with the martial

HOW HAS YOUR MARTIAL ARTS SCHOOL IMPACTED YOUR COMMUNITY?

My journey began with teaching in the community at local YMCAs. The families I met there became my first students when I took the leap into opening my first stand-alone martial arts school. I have always believed in giving back to my community, and this belief has been the cornerstone of our school's mission. We have organized numerous events, fundraisers, and donations, and have been actively involved in teaching in elementary schools. This commitment to community service is what has made us one of the top schools in New England, and I am proud of the positive impact we have had on our community.

arts. It complimented my wrestling very well. I continued the kickboxing and devoted my whole paycheck to signing up at multiple schools. My high school days included Kickboxing, Tae Kwon Do, Aikido, and Karate.

HOW HAS MARTIAL ARTS INFLUENCED YOUR LIFE?

I never realized how a teaching opportunity would help my own skillset. When you teach, you learn twice. Given the opportunity to instruct is what grew my passion into opening my own martial arts school at the age of 20 years old.

NATHAN
RAY

WORLD KARATE-DO
OF KNIGHTDALE
KNIGHTDALE, NC

❝

I fell in love with martial arts, the people, and seeing people and myself transform.

SCHOOL & TRAINING INFORMATION

Years in business: 38 years

Style of Martial Arts: Shisei Ryu

School website:
www.suprememartialartsknighdale.com

Belt Rank/Titles: 10th Degree Black Belt

Yrs. In the Martial Arts: 47 years

ORGANIZATIONS & AFFILIATIONS

International Karate Dojo Organization

Wanomichi-Takemusu Aiki

American Martial Arts Alliance

HOW DID YOU GET STARTED IN THE MARTIAL ARTS?

I was always drawn to the idea of martial arts. I would grab books about karate and other martial arts in the library. They just drew me in, and the same with TV and film. My uncles were military, and on a subliminal level, they had a big influence. I was later introduced to a master who shared that he thought I would have a great future in the warrior's way. He continued to share that if I chose that path, it would lead me worldwide to great success and prominence, and I would help to change and influence many lives. I believed him, and I chose, at 12 years old, to live the way of the warrior.

HOW HAS MARTIAL ARTS INFLUENCED YOUR LIFE?

Martial arts have influenced my life because they are part of my life! I became a martial arts business owner because I wanted to walk in the footsteps of my karate teacher. I grew up in my teacher's dojo and saw how he helped people. As an impressionable youth, I, too, wanted to have a professional and successful karate business. I was ten years old at that time.

I fell in love with martial arts, the people, and seeing people and myself transform. I trained hard and became a fierce tournament competitor, winning 1st Place in my first tournament. I went on to compete on the U.S. National Karate Team at the Pan American Championship and three more world championships. I retired from karate competition as a two-time World Champion (Venezuela and Okinawa, Japan).

As a young entrepreneur, I began my own dojo (karate school) as a freshman in high school. I am still excited to say that I can't wait to get up every morning and start the day by training my students. As an international competitor and super young business owner, I was frequently featured in newspapers and TV news outlets.

HOW HAS MARTIAL ARTS INFLUENCED YOUR LIFE? (CONT.)

After high school, I became an exchange student in Japan. I lived my dream and studied and taught karate while attending high school in Saitama, Japan. I graduated from North Carolina State University with a degree in Political Science and a minor in Japanese. I built and completed my dream dojo—our current 5,600-square-foot building. It is one of the most beautiful facilities dedicated to human transformation and success.

Only a few can say that they look forward to each new day and what training brings, as I can!

HOW HAS YOUR MARTIAL ARTS SCHOOL IMPACTED YOUR COMMUNITY?

My business has had a major influence on the community by pouring positivity through martial arts into both singles and families. Our work with children has given them an advantage in life by instilling discipline, respect, imagination, and gratitude into their lives. We fill voids where there are single parents who need support with raising their children. We work hand in hand with moms and dads to ensure that we provide a nourishing environment that is based on high moral standards and ethics. Environment shapes, so our primary work is to create a safe and productive environment for all of our clients. This is vital for proper association, which leads to opportunities in our community at large.

At the end of the day, our track record speaks for itself. We have been an example and a beam of guidance to students who have gone on to influence the world as scholars, doctors, lawyers, military, police, pro athletes, Olympians, politicians, and many more.

We are touching the world and making a difference for generations past, present, and future. We make a difference in the world, and that is an amazing gift.

RANDY
ROBINSON

ROBINSON
MARTIAL ARTS
MARION, NC

"

...I opened Robinson Martial Arts to give kids and adults an opportunity to embrace something positive...

SCHOOL & TRAINING INFORMATION

Years in business: 12 years
Style of Martial Arts: Sakura Ryu Karate
School website: www.rmakarate.org
Belt Rank/Titles: 10th Dan Grand Master
Yrs. In the Martial Arts: 52 years

ORGANIZATIONS & AFFILIATIONS

American Martial Arts Alliance
American Martial Arts Alliance Foundation
Kuro Bushi Martial Arts Organization
Karate for Christ
Dojo Organization
American Independent Karate Instructors
Association

HOW DID YOU GET STARTED IN THE MARTIAL ARTS?

My martial arts journey in Chinese Kempo began in 1972 under Professor Martin Buell in Aiea, Hawaii. I was drawn to martial arts because it was very physical, and my success would be completely up to me. I would get out of it exactly what I was willing to put in. At the time, I didn't realize what a difference it would make in my life.

HOW HAS MARTIAL ARTS INFLUENCED YOUR LIFE?

I quickly fell in love with martial arts. It was physical, it was rough, and I was learning at a rapid pace. But, after several months of training, Professor Buell must have sensed something was lacking in my understanding. He told me, "This is not about fighting. This is about making people's lives better - physically, morally, and spiritually. If you don't accept that, you should leave now." That changed my life forever.

HOW HAS YOUR MARTIAL ARTS SCHOOL IMPACTED YOUR COMMUNITY?

When my family relocated back to Western North Carolina, we found that the area had become infested with drugs. We were shocked and realized we had to do something, so my wife, Carolyn, our son, Scot, and I opened Robinson Martial Arts to give kids and adults an opportunity to embrace something positive rather than destroying themselves with drugs and violence.

Hopefully we are achieving our goal of building a better community - one student at a time.

Become an
AMAA
MEMBER!

VICTOR TERAN

INTERNATIONAL TAEKWON-DO ACADEMY
ARVADA, CO

" *I don't just teach kicking and punching; I also share life experiences with my students...*

SCHOOL & TRAINING INFORMATION
Years in business: 11 years
Style of Martial Arts: ITF Taekwon-Do
School website:
www.internationaltkdacademy.com
Belt Rank/Titles: 8th Dan
Yrs. In the Martial Arts: 42 years

ORGANIZATIONS & AFFILIATIONS
Kombat Taekwondo Colorado - President
Sport Karate West - Board Member
International Taekwon-Do Federation
All International Taekwon-Do Federation

HOW DID YOU GET STARTED IN THE MARTIAL ARTS?

Master Teran is the owner and master instructor at International Taekwon-Do Academy and the owner of RDX Supplements, a four-time American Martial Arts Hall of Famer, a Three-Time Martial Arts Hall of Honors Inductee, an Actor, Fight Choreographer, and Author. He's been featured in three iconic martial arts books produced by the American Martial Arts Alliance: Chuck Norris's Martial Arts Masters and Pioneers biography book, Changing Lives Tribute to Ernie Reyes, Sr. biography book, and Changing Lives Tribute to Bill "Superfoot" Wallace biography book.

Bringing his skills to magazines and commercials, he has built a solid reputation as an award-winning children's book author, writer, business owner, and martial arts instructor. Victor has been featured in Halo Dog Collar commercials, hotel commercials, and professional video/photoshoot training for law enforcement's escalation and de-escalation use of force. He's been featured in martial arts magazines and media articles/interviews, music videos, films, and a Toyota commercial. In addition, Master Victor Teran was ranked in the top three at the 2022 Health & Fitness magazine competition and is the President of Kombat Taekwondo in the State of Colorado.

Master Teran served and defended our great nation from late 1996 until August 2013. He served in Operation Enduring Freedom and Operation Iraqi Freedom, serving in Iraq for 10.5 years. He is currently an 8th-degree Master Instructor Trainer, U.S Marine Corps Combat Veteran, Sergeant in the United States Marine Corps, Diplomatic Private security for Blackwater and Triple Canopy, Agent-in-Charge, direct hire for the U.S. Department of State in the Diplomatic Security Service, and Ambassador for the American Military University.

Master Teran was first introduced to Taekwon-Do at age five in New York City. He's presently training under his Great Grandmaster, Kwang Duk Chung, in New York. Master Teran became a black belt at age 13, where he started his initial training as an assistant instructor, teaching children ages 8-12 and assisting the adult classes under his instructor's supervision.

At the age of 15, Master Teran had the opportunity to compete at the Tri-State Championship in Virginia, taking Gold in sparring and silver in the Grand Master Championship. Silver medalist at the All-American Grand National Championship in New Jersey. Gold medalist at the 10th Metro Championship in New Jersey in 2015.

His hard work, dedication, and determination have helped him learn and appreciate Taekwon-Do as an art. He has been given the opportunity to travel to Seoul, Korea, to train with the Korean Olympic Team.

Upon his return to the United States, Master Teran was offered six more months to train in Seoul with the Olympic committee, as well as an opportunity to travel to Colorado Springs for the United States Olympic team trials. Master Teran later joined the United States Marine Corps, attending Marine Corps Boot Camp in Parris Island, South Carolina.

Upon graduation, Master Teran was stationed in Camp Lejeune, North Carolina, taking on a new challenge as an Infantryman. In early 1999, he came across a Taekwon-Do Club where he continued his training, and within several weeks, he became the Chief Instructor for the U.S. Marine Corps Taekwon-Do team. Master Teran's main focus was on "fighting" drills while he was waiting for the approval to participate in the Pan American Games in late 1999.

In 2002, Master Teran attended the Marine Corps Martial Arts Program. Through hard work, blood, and sweat, he was able to move up the ranks and graduated as a Marine Corps Martial Arts/Close Combat Instructor trainer, teaching self-defense and combative to thousands of Marines. Master Teran became a close combat instructor (hand-to-hand) and a Military Operation in Urban Terrain instructor (Urban Warfare), Enemy Prisoner of War instructor, and attending advanced Sniping and Counter Sniping instructor courses. Additionally, he attended many tactical courses, including intensive weapons training, tactical operations, medical training (John Hopkins), and multiple high-threat evasive driving courses.

In 2003, Master Teran deployed to Iraq to fight the War on Terror. In March 2004, he was honorably discharged and initially joined the U.S. State Department as a security specialist in private security firms. Later, he transitioned to the Federal Agency full-time and was stationed in Iraq, conducting high-threat personal protection for high-level dignitaries.

Master Terans promotions and titles include Personal Security Specialist, Tactical Commander, Quick Reaction Force Commander, Advance/Reconnaissance Commander, Air Recon and Reaction Force, Shift Leader, Detail leader/Unit Support Coordinator, and finally Agent-in-Charge for the U.S. Ambassador/ Consul General protective detail in Iraq. In addition to other high-level Diplomatic Advisors under the U.S. Department of State — U.S. Foreign Government relations.

HOW HAS MARTIAL ARTS INFLUENCED YOUR LIFE?

Master Teran is always seeking self-improvement, and whoever is part of his team, he will ensure to do the same for them. He says, "Our training is reality-based, as well as the art of Taekwon-Do. I don't just teach kicking and punching; I also share life experiences with my students that have helped me become a better person. I teach the D.O. in Taekwon-DO. We do this as a way of life and train as martial artists, elevating our martial spirit in every training session. For my students to progress and learn about the D.O., I must continue to train and learn from Great Grandmaster Kwang Duk Chung—a pioneer in martial arts and direct disciple of General Choi Hong Hi."

HOW HAS YOUR MARTIAL ARTS SCHOOL IMPACTED YOUR COMMUNITY?

Master Teran has previously partnered with Play4Autism Foundation in New Jersey to train children with autism spectrum disorder and recently partnered with the "Dear Jack Foundation" in Colorado, which provides programs to adolescent and young adult cancer patients, survivors, and families. Master Teran says, "This is a special project because it is all about giving back to our community in the belief that the opportunity to learn martial arts should be available to everyone, no matter their condition, setbacks, or limitations."

PERSONAL & PROFESSIONAL ACCOLADES

Master Teran's dojang, International Taekwon-Do Academy, has received many impressive accolades, including his own personal accolades:

- 2024 Appointed as Colorado's President of Kombat Taekwondo
- 2024 Official "Kombat Taekwon-Do" Licensed Training Center - Colorado
- 2024 Official "Kombat Taekwon-Do" Licensed Referee - Colorado
- 2024 "Best Martial Arts" School - Colorado Community Media
- 2024 - Invited as Team USA at the World Taekwon-Do Championship - Kazakhstan
- 2023 & 2024 World Taekwon-Do Championship Title
- 2023 "Best Martial Arts" School in Arvada — Quality Rating +95%
- 2023 "Best of Arvada" — Colorado Community Media
- 2023 Colorado Parent's Favorite Family Favorites Nominee
- "Best of Jersey City" New Jersey — 6 Consecutive Years
- Business Hall of Fame — 8 Consecutive Years
- "Best School" in New Jersey's Martial Art Games — 7 Consecutive Years
- Martial Arts Excellence Award — 4 Consecutive Years
- Ranked Top Ten "Best Master Instructor" in New Jersey - 3 Consecutive Years
- United States Martial Arts Hall of Fame Inductee
- New Jersey Metro Championship — 5 Consecutive Years
- New Jersey State Championship — 4 Consecutive Years
- Colorado State Championship — 2 Consecutive Years
- United States National Championship — 8 Consecutive Years
- Junior Olympic Championship — 2 Consecutive Years
- AITF Training Director - Colorado
- "Letter of Proclamation" from the Jersey City Mayor's office. Letter from New Jersey Gov. Chris Christie and Gov. Jared Polis from Colorado. Two Outstanding Leadership Awards signed by Mayor McCormac - Woodbridge, New Jersey

Who's Who
Author Awards

RITA HUNDLEY
HARRIS

> **"**
> *Many things will distract you in life;*
> *however, martial arts develop your*
> *focus and help you perfect tasks until*
> *they are second nature to you.*

WHY THE MARTIAL ARTS?

At the age of three, my parents placed my twin and me in the Dutchess Community College Laboratory Nursery School, where they studied twins. Interestingly, their observations of me were, "Rita is compassionate and observant of other children with special needs, and her muscular coordination is exceptionally good. This is evidenced by the ease with which she uses her body." Our second year of twinship studies stated, "Rita enjoys being outdoors where she has more space and freedom to move. She uses her body easily and gracefully when she climbs, jumps, runs, or pumps herself in the swing."

My parents were licensed social workers who raised four children in Washington, D.C. They had a simple goal for their four children: to obtain our education, participate in structured community programs, and serve others. Like most children, we were exposed to our recreation centers, and we were enrolled in Howard University's summer gymnastic and swimming programs. My father believed his children should be able to protect themselves as we traveled throughout the D.C. area. So, my martial arts training started at eight years old. Many commercial dojangs in Washington, D.C, had established names and wore fancy uniforms; however, my parents had a strict budget and only allocated $3 monthly for martial arts training. I learned early that I could be an instructor and waive my fees. Learning and practicing martial arts at Banneker Recreation Center taught me that it was not the fancy martial arts school with the most students, but the martial arts instructors and their life lessons were the most important.

At twelve years old, my twin brother and I earned our black belt in Tae Kwon Do under the tutelage of Sensei Robert Morton at Banneker Recreation in Washington, D.C., adjacent to Howard University. As soon as I began training seriously in martial arts, I realized I was different from my siblings. The difference was that my physical and mental attributes inclined me towards martial arts and sports. Some of my physical characteristics were that I could hit hard,

kick high, run fast, jump high, and climb almost any tree. Mentally, I had the heart and mindset of a champion before I knew what that meant.

"Champions do not become champions when they win the event, but in the hours, weeks, months, and years they spend preparing for it. The victorious performance itself is merely the demonstration of their championship character."~ Alan Armstrong

I began my competitive martial arts training at age 12, and soon, I would compete at 16 in the women's division. I won numerous local, state, and national U.S. martial arts tournaments. I attended Notre Dame Academy, a private girls' school in Washington, D.C. I competed in Track and Field events and participated on the Pom-Pom Team in swimming and karate. In my senior year, I won "Athlete of the Year." In the same year, I was recognized by the Mid-Atlantic Martial Arts Practitioner for Outstanding Black Belt Kata Award Winner. Over and over, I repeatedly won in my chosen sports and proved that being a woman has no bearing on excellence.

In the 80s and 90s, getting martial arts recognized in most academic circles did not align with typical sports such as basketball, track and field, volleyball, etc. Therefore, getting martial arts recognized in high school and college was challenging; however, I soon earned respect and could couple education with martial arts.

TRAINING INFORMATION

- Belt Ranks & Martial Arts Styles: Tae Kwon Do - 7th Degree
- Instructors/Influencers: Sensei Robert Morton, Sensei Ralph Hundley, Sensei Charlie Neal, Grand Master Johnny D. Houston (Current)
- Birthplace/Growing Up: Queens, NY / Washington, DC
- Yrs. In the Martial Arts: 51 years
- Yrs. Instructing: 35+ years
- Instructor

PROFESSIONAL ORGANIZATIONS

- American Psychological Association (APA) Member
- Psi-Chi National Psychology Honors Society (Member)
- National Association of Housing and Redevelopment Officials (NAHRO)
- National Association of Housing Counselors and Agencies, Inc. (NAHCA)
- The Order of the Eastern Star - Past Grand Matron
- Union Wesley AME Zion Church — Vice-Chair of UW Housing Development

PERSONAL ACHIEVEMENTS

- Wife to Don Harris since January 28, 1992
- Mother to DeVyn Walter and Daelyn Edward Harris
- Obtained a double major in Biology and Psychology
- Mary Baldwin College Athletic Hall of Fame for Martial Arts
- Received a Master's Degree in Clinical Psychology
- An active member of Union Wesley AME Zion Church for 54 years
- 39 years in the Affordable Housing Industry profession
- Community Advocate for Seniors, Veterans, the Homeless, and the Disabled since 1986
- Requested Martial Arts Judge at various Martial Arts Tournaments

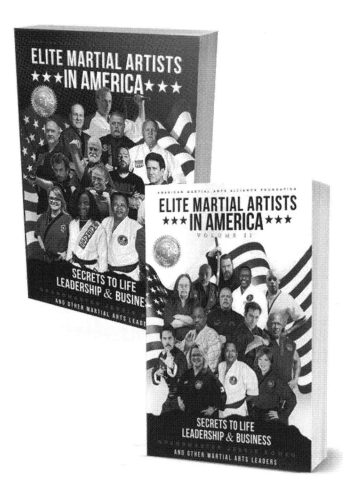

MAJOR ACHIEVEMENTS

- 1982 Most Athletic - The Academy of Notre Dame
- 1982 Mid-Atlantic Practitioner Outstanding Black Belt Kata Award
- U.S. Capital Classics First Women's Sparring Grand Champion 1982-1983
- National Regional PKL Rating, ranked #1 in Forms and Fighting
- Defending Champion - Everhart's Tri-Area Karate and Kung Fu Championship
- 1986 Athlete of the Year, Mary Baldwin College
- 1985 & 1986 Krane New England Open Black Belt Superstar Finalist
- Fighting Strategy Seminars
- Self-Defense Seminars
- 1997 3rd Annual Living Legend Awards — Sensei Robert Everhart, Kenpo Karate Washington, D.C.
- 2010 Mary Baldwin College — Hall of Fame
- 2011 U.S. Capital Classic — Hall of Fame
- 2012-Present Union Wesley AME Zion Board of Trustees
- 2017 Leadership Tomorrow Inductee
- 2017 Who's Who In The Martial Arts-Legends Edition
- 2019 Montgomery County Lead for Impact Inductee
- 2022 Montgomery County Illuminate Your Leadership Inductee
- 2022 USHOFMAA 2022 International Hall of Honor Inductee
- 2023 Co-Author of International Best Seller *Elite Martial Artists in America: Secrets to Life, Leadership & Business, Vol. I* by GM Jessie Bowen
- 2023 Women's Hall of Honors
- 2023 AmeriCorps and the Office of the President's Lifetime Achievement Award for volunteer service
- 2023 Panelist to elect Hall of Fame Inductees for the 2023 Mary Baldwin Universities Hall of Fame
- 2024 - Volunteerism of 500 plus hours of Community Service hours to residents of Wesley House senior residential apartments

While at Mary Baldwin College in Staunton, Virginia, where my skills continued to shine, I represented the college at competitions locally and nationally. In my senior year, I was selected not only by my classmates for Who's Who of Colleges and Universities but also by the college's athletic department and the student body, who chose me as "Athlete of the Year" in 1986.

Upon graduating from college, I continued participating in tournaments and ranking tests. Since I started in martial arts, the wins kept coming, but the losses taught me my greatest lessons. Martial arts taught me not to be obsessed, mad, or overthink my decisions when I lose. The most important takeaway from starting in martial arts through today is that failure begins the learning process. My experience in martial arts taught me mental and physical conditioning. The lessons in martial arts taught me to align my priorities, exercise self-control even when the going gets tough, develop a stick-to-itiveness attitude, and always finish whatever I start.

HOW HAS MARTIAL ARTS IMPACTED YOUR LIFE?

The impact of martial arts was not just for discipline, confidence building, or protecting myself from bullies. Martial arts helped me cope with skills to respond to agonizing, unbearable, or unjust situations. Unfortunately, we encounter bullies at work or in the community in childhood and adulthood. I have always wanted to use martial arts to improve my self-preservation skills. Awareness that I would know what to do in difficult situations without overthinking is one of the most impactful lessons I learned.

A second way that martial arts have impacted my life is with focusing, memory retention, and developing what is now referred to as mindfulness. Learning the offensive and defensive patterns required in performing

MAJOR ACHIEVEMENTS

- 2024 Panelist to elect candidates for a new cohort of Leaders for Montgomery County, Maryland Lead for Impact
- 2024 Presenter in the Housing Opportunities Commission - Strategic Plan Video
- 2024 Co-Author of International Best Seller *Elite Martial Artists in America: Secrets to Life, Leadership & Business, Vol II*, by GM Jessie Bowen

HOW HAS MARTIAL ARTS IMPACTED YOUR LIFE? (CONTINUED)

Kata's helped me in school and life to buckle down and keep my head in the game, especially through adversity. In life, building not only your physical but also your mental strength is essential. Martial arts improve your overall memory. Through repetition of most sports techniques, you will improve your muscle memory. Many things will distract you in life; however, martial arts develop your focus and help you perfect tasks until they are second nature to you. Finally, martial arts teach you calmness and peace of mind through meditation, intentional breathing techniques, and practicing patience. Anchoring into your spiritual power makes the above only that much greater. As for me, my soul is anchored in the Lord.

The third impact of martial arts in my life was to be of volunteer service and always be concerned for others. I dedicated my life to volunteering to serve the homeless community, persons with disabilities, veterans, seniors, and many other needy populations.

Finally, the impact of martial arts in my life is to continue staying active in the Tae Kwon Do community by conducting self-defense seminars and volunteering as a referee for local and national martial arts tournaments. I am incredibly grateful to impart any wisdom to those practicing or participating in the youth-only tournaments.

MARVIN KING

" *Martial Arts have become who I am. Everything is based on the philosophy of martial arts.*

WHY THE MARTIAL ARTS?

My martial arts journey started as an adolescent in the 60s when martial arts schools were traditional, tough, and gritty. As a new student in my first karate class, I was paired with a bigger student who choked me out by applying too much neck pressure during a basic choke escape drill. That first experience was painful and nearly caused me to quit. But I didn't. During those early days in the dojo, I quickly learned that you need discipline, patience, and courage to earn a black belt. I remember falling a lot, picking myself up, and pushing my physical limits as my Sensei drilled us in the art of kicking, punching, sparring, and self-defense. I eventually earned a green belt in Tae Kwon Do with discipline and hard work, but because the school was far from home and expensive, I stopped training there. Being removed from the dojo was disappointing, but unbeknownst to me then, that transition would be what ignited my great love, commitment, and journey in martial arts. It also reminded me of what my parents taught me about not settling for the status quo and to keep moving forward.

My turning point was when I realized that being a martial artist was not about a school or a system but about practice, discipline, consistency, perseverance, and patience!

Curious to know more, I researched books and literature and accumulated and absorbed everything on the subject. I learned about strength training, kinesiology, bodybuilding, philosophy, meditation, and diet. Bruce Lee movies also inspired me. I appreciated the variety in martial arts systems and was humbled to know that each system offered abundant knowledge, tradition, and history.

By age 12, I transformed my body by consuming healthier foods and adding weight training and meditation to my martial arts practice. During the '70s, I took karate classes in gyms and auditoriums and trained with accomplished Tae Kwon Do Black Belts. 1980, I joined the International Shuai-Chiao Academy in Cleveland, Ohio, with Master Chi-Hsiu Daniel Weng, Ph.D. Master Weng often hosted his teacher, Grandmaster Ch'ang Tung-Sheng (aka The Flying Butterfly), when he visited from Taiwan. I was humbled after witnessing the power, balance, and

- Belt Ranks & Martial Arts Styles: Tae Kwon Do, Traditional Shuai-Chiao with Grandmaster Chi-Hsiu Daniel Weng Ph.D., and Grandmaster Ch'ang Tung-Sheng (aka The Flying Butterfly), Ch'ang style T'ai-chi-ch'uan and Hsing Jing (Ch'ang's "essence of Hsing-I"), Shaolin Do Kung Fu, Hung Fut Southern Shaolin Kung Fu, Krav Maga, Target Focus Training (TFT), Korean Sulsa, Ju-Jitsu, Sun Style Tai Chi Chuan

- Instructors/Influencers: Grandmaster Ch'ang Tung-Sheng, Grandmaster Chi-Hsiu Daniel Weng, Ph.D, Grandmaster Sin Kwan The 8th Generation, Grandmaster Tai Yim, Grandmaster Bryant Fong, Master Tim Larkin, Pavel Tsatsouline

- Birthplace/Growing Up: Cleveland, OH

- Yrs. In the Martial Arts: 50 years

- Yrs. Instructing: 40 years

- School owner & Instructor at Bowie Kettlebell Club Health & Wellness Center

PROFESSIONAL ORGANIZATIONS

- Project Management Institute (PMI): Project Management Professional (PMP), 2012 to present

- Project Management Institute (PMI): Agile Certified Practitioner (PMI-ACP)

- Duke Certified Lean and Agile Practitioner (DCLAP) Project Manager

PERSONAL ACHIEVEMENTS

- 2- Time Published Author

- 2-Time Marine Corp Marathon Finisher

- 1-Time Philadelphia Marathon Finisher

MAJOR ACHIEVEMENTS

- Author of *The Art of Being Well, Healthy Strategies for Daily Living.*

- CEO/Owner of the Bowie Kettlebell Health and Wellness Center, teaching Kettlebells, Joint Mobility, Strength Stretching, Qigong, and Martial Arts Science.

- 2024 Amazon and International Bestselling Co-author for *Elite Martial Artists in America: Secrets to Life, Leadership, and Business* Compilation Book

- 2023, Who's Who International Hall of Honors Legends Award

grace of these masters and was excited to finally learn Chinese Kung Fu. Shuai-Chiao training included the Ch'ang style T'ai-chi-ch'uan and Hsing Jing (Ch'ang's "essence of Hsing-Yi"). I stayed with Shuai-Chiao, practiced hard every day, and was honored to earn my first black belt from the late grandmaster in 1982. I successfully competed in many Shuai-Chiao and Karate tournaments in the years following my training and was appreciative when tournament rules were changed to accommodate more fighting styles.

Today, I'm focused on the "Wellness Lifestyle" and the minimalist approach to Reality-Based Self Protection, Qigong, Tai Chi, and the development of functional strength best achieved from hardstyle kettlebell exercises. Under the guidance of kettlebell and strength expert Pavel Tsatsouline, I earned the Level 1 and Level 2 Russian Kettlebell Challenge (RKC) Certifications. I was fascinated and awestruck by how quickly the Kettlebell 1-Arm Swing and Turkish Get Up (TGU) improved martial artists' fighting endurance and power. I immediately implemented the RKC strong man philosophy and minimalist training methods in my martial arts practice with immediate positive results. Hardstyle kettlebell swings teach the martial artist how to generate explosive hip power while relaxing the arms and anchoring the feet. Like the Yin/Yang, the TGU (Yin) develops the elusive soft elements of strength while the kettlebell swing (Yang) accentuates the martial artist's ability to generate explosive power.

In 2014, I created the Bowie Kettlebell Club (BKC), a strength and holistic wellness-based school that teaches and trains students to be functionally fit at any age using Joint Mobility, Kettlebells, Qigong, and Martial Arts. In 2020, during the COVID-19 pandemic, the business went virtual and officially changed its name to the "Bowie Kettlebell Club Health and Wellness Center." The program expanded internationally to represent and show others that the goal of a really good fitness program is to teach the "Art of Being Well." We call this approach to wellness "Forever-Young-Forever," which has become the philosophy behind the training method. Like the martial arts progression from beginner to advanced, the student learns that the art of being well is more about the little things you do every day to remain functionally youthful for a lifetime. Self-protection classes at the BKC focus on understanding actual violence and the simple tools anyone can use to protect themselves. No previous training or martial arts prerequisites are required for this class. The BKC "Loaded Yoga" and "Forever-Young-Forever" Programs are a creative blend of Kettlebells, Joint Mobility, Strength Stretching, Qigong, and Martial Art exercises that, when done regularly, will improve each person's ability to maintain a state of athletic readiness. The programs can also be adapted to complement any training method.

I'm humbled by this opportunity to serve others and live by a simple philosophy, "You don't have to please anyone! You only have to be the best you that you can be!" So, "Find a path, stay humble, and always march forward courageously!"

MAJOR ACHIEVEMENTS

- 2022, Martial Arts Author of the Year Award for; "The Art of Being Well, Healthy Strategies for Daily Living"
- Certified Wellness Coach
- 2021, President Joe Biden Ameri Corps Lifetime Achievement Award
- 2021, "Outstanding Martial Arts Instructor" award from the American Freestyle Karate Association (AFKA)
- 2021, American Martial Arts Alliance Board of Advisors
- 2021, Inducted into the Argentina International Martial Arts Hall of Fame.
- 2020, Represented the United States Instructors in the first "World Martial Arts Live" International event in which over 40 countries were represented.
- 2020, "Lifetime Martial Arts Achievement Award" from the American Freestyle Karate Association (AFKA)
- 2020 Action Martial Arts Hall of Honors Inductee and received the (40-Year Martial Arts Golden Lifetime Contributions Award.
- Featured in the 2020 Action Martial Arts Hall of Honors World History Book.
- 2019 Inductee into the American Martial Arts Alliance (AMAA) Who's Who Legends Hall of Honors
- Featured in the 2019 Martial Arts Masters and Pioneers Biography Book
- Black Sash in Hung-Fut Kung Fu with 8th Generation Grandmaster Tai Yim
- 1995, World Kung Fu Federation (WKF) National Forms and Weapons Grand Championship
- 1982, Black Belt in Shuai-Chiao from Grandmaster Ch'ang Tung-Sheng and Master Chi-Hsiu Daniel Weng, Ph.D.
- Member of the first-generation USA Shuai-Chiao Black Belts
- Brown Belt in Shaolin Do, where I learned the Qigong breathing meditations under Grandmaster Sin Kwan
- National Council of Strength and Fitness (NCSF) Certified Professional Trainer (CPT) 1999 to present
- Russian Kettlebell Challenge (RKC) Level 1 Certification - 2006 to present with Kettlebell and strength expert Pavel Tsatsouline
- Russian Kettlebell Challenge (RKC) Level 2 Certification — 2009

HOW HAS MARTIAL ARTS IMPACTED YOUR LIFE?

Martial Arts have become who I am. Everything is based on the philosophy of martial arts. The ability to incorporate my skills learned in martial arts into everyday living has inspired me to write my first book entitled "The Art of Being Well, Healthy Strategies for Daily Living." Martial arts have inspired me so much that I cannot remember when I haven't practiced martial arts in some capacity each day. I look forward to fellowshipping with my martial arts like-minded friends for years to come.

BRENDAN
WILSON

"
Martial arts have helped me focus on becoming a better leader, filmmaker, novelist, and diplomat.

I won the silver medal at the US Open held in Las Vegas in my age group in 2009, and in 2010, I was selected to be an international judge for the US Open. I have competed in numerous tournaments over my career, and in 1996, I was the AAU Louisiana State Champion for sparring, forms, and musical forms. In the mid-1990s, I was ranked in competition by the National Black Belt League and Sport Karate International Magazine. In 2022, I was inducted into the Bill Wallace AMAA Hall of Honors and received the *Changing Lives* Award and the *International Impact Award.*

Contribution: I am the founder of the martial arts style of Aristos, a style based upon Korean hard-style techniques and the philosophy of classical Greece. I have trained students from 13 countries.

I n 1974, I got cut from the high school varsity baseball team. That day, I went to Roberts Karate in Alexandria, Virginia, and began training in Tae Kwon Do. Later, while at university, I trained at Tong's Studio of Tae Kwon Do in Harrisonburg, Virginia, where I received my first dan in 1980. Upon graduation, I entered the Army as a 2nd Lieutenant and qualified as a US Army Ranger, during which I also trained in combative military techniques. While in the Army, I continued my training, including a year in the Republic of Korea. I was the coach and team captain for two military martial arts teams: one from the 101st Airborne Division and one from the XVIII Airborne Corps. Additionally, I trained the NATO commander's close protection team in weapons-disarming techniques while overseas. Finally, while serving in Iraq as a diplomat, I trained personnel at one of the allied embassies.

HOW HAS MARTIAL ARTS IMPACTED YOUR LIFE?

Martial arts have helped me focus on becoming a better leader, filmmaker, novelist, and diplomat.

Studying martial arts has been a wonderful journey for me, and that journey continues. The feeling I have is gratitude, which is the most significant measure. I am grateful for the discipline that helped me through some of the toughest military training in the world. Six years of Tae Kwon Do training helped me get through the US Army Ranger School. My martial arts instructor in college would say during a grueling session when students dropped out from exhaustion that "if you can't go on, make sure it is your body that has failed you, not your spirit." In Ranger School, we were driven 22 hours a day and given so little food that many dropped 30 pounds in nine weeks. In the year I attended, five students died from exhaustion and exposure. It was a modern Shaolin Temple. When I felt I couldn't go on, I remembered my instructor telling me that the spirit decides.

I am also grateful for the great people I have met and trained with over the years: soldiers, martial artists, and competitors from many countries. A bond forms with sweat, effort, and the occasional tear.

TRAINING INFORMATION

- Belt Ranks & Martial Arts Styles: Taekwondo-8th Dan
- Instructors/Influencers: Stan Alexander, Gary Harvey, GM Sugman Park, GM Jackie Kwon, Larry Wilk, GM George Petrotta, GM Song
- Birthplace/Growing Up: Hampton, VA / Military Family (moved many times)
- Yrs. In the Martial Arts: 50 years
- Yrs. Instructing: 43 years
- School owner, Manager & Instructor at Aristos Martial Arts, LLC

PROFESSIONAL ORGANIZATIONS

- Superfoot System Affiliate
- International Sungjado Association
- Kukkiwon
- Jung Do Kwan Association
- International Chang Hon Taekwondo Federation

PERSONAL ACHIEVEMENTS

Martial Arts Awards:

- Grandmaster of the Year Award, AMAA Magazine, 2024
- Outstanding Contribution to Military Martial Arts, Action Martial Arts Hall of Honor, 2024
- Inducted into the Who's Who in the Martial Arts Hall of Honor, AMAA, 2022
- Changing Lives Legacy Award, AMAA, 2022
- International Impact Award, AMAA, 2022
- Silver Medal, US Open, United States of America Taekwondo (USAT), Las Vegas, NV, 2009
- Gold Medal, AAU Louisiana State Championship, Forms, Sparring, Musical Forms, 1995
- Ranked 4th, Dixie Region, National Blackbelt League, and Sport Karate International, 1993

Certifications:

- International Referee, Pan American Taekwondo Union (PATU)
- Served as International Referee for the US Open competition in 2010, Las Vegas, NV

PERSONAL ACHIEVEMENTS (CONTINUED)

Martial Arts Leadership:

- Team Coach and Captain for two military competition teams
- Taught NATO Commander's close protection team in weapons disarming techniques
- Founded the NATO Military Taekwondo Association
- Founded Aristos Martial Arts, LLC

Martial Arts Publications

- Warrior Goddess: Book Two in the Mei Ling Lee Trilogy, Elite Publications, 2024
- Leadership, Ethics, and Reality: The Art of Getting Things Done, Elite Martial Artists in America, Co-author, 2024
- The Achilles Battle Fleet: Book One in the Mei Ling Lee Trilogy, Literate Ape Publications, 2021
- WTF Poomsae: Time for a Course Correction; Totally Tae Kwon Do, May 2010
- Paradise Lost: Tae Kwon Do and the Art of Simplicity; Totally Tae Kwon Do; June 2009, Co-author
- State of the Art in Tae Kwon Do: ITF versus WTF, Totally Tae Kwon Do; May 2009
- The Principles of War and the Martial Arts, Inside Martial Arts, Summer 1995
- Tournament Blues, Martial Arts Masters, May 1995
- Perseverance: A Day at Ranger School, Inside Karate, December 1994
- The Essence of What is Real, Masters Series, September 1994

Martial Arts Films:

- Aristos Documentary, Athens, Greece, Equal Productions Greece, producer, writer, actor, 2014
- Aristos Training Video, Athens, Greece, El Oso Diablo Productions, LLC, producer, writer, actor, 2014

MAJOR ACHIEVEMENTS

- Publication of two bestselling martial arts novels
- Wrote and produced two award-winning films: Doug's Christmas, 2014, and A Child Lies Here, 2011. El Oso Diablo Productions

Military Service:

- Retired as Lt. Col. with 25 years of service
- US Army Ranger, Paratrooper, Air Assault Qualified
- Commanded a Firebase in the Republic of Korea
- Served in 101st Airborne Division and 18th Airborne Corps

Diplomat Service:

- NATO Defense Planner for 15 Years
- Served in Iraq, Bosnia, Libya, Ukraine, Belarus, Russia, and Korea

Education:

- Juris Doctor (JD), Northwestern California University School of Law, 2022
- Doctor of Philosophy (Ph.D.), International Relations, Berne University, 1999
- Masters of Business Administration (MBA), Oklahoma City University, 1988
- Bachelor of Science in Economics (BS), James Madison University, 1981

Become an
AMAA MEMBER!

AMAAF

Alumnus & Inductees

DANA ABBOTT

"
The path of the sword has taught me the importance of dedication, focus, and continuous self-improvement.

WHY THE MARTIAL ARTS?

I began my studies in the Fall of 1978 in the southwestern town of Prescott, Arizona. It was in this quaint setting that my journey into martial arts began, specifically Korean karate, which I learned through the Police Athletic League (PAL) at the armory next to the courthouse. The very same courthouse that had gained fame as the filming location for the iconic martial arts movie of the 1970s, "Billy Jack," where Billy Jack's unforgettable kick to the guy's head took place. During this time, I worked as a surveyor for Yavapai County, Arizona, immersing myself in the study of martial arts while embracing my professional career.

As I delved deeper into my martial arts journey, I relocated to Tokyo, Japan, and found myself greatly influenced over the next 15 years by the teachings of several esteemed sword masters. These masters were seasoned combat veterans who had served in the Japanese Imperial Army during World War II.

With their guidance, I began to grasp the essence of swordsmanship, training in various disciplines such as kendo, kenjutsu, iaido, and tameshigiri. My masters, including Abe Shinobu, Shizawa Kunio, Tanabe Tetsundo, Tabuchi Mitsunobu, and Nakamura Taizaburo, who was knighted by the Emperor of Japan, imparted their wisdom, shaping my understanding of the way of the sword. As a 7th Dan in Japanese swordsmanship, specializing in Kenjutsu and Toyama-Ryu Iai Batto-do, my expertise is highly respected in both Japan and the United States, where I currently reside. My extensive training and certification were obtained through Japan's esteemed Martial Arts University, Nihon Taiiku Daigaku, under the Japanese Department of Education and Recreation. Throughout my career, I have had the privilege of crossing swords with formattable opponents, who made me a stronger martial artist.

Reflecting on my journey, I am often asked about my experiences learning kenjutsu from the great sword masters in Japan. Many seek my guidance on mastering techniques and understanding the mental

TRAINING INFORMATION

- Martial Arts Rank: Toyama-Ryu Iai-Batto do - 7th Degree Black Belt
- Instructors/Influencers: Abe Shinobu, Shizawa Kunio, Tanabe Tetsundo, Nakamura Taizaburo, Tabuchi Mitsunobu, and the great samurai movie actor, Mifune Toshiro
- Yrs. In the Martial Arts: 46 years
- Yrs. Instructing: 26 years
- School owner at Samurai Sports

HOW HAS MARTIAL ARTS IMPACTED YOUR LIFE?

Martial arts have left an indelible imprint on my life. Over 45 years of learning, practicing, and contemplating the art of the sword, I have been profoundly influenced by the traditions passed down by my sword masters. Each movement, technique, and transition has shaped my adult life, fostering discipline, perseverance, and a relentless pursuit of perfection. I envision myself as a protector, dedicated to maintaining consistency and good health well into my centenary years. The lessons and values instilled in me by martial arts guide my everyday actions and decisions. They have become an integral part of who I am, influencing my physical abilities, mindset, and character.

The path of the sword has taught me the importance of dedication, focus, and continuous self-improvement. It has given me the tools to overcome challenges and embrace a balanced and harmonious way of life. With each passing year, I strive to embody the principles of martial arts more fully, always seeking to deepen my understanding and refine my skills.

As I progress along this lifelong journey, I am grateful for the profound impact the martial arts have had on me. They have shaped my perspective, my values, and my aspirations. I carry the spirit of the sword with me, embracing its teachings and using them to guide me on the path of personal growth and enlightenment.

aspects of swordsmanship. In response, I paint a vivid picture, sharing the mental images that offer insights into the mindset of a Japanese swordsmanship student. My dedication to traditional practice and an unwavering pursuit of perfection set me apart. While some martial artists lean towards a less physically demanding approach, I remain committed to the age-old adage that practice makes perfect.

I firmly believe that one's dreams and desires, combined with motivation and determination, hold the key to achieving proficiency and mastery. My lifelong devotion to Japanese swordsmanship has propelled me to the forefront of my field, leaving an indelible mark on the martial arts community and igniting a passion for the ancient traditions I hold dear. I am grateful for the opportunities to share my knowledge and experiences, and I hope to continue inspiring others on their own martial arts journeys.

HOW HAS MARTIAL ARTS IMPACTED YOUR LIFE? (CONTINUED)

My martial arts career boasts numerous accomplishments and accolades. Notably, in 2004, I was honored to be inducted into Black Belt Magazine's prestigious Hall of Fame, a testament to my expertise and contributions to the martial arts industry. Yet, my proudest achievement lies in the present, as I have reached the same age as my masters before me, embodying their teachings and becoming a reflection of their wisdom. Through years of sword fighting and relentless practice, I have attained a sense of calm and peacefulness, cultivating a mindset that I believe will carry me well into old age. My dedication and skill have earned me recognition as a leader in the martial arts world. I have been fortunate to receive numerous honors and awards, including the Black Belt Magazine Hall of Fame, the Golden Shuto Award, the Elite Black Belt Hall of Fame, and the Martial Arts History Museum recognition, among many others. I have been commended for my dedication to preserving the spirit of Budo, and my achievements have been acknowledged with Lifetime Achievement Awards and the AMAA Who's Who in the Martial Arts, to name a few. It is a humbling experience to be recognized for my contributions and to know that my passion for martial arts has made an impact. I will continue to strive for excellence and share my knowledge and love for martial arts with others, carrying on the legacy of my master's and inspiring future generations.

Become an
AMAA MEMBER!

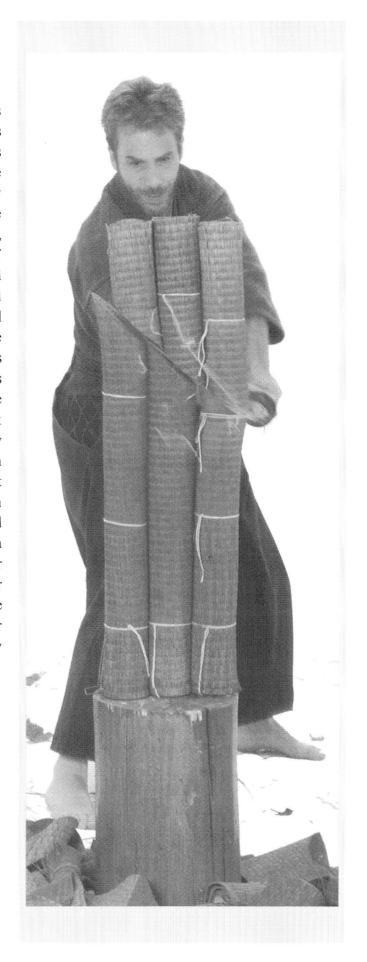

CHRIS ANDERSON

"
The dojo is the only place where I can go to shut out everything wrong in my life and focus only on my karate.

Murfreesboro, Tennessee. I've been studying Wado-Ryu Karate at Bill Taylor's Bushido School of Karate for 25 years and counting. I taught classes as an assistant instructor (SWAT) for three years while training to become a black belt, and then I taught for two additional years after earning my first-degree black belt. I received my first-degree black belt (Sho Dan) in December 2003 and my 5th-degree Black Belt (Go Dan) in April 2021. I still attend class twice weekly to hone and sharpen my skills, and I'm working toward earning my 6th-degree Black Belt (Roku Dan). I plan to continue training in the martial arts as long as I live. Martial arts is more than just a hobby for me. It has become an essential part of my life.

HOW HAS MARTIAL ARTS IMPACTED YOUR LIFE?

Studying martial arts has played an incredibly positive role in my life. Studying martial arts has transformed me into a disciplined, self-confident, respectful, humble, patient, and tenacious individual. It has made me mentally and physically tough and kept me physically fit. Studying martial arts has helped me in college, graduate school, careers, and in my personal life. Before studying martial arts, I sometimes gave up

WHY THE MARTIAL ARTS?

I had been interested in studying martial arts from an early age, especially after seeing the original Karate Kid film in the theater in 1984. I officially began studying martial arts in 1997. While attending Middle Tennessee State University in Murfreesboro, Tennessee, I enrolled in self-defense, beginner karate, and advanced karate over the following three semesters. After completing advanced karate, I enrolled in a local Taekwondo studio and studied Taekwondo for the next two years, earning a 2nd Degree Red Belt (2nd Gup). I then decided to switch styles in 1999 to my current style of Wado-Ryu Karate at Bill Taylor's Bushido School of Karate in

HOW HAS MARTIAL ARTS IMPACTED YOUR LIFE? (CONTINUED)

quickly on specific tasks or obstacles for fear of failure. Learning new techniques, memorizing sometimes lengthy and difficult patterns/katas, sparring against bigger and stronger opponents, and passing difficult belt exams gave me the confidence I needed to never give up and continuously pursue my goals and aspirations. Studying martial arts has also kept me focused and mentally strong during challenging seasons of my life. The dojo is the only place where I can shut out all the negatives in my life and focus only on my karate. In addition, the longer I study martial arts, the more I find myself becoming increasingly humble, calm, respectful, and patient with others as well as myself. Studying martial arts has given me confidence and a sense of peace, knowing I can defend myself and my loved ones if a situation arises in this unpredictable world. Lastly, studying martial arts has brought many friends and amazing individuals into my life, including classmates and instructors. If I had to change anything about my study of martial arts, I would have started studying much earlier in life.

TRAINING INFORMATION

- Martial Arts Styles & Rank: Taekwondo - 2nd Degree Red Belt, Wado Ryu - 5th Degree Black Belt (Go Dan)
- Instructors/Influencers: Bill Taylor, Steve Holt, William Herzer, Newton Harris, Ronald Tucker, Paul Caruthers, Thomas Bain
- Birthplace/Growing Up: Nashville, TN / Smyrna TN
- Yrs. In the Martial Arts: 27 years
- Yrs. Instructing: 5 years

PROFESSIONAL ORGANIZATIONS

- United States Eastern Wado-Ryu Karate-Do Federation
- Black Belt Club Member
- SWAT (Assistant Instructor)
- Lifetime Black Belt Member of the American Martial Arts Alliance

PERSONAL ACHIEVEMENTS

- Earning my 5th Degree Black Belt (Go Dan) and becoming an official sensei
- Being awarded an Excellence in Teaching Award when I helped teach classes at my dojo as an assistant instructor
- Training numerous times with Wado-Ryu Grand Master Sensei Kazutaka Otsuka
- Attending multiple seminars and training with World Kickboxing Champion Bill "Superfoot" Wallace
- Training with Heavyweight Kickboxing Champion Joe Lewis

MAJOR ACHIEVEMENTS

- Being selected to have my martial arts biography published in the AMAAF Special Tribute to Bill "Superfoot" Wallace edition of the Changing Lives Series Biography Book, Volume 7, in 2022. My martial arts biography is also featured in the Who's Who in the Martial Arts Special Edition Third Series Honoring Cynthia Rothrock, July 13, 2023. In addition to being included in these two books, I was mentioned in Martial Arts Extraordinaire Magazine, Issue 6, April 25, 2023 for being named a new black belt member of the American Martial Arts Alliance, LLC. I was also mentioned in Martial Arts Extraordinaire Magazine, Issue 8, February 29, 2024 for being named an American Martial Arts Alliance Alumnus, inductee, and future leader.

MATEO
BASSI

❝

Studying martial arts has allowed me to visit many countries and meet different martial arts practitioners.

HOW HAS MARTIAL ARTS IMPACTED YOUR LIFE?

Studying martial arts has allowed me to visit many countries and meet different martial arts practitioners. I have gained knowledge and appreciation for all martial arts styles.

TRAINING INFORMATION

- Martial Arts Styles & Rank: Sibpalki-7th Dan, Hapkido-2nd Dan, Taekwondo WTF-1st Dan
- Instructors/Influencers: Pedro Alejo Barberan, Oscar Tajes
- Birthplace/Growing Up: San Luis, Argentina
- Yrs. In the Martial Arts: 40 years
- Yrs. Instructing: 20 years
- Instructor and School owner at Dan Gun Sipbalki Kwan

PROFESSIONAL ORGANIZATIONS

- Asama Association

PERSONAL & MAJOR ACHIEVEMENTS

- Hall of Fame Argentina Embassy
- Asama Association, President
- Dan Gun Sibpalki Kwan, Director
- "Represent Yourself in Argentina" from the World Master Elite Association

WHY THE MARTIAL ARTS?

When I was 14, a friend introduced me to Taekwondo, and I quickly developed a deep passion for martial arts. My journey led me to the practice of Sibpalki, where I now proudly run my own Dan Gun Sibpalki Kwan School and Asama Association. I am honored to be recognized as a member of the Argentine Hall of Fame.

PEARCI
BASTIANY

"
Martial arts has had a tremendously positive impact on my life and has become one of my ministries.

Martial arts has created some of the most honorable and friendly relationships. The mental and physical attributes are phenomenal. After experiencing a robbery attempt, my self-defense training enabled me to handle the situation. Through martial arts, I was able to chase my dream of trying out for the Olympics. Most of all, it has given me the tools to not just be a black belt in martial arts but a black belt in life!

HOW HAS MARTIAL ARTS IMPACTED YOUR LIFE?

It has been an incredible journey in the world of martial arts. Martial arts has had a tremendously positive impact on my life and has become one of my ministries. It has allowed me to inspire people to lead more positive lifestyles.

WHY THE MARTIAL ARTS?

I started martial arts with Judo at the YMCA when I was six years old. I fell in love with it when the class bully grabbed me from behind, and I flipped him with a shoulder throw! I continued to train in many different styles until I met and trained with Grandmaster Billy Blanks. He helped turn me into a champion. When I relocated to California, he suggested I train with Great Grandmaster Ernie Reyes and Great Grandmaster Tony Thompson.

It has been a great martial arts journey to this day. Martial arts has had an enormous positive impact on my life. It has become one of my ministries. It has given me the gift to inspire people to live a more positive lifestyle. I have traveled and trained around the world.

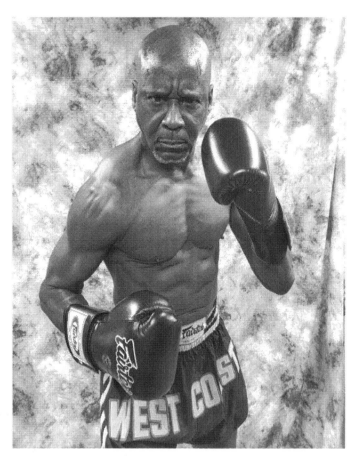

HOW HAS MARTIAL ARTS IMPACTED YOUR LIFE? (CONTINUED)

Through martial arts, I have had the opportunity to travel and train around the world, forming some of the most honorable and friendly relationships.

The mental and physical attributes of martial arts are phenomenal. Following a recent attempted robbery, my self-defense training equipped me to manage the situation effectively. Through martial arts, I was able to pursue my dream of trying out for the Olympics. Most of all, it has given me the tools to not just be a black belt in martial arts but a black belt in life!

TRAINING INFORMATION

- Martial Arts Styles & Rank: West Coast World Martial Arts Association - 9th Degree, Mixed Martial Arts - 9th Degree
- Instructors/Influencers: Great Grandmaster Ernie Reyes, Great Grandmaster Tony Thompson, UFC Champion Daniel Cormier, UFC/Bellator Champion Chris Cyborg, Grandmaster Billy Blanks, Grandmaster Benny "The Jet" Urquidez, Grandmaster Bill "Superfoot" Wallace, Grandmaster Cynthia Rothrock, Grandmaster Mark Gerry, Grandmaster Robert "Sugar" Crossan, Grandmaster Kru Phimsoutham and many other Grandmasters and Masters of Martial Arts

TRAINING INFORMATION (CONTINUED)

- Birthplace/Growing Up: Hartford, CT
- Yrs. In the Martial Arts: 50+ years
- Yrs. Instructing: 30+ years
- Instructor and School owner at West Coast World Martial Arts Association, Certified Personal Trainer

PROFESSIONAL ORGANIZATIONS

- USTU

PERSONAL ACHIEVEMENTS

- 2024 - Promoted to 9th degree black belt
- 2024 - AMAA Hall of Honors: 10th Anniversary
- 2024 - Gold Medal - 5X Body For Life Fitness Challenge Champion
- 2024 - Tae Bo Advanced Instructor Certification
- 2024 - IKF Muay Thai Championships - Katana demonstration
- 2024 - Spartan Race: Hawaii
- 2023 - Muscle and Fitness + (Fitness Expert)
- 2023 - Muscle and Fitness- Mr. Muscle and Fitness: Finalist
- 2020 - Martial Arts Masters Hall of Fame - The World's Greatest: Volume 24
- 1996 - US Olympic Trials at the Olympic Training Center: Taekwondo
- 1996 - US National Champion
- 1996 - 1997 - California State Taekwondo Champion
- 2020-2022 - Movie stuntman: *GI Joe Snake Eyes, Bay Lawz, Bizzare 2*

MAJOR ACHIEVEMENTS

- 2024 - Tae Bo Advanced Instructor Certification
- 2020 - Martial Art Masters Hall of Fame
- 2008-2024- 5X Ultimate Body for Life Challenge
- 1996 - Olympic Trials Competitor- Taekwondo
- 1996-97 - California National Taekwondo Champion
- 1989 - Bodyguard for Muhammad Ali
- 2008 - Bodyguard for Serena Williams
- 1993 - Bodyguard for Ice Cube

MICHAEL
BENNETT

"

Martial arts have helped me impact the youth of America...

HOW HAS MARTIAL ARTS IMPACTED YOUR LIFE?

Learning and studying martial arts impacted my life in many ways. I started off meeting great people to look up to, and it has given me the confidence to achieve anything I desire in life. My parents were my role models, but learning martial arts helped build my character into who I am today. Martial arts have helped me impact the youth of America by teaching them how to be productive, good citizens and stewards in their neighborhoods and how to become great parents.

TRAINING INFORMATION

- Martial Arts Styles & Rank: World Taekwondo -7th Dan, World Taekwondo Changmookwan -7th Dan, Ju Bushi Do - 5th Dan, Aikido -1st Dan, Kung Fu - Black Slash Belt
- Instructors/Influencers: GM Rafael Medina, GM Bobby Clayton, GM Carroll Baker, GM Robert Scott, GM Todd Angel, Sensei David, Sinfu Lee
- Birthplace/Growing Up: Shreveport, LA
- Yrs. In the Martial Arts: 55 years
- Yrs. Instructing: 42 years
- Instructor and Coach of Olympic Style Taekwondo to hundreds of champion students

WHY THE MARTIAL ARTS?

I started martial arts training because my mom was worried about me defending myself because my brothers were in college. So, my mother enrolled me in a Kung Fu class, which started my martial arts career. I learned not to be afraid of achieving my status as a great martial artist by watching Bruce Lee, Chuck Norris, Cynthia Rothrock, Sho Kosugi, Stephen K. Hayes, and many other great martial artists.

PROFESSIONAL ORGANIZATIONS

- United States Army (retired)
- Federal Police Officer (retired)
- United States Military Taekwondo Foundation
- Masonry

PERSONAL ACHIEVEMENTS

- Graduated in Computer Programming with a Bachelor of Science from Southern University A&M College in Baton Rouge, Louisiana
- Graduated in Criminal Justice with an Associate Degree of Science from Houston Community College in Houston, Texas
- Finishing my Bachelor's Degree in Criminal Justice at Texas Southern University in Houston, Texas
- Graduated with my Master's Degree from Fresh Anointing Christian Bible Institute in Reston, Virginia
- Graduated with my PhD from Fresh Anointing Christian Bible Institute in Reston, Virginia

MAJOR ACHIEVEMENTS

- Joined the United States Army for 24 years; deployed to Iraq 5 times; a tour in Afghanistan; a tour in Panama conflict; and other deployments.
- I joined the All-Army Taekwondo Team and became an All-Army Head Coach for the Taekwondo team.
- U.S. National Taekwondo Medalist
- U. S. Open Taekwondo Gold medalist 3 time
- U. S. Olympic Team Try-out (92', 96') in Taekwondo team
- 8th Army Taekwondo Gold medalist 3 time
- PKA Southeast Kickboxing Champion and many more championships
- Becoming a Police Officer, then became a Federal Police Officer
- Joined the Mason and moved up to the U. S. National Junior Warden, PHO Masonic Compacts of the United States of America
- Together, with Master Louis Davis and Grandmaster Rafael Medina Castro, we wrote the book "One Team One Fight One Family," which is a #1 Amazon Best-seller.

DALE
BLACKSTONE

"
*Returning to teaching [Martial Arts]
made me feel better, and now I'm
stronger.*

WHY THE MARTIAL ARTS?

I started martial arts because my mom told me to find a hobby for the summer of 1968. I looked at the recreation department and found karate classes. I liked them, so I went to Lee School of Karate. I've been in Taekwondo for 56 years.

HOW HAS MARTIAL ARTS IMPACTED YOUR LIFE?

Black belts asked me to teach after my wife passed, but I didn't want to; however, I did it anyway. Returning to teaching made me feel better, and now I'm stronger. When I feel bad, I always go and work out, which makes me feel better.

TRAINING INFORMATION

- Martial Arts Styles & Rank: 10th Dan - Tae Kwon Do Moo Duk Kwan, 10th Dan - Tang Soo Do Moo Duk Kwan
- Instructors/Influencers: Grandmaster Soo Woong Lee of Lee School of Karate
- Birthplace/Growing Up: Moscow, ID / Annandale, VA
- Yrs. In the Martial Arts: 56 years
- Yrs. Instructing: 51 years
- School owner, manager & instructor at Blackstone School of Karate Blackstone's Taekwondo

PROFESSIONAL ORGANIZATIONS

- Lee School of Karate
- Korean Tae Kwon Do Moo Duk Kwan
- The World Tae Kwon Federation
- Simba Do Jang
- World Korean Martial Arts Union
- United States Head of Family Martial Arts Association

PERSONAL ACHIEVEMENTS

- My greatest achievement was marrying Ginger Blackstone, my wife. She was my high school sweetheart, best friend, and business partner.

MAJOR ACHIEVEMENTS

- I opened Blackstone Karate School in 1981, received my 10th Dan in Tae Kwon Do Moo Duk Kwan, and taught. I still compete in tournaments (forms and weapons).

Become an
AMAA MEMBER!

KIMBERLY
BLAKE

"
I am blessed to continue my studies as a student, a Sensei, and a Professor on and off the mats.

HOW HAS MARTIAL ARTS IMPACTED YOUR LIFE?

Beginning my martial arts journey at 42 and still active after 20 years has taken me across many like-minded journeys and crossed paths with many amazing people. Seeding my journey into the lives of girls and women across the globe is very rewarding and enjoyable. I am blessed to continue my studies as a student, a Sensei, and a Professor on and off the mats. I have competed locally, regionally, nationally, and internationally. There is much to obtain and pass on to others I meet. This is my purpose.

WHY THE MARTIAL ARTS?

I began training in martial arts at 42 (currently 62). My interest in martial arts started at 13 when an after-school martial arts class was offered at my Jr. High School. Unfortunately, my father wouldn't consent because he said: "girls did not participate in combative sports." This was very hard for me to accept, but I still had my love for Bruce Lee and martial arts films.

It wasn't until I was 41 that my friend and mentor, Dr. Brenda Lloyd-Jones, asked me, "What is stopping you from achieving this dream now?" Realizing that nothing could stop me, I enrolled in Karate class at Apollo's Martial Arts right after my 42nd birthday.

TRAINING INFORMATION

- Belt Ranks & Martial Arts Styles: 5th Degree Black Belt in Karate, Kickboxing and Japanese Jiu Jitsu, 2nd Degree Black Belt in Ketsugo, 1st Degree Black Belt in BJJ
- Instructors/Influencers: Master Carlos Machado, Karate: Dale Cook, Randy M. Blake, Jr., Ketsugo: Dr. Patrick Sharp, Robert Hale
- Birthplace/Growing Up: Cleveland, OH
- Yrs. In the Martial Arts: 20 years
- Yrs. Instructing: 15 years
- Instructor

PROFESSIONAL ORGANIZATIONS

- Carlos Machado Affiliate Member
- IBJJF Athlete
- USA Martial Arts Hall of Fame
- Universal Martial Arts Hall of Fame
- Oklahoma Karate Association
- Sponsored by "The Athletes Sports Bag"
- Sponsored by " Elite Sports Company
- American Martial Arts Alliance Foundation

PERSONAL ACHIEVEMENTS

- Girls in Gis Ambassador
- Grappling Getaways Brand Ambassador
- Sponsored by "The Athletes Sports Bag"
- Sponsored by " Elite Sports Company
- Retired from BP Pipelines NA 12/31/20
- Became a grandmother for the first time on 2/3/21

MAJOR ACHIEVEMENTS

- First Female BJJ Blackbelt in the State of Oklahoma
- First African American Female BJJ Black Belt under Carlos Machado Affiliation
- Tulsa, Oklahoma Impact Woman of Color of the Year
- 2x World Champion BJJ Master
- Ranked #3 Internationally for BJJ Female Black Belt Master 6
- 22 State Championships
- Multiple National Championships
- 40+ Karate Grand Championships

MAJOR ACHIEVEMENTS

- Lifetime Achievement Award by the Whirlwind Classic Tournament
- 2nd Degree Black Belt Ketsugo under Harold Brosius
- 5th Degree Black Belt in Karate under Dale Cook
- 2017 USA Martial Arts Hall of Fame Inductee
- 2021 AAMA Inductee
- 2021 Universal Martial Arts Hall of Fame Inductee
- 2021 Sport Karate Museum Honoree
- 2021 Girls in Gis Black Belt Co-Instructor
- 2023 International Best-Selling Co-Author in the Elite Martial Artists in America Compilation Book: Secrets to Life, Leadership, and Business, Volume I
- 2023 United States Martial Arts Hall of Fame Inductee
- 2023 International Martial Arts Hall of Fame & World Moo Duk Kwan Tae Kwon Do Alliance
- 2023 Presidential Lifetime Achievement Award
- 2023 Karate Rank of 5th Degree recognized Internationally by the International Martial Arts Council of America
- 2023 International Best-Selling Co-Author in "Who's Who in The Martial Arts Honoring Cynthia Rothrock"
- 2024 IBJJF Europeans Champion (Black) Master 7
- 2024 IBJJF PAN AM Champion (Black) Master 7
- Currently Ranked #1 Internationally for IBJJF Female Black Belt Master 7

JESSIE
BOWEN

Self-discipline is a critical life skill that enables you to succeed in anything you choose to do.

have to tell students everywhere about the benefits of martial arts," Grand Master Bowen says. "These methods are meant to build from the ground up to meet the great achievements of the Lifetime Achievers and Pioneers who paved the way for today's martial artists."

GRAND MASTER JESSIE BOWEN: 4.9 DECADES OF FOCUS

Jessie Bowen started his study in the Martial Arts in 1975 under the direction of Grandmaster Jan Wellendorf, co-founder of Karate International of North Carolina. As with most individuals that begin to study the martial arts, he was intrigued. There wasn't a mystical impetus for Jessie Bowen, rather he was motivated by a "nobody better mess with me" desire for becoming a great martial artist. His initial reason for joining the martial arts school then was out of desperation, and at the age of 21 he made the conscious decision that he would no longer be picked on.

Through elementary, middle, and high school, he was picked on and almost lost his life several times. As he looks back on it now, it was never because he couldn't defend himself, it was because of the lack of courage. One of Hanshi Bowen's coworkers had threatened to

WHY THE MARTIAL ARTS?

In 2015, Grand Master Jessie Bowen started on a path to write the history of his generation in the martial arts and the pioneers who helped them move forward. Now, Jessie Bowen is taking an entirely new step in the Martial Artists Who's Who in the Martial Arts and Changing Lives Series Biography Book Series.

" This year, we're writing about the stars of today and tomorrow and letting everyone in our industry know about them, from newcomers to industry leaders. Then, we help these stars of today and tomorrow use the tools they beat him up, and Jessie then learned his threat came from a black belt in Taekwondo. Jessie had never heard of Taekwondo, but he had recently seen *Enter the Dragon* and saw what Bruce Lee did to his opponents. Jessie's initial thought was "I need to learn some form of self-defense NOW." That is the moment that changed his life and for decades now he has been committed to empowering others physically, mentally and spiritually.

Hanshi Jessie Bowen spent the first three years of his martial arts study as a student, instructor, and competitor. He began teaching the martial arts full time as an instructor for O'Sensei Wellendorf and built a reputation of his own in Sport Karate.

Hanshi Jessie Bowen became known throughout the Southeast for his martial arts skills in Form, Weapons, and Fighting. He then took his first career step. The American Martial Arts Association was the first martial arts organization to offer a business degree in Martial Arts Management. Hanshi Bowen was one of its first graduates. The program was mandatory for anyone wanting to own a Karate International Franchise.

His school, Karate International of Durham, was founded in 1980, by Hanshi Jessie Bowen, as a Karate International franchise school under the Karate International brand.

Since opening, Hanshi Bowen has promoted more than 400 students to black belt. He has been recognized by organizations throughout the country for his contribution to the martial arts. He was one of the first martial arts instructors to integrate martial arts into sports. He started with Coach Dick Crum, Football Coach at the University of North Carolina at Chapel Hill in the mid 80's. He was also a Martial Arts Performance Coach for four seasons under Coach Mack Brown, former UNC Football Coach. He was also a Personal Trainer for Duke University Basketball star, Carlos Boozer and others.

After winning more than 2000 trophies and awards in martial arts competitions, Hanshi Bowen believed the next evolution in martial arts performance was in the mind. He is a certified Life Coach, Sports Hypnosis Coach, NLP Coach, Silva Life System Seminar Facilitator, and Mindfulness Coach.

TRAINING INFORMATION

- Belt Ranks & Martial Arts Styles: 10th Degree Black Belt
- Instructors/Influencers: Jan Wellendorf, Joe Lewis, Bill Wallace, Dan McFarland
- Birthplace/Growing Up: Washington, NC
- Yrs. In the Martial Arts: 49 years
- Yrs. Instructing: 48 years
- School Owner (Karate International of Durham, Inc), Instructor, Manager, Author

PROFESSIONAL ORGANIZATIONS

- American Martial Arts Alliance
- Professional Karate Association

ACCOMPLISHMENTS & ACHIEVEMENTS

- Action Martial Arts Magazine Hall of Fame as the 2014 Ambassador of Goodwill to the Martial Arts Member Solution Financial Services Top Achiever Award
- NRC Business Man of the Year
- American Martial Arts Association Hall of Fame Leadership Award
- Established Mastermind-Sports Performance Virtual Coaching Service
- American Martial Arts Alliance Sport Karate Tournament Promoter of the Year
- Action Martial Arts Magazine Martial Arts Instructor of the Year
- Certified Sports Hypnotist
- Certified Silva Method Lecture Developer Trainer
- Certified Silva Method Lecturer
- American Martial Arts Freestyle Golden Lifetime Achievement Award
- American Martial Arts Association Hall of Fame Man of the Year Award
- National Business Advisory Business Man of the Year Recipient of Super Star Black Belt Hall of Fame Living Legend Award 2003
- 2002 World Cup, Karate World Champion
- Black Belt Super Star Hall of Fame, WHO'S WHO in the Martial Arts Award
- Universal Martial Arts Hall of Fame Inductee as Outstanding Grand Master of the Year

Hanshi Bowen learned to apply the principles of martial arts and sports mind game coaching into Bowling, winning over 40 amateur titles before becoming a PBA Member (Professional Bowlers Association) in 2002. He became the Bowling Instructor for Duke University and Performance Coach for NCCU Women's Bowling Team, winning NCCU's first CIAA title.

O'Sensei Jan Wellendorf sanctioned the advancement of Hanshi Jessie Bowen to 10th Degree Black Belt and assigned him the task of creating his own system of Martial Arts Aiki-Shinkai Karate. Aiki means to fit, join or combine energy. Aiki is a Japanese martial arts principle or tactic in which the defender blends (without crashing) with the attacker, then goes on to dominate the assailant through the strength of their application of internal dynamics or Ki energy to effect techniques. Shinkai means the opening of uncultivated land, new frontiers.

HOW HAS MARTIAL ARTS IMPACTED YOUR LIFE?

I started learning martial arts in 1977 without really understanding what it was all about other than fighting. I joined a martial arts program to learn self-defense and to avoid being bullied. Little did I know that joining Karate International North Carolina would take me on an incredible life journey.

Martial arts has had a profound impact on my life, particularly in terms of self-confidence. Prior to embarking on my martial arts training, I was a shy and timid individual who lacked belief in myself.

ACCOMPLISHMENTS & ACHIEVEMENTS

- United States Karate Hall of Fame inductee as Most Distinguished Grand Master of the Year
- United States Karate Hall of Fame Inductee as Most Distinguished Grand Master of the Year
- World Karate Union Hall of Fame Inductee as Grand Master of the Year
- United States Karate Hall of Fame Inductee as Grand Master of the Year
- Sport Karate Tournament Promoter of the Year
- Sports Coordinator for the US Olympic Committee and North Carolina Amateur Sports for the US Olympic Festival, Tae Kwon Do competition in 1987
- Sports Coordinator for North Carolina Amateur Sports in Karate and Bowling
- Professional Bowler - PBA Tour Member
- USBC Bowling Coach
- Bowling Instructor Duke University
- Director of the nationally ranked Durham Karate Open tournament since 1981
- Action Martial Arts Magazine Award- Organization of the Year
- Action Martial Arts Magazine award- Excellence in Radio & Media Coverage
- Masters of the Martial Arts Award
- Action Martial Arts Magazine Award- Contribution in Publishing in the Martial Arts
- AFKA Award-Excellence in Martial Arts Journalism
- 2021 - Presidential Lifetime Achievement Award
- 2021 - Grandmasters Hall of Fame
- 2023 - Action Martial Arts Magazine Excellence in Publishing in the Martial Arts
- 2023 - World Head of Family/Sokeship Council Leadership Award
- 2023 - London International Hall of Fame Media Publication of the Year Award
- 2024 -Action Martial Arts Hall of Honors Excellence in Publishing Award
- 2024 -Martial Arts Extraordinaire People Leadership Award

However, as I progressed in my training, I began to gain self-confidence with each passing day. The discipline and dedication required in martial arts helped me develop a positive mindset and believe in my abilities. I learned to overcome challenges and setbacks, which in turn boosted my self-confidence both inside and outside the dojo. It has provided me with the strength to face any obstacle that comes my way and the self-confidence to believe in myself.

Martial arts has transformed my life in ways I never imagined possible. Through martial arts, I have learned valuable life lessons such as discipline, perseverance, and resilience. These qualities have not only helped me excel in the martial arts arena but have also positively influenced other aspects of my life. Whether it is facing challenges at work or dealing with personal setbacks, I approach them with the same determination and self-confidence that martial arts has instilled in me.

Martial arts serves as a tool for shaping my life physically and mentally, and it all began with having a great teacher. My martial arts instructor, O'Sensei Jan Wellendorf, is the founder of Karate International North Carolina. I firmly believe that everyone's life has a purpose, and God places special people in our lives to help us discover our inner light. O'Sensei Wellendorf taught me more than just kicks and punches; he provided me with experiences that went beyond winning trophies. He laid the foundation almost 50 years ago for the person I am today, and for that, I am forever grateful.

Become an
AMAA MEMBER!

THE WHO'S WHO IN THE MARTIAL ARTS, MASTERS & PIONEERS AND THE CHANGING LIVES BOOK SERIES REPRESENTS NEW FRONTIERS, JOINING HIS PREVIOUS

- Hanshi Bowen has written 18 books on Mind-Body Personal Development Training including Zen Bowling the Psychology of Better Bowling; The New You Self Discovery System; and Zen Mind-Body Mindfulness Meditation Training.

- In 2017 he was the recipient of the Action Martial Arts Hall of Honors award for the Who's Who in the Martial Arts Book and the 2017 AFKA Hall of Fame Martial Arts Journalism Award.

- In 2019, the Action Martial Arts Magazine Hall of Honors presented another award for his Online Media Blog Talk Radio.

- In 2018 & 2019 Jessie Bowen also received the Action Martial Arts Magazine Hall of Honors Martial Arts Organization of the Year awards.

GUY
BRACALI-GAMBINO

> **"**
> *Martial Arts helped my confidence to communicate and teach people to help break through barriers.*

Kickboxing. In 1983 I moved to Oroville, California, and started work as a bouncer. During that time, I met my Chinese Kenpo instructor, 3rd Degree Black Belt Ron Cox. I trained with his Grand Master, Bruce Juchnik. Bruce became my Grandmaster in Chinese Kenpo and Kosho Shorei - Ryu Kempo. In 1989 I began training in Taekwondo NCTA, then on to WTF. In the late 80s, I was ranked in the PKL Professional Karate League and competed in the IMACF from 1984-1995. I won several awards as an instructor as well as a competitor. From 1993-1995 I competed professionally in the National Blackbelt League NBL.

My good friend/brother Paul Mendoza tried to form me as a point fighter from kickboxing which was hilarious. I was known to punch and kick guys through scoreboards and get disqualified in the first round. I got lucky if I advanced to the second fight. My coaching was great for my students, but I had too much full contact in my background. Paul significantly impacted my life as a fighter by understanding the full-contact point fighting as I describe today. A full-contact point fighter is like being a sniper with your hands and feet. You don't get a second chance against the wrong opponent. So, by becoming a better point fighter, I became more precise

WHY THE MARTIAL ARTS?

I was eleven years of age in 1976; I would read magazines about martial arts superstars. I did not think I would be trained by some of them, let alone be on their teams someday, daydreaming about being like them. Martial arts world champions such as 12X World Champion Tony Satch Williams, multiple-time World Champion Woody Sims on Bay Area's Best, and World Champion Tami Whelan on Team Full Contact.

During the Bruce Lee era, we grew up in a neighborhood called Santa Venetia/San Rafael, CA, and my best friend's older brother, Staff Sergeant Fred Montero, a known neighborhood martial artist, took me by the hand to my first class. My first instructor was a former Green Beret and Sensei, Gus Johnson. In my late teens, I studied Muay Thai and in my techniques and took control of the fight. Paul made the bay area's best national karate team in 1993. I followed shortly thereafter and made the team as the Number 2 super heavyweight; Woody Sims was number one, and I was their brick breaker. I began training with Tony Satch Williams, and we became a very close family. He lived with me during the summers. I then made Team Full Contact in 1994, Zane Fraiser (former Boston Celtics) was the #1 Super Heavyweight on the team, and I was the #2 Super Heavyweight and their brick-breaker. Then in 1995, I made Team USA Australia Goodwill Games, Olympic Center. I received an endorsement from US Congressman Wally Herger.

Several years later, I got into bail enforcement and training in the US Military as a master combative instructor and DOD Government Security Contractor. It was the best time in my life other than fathering my children, hanging out, training with, and competing on the same team with men and women I read about in Black Belt Magazine. I wanted to hit harder than Tony Satch Williams. One day he and I were sparring, and he got mad because he thought I hit him hard. He said, "Don't hit me like that again." I told him, "I barely hit you!"

Besides that, I trained my students who had nothing in a town where nothing existed. I kept them out of gangs and gained the respect of several gang members. I took them camping and boating and competed all over California and Nevada. We were a big family, and our National Demo Team was 4X National Champions.

My first NBL World Title was in 1993. I called my father from New Orleans to Tiburon, California, at the Caprice Restaurant to give him the good news. I called and said, "Dad, I got World Champion!" He said, "Of what?" I replied, "Martial arts." He said, "Call me when you get home." He was proudly waiting for me at the airport.

In 1987 my rival in the super heavyweight division, Master Rocky Ryan, and I fought bare-knuckle on military bases. In 1995 after making Team USA, I became very good friends with the coach and became like family to him. Master Lim Sison ranked me Godan

TRAINING INFORMATION

- Belt Ranks & Martial Arts Styles: Chinese Kenpo-5th Degree, Shorin-Ryu 5th Degree, Kosho Shorei Ryu Kempo-1st Degree, Tong Soo Do, Kickboxing, Muay Thai, Arnis, Tae Kwon Do

- Instructors/Influencers: Grandmaster Bruce Juchnik, Master Lim Sison, Gus Johnson, Tony "Satch" Williams, Master Ron Cox

- Birthplace/Growing Up: Bay Area, Marin County, CA

- Yrs. In the Martial Arts: 48 years

- Yrs. Instructing: 38 years

- Former School owner & Master Instructor, Bracali's Martial Arts academy Oroville, CA

PERSONAL ACHIEVEMENTS

- My five children
- Several wards from IMACF
- Best instructor of the year two years in a row IMACF
- Best Competitor of the Year IMACF
- Best Official of the Year for 2 years IMACF
- 2021 Best Choreography for Eryx and the Void IMDB

MAJOR ACHIEVEMENTS

- Master Combative Instructor
- Department of Defense Contractor
- Bail Enforcement Agent
- IMDb Martial Arts Military Choreography
- Brick Breaking World Records 109 two-inch concrete blocks in 9.1 seconds; the previous record holder was 100 blocks in 19 seconds.
- The first man to do a free dive 12 feet and break a two-inch block underwater.
- I prepared for the Navy Seal Legacy Foundation with my good friend, former Navy Seal Reuben (Red) Lowing as open water 30 meters deep, 6 inches of concrete with bull sharks, hammerheads, and tiger sharks in the Gulf of Texas to raise money for our fallen/Navy Seals in the summer of 2023.
- 2023 AMAA Who's Who in the Martial Arts Cynthia Rothrock Tribute Biography Book Inductee and Legacy Award Recipient.

He trained with Roy Jones, Sr., and Jr. and was Roy's sparring partner. Reuben boxed all Navy and spent ten years in the SEAL Teams. We became friends from the fight world and through other mutual friends throughout the teams and other special operation circles. Reuben has helped me out with PTSD and in my spiritual walk. I love him like my brother. One of the things I lacked in my martial arts career besides mercy was humbleness. And someone who has come to every one of my tournaments, every event. Every time I was doing some event, I owed all my success and growth to. And I believe they worked through Kirby DeLaunay to make this happen for me today. I had never thanked them once in my career nor given them recognition when they believed in me more than anybody.

On my knees, I humbly thank my Heavenly Father, His only begotten Son Jesus, and the entire heavenly family for what He has done and is doing in my life. And to my parents, Roger and Jacqueline Bracali, my sisters Patricia and Marlene and their families, my lovely ex-wives, my son, and my 4 daughters. Thank you, God Jesus, I love you.

HOW HAS MARTIAL ARTS IMPACTED YOUR LIFE?

It helped my confidence to communicate and teach people to help break through barriers. It helped me identify people's weaknesses and strengths in the development stages of martial arts or the combative world. I was able to pass on teaching and leadership to my daughters One of my daughters serves as an E6 in the United States Navy and is now an instructor. When she was not confident as a little girl, I am proud to say she has become the tip of the spear. Cora Rago Bracali-Gambino.

5th Degree blackbelt in Shorin-Ryu in 2012. In my life, I've had the privilege to meet several phenomenal people who were legendary martial artists: some pretty tough and solid individuals, special operations, Navy, Marine, and Army. A lot of people I met were from events.

One of whom is my close friend, my brother Reuben (Red) Lowing, who has significantly impacted my life. I trust him with my life. He is a phenomenal boxer.

JASON
BROOKS

"
Every aspect of my life is directly affected by my martial arts philosophies and training.

WHY THE MARTIAL ARTS?

Grandmaster Jason Brooks has been training in martial arts since 1977 as an understudy of Grandmaster John Natividad. Jason currently has three different black belt styles; Tang Soo Do, Karate-Do, and Krav Haganah. In 2021, Jason was awarded Bushinkai Ninjutsu Ni-dai Soki.

Jason's rich martial arts background lead him to join the United States Marine Corps, where he would come to serve as the lead instructor in the Marine Corps Martial Arts Program for his unit, 2D Marine Force Recon Battalion. Jason trained over 3500 active-duty Marines and Sailors and reserve forces in all aspects of NBC warfare.

As a Marine, Jason was deployed in Operation Iraqi/

Enduring Freedom as NCOIC of the Reconnaissance Operation Center in support combat operations. Staff Sergeant Brooks, along with his unit, received the Presidential Unit Citation for over 30 days of sustained Combat while in Iraq. In 2005, Staff Sergeant Brooks was medically retired from the Marine Corps due to the injuries he sustained during combat operations in Iraq.

In 2017, Jason started working at CRI Counter Terrorism Training School as a lead instructor, veteran outreach coordinator, and recruiter. Additionally, Jason is an adjunct instructor for the National Association of Chief of Police and trains police officers in advance officer survival. Jason was also on the UFC executive protection security team and has been on numerous motorcade details for the President and First Lady of the United States when they visited Las Vegas.

Currently, Jason Brooks is co-owner and lead instructor of Assault Counter Tactics. This personal protection company trains in all levels in the use of force for private and professional security.

Jason is certified to teach escaping captivity (SERE) survive /evade/ resist/ escape; tactical medicine; protective security formations; VIP protective techniques; tactical driving; convoy operations; tactical shooting (rifle, pistol, shotgun); counter-ambush techniques; counter-kidnapping; VIP rescue recovery; radio procedures; weapons retention; defense against edge weapons and knives; throwing knives; weapon disarmament; defense against grabs/holds; counter strangulation; ground defense; takedowns; strikes; punches; blocks; and kicks.

Jason has been nominated into two martial arts Halls of Fame in 2021; the Universal Martial arts Hall of Fame and the United States Martial Arts Hall of Fame.

HOW HAS MARTIAL ARTS IMPACTED YOUR LIFE?

Martial Arts has impacted my life by guiding my personal growth and mental development. Preparing me physically as well as mentally for Marine Corps Bootcamp is just one example. My career in the Marines, including my conduct in battle, directly reflects the discipline and physical skills attributed to my martial arts training. My life after the Marines is another example, as I am a Counter Terrorism Instructor, tactical shooting instructor, and master firearms instructor. Every aspect of my life is directly affected by my martial arts philosophies and training. My personal and business relationships are another area where my core martial arts beliefs of honor, integrity, and faith take hold and drive me forward. I can definitely say that I am a better person because of my martial arts lifestyle.

TRAINING INFORMATION

- Tang Soo Do, Karate Do, Krav Haganah Master Instructor, Bushinka Ninjatsu - Ni-dai Soki
- Instructors/Influencers: Grandmaster John Natividad, Grandmaster Rob Mancini, Rev. David LeBleu
- Birthplace/Growing Up: Las Vegas, NV
- Yrs. In the Martial Arts: 46 years
- Yrs. Instructing: 34 years
- Traveling Instructor

PROFESSIONAL ORGANIZATIONS

- Member - Veterans of Foreign Wars
- Member - Marine Corps Association
- Member - First Reconnaissance Battalion Association
- Member - Armed Forces Benefit Association
- Member - Jewish War Veterans Association
- Member - American Legion
- Member -Wounded Warrior Program Alumni
- Member -Iraqi and Afghanistan Veterans of America
- AMAA Foundation Member
- Traditional World Karate Association
- Sport Karate History General and Ambassador
- International Association of Law Enforcement Firearms Instructors

PERSONAL ACHIEVEMENTS

- Certified Peer Group Facilitator — Wounded Warrior Project
- Certified Peer Mentor — Wounded Warrior Project
- Peer Mentor — Veterans Court Treatment Program
- Certified Nevada Veterans Advocate
- Veteran Jobs Advocate
- Honor Award for Public Service by the American Police Hall of Fame

MAJOR ACHIEVEMENTS

- Combat Action Ribbon
- Navy Commendation Medal
- National Defense Medal
- Global War on Terrorism Service Medal
- Sea Service Deployment Ribbon
- Global War on Terrorism Expeditionary Medal
- Navy and Marine Corps Achievement Medal (3)
- Presidential Unit Citation
- Good Conduct Medal
- Distinguished Person Humanitarian Award
- International Leadership Award
- Williams Elite Hall of Honor Inductee
- Freelancer Writer for American Shooting Journal
- Concealed Carry Weapons Instructor

DENNIS BROWN

"

Martial arts has afforded me the opportunity to travel the world. In doing so, I have met so many amazing people...

WHY THE MARTIAL ARTS?

Grand Master Dennis Brown: Fifty-Eight Years and Still Training:

The high school that I attended in Washington, D.C. was an exceptional school. It was city champions in football, basketball, baseball and track and field. I was too small for football, too short for basketball, too slow for track, and still can't hit a baseball. I was looking for a sport that would work for me, and so I chose martial arts.

When asked about my martial arts career and how it all began, I have got to admit that it was not a conscious choice or planned desire. I was introduced to the arts in 1965 while attending Howard University. I was living in Drew Hall on campus while awaiting the up-and-coming school year and had heard that there was a karate class going on at the school gym, so I decided to go over to observe what actually turned out to be a Judo class run by an instructor that I believe was named Dr. Yang, who turned out to be Korean. While watching some of the throwing drills, I witnessed one of the students injure his leg when falling. Needless to say, I never went back for a second class and assumed that was not for me — wrong place at the wrong time. But I went on to join the University's Air Force ROTC Drill Team, where my drill sergeant, a gentleman we called "Hook," introduced me to Karate. I immediately realized that I enjoyed kicking a lot more than being thrown and hitting the mat.

And so, it began for me in the basement of a local junior high school across the street from the University, where I discovered a small group of guys training in something called Guo Shu or Kung Fu. It was not the most popular style at the time. In fact, few had ever heard of it – just a few guys who had ventured into China Towns in D.C. and NY to attend a limited number of classes for foreigners. Gaining the trust and respect of the Shi Fus was difficult for outsiders and in some cases took years.

So, most of my early training was whatever I could pick up from those few students who had ventured into China Town and what we could pick up from the Chinese theaters that showed Kung Fu movies from Hong Kong on the weekends. Our classes were mostly held in the city parks or any school gym that would allow us in on the weekend.

After years of moving around to wherever we could find space to train, I decided to attend one of the few formal schools available, Jhoon Rhee's Tae Kwon Do School, where I trained with many of his top black belts that he had brought with him from Texas who later went on to become his world champions. It gave me a foundation that would help me throughout my long career.

My formal training in Kung Fu actually started when I happened to see a small sign in the window of a Tracy's Karate School while driving through town that read," Kung Fu-Tai Chi." I stopped in for information where I met Willy Lin, who would become my Shifu and mentor from then 1971 until now, and allow me a front row seat to the evolution of martial arts in America.

Even though I was still a young kid in the 50s, I remember the martial arts in America was then all about Judo. It was a fighting art that had been brought back to the U.S. by the many soldiers that had been stationed in Japan during war time and were now returning home with these fighting and training skills. In the 60s, things started to change as men were returning from, what would be called the "Korean Conflict," with the Korean fighting arts which would become Tae Kwon Do. The schools were professionally run and would organize and dominate the times.

But just as many thought there was nothing else new, along came Bruce Lee and David Carradine and Chinese Kung Fu became the rage of the 70s and a new era of flash and excitement was born. No one could have foreseen the arrival of the Ninja Turtles in the 80s as Nin-Jit-Su dominated the martial arts scene and everyone, for the first time, wanted to wear a mask. But in the 90s, who could have predicted that Billy Blanks, a

TRAINING INFORMATION

- Belt Ranks & Martial Arts Styles: Tae Kwon Do (1st Degree Black Belt), Tien Shan Pai (Grand Master), Tai Chi Chuan, Chin-Na, Shuai Jiao
- Instructors/Influencers: Shifu Josephus Colvin, Grand Master Jhoon Rhee, Grand Master Willy Lin, Coach Wang Jin Bou
- Birthdate: 1948
- Birthplace/Growing Up: Alexandria, VA / West Virginia & Washington, DC
- Yrs. In the Martial Arts: 59 years
- Yrs. Instructing: 55 years
- School Owner

PROFESSIONAL ORGANIZATIONS

- Chairman, Wang QiHei Taijiquan Association of Hebei, China
- Senior Board of Director, Educational Funding Company, leading business consulting group for martial arts schools
- Senior Board Member, North American Sport Karate Association (NASKA), one of America's oldest martial arts circuits and sanctioning boards

PERSONAL ACHIEVEMENTS

- Recognized by Black Belt Magazine as one of the "25 Most Influential Martial Artists of the 20th Century."
- "Only non-Chinese featured in the 1998 Discovery Channel documentary, "The Secrets of the Warrior's Power."
- First African-American martial artist to appear on the covers of Inside Kung-Fu and Kung Fu Tai Chi magazines.
- Master instructor of Tai Chi, Chin-Na and other internal systems
- Redesigned and revolutionized the rope dart, which is arguably the most exotic Chinese weapon to master and he remains one of the few living experts.
- Founder/owner Dennis Brown Shaolin Wu-Shu Centers in Washington, D.C. area
- Wrote, hosted and produced one of the first martial arts talk shows, "Martial Arts Showcase," for Howard University that included special guest interviews and appearances from world renowned martial artists.

world champion fighter, would launch Tae Bo and no martial arts school would be able to survive without Cardio Kick Boxing.

2000 brought with it the decade of Jiu-Jitsu. Not just Jiu-Jitsu, the Brazilian Jiu-Jitsu. Not just Brazilian, but Gracie Brazilian Jiu-Jitsu, and it was crowned the ultimate system of fighting. 2010 claimed to have brought together the best of all the previous decades of fighting arts, including American Boxing. MMA arrived displaying all of what we have learned.

But, if we have really learned anything, it is that each generation evolves and changes. This is the generation of internal thinking. Wars will include strong minds as well as bodies. My 55+ years of martial arts tells me this is the decade of the Art of Tai Chi Chuan "The Grand Ultimate Fist," the development of the Mind, Body and Spirit.

HOW HAS MARTIAL ARTS IMPACTED YOUR LIFE?

Martial Arts makes it possible for me to pursue my dream of helping others to see and experience the benefits of the positive influence and impact that it can have on your life, as it has on mine. I have a wonderful family. Martial arts has afforded me the opportunity to travel the world. In doing so, I have met so many amazing people who continue to share their knowledge, friendship and love. I am blessed and thankful.

MAJOR ACHIEVEMENTS (CONTINUED)

- City of Washington, D.C. proclaimed September 11, 1982 as Dennis Brown Day for his ongoing work in the community.

- Represented kung fu and wushu in the Wesley Snipes TNT documentary, "A Tribute to the Masters of the Arts."

- Featured in historical documentaries: "The Black Kung Fu Experience," "Urban Dragons," and "How I Made It in America."

- Appeared on the covers of every major national martial arts publication of the last five decades.

- First African-American to train in the People's Republic of China, an historical first.

- Starred in movies in Taiwan, Hong Kong and Bangkok landing the lead role in a major kung fu movie and becoming the only non-Chinese to be directed by legendary Shaw Brothers director Chang Cheh, who started the kung fu movie craze of the 60s.

- June 2017 was honored to be appointed Chairman of the Wan Qihe Taijiquan Association of Hebei Province in the People's Republic of China for the United States, and the only American to represent China's leading style of Tai Chi and meditation in the U.S.

- August 13, 2007, at a simple tea ceremony rarely held in public, Grand Master Willy Line passed along "The Robe and Bowl" of Tien Shan Pai to his disciple of over 40 years, declaring Dennis Brown as Grand Master of the system. He is now officially YiBen, or heir apparent to the world-famous fighting system, which originated in the Tien Shan Pai mountains of northeastern China.

- Promoter of the long-running US Capitol Classics China Open international martial arts competition.

- Certifications from Jiangsu Sport Center in Nanjing and the Beijing Institute of Physical Education

- Inducted into Karate's Black Belt Hall of Fame and Kung Fu's Inside Kung Hall of Fame

GREGG "SHOGUN" BROWN

> *"Martial Arts put me in a position to meet influential people and made me a better husband, father and friend.*

WHY THE MARTIAL ARTS?

I started martial arts when I was six years old in 1969, in the brutal homicide streets of Kansas City, Missouri. I started Martial arts to protect my life and my loved ones because I witnessed the tragedy around me, and I did not want that to happen to me or my family. My older brother, when I was 17 and he was 25, was murdered by his best friend; he was shot five times in the face with a 357 magnum. I always trained hard and I learned as much as possible, but after that happened, I became deeply serious about martial arts and have studied several systems ever since.

HOW HAS MARTIAL ARTS IMPACTED YOUR LIFE?

Martial arts has saved my life. I grew my Christianity through Jesus Christ. Martial arts put me in a position to meet influential people and made me a better husband, father and friend

TRAINING INFORMATION

- Belt Ranks & Martial Arts Styles: "Hanshi" Shin Do Ryu Kempo Karate - 9th Dan Red Belt, "Kyoshi" Okinawan Kenpo Karate - 8th Dan, Go Shin Budo Kai - Bakufu-Do-Kumite - 8th Dan, Aiki-Bu-Jitsu - 7th Dan, Chi'na 18 Postures Ki Gung - 8th Black Sash, Taiko Ryu Aiki Jiu Jitsu - 4th Dan, Hapkido - 1st Dan

- Instructors/Influencers: Dr. Supreme Grandmaster James V Debrow III, Hanshi Dan Kennedy, Professor Eduardo Rodriguez, Hanshi Terry Bryan, Professor Ken Baker, Dr. M. Cooper

- Birthplace/Growing Up: Kansas City, MO

- Yrs. In the Martial Arts: 55 years

- Yrs. Instructing: 40 years

- Business School Owner for over 20 years 8,000 sq. ft. to over 300 students at Shogun Martial Arts Center International LLC

PROFESSIONAL ORGANIZATIONS

- Leader and Officer - James Debrow III Fighting Tigers

- Board Member and High Rank Official - U.S.K.K

- Mentor and Officer Elite Presidential Award - Dr. John Williams

PERSONAL ACHIEVEMENTS

- Dojo of the Year Award

- Okinawan Kenpo Karate Practitioner of the Year Award

- 3 Time Grandmaster of the Year Award

- Debt-Free Martial Arts School Start-up Business Mentor 6 Time Hall of Famer

- Lifetime Achievement Award Presidential Award

- Soke of the Year Award

MAJOR ACHIEVEMENTS

- Personal Trainer and Health Design Program

- Self-made millionaire in 1999

- Opened a Dojo during a recession with no bank loan or SBA loan - 2003

- Mentorship for CEO

Become an
AMAA MEMBER!

REGINALDO
BROWN

"

I spent many decades in physical transition to physical and mental humbleness and success.

WHY THE MARTIAL ARTS?

I began my martial arts training in boxing with the permission of my mother and first martial arts instructor, Spec. 5 Iris Brown, a Vietnam veteran. I learned practical self-defense under the Reverend Sergeant First Class United States Army Theodore Brown, my father. He is a combat veteran who served in World War II and the Korean and Vietnam conflicts and earned the Bronze Star in each campaign. Additionally, I received Judo training from Sensei Steve, a young blackbelt in Aberdeen, Maryland, from 1964 to 1965.

While at A.P.G., I continued my martial arts training and picked up baseball, soccer, track and field, basketball, football, and swimming. I also started training in Shotokan Karate under the guidance of the illustrious Hall of Famer, Sosai Reno Moralez. After several years, I was honored to receive the rank of 6th dan. I trained in Kung Fu, Tai Chi, and Tae Kwon Do while attending college in New York City from 1973 to 1975. Years later, it all came together when I was

invited by the Hall of Famer, the illustrious Shinan Antonio Pereira, founder and director of Tremont School of Judo, Jujitsu, Karate, and Tae Kwon Do in the Bronx, New York, to train at his school. Years later, I received the Jujitsu rank of Menkyo and a black belt in Judo. I served as an active Judo, Karate, and Tae Kwon Do coach for the competitor teams in the 1980s and 1990s. In 1988, I became a certified Judo coach by the U.S.J.A. and an active member of the United States Judo Association as a Gold Life Member.

In 2000, I was invited to train under the illustrious Shinan Hector M. Negron, a Hall of Famer and the founder and director of San Yama Bushi Ryu Judo, Jujitsu, Karate, and Tae Kwon Do School in New Rochelle, New York. Years later, I received the rank of Kaiden, Shihan. Additionally, I have received numerous rank validations from Grandmaster Jack Papasan Stern, as well as multiple certificates and recognition from Hall of Famer Shihan/Kyoshi/Sensei Zurriane Bennett (author, veteran, law enforcer, founder, and director of the Sanyama Bushi Jujitsu Combination Goju Karate schools in Woodbridge, Virginia). The late Kyosah/Shihan Jamal C. Brown has been my inspiration on this journey, before and now, and for that, I thank him.

HOW HAS MARTIAL ARTS IMPACTED YOUR LIFE?

I spent decades undergoing physical, mental, and spiritual transformation toward humility and success. All the instructors mentioned above (and some unmentioned) were my teachers. My spiritual growth and understanding of this journey is my destination.

TRAINING INFORMATION

- Belt Ranks & Martial Arts Styles: Judo-3rd Dan, Shotokan -6th Dan, Jujitsu -9th and 10th Dan
- Instructors/Influencers: Iris Brown, Theodore Brown, Sensei Steve, GM Renzo Moralez, Shinan Antonio Pereira, Shinan Hector Negron
- Birthplace/Growing Up: Bronx, NY
- Yrs. In the Martial Arts: 60 years
- Yrs. Instructing: 44 years
- Former School owner & Instructor at Phase Piggy Back Judo, Argus Community Inc. Judo

PROFESSIONAL ORGANIZATIONS

- United States Judo Association - Life Gold Member
- Combat Jujitsu Combination Builders (with the Spirit of the late Co-Founder Kyoshi/Shihan Jamal C. Brown)

PROFESSIONAL ORGANIZATIONS (CONTINUED)

- Associate member of the illustrious Martial Arts Grandmasters International Council Inc. (with the late great Hall of Famer Soke Papasan Canty): Yonkers, New York
- Member of the prestigious United States Martial Arts Association (by the late great Shihan Phil Porter)
- Member of The United States Head of Family Martial Arts Association and International Hall of Honor Hall of Champions (by Dr. Joe Parrish-Founder and President I.H O.H.H.O.C.)
- Recognized by the United States Martial Artist Association (by Hall of Famer Supreme Grand Master William A. Rankin-10th dan)

PERSONAL ACHIEVEMENTS

- Eagle Scout Troop 79: Murnau, Germany
- Co-founded Combat Jujitsu Combination Builders and Two Fish and Five Loaves Martial Arts Fellowship Association (with the spirit of the late co-founder Kyoshi/Shihan Jamal C. Brown)
- Chartered Phase Piggyback Judo Club and Argus Community Inc. Judo (the first chartered judo clubs in Harlem, New York)

MAJOR ACHIEVEMENTS

- Member of the Eastern United States International Martial Arts Association Hall of Fame (by Hall of Famer Soke John C. Kanzler)
- Member of the North American Black Belt Hall of Fame (by Hall of Famer Dr. Rocky Farley PHD Grandmaster Soke)
- Member of the United International Kung Fu Federation Hall of Fame (by the late great Hall of Famer Sijo George Crayton Junior)
- Member and Hall of Famer of The World Martial Arts League (by Hall of Famer Grandmaster/Professor Amin Hassan and Grandmaster and Hall of Famer Klaus Schumacher C.M.D. & Phd)
- Received community and martial arts recognition (by The Greater Harlem community supporter and provider and Hall of Famer martial artist Master/Sensei Abukarriem Shabazz)
- Recognition for over 13 years by the Action Martial Arts Magazine Hall of Honors (by The illustrious Hall of Famer Grandmaster Sifu Alan Goldberg)

JAMES CLARK

"
As an instructor, teaching young people and senior citizens is my way of helping others into a brotherhood like no other.

job may be the most physically demanding and mentally stimulating in the Army. He has to be tough but also has to be fair. He sometimes has to rant and rave, but he must also be understanding. He has to be demanding, but he also has to be compassionate. Throughout my life, I have been very fortunate. I was born and raised in Parkton, NC, right outside of Fayetteville and Fort Bragg, on January 22, 1948—the older of two children of Mr. and Mrs. Albert W. Clark. I attended elementary school in Partition and Lumber Bridge, NC, where I graduated from Oak Ridge High School. After being captain of the basketball team and selected all-conference honors in 1966, the summers and weekends were spent bagging groceries and working on my uncle's farm.

In September of 1966, I found myself with a basketball scholarship, but I had little desire to spend four years in college, so I signed up for Airborne Infantry training. If I was going, "I wanted to go all the way," I took basic training at Fort Bragg and was selected to attend the Leadership Training Course at Fort Gordon, where I also had Infantry Advanced Individual Training. I then transferred to Fort Benning, GA, for Jump School. All of the schools were good for me and good to me. The Army's drill

WHY THE MARTIAL ARTS?

A drill campaign hat tilted low on the forehead. Pistol belt cinched tight around the waist. Perfectly pressed fatigues with all kinds of badges and the ever-present whistle on a cord. Underneath it all was a demon in the shape of a man whose ONLY pleasure was making life miserable for hundreds of trainees. That's my generation's impression of Drill Sergeants and of the Army in general. But I did not believe it...or maybe I did, and I just believed in myself a little bit more.

In any case, here I am with my campaign hat and pistol belt, and I have found out the Drill Sergeant's sergeant image I grew up with might have been a little more accurate than now, but all that gruffness and barely restrained fury even then concealed an individual deeply concerned for his troops' welfare. They will hate one side of you and still realize that you are on their side. You belong to your troops, and they begin to take pride in you. And, incidentally, in themselves.

I consider that the main function of today's entry-level training program is to take civilians with various levels of education and degrees of motivation and turn them into technically proficient, highly self-confident soldiers, men with pride in themselves, in their profession, and in their country. Nearly all of the trainee standards are higher now than they were 14 years ago. Physical training, rifle marksmanship, and skill proficiency testing requirements are stringent, giving the troops valuable skills and, more importantly, self-confidence.

The pride my drill sergeants gave me was more than a valuable luxury; it was a necessity. B co, 1STBN, 504Th Abn INF at Fort Bragg, and the 101ST ABN Division at Fort Campbell provided a training program before going to Vietnam. I also obtained leadership experience while stationed with B CO, 2nd BN, 501st Abn INF, as a Specialist Four Squad Leader; I arrived in Vietnam in December 1967, was promoted to E-5 in January 1968, and was hospitalized for wounds received in the 68 Tet Offensive in February. I was released from the hospital in March 1968, lucky to have a good leg again and with a Purple Heart. I returned to Fort Benning, GA, for Jumpmaster Training, Pathfinder School, and the Instructor Training Course. I had a tour at Fort Wainwright, Alaska, and attended NCO Academy as an E-6, then I shipped out for another overseas tour. Camp Caser, Korea, isn't a bad place to be. I was NCOIC of the 2nd Replacement Detachment and served a 45-day tour as First Sergeant. I was both a student and later an instructor in the Art of Tae Kwon Do. I attended an Instructor Course for Tae Kwon Do during my tour, and that instruction paid off. I captured the 2nd Infantry Division Middleweight Championship and was awarded the 2nd Infantry Division Sweater. I count it as one of my most valued possessions.

I was transferred from Korea to Fort Benning, GA, as an Airborne Instructor for two years. This was the period of 1976-1978, with time out for the ANCOES Course as an E-7. My next assignment was with Echo Co, 1st Battalion, 1st Infantry Training Brigade at Fort Benning, where I attended Drill Sergeant School. I was assigned to E-1-1 as a Senior Drill Sergeant, where I was awarded twice the Distinguished Drill Sergeant Award

TRAINING INFORMATION

- Belt Ranks & Martial Arts Styles: 5th Dan Black Belt-Tae Kwon Do, 7th Degree-Chinese Goju
- Instructors/Influencers: Grandmaster James Debrow, Sensei James E. McCall, Mr. Lee
- Birthplace/Growing Up: Fayetteville, NC / Parkton, NC
- Yrs. In the Martial Arts: 50+ years
- Yrs. Instructing: 48 years
- Instructor

PROFESSIONAL ORGANIZATIONS

- Jones County Sheriff's Office Instructor
- 555th Parachute Infantry Triple Nickel Organization
- Purpleheart Association

PERSONAL ACHIEVEMENTS

- 2nd Infantry Division Champion
- Fort Benning Heavyweight Champion
- Fort Benning Grand Champion
- Participated in 30-plus tournaments, placing 1st, 2nd or 3rd

MAJOR ACHIEVEMENTS

- Volunteer to teach self-defense to women for 40-plus years so they can survive an attack. I do this because a friend was raped and murdered, and I don't charge to teach these classes I teach these classes now and will teach as long as possible
- Give lectures on SAFETY for Jones County at churches and senior citizens groups

and Honor Drill Sergeant Award, at Fort Benning, GA, Drill Sergeant of the Year. I have also been fortunate to have been awarded the National Defense Ribbon, ARCOM, Good Conduct Ribbon (4th Award), and the Combat Infantry Badge.

I've developed interests in bowling, horseback riding, table tennis, pool, jogging, basketball, and coin collecting. I've never lost my love for martial arts and teach whenever possible. I also started teaching women self-defense classes because, during my time in the military, a young female soldier was raped and murdered at Fort Benning, GA. I still teach advanced self-defense classes for women so they can defend themselves against a much stronger opponent/attacker and survive.

I think I've earned my campaign hat, and now I wear it tilted low with a pistol belt cinched tight around my waist. I rant and rave sometimes, but the soldier has a challenge that has to be met on a one-to-one basis. All recruits are different now; I see a drill sergeant from the inside. I see and must be treated as such. A man has to have pride in himself, but a soldier must be proficient and disciplined. The challenge lies in making a soldier out of a man while ensuring he remains a man. The drill sergeant must care, and his men must know he does. Without the desire and ability to fulfill these

requirements, the drill does not measure up to the standards expressed by the motto, "This we'll defend."

I am married to Tanisha Farley-Clark. My children are Kimberly Clark, whom I trained in martial arts; SSG James A. Clark II, whom I trained in martial arts and boxing, where he had a first-round knockout; Brandon M. Clark, whom I trained in Basic Self Defense; SPC Arnez Pitts; and PFC Ashunti Pitts.

I retired from the U.S. Army after 21 years as a First Sergeant in October 1987 and from the Jones County Sheriff's Office; and Retired as a Captain after 22 years in August 2023.

HOW HAS MARTIAL ARTS IMPACTED YOUR LIFE?

When I was a young man, around 12 years old, watching TV, I saw this man defeat two men. A lady who witnessed the fight asked, "Where did you learn to fight like that?" He said, "I learned Judo in Japan." From that day, I said I would learn Judo if I ever visited Japan.

So, I ordered books on how to learn Judo. My cousin and I would practice from the book, throwing and taking each other down. When I joined the Army, I trained in hand-to-hand combat.

Then came the Bruce Lee movies; I was hooked and wanted to learn martial arts. In 1974, I was stationed in South Korea. I started training with Mr. Lee, went on to get my black belt, and won the 2nd Infantry Division Championship. I started teaching martial arts in 1975. I still teach today for the Jones County Sheriff's Office in Gray, GA. I also teach women's self-defense classes for the Sheriff's Office.

As an instructor of the arts, it's a way to give back and help people with self-confidence. As an instructor, teaching young people and senior citizens is my way of helping others into a brotherhood like no other. Martial arts help everyone on the job and in school. It helps them to think fast, which makes them better students. People who learn the arts can teach others in the future. They will pass down the teachings from past and future masters, and some will become masters.

According to my reading, the oldest known art is Tae Kwon Do, which dates back to 2300 BC. Other arts may be older, but they are not in the history books. Overall, it's the best way to help keep martial arts alive forever!

DANIEL
CLINKSCALES

"

Martial arts have given me a way of life that has impacted how I conduct and attend to every life issue.

Afterward, I met Claude Battle, and he showed me different things in fighting that I later found out were Kyokushin. Claude would pass my house daily and ask if I wanted to accompany him to the dojo at The Academy of Music on the 2nd floor. At that time, it was the US headquarters of Grand Master Oyama. Claude and I would train off and on until my other friends in the neighborhood of Bedford Stuyvesant told me about other martial arts classes in the hood. My cousin, the Warrior Prince Katan, and I would visit local classes, and we joined the Tompkins Dojo (EP System Self Defense Club). This would widen my range of understanding of the many other systems around. The EP System Grand Master was GM Edward Pough, which is now led by Grand Master Michael "Bouncy" Baily.

WHY THE MARTIAL ARTS?

My first introduction to martial arts was in Judo by my father (Grady Clinkscales, a decorated World War II Veteran). He would demonstrate his Judo tricks on my friends and me when we were boxing and/or wrestling. He would say, you guys don't know anything about fighting. Then, he would say, "Let me show you what we did in the Army, Baby Boy." Then, he would quickly strike with a front kick, Judo chop, and take down. My friends and I would practice these moves with each other. This led me to meet Mr. Williams, a Judoka who started showing us Judo at the Boys Club.

TRAINING INFORMATION

- Belt Ranks & Martial Arts Styles: Shotokan/ EP System Jitsu - 9th Degree- Hanshi, Traditional Shotokan-5th Dan, Danha Kai Samurai Karate-Do Ryu-9th Dan, Master Level-Tomaya Ryu Batto Do, Muso Shindo Ryu

- Instructors/Influencers: GM Edward Pough/ GM Michael "Bouncy" Bailey, Prince Katan "The Warrior Prince" Ben Yedudah, Shihan Louis Correa, H. Kanazawa, Soke, Grand Master F.J. Hamilton, Soke Fumio Demura, Sensei Claude Battle

- Birthplace/Growing Up: NYC

- Yrs. In the Martial Arts: 62 years

- Yrs. Instructing: 56 years

- School owner & Instructor

PROFESSIONAL ORGANIZATIONS

- Danha Kai Samurai Karate-Do
- United States National Karate Association
- S.K.I.F.
- Shotokan Karate-Do of Japan
- Japan Karate federation
- A.A.U
- NASKA

PERSONAL ACHIEVEMENTS

- 2022 - AMAA Hall of Honor
- 2021 - The Philadelphia Historic Martial Arts Society
- 2021 - International Hall of Honor - Hall of Champions Honoree
- 2019 - Martial Arts Press Conference Hall of Fame
- 1996 - United International Kung Fu Federation - Diamond Achievement Award

The neighborhood was full of martial artists who would come through Tompkins Park, The Bedford Boys Club, PS 25, and JHS 258. I would meet and cross-train with people like Charles Crandle, Isshin Ryu, Little John Davis and Prof Mo, Bouncy and Bo Pee, Marvin Gantt, Tom Windley, Lamunba, Prince Katan, and Prince Shem, just to name a few (1960's).

After high school, I would leave my family to move to South Jamaica, Queens. There, I met and trained with new friends and developed new relationships in martial arts, but I still kept my roots with The EP System.

In Queens, I met instructors Kim & Joo Soo Chang of Chang's Tae Kwon Do, and I trained from 1971 through 1973. I later met instructors in Kenkojuku, Master Miyazaki Takahashi, Hamilton, Correa, Sijo Geoge Crayton, Baron Clark, Warren Bailey, Roosevelt Mumford Kelley, and Prof. Moses Powell. I ran into a good friend from "Tong's Dojo," Master Speedy Leacock (Black Magic Dojo), Robert Wallace, Hector Payne, and a few great martial artists I would train with.

During these years, I would join karate associations such as Japan Karate Federation # A-TE-NY-004, 12-10-1993, Master Fumio Demura; Shotokan Karate-Do of Japan, rank San Dan (3rd Degree, Black Belt) 05-15-1993; United States National Karate Association # 1-2100-1-97-115, 12-14-1997; Shotokan Karate-Do International Federation, 08-01-1999, San Dan (3rd degree, Black Belt) # 32277; Soke H. Kanazawa, and Ep System Inc Self Defense Club, Hanshi (9th Degree Black Belt) GM Michael "Bouncy" Bailey, 10-13-2018; Son of The Ancient Arts of Abraham, 4th Degree Black Belt, 09-25-1983. Japan Karate-Do Itosu -Kai International, Master Seminar Special Training Certificate 1992 & 1993 Tomaya Ryu Batto D0. Master Fumio Demura; NASKA 1991; A.A.U. 1980 D.A.R.T; Advanced Marksmanship & Small Unit Tactics Certified 11/2019.

Currently, I am the founder of The Danha Kai Samurai Karate Do Jitsu Dojo and Chief Head Instructor with Branches in New York City, Pennsylvania, Connecticut, and Florida.

Over the years, I have competed in Kumite, Kata, Weapon, Self Defense, and Team Kumite and won many awards in the AAU, Open Tournaments, Traditional Invitational, and SKIF Tournaments.

I've been inducted Five (5) times into the Hall of Fame/ Honors; 1996 United Kung Fu Federation; 2019 Martial Arts Press Conference; 2021 The Philadelphia Martial Arts Society & International Hall of Honor/Hall of Champions, Action Martial Arts Hall of Honors and numerous of other awards and honors in the martial arts.

HOW HAS MARTIAL ARTS IMPACTED YOUR LIFE?

Martial arts impact my life because they are a way of life for me. They keep me focused on everyday life at home with the family and with co-workers/customers at the office.

The physical part of training keeps me fine-tuned with my abilities to be able to teach and demonstrate the applications of:

MAJOR ACHIEVEMENTS

- Numerous Kata, Kumite, and Self Defense awards
- A.A.U Silver & Gold Medals
- SKIF Kumite Gold Medal
- SKIF Kata Silver Medal
- SKIF Team Kumite (Capt) Gold Medal
- Empire State Nationals - 1st Place Self Defense
- Fred Hamilton - Battle of the Zodiac - Kata and Kumite 1st Place
- Ron Bourand - Goju Championship - 1st Place Kumite & 1st Place Weapon
- Long Island University for "Head Injury and Head Gear in Karate" symposium
- Long Island University - International Instructors Certification Program

HOW HAS MARTIAL ARTS IMPACTED YOUR LIFE? (CONTINUED)

1. I can explain to the class the three major actions of punching and breathing.

2. I can explain the application of kicking utilizing the hip, pivot action with muscle control, and breathing.

3. I can explain the application of stances and the ranges of weight variations in hip action with expansion and contraction.

4. I can explain blocking, breathing, and muscle control applications.

5. I can explain the importance of meditation in connecting the mind, body, and spirit.

It is always a blessing for me to welcome new students, as it may be for the first time, people who are returning after years of being off, and or advanced students who are looking to advance. This is my energy flow that keeps me going, and at times, I am amazed at how fast the younger one learns things.

Thus, martial arts have given me a way of life that has impacted how I conduct and attend to every life issue.

KEITH L.
COLLINS

"
Martial Arts allowed me to teach children for several years, where I am most satisfied.

WHY THE MARTIAL ARTS?

I began the study of martial arts, K.I. Kajukenpo Karate and Minna Jujutsu in April 1973. I graduated from Bedford (Ohio) High School in 1978 and earned my 1st dan black belt in Isshin Ryu Karate in August 1978. I enrolled at Wilberforce University from 1978 to 1981.

I have been married to Sherida for 42 years, and we have four children and four grandchildren. I retired from the First African American law enforcement office for the City of Bedford, Ohio, on February 9, 1990; I had a thirty-year law enforcement career. I've trained police cadets at Cuyahoga Community College Basic Police Academy in subject control, defensive tactics, aerosol restraints, TASER, and handcuffing.

I was the Chief DT Instructor for Bedford Police Department for ten years and received a Bachelor of Criminal Justice Administration from Tiffin University in May 2010. I also hold a Master of Divinity from the United Theological Seminary in May 2023 and am a former Juvenile Detention Officer and Substitute teacher.

I currently teach martial arts to K-8 at a charter school in Cleveland, Ohio.

HOW HAS MARTIAL ARTS IMPACTED YOUR LIFE?

I was an angry teenager. Martial arts initially helped me to control that anger. As I grew older, martial arts increased my discipline and self-control, which helped during my pledge period in college, my police academy experience, and my law enforcement career. During my career, there were numerous times my self-control and discipline allowed me to conduct myself in a professional manner. It has also allowed me to teach children for several years, where I am most satisfied.

HOW HAS MARTIAL ARTS IMPACTED YOUR LIFE? (CONTINUED)

It has also impacted me by allowing me to continue learning and studying the martial arts. I have learned from numerous martial artists and law enforcement trainers such as Hock Hockheim - Scientific Fighting Congress, Gary Klugewicz — Active Counter Measures, Ron Shaw — Isshin Ryu Karate, Bruce Crutchfield — Silat, and Londale Theus — Krav Maga. These are just a few of the trainers. I also had an opportunity to train with Bill "Superfoot" Wallace when I was fifteen. I was also in the 1978 AAU Ohi/Lake Erie Taekwondo Team with Billy Blanks. I was seventeen at the time.

The highlight of my martial arts career is being a co-author of the second volume of the *Elite Martial Artists in America: Secrets to Life, Leadership, and Business* compilation book and being nominated for the 2024 10th Anniversary Who's Who Legacy Award.

TRAINING INFORMATION

- Belt Ranks & Martial Arts Styles: Goshin Budo Bujitsu-8th Dan, American (Ferguson)-5th Dan, Isshin Ryu-3rd Dan, K.I. Kajukenpo Karate-San Kyu, Minna Jujutsu-San Kyu, Yang Style TaChi an Qigong-Beginner Level
- Instructors/Influencers: Grandmaster Leaston Chase IV (Late), Grandmaster Muhammad Sallahudin (Late), Grandmaster Ken Ferguson, Professor Andrew Torak, Sigung Robert Fleeming, Sensei Len Uronis
- Birthplace/Growing Up: Cleveland / Oakwood Village, OH
- Yrs. In the Martial Arts: 50 years
- Yrs. Instructing: 40 years
- Instructor

PROFESSIONAL ORGANIZATIONS

- AAU Karate
- USA Karate Federation
- Cleveland Martial Arts Hall of Fame
- International Law Enforcement Educators Association
- American Society of Law Enforcement Trainers Association (Defunct)delta
- Alphia Phi Alpha Fraternity, Inc. Delta Alpha Lambda Chapter

PERSONAL ACHIEVEMENTS

- Bachelor of Criminal Justice Administration - 2010
- Tiffin (Ohio) University
- Master of Divinity - 2023
- United Theological Seminary

MAJOR ACHIEVEMENTS

- USA Karate Hall of Fame 2014
- Cleveland Martial Arts Hall of Fame 2015
- International Hall of Honor Hall of Champions 2021
- Elite Publications' *Elite Martial Artists in America: Secrets to Life, Leadership, and Business*, International Best-selling Co-author, 2024

KEVIN
COMBS

" Martial arts is more than just physical training for me; it's a stress reliever from my stressful, demanding career.

WHY THE MARTIAL ARTS?

I have always been interested in martial arts. I remember watching David Carradine in the TV show "Kung Fu" and being very intrigued. Years later, after injuring my lower back, I was advised to undergo physical therapy, which included stretching techniques. This presented me with the opportunity to pursue my dream of joining the martial arts community.

I started my training under the direct supervision of Grand Master Py K. Eun at the Tennessee Taekwondo Judo College in Knoxville, Tennessee. I continued my training at this dojo until I had to leave Knoxville to attend medical school in Pikeville, Kentucky, and then residency in Norton, Virginia.

After a brief pause in my martial arts training, I resumed training at a dojo in the same town where I currently practice internal medicine in Tazewell, VA. I

study under Master Kasey Addair in the Oh Do Kwan art. During this time, I achieved the rank of 3rd dan in Taekwondo and became a respected instructor for new students at the dojo.

This has been a very rewarding time at the dojo. We are actively involved in the community, regularly performing demonstrations at the annual local fair and other community events, as well as participating in local tournaments.

Our martial arts dojo regularly participates in the Karate College in Radford, VA. We take part in all of the classes offered at this college camp, which provides a unique opportunity for our students to learn a wide variety of martial arts from around the world. My personal favorite class is Krav Maga. Over the years of attending this college camp, I have made several friends from across the country. I always look forward to the next installment so that I can see them again. It feels like an annual family reunion!

HOW HAS MARTIAL ARTS IMPACTED YOUR LIFE?

Martial arts is more than just physical training for me; it's a stress reliever from my stressful, demanding career. There have been numerous occasions when I felt emotionally and physically drained after a tough day at work. Teaching classes at my dojo, including self-defense, for 2 hours helps me unwind. After this intense workout, I feel much better about the day and sleep well at night.

Martial arts has not only helped me but also some of my patients to better cope with the stress of the world we live in, especially post-COVID.

TRAINING INFORMATION

- Belt Ranks & Martial Arts Styles: Kukkiwon Taekwondo—1st Dan Black Belt, Hapkido—1st Dan Black Belt, Oh Do Kwan—3rd Degree Black Belt, Tai Jutsu—2nd Degree Brown Belt
- Instructors/Influencers: Master Kasey Addair, Grand Master Py K. Eun
- Birthplace/Growing Up: Knoxville, TN
- Yrs. In the Martial Arts: 30 years
- Yrs. Instructing: 8.5 years
- Instructor and Physician

PROFESSIONAL ORGANIZATIONS

- American Medical Association
- American Osteopathic Association
- American College of Osteopathic Physicians
- American College of Physicians
- Sons of the American Revolution

PERSONAL ACHIEVEMENTS

- Chapter Surgeon and Chapter Vice President in the Virginia Society of the Sons of the American Revolution, Abingdon Chapter.
- Medical Director for Legacy Hospice, Legacy Palliative Care, Divine Home Care, and Tazewell Veterans Affairs Clinic.
- Edward Via College of Osteopathic Medical School, Associate Professor of Family Medicine.
- Carilion Tazewell Community Hospital Director

MAJOR ACHIEVEMENTS

- My most significant personal achievement in martial arts is guiding a beginner white belt student from day one to achieving 1st dan in the Oh Do Kwan dojo.

JOHN CONNELLY

"

I hope to be able to continue to share the lifelong benefits and joy of Martial Arts...

WHY THE MARTIAL ARTS?

Amazingly, I started training in 1986 near where I currently teach, as a young boy of 10 years of age. I was introduced to the arts by my friends. Once starting training, it became a part of my life, which has turned into an ongoing lifetime of continuous training and personal development.

I've benefited well from consistent and regular training, which has given me immediate and long-term benefits while creating lifelong friendships and gaining essential life skills such as discipline, respect, and courtesy. Martial arts has provided me with a family outside of my own, spanning nationally and internationally, with like-minded martial artists and their families, many of whom I consider my brothers and sisters in the arts and life.

When growing up, I lived in the countryside; it was hard to join a club. However, it all changed when my brother's friend's father noticed that I also wanted to train and eventually would take me to class with his son, opening the door to my love of the arts.

Martial arts have enabled me to learn to focus, have greater self-control, better interpersonal skills, and gain more confidence while providing the fortitude and skills to handle challenging situations arising in the dojang (training hall) and outside the dojang, including work and personal life. Throughout my life, during various difficult and challenging times, I have been fortunate enough to have my martial arts friends and family there to help me overcome these personal and challenging life obstacles.

When I started this journey, it was about mastering the required movements and strengthening the mind and body while creating a strong spirit. Continually working on my martial arts journey has never been easy, and I will continue to strive forward on this path for the rest of my life.

Challenges faced me when I was young; I was losing my balance and coordination as I contracted an illness that caused my throat and ears to require surgery. The ear operation was the cause of my loss of balance, coordination, and a significant amount of hearing in both ears. Training in martial arts has helped me overcome many life hurdles and strengthened my body, mind, and spirit. It has brought balance and harmony into my daily life, and I am truly blessed and thankful. *Gamsahamnida* — Thank you

HOW HAS MARTIAL ARTS IMPACTED YOUR LIFE?

Martial arts have allowed me to learn, develop, and harness the skills required to become a leader in the dojang and the workforce. It allows me to teach martial arts and other classes for the community, benefitting everyone by increasing inclusiveness and social awareness and harnessing the value of community by participation. This is achieved by training together, supporting each other, and achieving set common goals as a community team.

These skills have also been effective in my working life, allowing me to gain greater positions of responsibility and authority. Being taught and exposed to the skills of face-to-face teaching and coaching early in life, extended by volunteering at competitions and fundraising events, being an integral part of the community and social groups, and assisting in planning community events, has helped to pave the way to success.

TRAINING INFORMATION

- Belt Ranks & Martial Arts Styles: Taekwondo — 6th Dan, Tang Soo Do — 6th Dan, Hapkido
- Instructors/Influencers: Grand Master Jean Kfoury, GM Hae Man Park, GM Don Oi Choi, GM Cynthia Rothrock, GM Brad Hope, GM Trevor Stone
- Birthplace/Growing Up: South Australia
- Yrs. In the Martial Arts: 38 years
- Yrs. Instructing: 29 years
- School Owner and Instructor at SMAC Tang Soo Do

PROFESSIONAL ORGANIZATIONS
- Cynthia Rothrock Association
- The Korean Taekwondo Moo Duk Kwan
- World Hapkido Martial Arts Association
- Australia Taekwondo Association
- Sports Taekwondo Australia Association
- Taekwondo Australia Association
- Martial Arts Australia Association
- Kukkiwon + World Taekwondo
- The World Taekwondo Chung Do Kwan Federation

PERSONAL ACHIEVEMENTS
- Martial arts has enabled me to overcome many obstacles in my life, allowing me to grow and succeed. Ranging from personal sickness to the challenges of growing up through the years, getting married, having kids, and, in the future, grandkids.
- I've learned the fortitude and resolve to mourn and support friends and family through loss and tragedies. Be it through natural or unnatural means, while also being able to celebrate milestones with my family, martial arts family, and friends here and abroad.
- My success has ranged from in the club to local, national, and international competitions, continuing into my work and personal life.
- Martial arts has given me a purpose, and with that purpose, I have been able to use it to harness success.

MAJOR ACHIEVEMENTS

- Internationally recognized Author, Mentor, and Coach.
- Master Functional Trainer
- 2024 National re-nominated for the Social Value & Community Impact Award
- 2024 International Best-selling Co-author - Elite Publications' Elite Martial Artists in America: Secrets to Life, Leadership, and Business compilation book
- 2023 Ausactive Nationalist Finalist: Social Value & Community Impact Award
- 2023 Martial Arts Australia — nominated for Master of the Year
- 2019 Seniors Martial Arts Playford City Community Award
- 2018 International Master's Gold Medalist
- 2017 US Open Bronze Medalist
- 2017 Author Award
- 2016 International Masters - Medalist
- Represented Australia in Korea in 2016 at the Kukkiwon headquarters
- 2011 Total Taekwondo Coach of the Year

HOW HAS MARTIAL ARTS IMPACTED YOUR LIFE? (CONTINUED)

I have competed in martial arts tournaments and garnered national and international medals in fighting and power-breaking competitions. This success can be attributed to the many promotional opportunities presented to me, my students, and my club in the last few years.

Standout events include being involved in national television appearances, national radio, and printed media (newspapers), as well as receiving national and international community and martial arts awards. Recently, this has extended to international achievements as an author/illustrator of a set of children's books and co-authoring with Elite Publications in Elite Martial Artists in America: Secrets to Life, Leadership, and Business, which became an International Bestseller for the promotion of martial arts across America and the rest of the world.

Martial arts has changed my life in many positive ways and will continue to do so. I hope to be able to continue to share the lifelong benefits and joy of martial arts, to the martial arts family and the rest of the world.

Become an
AMAA MEMBER!

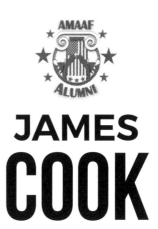

JAMES COOK

"
The Rank means nothing. The Knowledge means everything…

WHY THE MARTIAL ARTS?

Growing up in Cleveland, Ohio, in the 1950s was not easy. We had a coal and wood-burning pot-bellied stove in the middle of the kitchen and a pump on the sink. We were poor, but it was a good thing we didn't know it. As a kid, I looked like Steve Urkle, with glasses and tape hanging on my nose, high-water pants with suspenders, and penny loafers. I was the target of bullies in elementary school and junior high. One day, I watched an old "Ozzie & Harriet" episode, and Ricky Nelson was bullied in school. He decided to take karate from a gentleman named Ed Parker.

That was the first time I saw martial arts. I was 10, and we lived around the corner from Corey Recreation Center, where I used to take magic classes. The instructor didn't show up one day, so I wandered around the center for the first time.

It was then that I passed a room full of people wearing pajamas with different-colored belts. I watched for a moment and realized that it was Judo, a way to learn how to defend myself.

At first, I was just another clumsy kid with three legs, but under the instruction of Mr. Bob Howard, I slowly turned into a swan. I finally made it to the green belt and was proud.

One day after class, I walked out without my shoes. As I returned to get them, I looked in and saw Mr. Howard and his brother kicking and punching. It was confusing because, in Judo, there are no kicks or punches. This was karate. In those days, you could not take karate before age 18. Mr. Howard got around it by making me a mascot.

As I remember, Mr. Howard took me to my first tournament, where I watched Bill Hayes, Russell Benefield, Joe Pennywell, and the Great Zenpo Shimabuku. This was back in the day when you fought with only tape on your fist, and the technique had to be within two inches from the target to be called a point. The control of these fighters was amazing. I watched with amazement as Master Shimabuku countered his attackers with the most fantastic jump spin thrust kick that was perfectly timed. After the tournament, I ran to the dressing room to ask him about the kick. He spoke no English, so I motioned, attempting to do the kick.

He positioned me, gently grabbed me by my collar and belt, and lifted me in the air, turning and sitting me back down again. I never forgot that, and the technique became one of my trademarks.

TRAINING INFORMATION

- Belt Ranks & Martial Arts Styles: Kodakan Judo-3rd kyu, Shotokan-4th Kyu, Goju-4th Kyu, Bak Me Pai Gung Fu - 4th Level, Ishinryu, O'Do Gwan Tae Kwon Do-3rd Dan, Northern Praying Mantis-8th Level "8th Dan"
- Instructors/Influencers: Bob Howard, Clifford Yates, John Custer, Wally Cowper, Tiger Division (VIETNAM) 66-67, Ku Muc Whe, Do Hak Soo-Chun Gwon Ho - Juno Ho Ming
- Birthplace/Growing Up: Cleveland, OH
- Yrs. In the Martial Arts: 63 years
- Yrs. Instructing: 55 years
- Instructor

PROFESSIONAL ORGANIZATIONS

- USKA
- PKA
- American Black Belt Association
- Southwest Karate Association
- Chan Moo Kwon World Association
- United States Association of Martial Arts·
- World Chinese Martial Arts Federation

PERSONAL ACHIEVEMENTS

- Cleveland Martial Arts Hall of Fame
- Pennsylvania Karate Lifetime Achievement Award
- Who's Who Legend Award
- Joe Lewis Eternal Warrior Award
- PKA Warrior Award
- Karate Hall of Fame Award Cal.
- National Martial Arts Hall of Fame Award
- Masters Hall of Fame Lifetime Achievement Awards
- Sport Karate Museum Dragon Image Fighting Award
- USA Martial Arts Legend Award

MAJOR ACHIEVEMENTS

- 1977 - Top 10 Fighter in the U.S. - Official Karate Magazine
- 1977 - Top 3 World Weapons Expert - Official Karate Magazine
- 1977 - United States Karate Association Grand Champion - Pittsburgh, PA
- 1978 - Battle of Atlanta Middleweight Champion
- 1979 - International Middleweight Champion - Venezuela
- 1980 - International Grand Champion Venezuela
- 1980 - Karate Hall of Fame Inductee
- 1981 - Martial Arts Hall of Fame Inductee
- 1996 - Top Fighter and form competitor Knoxville Pro AM
- Top Tournament Achievements
- International Weapons Champion - Venezuela
- International Forms Champion - Venezuela
- International Weapons Champion - Venezuela
- Battle of Atlanta Weapons Champion
- Over 1,500 1st places and awards to date

AMBER
CRABTREE

"Studying martial arts gives me focus, not just on myself, but on what actually matters in life and how precious life is.

HOW HAS MARTIAL ARTS IMPACTED YOUR LIFE?

The respect, self-discipline, and warriorship that martial arts have taught me have and continue to impact every aspect of my life; it has made me a much better person. Studying martial arts gives me focus, not just on myself, but on what actually matters in life and how precious life is. Through the worst times in my life, martial arts was there. No matter what was going on, training until it took everything I had to walk to the car always made everything manageable; in those sweaty, grueling hours, nothing else existed. I am genuinely not sure if I would have survived without it.

WHY THE MARTIAL ARTS?

I began martial arts when I was a young teenager suffering from a family loss and not knowing how to deal with my emotions. I had so much anger inside; I remember asking about punching bags and saving up to buy one when I was fourteen after watching my now brother-in-law beating his punching bag up. Unbeknownst to me, this was only the beginning. As I got older, I trained primarily to protect myself, and as a smaller female, I knew martial arts was key. Since then, I have trained in Kung fu, Brazilian Jiu Jitsu, axe throwing, Six Harmonies Drunken Boxing, bodybuilding, and every weapon I could get my hands on. Twenty-six years after my initial desire began, I still train almost every day.

TRAINING INFORMATION

- Belt Ranks & Martial Arts Styles: Kung Fu - 7th Degree Black Sash, Brazilian Jiu Jitsu - Blue Belt
- Instructors/Influencers: Grandmaster Tim Pickens, Professor Brian Cooley (Gracie Barra)
- Birthplace/Growing Up: Monticello, KY
- Yrs. In the Martial Arts: 26 years
- Yrs. Instructing: 8 years
- Instructor

PROFESSIONAL ORGANIZATIONS

- IBJJF

PERSONAL ACHIEVEMENTS

- Tri-Beta Biology Honor Society, Underwood-Alger Biology Scholars Award
- Phi Kappa Phi Honor Society
- Vincent Qui Patitur Honor Society
- Phi Theta Kappa Honor Society
- Graduated from Berea College with Honors
- American Council on Exercise Certified Personal Trainer
- National Academy of Sports Medicine Weight Loss Specialist
- National Academy of Sports Medicine
- Group Personal Training Specialist
- I am currently finishing my Ph.D. so that is my "in progress" personal achievement
- I also have some bodybuilding competition awards

MAJOR ACHIEVEMENTS

- Competitive Placings: six gold, four silver, and one bronze

LOUIS E. DAVIS

> **"**
> *God will always be my primary ally.*
> *My thoughts and feelings about this go*
> *beyond words.*

WHY THE MARTIAL ARTS?

Louis Edward Davis was born in Chicago, Illinois, on October 11th, 1970. In August of 1977, his family migrated to Minneapolis, Minnesota. By late 1985, he began training in martial arts at the age of 15, and by the summer of 1986, he began competing in local point karate tournaments, some of which were hosted by Pat Worley. During the 1993 USTU National Championships held in St Paul, Minnesota, Louis came into contact with the All-Army Taekwondo team. After searching the venue, he learned that a team existed representing each branch of the US Armed Forces. After vowing (to himself) to become a member of one of these teams, he enlisted the following year. In 1995, while at his first duty station, Fort Hood, Texas, he was approached by Sergeant Michael Bennett, a member of the All-Army Taekwondo Team competing in the heavyweight division. Under Sergeants Bennett and Todd Angel's guidance, Louis went from an awkward novice to one of three Fort Hood Taekwondo team captains.

In late April 1997, Louis, along with fellow Fort Hood

Taekwondo teammates John Swan, Nicolau Andrade, Ryan Lundy, Howard Clayton, and, of course, Sergeant Bennett and Sergeant Angel, attended the 1997 All Army and Armed Forces Taekwondo trial and selection camp held at Fort Indiantown Pennsylvania. On April 27th, Louis took the silver medal in the welterweight division during the Armed Forces Championships, securing a place on the 1997 Army team.

In December 1997, Louis relocated from Fort Hood, Texas, to Harvey Barracks in Kitzingen, Germany. By October 1998, Louis began to establish himself as a competitor throughout the Bavarian (Bayern) area, winning the Bavarian Championships later that same year, holding said title until 2000. During this time, Louis received phone guidance from coach Rafael Medina on how to maximize his training and improve his skill set. One of these many phone conversations led him to Georg Streif, the head coach of the German Armed Forces and German national team. Georg had invited him to attend one of his training camps, which greatly improved Louis' growing abilities.

In 1999, Louis returned to Fort Indiantown Gap. He secured a place on the team after defeating Daryll Woods in the finals and defeating London Arevalo of the Air Force Taekwondo team during the Armed

Forces Championships. In 2000, Louis began visiting Pickens, South Carolina, and entered a mentorship with former All-Army and national champion Reginald Perry. It was here that Louis began to research the history of the All-Army team.

The following year, Louis returned to "The Gap," securing a position as one of two middleweights on the Army team and by January of 2003, relocated from Germany to South Korea, joining All-Army teammates Kevin Williams and Johnny Birch as a member of the 2nd Infantry Division's taekwondo team. During this four-year tenure in Korea as a member of the 2nd Infantry Division's Taekwondo Team, Louis quickly established himself as a talented competitor, winning any competition held by Camp Casey or Camp Hovey, respectively, winning both the 2003 and 2005 Friendship Cup (AKA the Commander's Cup), the 2003-2005 Area 1 Championship, and the 8th Army Championship. In 2005, Louis took Gold in the USA Taekwondo National Championships in San Jose, California, and his second National Medal (Silver) in Austin, Texas, in 2009.

In early to mid-2007, Louis was asked by Rafael Medina to attend the inaugural Taekwondo Hall of Fame banquet in Teaneck, New Jersey, as a representative of the US Armed Forces, later becoming a technical advisor. Louis himself received recognition from the Hall of Fame for his efforts as a competitor. Louis continued to work as a technical advisor representing the US Armed Forces until 2015.

After retiring from both the Army and Taekwondo competition, Louis returned to Minneapolis, Minnesota. There, he volunteered his knowledge and experience as a coach in support of a collective of Taekwondo school owners within the Twin Cities metro area. He also connected with his former All-Army coaches and teammates, who operate Taekwondo schools themselves. Currently, Louis is a D-Level referee and coach under USA Taekwondo, as well as a coach under the Amateur Athletic Union.

In addition to coaching, Louis researched the history of the All-Army and Armed Forces Taekwondo Program by locating many of its pioneers, former champions, and team members. He combined the knowledge he had

TRAINING INFORMATION

- Belt Ranks & Martial Arts Styles: 2nd Degree Black Belt-Olympic Freestyle Taekwondo Intermediate Level
- Instructors/Influencers: GM Michael R. Bennett, GM Todd Angel, GM Rafael Medina, GM Bobby Clayton, GM Bongseok Kim, Sifu Gary D. Eshelman
- Birthplace/Growing Up: Chicago, IL / Minneapolis, MN
- Yrs. In the Martial Arts: 39 years
- Yrs. Instructing: 11 years
- Instructor

PROFESSIONAL ORGANIZATIONS

- USA Masters Taekwondo Team

PERSONAL ACHIEVEMENTS

- Retired Army (20 years) Associate Degree
- Computer Support & Network Administration
- Associate Degree in Computer Forensics

MAJOR ACHIEVEMENTS

- 1996 — 1997 Fort Hood Taekwondo Team, one of three team captains
- 1996 Fort Hood Championships — Bronze
- 1997 Armed Forces Championships — Silver
- 1997 Fort Hood Championships — Gold
- 1998 Bavarian Regional Championships — Gold
- 1998 Bavarian Championships — Gold
- 1998 Italian Open — Gold
- 1999 All Army Championships — Gold
- 1999 Bavarian Regional Championships — Gold
- 1999 Bavarian Championships — Gold
- 2000 Bavarian Regional Championships — silver
- 2000 Bavarian Championships — Gold
- 2001 All Army Championships — Silver
- 2002 South Carolina State Championships — Gold
- 2003 South Carolina State Championships — Gold
- 2003 Commander's Cup Korea — Gold

gained and co-authored the #1 Best-seller One Team. *One Fight. One Family: The History of the Armed Forces Taekwondo Team* with Grandmasters Michael Bennett and Rafael Medina.

HOW HAS MARTIAL ARTS IMPACTED YOUR LIFE?

The quote, "When the pupil is ready, the master will appear," best describes how Louis's continued study of martial arts has impacted his life. What began as a quest for the tools to seek justice for the abuse he suffered in a group home became a journey that would enrich his life in ways that he could not fathom.

Martial arts offered Louis more than a physical form of unarmed combat. It allowed him to dodge the pitfalls that befall the average young black man at that time. It accepted him without judgment nor prejudice and opened the doorway to the world, which led him to enlist in the Army in hopes of studying abroad in a country where one of these arts originated. Its discipline coincided with the discipline instilled in Louis by the Army. It offered him purpose, direction, and motivation. It became his constant friend and a secondary ally. Louis says, "God will always be my primary ally." His thoughts and feelings about this go beyond words.

MAJOR ACHIEVEMENTS

- 2003 Area 1 Championships Korea — Gold
- 2003 8th Army Championships Korea — Gold
- 2003 Mid Atlantic Championships — Gold / Grand Champion
- 2003 World Taekwondo Hwarang Festival, Jincheon Gun — Bronze
- 2004 Jeju Island Invitational — Bronze
- 2004 Area 1 Championships Korea — Gold
- 2004 8th Army Championships Korea — Gold
- 2005 Commander's Cup Korea — Gold
- 2005 Area 1 Championships Korea — Gold
- 2005 8th Army Championships Korea — Gold
- 2005 USA Taekwondo National Championships — Gold
- 2007 USA Taekwondo National Qualifier — Silver 2009
- USA Taekwondo National Qualifier — Bronze 2009
- USA Taekwondo National Championships — Silver
- 2011 Armed Forces Championships — Bronze
- 2012 Armed Forces Championships — Gold
- 2013 Armed Forces Championships — Bronze
- 2021 US Masters Cup - Gold
- 2023 Asian Pacific Masters Games - Gold
- 2012 - 2015 Taekwondo Hall Of Fame Technical Advisor
- 2022 - Taekwondo Hall Of Fame Inductee
- 2023 - AMAA Who's Who in the Martial Arts Hall of Honors Inductee
- 2023 - Co-authored the #1 Best-seller *One Team. One Fight. One Family: The History of the Armed Forces Taekwondo Team* with Grandmasters Michael Bennett and Rafael Castro Medina.
- In April 2024, the government of Humacao, Puerto Rico, recognized the authors of the book One Team, One Fight, One Family for their work as bestselling authors. The book is currently on display at the Center for Arts, Culture, Literature, and Tourism, located in Humacao, Puerto Rico.
- May 2024 - The authors were also featured on the Master's Alliance Podcast hosted by Olympic Gold Medalist Grandmaster Herb Perez. https://bit.ly/4cJyi3T

KENNETH
DAY, SR.

"
I've learned discipline, which motivates me to share the knowledge and techniques I've learned over the years.

I was diagnosed with cancer in 1990. I endured radiation and chemotherapy, including two recurrences of the cancer in 1992 and 1998. To this day, Tae Kwon Do has been an important part of my life and has made me the person that I am today. I strive to be fair, compassionate, and loyal in everything that I do, and that is how I live my life. I have mentored other cancer patients and young martial arts students, instilling them with determination and the spirit to never give up, whether it be in athletics or health-related situations.

WHY THE MARTIAL ARTS?

I come from a family of twelve children living in a two-bedroom house. My mother died when I was just fourteen years old. In 1974, I took my first Tae Kwon Do class under Grand Master Myuang Hak Kang, located in Arlington, VA, and the Grand Master is still teaching classes today. I studied Tae Kwon Do in 1976 with Grand Master Jhoon Rhee and trained with Jangs Tae Kwon Do from 1976 until 1981. My training continued in Maryland with Grand Master Dongju Lee at the Lee Karate Studio and Grand Master Apollo Ladra at Apollo's East Coast Tae Kwon Do School.

HOW HAS MARTIAL ARTS IMPACTED YOUR LIFE?

Martial arts have had a significant impact on my life over the years. They keep my body in shape and keep me busy. I've learned discipline, which motivates me to share the knowledge and techniques I've learned over the years. When I was young, I watched Bruce Lee movies and practiced the moves he used to do. I am honored to have been taught by one of Bruce Lee's good friends, Grand Master Jhoon Rhee.

Become an
AMAA
MEMBER!

TRAINING INFORMATION

- Belt Ranks & Martial Arts Styles: Tae Kwon Do (3rd Degree Black Belt)
- Instructors/Influencers: Grand Master Myuang Hak Kang, Grand Master Jhoon Rhee, Master Cleanzo Vollin, the late Master Instructor Andre Yamakawa, Grand Master John Chung, Grand Master Dongju Lee, Master Apollo Ladra Grand Master Michael Coles
- Birthplace/Growing Up: Washington, DC / Arlington, VA (Green Valley)
- Yrs. In the Martial Arts: 50 years
- Yrs. Instructing: 17 years
- Instructor

PROFESSIONAL ORGANIZATIONS

- The World Cup Martial Arts Organization

PERSONAL ACHIEVEMENTS

- I am a 34-year cancer survivor
- I retired after 32 years of working at Giant Food
- I have been the Roving Chief for Anne Arundel County Public Schools for 24 years

MAJOR ACHIEVEMENTS

- In August 2017 and June 2019, I received the AMAA Who's Who Legend Award.
- In 2020, I received the AMAA Ambassador of The Year Award.
- In 2020, I received the Golden Year Award from the World Cup Martial Arts Organization.
- 2022 AMAA Hall of Honors Tribute to Bill "Superfoot" Wallace Biography Book Inclusion and Award
- 2023 AMAA Hall of Honors Tribute to Cynthia Rothrock Biography Book Inclusion and Award
- 2023 Masters Martial Arts Hall of Fame Award - Expo 17 - Sifu Cliff Kupper
- 2023 Lifetime Achievement Community Service Volunteer Award by President Joe Biden

JAMES
DEBROW III

"

Martial arts have added significant value to my life by imparting the following skills: discipline, respect, motivation...

HOW HAS MARTIAL ARTS IMPACTED YOUR LIFE?

Martial arts have added significant value to my life by imparting the following skills: discipline, respect, motivation, trust, leadership, communication, teamwork, teaching, followership, emotional control, physical fitness, mental fitness, resiliency, character, spirituality, improved attention span, calmness, loyalty, commitment, honesty, tenacity, competitiveness, goal orientation, cognition, and motor performance.

Martial arts have allowed me to interact with people from various backgrounds, including both men and women from domestic and international communities. I have worked with at-risk students from elementary, junior high, and high school, assisting many of them in staying in school and graduating. Additionally, karate has provided me with a source of income.

WHY THE MARTIAL ARTS?

My father and two uncles were professional boxers and black belts. As a result, I started training in boxing and martial arts at the age of four in 1959. My first of four black belts was given to me by my father and uncles. Additionally, I pursued martial arts training during my time in the United States Army in the Republic of Korea (ROK), Okinawa, and Tokyo, Japan. I was promoted by Dr. Al Francis, a 10th Dan black belt from the Al Francis Karate Organization, from 5th Dan to 10th Dan black belt in San Antonio, Texas (1985-2020).

TRAINING INFORMATION

- Belt Ranks & Martial Arts Styles: Judo/Jiu-Jitsu, Tae Kwon-Do, Japanese Karate, Judo, Aikido, Hapkido, Tang Soo Doo & Tai Chi - 10th Dan Black Belt

- Instructors/Influencers: James Debrow, Jr., Herbert Debrow, Johnny Davis, Masters Choi, Kim & Chang, Dr. Al Francis, Dr. Abel Villareal, Professor Charles Dixon, Late Grand Master Richard Dixon, Grand Master Mike Filmore, Dr. Dan Roberts

- Birthplace/Growing Up: San Antonio, TX

- Yrs. In the Martial Arts: 65 years

- Yrs. Instructing: 57 years

- School Owner, Manager and Instructor at James Debrow Fighting Tiger School, LLC, School of Champions, Police and Military Combat Instructor: Physical Fitness & Defensive Tactics, Instructor/Coordinator - Texas Department of Public Safety (State Trooper) Agency-wide

PROFESSIONAL ORGANIZATIONS

- Al Francis Karate Organization; Shinjimasu International Martial Arts Association; Global Tae Kwon Do Association

- Tae Kwon Do, Yong Moo Kwan Federation, and the World Moo Duk Kwan Alliance-United States Branch of Tae Kwon Do Association, etc.

- Shinjimasu Martial Arts Association

- Black Dragon Martial Arts Association

- US International Korea & Japan Union

- National Sport Karate Museum

- World International Supreme Red Belt Council

- United States Military Martial Arts Association

- International Wing Tsun Tiger Kung Fu Association

- Traditional World Karate Association

- International Soo Bak Kee Federation

- International Supreme Elite Warrior's Council

- United States Kali Association, Inc.

- US International Senior Grandmasters Council

- World Blackbelt Club Council

- Vic Moore International Karate Schools

- United States Kajukenbo Association

HOW HAS MARTIAL ARTS IMPACTED YOUR LIFE? (CONTINUED)

Martial arts played a crucial role in my promotion to sergeant at the Texas Department of Public Safety-State Trooper Training Academy. I dedicated over eight years to serving in the state police training bureau. Karate has been a lifelong passion for me and continues to be so. Currently, I am developing a program aimed at assisting children in improving their memory, attention span, and concentration skills.

Martial arts has been the best thing that has ever happened to me!

PERSONAL ACHIEVEMENTS

- Shinjimasu International Martial Arts Association, United Federation of International Grand Masters, Letter of Recognition and Inauguration, Recognized as a 10th dan black belt, Professor of Martial Arts, Lifetime Member on June 22, 2019, by Soke Charles Dixon, 10th dan, Chairman of the Counsel and the Shinjimasu Board of Directors, Temple, Texas

- International Police Tactical Training Academy, Appointed International Director of Training of the International Police Tactical Training Unit on June 26, 2020, by the President, Grand Master Robert J. Fabrey, 10th dan black belt and President, United States Karate Federation, National Headquarters, St. Portia, Florida

- Been promoted and a registered member of the United States Karate Federation (1997 to current)

- Philadelphia Historic Martial Arts Society, Martial Arts Hall of Fame Inductee Class of 2020

- United States Martial Arts, Martial Arts Hall of Fame Inductee Class of 2020 and Membership. International Martial Arts Council of America. Hot Springs, Arkansas

- The Universal Martial Arts Hall of Fame Inductee Class of 2020 and Membership

- Assigned to the Legendary Texas Department of Public Safety — Texas Highway Patrol Training Academy Staff as a Sergeant 1993/Coordinator: developed and implemented the Police Defensive Tactics Full-Contact Program (first and only grandmaster level karate boxer (9th & 10th dan black belt to date)

MAJOR ACHIEVEMENTS

- Physical fitness and defensive tactics coordinator for the Texas Department of Public Safety-State Trooper Training Academy agency-wide (1994-2003)

- Developed and implemented the physical fitness and wellness program and the defensive tactics program for recruiting school cadets and agency incumbents

- Use-of-force expert/policy developer

- Court-certified use-of-force, assigned to develop, implement, and instruct in the new Texas Concealed Handgun Program at the Texas Department of Public Safety as approved by the Texas legislatures.

- Philadelphia Historic Martial Arts Society - Martial Arts Hall of Fame inductee: class of 2020

MAJOR ACHIEVEMENTS (CONTINUED)

- United States Martial Arts - Martial Arts Hall of Fame Inductee: class of 2020

- Universal Martial Arts Hall of Fame Inductee: class of 2020

- Texas Amateur Martial Arts Association- Executive Committee Chair

- The World Moo Duk Kwan Do Alliance appointed as Central Director of the National Hapkido Association

- International Police Tactical Training Academy of the International Police Tactical Training Unit

HALL OF FAME & HALL OF HONORS INCLUSIONS

- USA Martial Arts Hall of Fame

- The Eastern U.S.A. International Martial Arts Association

- World Moo Duk Kwan Tae Kwon Do Alliance Hall of Fame

- United States Martial Artist Association-International Black Belt Hall of Fame

- Filipino Martial Arts Hall of Fame

- United States Martial Arts Hall of Fame

- All Federal Karate Organization / Al Francis Karate Organization

- The National Martial Arts Hall of Honor

- The Philadelphia Historic Martial Arts Society Hall of Fame

- International Hall of Honor Hall of Champions

- Internacional Hall of Fame-Argentina

- Masters of Martial Arts Hall of Fame

- Grandes Mestres das Artes Marciais, Erich Fromm University, Brazil

- Master Black Belt Book, Brazil

- Doni Mega High-Performance Athletes

- Molum Combat Arts Honor Society Yap Suk Dai JI Award

- The American Martial Arts Alliance Foundation

- The AMAA Legacy Metaverse Museum

GEORGE
DILLMAN

"
Martial arts have given me many opportunities, including being a 1969-1972 Winningest Tournament Competitor...

WHY THE MARTIAL ARTS?

George A. Dillman, 10th Degree Black Belt in Ryukyu Kempo Tomari-te, honored by *Black Belt Magazine* as "1997 Instructor of the Year," is one of the USA's best-known and well-established martial arts personalities. Dillman came to the attention of the martial arts press when he began competing in the early 1960s. By the middle of that decade, he started running his own tournament, the Northeast Open Karate Championships. This competition was held annually -the first kick-off in Palmer Park, Maryland, in 1966. The site was moved to Suitland, Maryland, in 1967 and moved again to Reading, Pennsylvania, in 1968, where it was held until 1996.

Official Karate magazine (Nov. 1982) described Dillman as "one of the winningest competitors karate has ever known." Dillman was a four-time National Karate Champion (1969-1972) and was consistently ranked among the top ten competitors in the nation by major karate magazines during this period. During his nine-year competitive career, Dillman won a total of 327 trophies in fighting, forms, breaking, and weapons.

Dillman began serious martial arts training in 1961 with Harry G. Smith. He went on to study with Daniel K. Pai, Robert Trias, and Seiyu Oyata. Dillman has always considered himself a student, never a master of the arts. To this end, he and his students have traveled throughout the United States to meet and train with various martial arts experts.

Because of his perseverance, Dillman's martial arts talents have earned him widespread U.S. media coverage. He has appeared on 35 national TV shows, including *Real People, Mike Douglas, PM Magazine, Evening Magazine, and NBC's Sports Machine.* Dillman has also been featured five times in *Ripley's Believe It or Not* and has been the subject of over 300 newspaper and magazine articles. Dillman, who was a professional boxer for three and one-half years, is the only person known to have trained with both Bruce Lee and Muhammad Ali. In May of 1988, Dillman was inducted into the Berks County Sports Hall of Fame. He was the first martial artist to be included. In 2003, he was inducted into the Schuylkill County Sports Hall of Fame.

TRAINING INFORMATION

- Belt Ranks & Martial Arts Styles: 10th Degree Black Belt in Ryukyu Kempo Tomari-te
- Instructors/Influencers: Harry G. Smith, Jhoon Rhee, Daniel K. Pai, Hohan Soken, Remy Presas, Wally Jay, Leo Fong
- Birthplace/Growing Up: Philadelphia / Pottsville, PA
- Yrs. In the Martial Arts: 66+ years
- Yrs. Instructing: 55+ years
- School Owner of Dillman Karate International, with over 200 schools around the world

PROFESSIONAL ORGANIZATIONS

- USKA
- Seiyu Oyata Ryukyu Islands

PERSONAL ACHIEVEMENTS

- Married Suzanne John Dillman in 2006. She is the daughter of a famous drummer, who starred in MGM Movies, and then the TV show "Lucky Strike." He was also the main drummer for "Louis Armstrong."
- Listed in Martial Arts Museum in Okinawa
- Featured in a best-selling book out of Okinawa (History of Okinawan Karate)
- Schuylkill County All Sports Hall of Fame for Baseball and Boxing
- Berks County All Sports Hall of Fame branch of Pennsylvania Sports Hall of Fame
- 1997 Black Belt Magazine "Instructor of the Year"

MAJOR ACHIEVEMENTS

- Worked out with and trained the great Muhammad Ali for his comeback fights
- Personal friends with Bruce Lee and Muhammad Ali

Dillman traveled the world teaching seminars on pressure points and tuite (grappling) hidden within the traditional movements of the old martial arts forms. It is his research and scientific dissection of the old forms that is earning him the most notoriety. Never one to shy away from controversy, Dillman has rediscovered a formerly secret level of meaning for Kata movements and has made that interpretation understandable to all. He has produced a DVD instructional series on pressure points and has written seven books with Chris Thomas: *Kyusho-Jitsu: The Dillman Method of Pressure Point Fighting; Advanced Pressure Point Fighting of Ryukyu Kempo; Advanced Pressure Point Grappling: Tuite; Pressure Point Karate Made Easy; Little Jay Learns Karate; Humane Pressure Point Self-Defense; and Pressure Point Fighting Secrets of Ryukyu Kempo.* The books have been said to be "the definitive martial arts books of the century" and "unparalleled among current martial arts literature."

George Dillman

Oyata Sensei

SPECIAL 2012 HALL OF FAME ISSUE
BLACK BELT
WORLD'S LEADING MAGAZINE OF MARTIAL ARTS

Happy Birthday
ALMOST 70, DILLMAN STILL GOING STRONG!

▲ Renowned for his knowledge of pressure-point fighting techniques, George Dillman has changed the way the martial arts are practiced in *dojo* across the United States and in 30 foreign countries. Through his books and DVDs, as well as a seemingly never-ending series of seminars with Remy Presas and Wally Jay, Dillman spread his arts of *tuite*, *Ryukyu kempo* and *kyusho-jitsu* to students of self-defense for decades. And although he's about to

turn 70, the Reading, Pennsylvania-based *Black Belt* Hall of Fame member is showing few signs of slowing down.

A former tournament standout, Dillman has made it his mission to reveal fighting techniques that have been hidden in *kata*. After having their eyes opened, numerous seminar attendees have said the experience breathed new life into their training.

In addition to his accomplishments in competitive karate, Dillman has a martial arts résumé that includes teaching *nunchaku* moves to Bruce Lee, wrestling with a black bear and breaking enough ice to shatter a world record.

Although his ice-breaking days are behind him, Dillman says he's not even thinking about retiring. He will, however, scale back the size of the seminars he teaches at schools that belong to his Dillman Karate International organization. In the meantime, he's working on another book.

On November 16-17, 2012, friends, associates and students will gather in Indianapolis for a two-day seminar and party—which will also mark the release of a new biography. Although *Black Belt* is, unfortunately, unable to attend, the staff joins the entire membership of DKI in wishing Mr. Dillman a happy birthday and many more to come. ✂

NOVEMBER 2012 | BLACK BELT 15

HOW HAS MARTIAL ARTS IMPACTED YOUR LIFE?

Martial arts have given me many opportunities, including being a 1969-1972 Winningest Tournament Competitor, meeting many famous people such as Johnny Cash, Charles Bronson, Troy Donahue, and Cameron Mitchell, and appearing on 32 National TV shows, including the number one show in 1980 with over 25 million viewers. Breaking Ice was the close of that show for ten years.

It has also allowed me to join the YMCA boxing team (Friends of Boxing - FOB) in 1958. I fought other boxing clubs throughout Pennsylvania and finished with a 27—3 record. In 1960, I joined the U.S. Army, and the requirements were 21 hours of hand-to-hand combat. The kicking part added to my boxing went well. I took lessons at Brown Gym in Fort Knox, Kentucky, after transferring to New Cumberland Army Depot and found Ralph Lindquist, a student of Harry G. Smith. He was a member of the United States Karate Association (USKA).

Become an
AMAA MEMBER!

GREG
DILLON

"
The Martial Arts has changed my life and taken me all over the world.

HOW HAS MARTIAL ARTS IMPACTED YOUR LIFE?

Martial arts have changed my life and taken me all over the world. I have met and made friends with people from all walks of life.

TRAINING INFORMATION

- Belt Ranks & Martial Arts Styles: Katai Te Ryu Karate-5th Dan, Ryu KyuKempo Karate-10th Dan
- Instructors/Influencers: Master Gene Gross, Professor George Dillman
- Birthplace/Growing Up: Washington / Otwell, IN
- Yrs. In the Martial Arts: 53 years
- Yrs. Instructing: 45 years
- Instructor at Dillman Karate International

PROFESSIONAL ORGANIZATIONS

- I Change Nations
- Black Belt Speakers
- Oakland City University Alumni
- Federation of United Martial Artist Crusade against Crime
- Dillman Karate International

WHY THE MARTIAL ARTS?

At age 15, I was very fit and athletic. Growing up on a farm, I met a Japanese man who was studying at a local university. One instructor led me to another that brought me to competitions—eventually leading me to Professor George Dillon who changed my life forever. From there, I was able to meet a King and world leaders, and I've been able to share and instruct hundreds of students around the globe.

PERSONAL ACHIEVEMENTS

- Honorary Doctorate of Humanities from United Graduate College International
- World Civility Ambassador by I Change Nations Distinguished Leadership Award

MAJOR ACHIEVEMENTS

- Black Belt Speakers Certified
- Medical First Responder certified with Indiana Department of Homeland Security
- Royal advisor to King Ommessa of Ghana

Become an
AMAA MEMBER!

STEVEN
DIRTON

"
Engaging in Martial Arts has provided me with valuable insights into setting and achieving a wide range of goals.

HOW HAS MARTIAL ARTS IMPACTED YOUR LIFE?

Engaging in martial arts has provided me with valuable insights into setting and achieving a wide range of goals. This includes understanding the principles of discipline, focus, and perseverance, all of which have been instrumental in my career in law enforcement. Additionally, the practice of martial arts has deeply enriched my personal and family life, fostering a sense of balance, respect, and mental fortitude that extends into many other aspects of my daily endeavors.

WHY THE MARTIAL ARTS?

My journey in martial arts began at the age of thirteen when I was captivated by the legendary Bruce Lee's performance. His mastery inspired me to embark on my own path of martial arts excellence, leading me to the art of Kajukenbo.

My dedication to martial arts extends beyond personal achievement. Over 50 years after my honorable discharge from the United States Air Force, I became the six-time heavyweight champion of South Carolina from the late 1980s to the mid-90s. More importantly, I have had the privilege of training numerous students who have become martial arts champions in their own right.

TRAINING INFORMATION

- Belt Ranks & Martial Arts Styles: Kajukenbo - 9th Degree Grandmaster
- Instructors/Influencers: Sifu John Reid, Senior Grandmaster Donald K.
- Birthplace/Growing Up: Greenville, SC
- Yrs. In the Martial Arts: 53 years
- Yrs. Instructing: 45 years
- School owner, Manager & Instructor at Dirton's Kajukenbo Martial Arts, maintaining Martial Arts at its highest level

PROFESSIONAL ORGANIZATIONS

- American Kajukenbo Association

PERSONAL ACHIEVEMENTS

- One-year PKA kickboxer
- Six times point's fighting champion

MAJOR ACHIEVEMENTS

- Four times Hall of Fame

JONATHAN
EDMONDSON

"Martial arts training has given me the opportunity to see what's in my hands. My abilities, gifts, and talents have fully matured through martial arts training.

leave and went to the dojo and started training in the style of chosen do with Grandmaster Micheal Willett, a biblical martial arts system.

WHY THE MARTIAL ARTS?

I started training in martial arts in 1973 after watching Bruce Lee as the Green Hornets counterpart. Bruce Lee was small in stature yet had the biggest life within martial arts. His techniques were of power and control. He was the answer to my perpetual melancholy of existence because of being bullied growing up in school.

I started training in an after-school program at John F. Kennedy High School in The Bronx, New York. My first instructor's name is Jack Von Schemberger. He was an instructor in the style of Taekwondo. My family moved to Queens, New York, in 1975. I met Grandmaster Doctor Michael, and he has been my instructor, friend, and mentor ever since he was an instructor in the style of GoJu Ryu. Then, I joined the US Army in 1988. In 1991, after fighting in combat on the front lines in Iraq Desert Storm, I came home on

HOW HAS MARTIAL ARTS IMPACTED YOUR LIFE?

My training in martial arts has allowed me to address some of my most inner deficiencies. Self-esteem issues have been addressed, and I have gained the confidence to overcome any obstacle in life. Martial arts training has given me the opportunity to see what's in my hands. My abilities, gifts, and talents have fully matured through martial arts training.

PROFESSIONAL ORGANIZATIONS

- Former board member of Ebony Horsewomen - Hartford, Connecticut
- Former board member of the African American Network of the Poconos
- Former board member of In the Name of Love Food Pantry
- Board member of New Beginning School in Jamaica, West Indies
- Board member of New Beginnings Food Pantry in Orlando, Florida

PERSONAL ACHIEVEMENTS

- Co-author of the book *Man by Choice, Male by Birth*
- Co-author of the book *Fatherhood Fight or Flight*
- Co-author of the book *Elite Martial Artist in America: Secrets to Life, Leadership, and Business, Vol II*
- Author of the book *Help Take My Clothes Off: Just Don't Leave Me Naked and Exposed*
- Proprietor of Super Sunday Power Talk
- Co-host of the Mob Show Podcast
- Overcoming many learning challenges, including not knowing how to read

MAJOR ACHIEVEMENTS

- 9 Time Action Martial Arts Hall of Fame Inductee
  ◊ 2011 Golden Exemplary Dedication to the Martial Arts
  ◊ 2013 Excellence in Teaching the Martial Arts
  ◊ 2015 Ambassador of Goodwill to the Martial Arts
  ◊ 2016 Military Contributions as a Martial Artist
  ◊ 2019 Esteemed Martial Artists
  ◊ 2020 Recognition as a Humanitarian
  ◊ 2021 Elite Esteemed Warrior
  ◊ 2023 Excellence in Teaching Martial Arts
  ◊ 2024 Platinum Lifetime Contributions in the Martial Arts.
- Universal Martial Arts Hall of Fame Supreme Sokeship Council inductee, 2015
- African American Network of the Poconos Man of Valor Award, 2015
- Community Activist Pocono, Pennsylvania
- Cast member of the musical *So Amazing*

TRAINING INFORMATION

- Belt Ranks & Martial Arts Styles: 8th Dan-Chosen-do System of Karate
- Instructors/Influencers: Jack Von Schemberger, Grandmaster Micheal Willett
- Birthplace/Growing Up: Bronx NYC /Queens NYC
- Yrs. In the Martial Arts: 49 years
- Yrs. Instructing: 35 years
- Instructor, Motivational speaker

JOHN
FALVO

" Martial arts has been my steadfast companion, guiding me through life's highs and lows.

WHY THE MARTIAL ARTS?

I got started in martial arts because I was a quiet, timed, and shy person who lacked confidence. I wanted to know how to protect and look after myself, be physically strong, and be in good fitness.

Bruce Lee was a big inspiration, especially watching all the martial arts movies that my local video store had on offer to rent. He was so fit, fast, and powerful, and he was often overlooked and underestimated, but he never gave up the fight.

Once I got started in martial arts, I soon started to learn that there was so much more to martial arts than I ever thought. It was not just kicking and punching but a whole new world revolving around mental strength, self-discipline, respect and camaraderie.

Studying martial arts inspired me to dream of one day achieving my black belt. I didn't have natural ability; I needed to be more coordinated and always struggled to put things together, especially my katas. A martial artist, to me, was someone humble, disciplined, strong, respectful, dedicated, loyal, and courageous. It only took one lesson for me to embark on this journey. It has taught me so much about myself physically, mentally, and spiritually.

HOW HAS MARTIAL ARTS IMPACTED YOUR LIFE?

Studying martial arts has impacted my life by allowing me to achieve things that I never dreamt possible. It has empowered me and taught me to never give up on working hard to achieve things. To persevere no matter how hard things are on the mind or body.

From my teenage years to the present, martial arts has been my steadfast companion, guiding me through life's highs and lows. It has instilled in me a passion and drive, propelling me to achieve goals I once deemed impossible. It has not only transformed me physically and mentally but also paved the way for me to become an instructor, a role I cherish.

Now, passing on what martial arts gives me to help others achieve the same and set their own personal goals. It has allowed me to overpower and beat insecurities in life. Becoming both mentally and physically stronger than I ever have been. For all of this I am truly grateful to my Instructor Master Gatt and our Master Chief Instructor Grand Master Donato.

TRAINING INFORMATION

- Belt Ranks & Martial Arts Styles: Tae Kwon Do Kwon Bop Do Federation - 5th Degree Blackbelt, Bunbu Ichi Nihon JuJitsu - Shodan 1st Dan, Ben Kan Ryuha Nihon Kobu Justu - Shodan 1st Dan

- Instructors/Influencers: Grandmaster Master Ell Gatt, Grand Master Nick Donato

- Birthplace/Growing Up: Annandale, Sydney, Australia

- Yrs. In the Martial Arts: 34 years

- Yrs. Instructing: 29 years

- Instructor

PROFESSIONAL ORGANIZATIONS

- Kwon Bop Do Federation

- International Tae Kwon Do Confederation

PERSONAL ACHIEVEMENTS

- Being promoted to Technical Advisor in 1997 and also being part of the Senior Board of Instructors

MAJOR ACHIEVEMENTS

- World Head of Family Sokeship Council - Instructor of the Year Award 2010

Become an
AMAA MEMBER!

AL FARRIS

" *My philosophy is to Touch Lives, Change Lives, and Save Lives!*

WHY THE MARTIAL ARTS?

Growing up, GM Farris lived in a low-income and high-crime community. The area he lived in constantly had violence, drugs, assaults, and people just trying to get by in life. He watched the police and criminals exchange gunfire at times, thinking this was normal. He was jumped and attacked growing up. He was bullied all through school. He had an extraordinarily strong motivation to learn martial arts.

After searching for a martial arts system, GM Farris found a Shaolin Kung Fu school to begin his training. He realized his training would be a lifelong journey. He also realized that one system might not be enough for every situation that would be encountered in life. Hence, he realized that mixed martial arts was the path for him to follow.

Forty-four years later, GM Farris is beyond thankful for the instruction, teaching, and systems he has been blessed to learn.

Grandmaster Farris serves as a Commander of the Training Division for his law enforcement agency. He is a Law Enforcement Instructor, Rangemaster, Senior Firearms & Head Defensive Tactics Instructor, and Self-Defense Instructor. He holds three Master Use of Force certifications in law enforcement and instructs the Force Continuum. He has been recognized as a Use of Force Subject Matter Expert. Grandmaster Farris currently trains first responders, law enforcement, and various United States military units. Their training includes de-escalation, defensive tactics, use of force, less lethal, and stopping a threat. The classes range from basic, intermediate, advanced, tactical, force-on-force, and edged weapons. Grandmaster Farris provides them with training in a range of styles and systems. He is certified to instruct in over seventy specific areas of law enforcement and martial arts applications. Grandmaster Farris has had the opportunity to train with and train agents/officers from the Bureau of Alcohol Tobacco and Firearms (ATF), Federal Bureau of Investigation (FBI), Drug Enforcement Administration (DEA), United States Secret Service (USSS), United States Marshals Service (USMS), local, state, federal law enforcement agencies, federal law enforcement agencies, swat teams, dignitary protection teams, training divisions, and various agencies throughout the United States of America during his tenure. Many of his training courses and instruction to these specific units are confidential. The training he provides is based upon real-life, real-world, combat-proven applications.

His students and peers refer to him as The Gold Standard in the World of Martial Arts Applications.

Grandmaster Farris is currently one of the highest-ranking martial artists in the world who actively serves as a law enforcement officer.

HOW HAS MARTIAL ARTS IMPACTED YOUR LIFE?

Studying martial arts made such a positive impact early on in Grandmaster Farris's life. Once he began a career in law enforcement, he could see a tremendous need for various forms of martial arts training. As an officer, he would run into criminals who refused arrest and seemed to feel no pain. The bad guys do not always comply with law enforcement officer requests. GM Farris realized that an officer must be well-rounded in this career. Our adversary may see us as a hurdle or roadblock to freedom. So, with all respect, it is quite clear that law enforcement officers will need a complete, well-rounded martial arts system or defensive tactics system! Martial arts have saved his life on numerous occasions. Once he began to see how much of an impact it had had on him and others, Grandmaster Farris developed a unique system for law enforcement, military, and first responders. He devoted decades to studying, analyzing, and developing a system that has worked very well. He incorporated the techniques utilized in self-defense to contain, restrain, control, and submit violent individuals.

They would then be taken into custody without injury to the officer or threat most of the time - a unique system for a warrior of today. Hence, the Modern Warrior System 360 came about and has saved many lives in law enforcement and the community. The training he has provided during the civil unrest, protests,

TRAINING INFORMATION

- Belt Ranks & Martial Arts Styles: Shaolin Kung Fu,10th Degree Black Belt, Grandmaster, The Modern Warrior System 360, Mixed Martial Arts, Grandmaster-Soke, International Taekwondo Confederation, 9th Dan — Grandmaster, Jiu Jitsu, Law Enforcement Instructor, Edged Weapons, Law Enforcement Instructor, Krav Maga, Law Enforcement Instructor

- Instructors/Influencers: Grandmaster Paul Newton, Grandmaster Henry Cook, Rokudan Earl Cheatham, Grandmaster Kong Young II, Grandmaster G Ong, Grandmaster Rick Stanford, Grandmaster John Pellegrini, Various instructors, masters, and grandmasters over the last 44 years

- Birthplace/Growing Up: USA

- Yrs. In the Martial Arts: 44 years

- Yrs. Instructing: 43 years

- School Owner at The Modern Warrior System 360 - designed for law enforcement, military, and first responders.

PROFESSIONAL ORGANIZATIONS

- World Taekwondo Order (WTO)

- International Taekwondo Confederation (ITC)

- Vice President Tactical Defense Solutions

- Director of the ITC Law Enforcement Board

- Co-Director of the ITC Advisory Board

- Co-Director of the Tactical Technology Board.

- Martial Arts Hall of Fame

- Martial Arts Hall of Fame, Alliance

- United States Martial Arts Hall of Fame

- International Council of Grandmasters

- International Congress of Grandmasters

- Action Martial Arts Hall of Honors

- Master's and Pioneer, the American Martial Arts Foundation

- American Freestyle Karate Association (AFKA)

- International Martial Arts Head Founders Grandmasters Council,

- International Martial Arts Council of America

- American Martial Arts Alliance Foundation

HOW HAS MARTIAL ARTS IMPACTED YOUR LIFE? (CONTINUED)

and riots over the last three years has saved many lives. He has assisted in developing a program to stop active shooters in our country that have gone national. Grandmaster Farris believes in helping people. His philosophy is clear and straightforward, "Touch Lives, Change Lives, and Save Lives!"

LAW ENFORCEMENT AWARDS

- The Medal of Honor
- The Medal of Valor
- The Veteran of Foreign Wars Award
- The Millennium Maker Award
- The Medal of Honor
- Deputy of the Year Award
- Life-Saving Award
- Exemplary Performance

PROFESSIONAL ORGANIZATIONS

- American Martial Arts Alliance Foundation, Board of Advisors
- Combat Hapkido
- The International Spartan Hall of Warriors

PERSONAL ACHIEVEMENTS

- Achieved a Black Belt in Shaolin Kung Fu
- Practicing martial arts for 44 Years
- Serving in Law Enforcement for 39 Years with Dignity, Honor, and Pride
- Top Gun Award
- Bachelors in Business and Marketing
- Masters in Philosophy
- Ph.D. in Philosophy

MAJOR ACHIEVEMENTS

- Shaolin Kung Fu, 10th Degree Black Belt, Grandmaster
- The Modern Warrior System 360, 10th Degree Black Belt, Grandmaster - Soke
- International Taekwondo Confederation, 9th Dan - Grandmaster
- Inducted into the Martial Arts Hall of Fame
- Inducted into the Hall of Heroes
- Inducted into the United States Martial Arts Hall of Fame
- Inducted into the Action Martial Arts Hall of Honors, Modern Warrior Award
- Master's and Pioneers, the American Martial Arts Foundation.
- Grandmaster of the Year Award
- International Grandmaster of the Year Award
- Law Enforcement Defensive Tactics Instructor of the Year Award
- American Freestyle Karate Association (AFKA), Modern Warrior Award
- Law Enforcement Officer of the Year
- Grandmaster of the Year - Law Enforcement
- Officer of the Year Award - Law Enforcement
- AMAA Changing Lives Award
- Law Enforcement Superior Leadership

PUBLICATIONS

- 2020 - Action Martial Arts Hall of Honors World History Book by Sifu Alan Goldberg & Grandmaster Jessie Bowen

- 2020 - American Martial Arts Alliance Foundation Martial Arts Masters & Pioneers - Tribute to Grandmaster Chuck Norris by Grandmaster Jessie Bowen - Inclusion and Cover Feature.

- 2021 - Action Martial Arts Hall of Honors World History Book by Sifu Alan Goldberg & Grandmaster Jessie Bowen

- 2021 - American Martial Arts Alliance Foundation the Changing Lives Series - Tribute to Grandmaster Ernie Reyes by Grandmaster Jessie Bowen - Inclusion and Cover Feature.

- 2022 - Action Martial Arts Hall of Honors World History Book by Sifu Alan Goldberg & Grandmaster Jessie Bowen

- 2022 - American Martial Arts Alliance Foundation, the Changing Lives Series - Tribute to Grandmaster Bill "Superfoot" Wallace by Grandmaster Jessie Bowen - Inclusion and Cover Feature.

- 2023 - Action Martial Arts Hall of Honors World History Book by Sifu Alan Goldberg & Grandmaster Jessie Bowen

- 2023 - Elite Publications' Elite Martial Artists in America: Secrets to Life Leadership & Business, Volume 1 - #1 International Bestselling Co-author

MAJOR ACHIEVEMENTS

- Officer of the Year

- American Freestyle Karate Association (AFKA), Law Enforcement Officer of the Decade

- Grandmaster of the Year Award Hall of Honors

- Honorable Elite Modern Warrior Award Hall of Honors

- World Taekwondo Organization, Hall of Honor, Leaders of Martial Arts Award

- The American Martial Arts Alliance Who's Who in the Martial Arts Metaverse Museum

- The International Taekwondo Confederation (ITC) promoted him to 9th Dan and Grandmaster. The ITC appointed him as the Director of the Law Enforcement Board, Co-Director of the Advisory Board, and Co-Director of the Tactical Technology Board. Grandmaster Farris now serves as the ITC Vice President of Tactical Defense Solutions.

- Grandmaster Farris serves the United States Martial Arts Hall of Fame on the International Martial Arts Head Grandmasters Council.

- Grandmaster Farris serves on the American Martial Arts Alliance Foundation Board of Advisors. These are all honors of a lifetime.

PUBLICATIONS (CONTINUED)

- 2023 - American Martial Arts Alliance Foundation Who's Who in the Martial Arts - Tribute to Grandmaster Cynthia Rothrock by Grandmaster Jessie Bowen - Inclusion and Cover Feature.

- 2024 - Action Martial Arts Hall of Honors World History Book - Tribute to Soke Michael DePasquale by Sifu Alan Goldberg & Grandmaster Jessie Bowen

- 2024 - Elite Publications' Elite Martial Artists in America: Secrets to Life Leadership & Business, Volume 2 - #1 International Bestselling Co-author

ALF FERLITO

> *Studying Martial Arts has been an enormous mental, physical, and spiritual awakening.*

A couple of months went by, and I went stir-crazy. I had to do something. I worked part-time at my weekend job, so I didn't fall into any state of depression or anxiety. Most people know that being left alone with ill thoughts can lead to trouble.

At that point, due to the major disruption to my life, was lost and had little direction until I met someone who would change my life forever. She gave me the courage to begin a journey. We can laugh about it now, but I was a bit of a handful at first! Angry at life. It was not easy for them at all, and it was an absolute mission for my instructors to get my head right. But, almost two decades down the track, here I am. I am grateful to Grand Master Donato, Master Gatt, and everyone else at Personal Defence Studios The Pit Martial Arts Centre, for giving me the great life I've led all these years after beginning my transformation.

WHY THE MARTIAL ARTS?

I started martial arts at a time in my life when, I could now confidently say, I was truly lost and had no direction. Basically, I met great people who encouraged me to embark on the martial arts journey. It sounds cliche, but every bit of it is true!

In the early 2000s, I was a mature aged university student studying psychology and sociology. It was my dream to further my education and expand my mind. Unfortunately, near the end of my degree, I was diagnosed with a life-threatening illness that halted any plans of me graduating. The only thing I was allowed to do was recover, rest, and regroup.

HOW HAS MARTIAL ARTS IMPACTED YOUR LIFE?

Studying martial arts has been an enormous mental, physical, and spiritual awakening. It has made me evolve and be more in tune with myself, the world around me, and the ones I love.

It has taught me that I'm a struggler, which may seem negative, but in truth is a great blessing because the lesson has been that I can overcome anything.

It has taught me that I'm not the most talented, not the smartest and not at all better than anyone else. But with the help of others, a great community to back you and having a mindset of service to others we all can be great.

It has made me appreciative of what great people like Grand Master Donato and Master Gatt do for individuals in society and for society as a whole.

It has taught me that without our great leaders, the great community of Personal Defence Studios The Pit Martial Arts Centre, and those people who truly understand me, I would not be half the person I am today.

TRAINING INFORMATION

- Belt Ranks & Martial Arts Styles: Kwon Bop Do TKD — 4th Degree Black Belt, Japanese Weaponry — Kobujutsu (Ben Kan Ryuha) — 1st Degree Black Belt, Japanese Ju Jitsu (Ben Kan Ryuha) — 2nd Kyu, Tai Chi Qigong — Level 2 Certificate

- Instructors/Influencers: Grand Master Nick Donato, Master Ell Gatt

- Birthplace/Growing Up: Sydney NSW, AUS

- Yrs. In the Martial Arts: 19 years

- Yrs. Instructing: 15 years

- Instructor

PROFESSIONAL ORGANIZATIONS

- Personal Defence Studios The Pit Martial Arts Centre

PERSONAL ACHIEVEMENTS

- 2020 GM Gary Wasniewski's International Martial Arts Instructor Award.

- Inducted in the 15th Anniversary London Hall of Fame for contributions to martial arts worldwide.

- 2023 World Head of Family/Sokeship Council award — Orlando, Florida - 31st Annual International Event

- Outstanding Instructor Award — GM F Sanchez & PDS International

MAJOR ACHIEVEMENTS

- Being in service to others in an amazing community - Personal Defence Studios The Pit Martial Arts Centre

Become an
**AMAA
MEMBER!**

RANDALL FLAHERTY

"

Martial arts has absolutely impacted my life. It has increased my overall confidence and raised my mental alertness regarding tactical training.

WHY THE MARTIAL ARTS?

Grandmaster Randall Flaherty's father, Robert Flaherty, verbally planted in him mental pictures of excellent martial arts practitioners who possessed skills of incredible accuracy, hand speed, and power, and others who were skillful at breaking bricks, or as Randall's father put it, "able to walk through walls."

Needless to say, the stories of human speed development, and the stories of crashing through walls with extraordinary human power, and the descriptions of precision fighting techniques planted the seeds for learning and developing such skills in Randall's eight-year-old brain. His father, created a "superhero image" of martial artists who possessed incredible skills, especially in his stories of Kenpo Karate in action.

Randall was a shy kid and, at times, would ask his father to sign him up for karate classes. Most often,

Randall was met with the same answer, "NO, you might misuse the art." His father refused to sign him up for karate classes because he thought his son might bully others and misuse karate. Randall just couldn't understand why his father would think he would misuse the art by hurting others when he himself would run from bullies! It wasn't until much later in his martial arts journey and life that Randall realized that his father was instilling in him the proper mindset for learning and developing. In fact, many humbling quotes from his father still resonate with Randall today, like the quotes: Son, it doesn't matter how big (good) you get; there is always someone better," and "Wherever there are two or three that are known, there is always one who is unknown." A son's continued response to the previous quote: "Train hard, in case you ever meet the unknown!"

Randall started his training in Kentucky in 1979 and joined his first official karate studio called the "DOJO," where he was introduced to basic karate movements, like the no telegraphic slip-kicks.

In 1980, after moving from Kentucky to California, Randall joined Kenpo Karate, Kung fu, and Judo classes at the International Martial Arts Academy, located in San Jose, California. At the Academy he received both group and private lessons directly under the tutelage of the Chief Instructor and Owner, Angel Martial.

In 1985, Randall received his 1st Degree Black Belt from Angel Martial's International Martial Arts Academy (IMAA). Before receiving his Black Belt, Randall was required by the business owner and other instructors to break 3 boards stacked with a single reverse punch or chop. The reverse punch was chosen and the Black Belt was earned!

A year later, Randall was featured in local newspapers and a Spanish television commercial with his life-long martial arts friend and martial arts brother, Ricardo Chaverri. At this time, the kata performed by Randall, to stimulate public martial arts interest, was called "Mass Attacks."

He studied Wushu Kung fu in 1987 directly under the tutelage of Master Jin Sun Ding. According to the Master, "If you lose a competition, then you are not recognized within the Wushu Institute." Randall's Wushu Master Instructor never lost a competition.

In 1988, he trained at the Jet Center in Los Angeles, California, under the instruction of kickboxing champion fighters, legends, and movie actors. The time Randall spent training at the center was priceless and would never be forgotten.

He opened his first martial arts school, Flaherty's Kenpo Karate Association, or "FKKA" in 1991. Located at 225 LaPala Shopping Center in San Jose, CA., the FKKA offered family self-defense training to people from all walks of life and from most age groups.

In 1996, he opened another martial arts business, located on Piedmont road in San Jose, and was featured in local Bay Area magazines and newspapers.

In 2000, he opened another martial arts business, located on Toyon Ave., while at the same time, developing after-school karate programs for elementary school-age students, continuing the process of developing effective and efficient FKKA self-defense programs for participants of all ages.

In 2007, Randall moved Flaherty's Kenpo Karate Association to Stockton, California, and in 2012, he

TRAINING INFORMATION

- Belt Ranks & Martial Arts Styles: Kenpo, Karate, Judo Kung fu, Boxing, Kickboxing, Self-defense, Tae Kwon Do, and Arnis. Current Rank: 10th Degree Black Belt
- Instructors/Influencers: Robert Flaherty, Angel Martial, Roland Gonzales, Benny Urquidez, Bill Wallace, Jin Sun Ding and many others not mentioned
- Birthplace/Growing Up: San Francisco, San Jose, and Kentucky
- Yrs. In the Martial Arts: 45+ years
- Yrs. Instructing: 42+ years
- School owner at Flaherty's Kenpo Karate

PROFESSIONAL ORGANIZATIONS

- Flaherty's Kenpo Karate Association (Team FKKA)
- Better Business Bureau (A+ Rating), since 2010 & 2023 Torch Award recipient
- Original USA Martial Arts Hall of Fame, Inductee
- Action Martial Arts Magazine, Inductee
- American Freestyle Karate Association, Inductee
- Professional Karate Association (i.e., PKA Worldwide), Lifetime Member

PERSONAL ACHIEVEMENTS

- Celebrating 45 years in the martial arts (1979 to 2024)
- Achieving 10th Degree Black Belt (Grandmaster Status)
- Promoting over 100 Black Belt Graduates
- Teaching and interacting with, over the years, tens of thousands of excellent parents, families, students, and instructors.
- Meeting with and supporting wonderful Hall of Fame Organizations, like the American Martial Arts Alliance Foundation (AMAAF), along with many others.

MAJOR ACHIEVEMENTS

- Earned a 1st Degree Black Belt in 1984 at the International Martial Arts Academy, located in San Jose, CA.
- In 1986, became the Sales Manager and Senior Trainer for the International Martial Arts Academy.
- In 1991, opened the first Flaherty's Kenpo Karate business, located in San Jose, CA.

became the founder of the updated Flaherty's "Brotherhood" and "Sisterhood" of Arnis. (A Filipino stick, swords, and knife fighting system.)

In 2022, Grandmaster Randall Flaherty received the American Martial Arts Alliance's "Changing Lives Series Legacy Award." It always gives the Grandmaster pleasure attending the AMAA events and visiting his martial arts friends from around the world.

In 2023, there were 24 finalists, and Flaherty's Kenpo Karate was selected as one out of five businesses to receive the Better Business Bureau's of Northeast California's Inaugural Torch Award for Ethics," presented during the BBB's Annual Award Ceremony event night, located in Sacramento, CA.

HOW HAS MARTIAL ARTS IMPACTED YOUR LIFE?

As stated in a few volumes of the American Martial Alliance books, along with other news articles and publications, and over my decades of training and teaching, martial arts has absolutely impacted my life. It has increased my overall confidence and raised my mental alertness regarding tactical training. Building on the detailed skills of Kenpo Karate insights, principles, theories, and concepts, along with both tournament and

MAJOR ACHIEVEMENTS

- In 1996, earned a 6th Degree Black Belt from the International Martial Arts Academy, San Jose, CA., and opened a new business location.

- In 2000, developed, organized and managed for six years the "Young Karate Masters Program" for elementary school age children in the Alum Rock School District.

- In 2004, received the USA Martial Arts Hall of Fame "Master of the Year" award.

- In 2005, received "Honorary Chairman" and "Businessman of the Year" National Leadership Awards from the U.S. Congress.

- In 2006, received the USA Martial Arts Hall of Fame, "Pioneer Award."

- In 2008, received the USA Martial Arts Hall of Fame, "Silver Life Award."

- In 2011, received the "Distinguished Service to California Award" from the state capital, Sacramento, CA. In addition, Flaherty's Kenpo Karate was voted #1 for the "Best Martial Arts Studio" of San Joaquin County, CA.

- In 2012, as a result of years of degree promotions, dedication, and commitment earned 10th Degree Black Belt (i.e., "Grandmaster" status), and received the USA Martial Arts Hall of Fame, "Kenpo Grandmaster of the Year" award.

- In 2013, Flaherty's Kenpo Karate Association received the "Best of Stockton Award." According to the Stockton Award Program Management, nationwide, only 1 in 70 (1.4%) 2013 Award recipients qualified as winners.

- In 2016, celebrated 25 years in the martial arts business industry as "Flaherty's Kenpo Karate" (aka: Team FKKA).

- In 2017, received the USA Martial Arts Hall of Fame, "Grandmaster of the Year" award. In addition, received a beautiful three Samurai Sword Set with stand, and Tonfa Set from the Hall of Fame CEO and owner.

HOW HAS MARTIAL ARTS IMPACTED YOUR LIFE? (CONTINUED)

street fighting applications also found in other martial arts systems, has had an enormous impact on my life.

Like millions of martial arts students worldwide, I have chosen to learn Kenpo Karate because it is a skill that fits best for my individual self-defense needs and is so versatile. Those who have studied a variety of martial arts systems tend to come back to Kenpo, seeing it as a personal and practical style that works well in many different circumstances. That's why I decided, back in 1991, to open a business entity called: "Flaherty's Kenpo Karate." The positive relational impact I have gained through meeting and training with outstanding people from all walks of life with consistency, dedication, perseverance and patience for learning is priceless, gratifying, and rewarding. And, as always, my ongoing advice as FKKA'S Grandmaster to anyone beginning in the martial arts and to our young future leaders is: "Don't give up. Keep going, and one day, your accomplishments will positively impact many lives, especially your own."

On behalf of the entire FKKA team, we at Flaherty's Kenpo Karate want to offer a warm thank you to the entire staff of the American Martial Arts Alliance Foundation for the many induction years, book inclusion opportunities, and excellent awards. Grandmaster Randall Flaherty is proud to take part in this year's "AMAA Legacy Book 10th Anniversary Edition."

MAJOR ACHIEVEMENTS

- In 2019, received crystal & plaque awards for "Best in Martial Arts Training for Eight Consecutive Years" by the Business Hall of Fame (Presented by Stockton Award Program). In addition, became inducted into the American Martial Arts Alliance (i.e., AMAA) Masters & Pioneers Autobiography Program. Flaherty's Kenpo Karate Academy was again voted #1 for "Best in Martial Arts Training" of San Joaquin County. And to finish this year with a bang, in December, Grandmaster Flaherty's students presented him with a monumental "Award of Excellence" for a lifetime of inspiration, motivation, and outstanding teaching.

- In 2020, named "Ambassador of the Year" and "School of the Year." by the American Martial Arts Alliance, and was also inducted into the American Freestyle Karate Association Hall of Fame, USA Martial Arts Hall of Fame, and the Stockton's Business Hall of Fame. In addition, received a "Distinguished Renowned Martial Artist Award" from Action Martial Arts Magazine.

- In 2022, was inducted into the American Martial Arts Alliance's "Who's Who in the Martial Arts Hall of Honors" and received the "Changing Lives Series Legacy" Award.

- In 2023, received from the Action Martial Arts Magazine Hall of Honors a certificate of "Respect and Honor," along with the Magazine's "21st Annual Trophy and Banner." In addition, Flaherty's Kenpo Karate Association won the 1st Annual Better Business Bureau of Northeast California's Inaugural "Torch Awards" for Ethics.

Become an
AMAA MEMBER!

REBECCA
FORREST

"

My goal for the future is to be able to impact others' growth in martial arts and their personal lives.

WHY THE MARTIAL ARTS?

I was introduced to Isshinryu Karate on October 29, 2009, when I met Master Kyle Forrest. He told me that he owned a karate dojo, Kyle's Isshinryu Academy, and I told him that I would tell my son about it, who was 12 at the time. My son said he would like to try it, so we went to his first class.

As time went on, I became the Office Director for Kyle's Isshinryu Academy, so I could see everyone training and learning. I started my training in 2012 because I was always going and supporting our students who were competing at the time, and I decided that I wanted to try it out, too. I ended up training hard and attending my very first tournament at 41 in 2013. I won two fourth place trophies, and after that, the tournament bug must have bitten me because I was ready for the next tournament. I trained hard and helped to motivate our other students who were training for the upcoming tournaments. The more I trained, the more knowledge I received. I began to think about when I was younger and wished I had

found karate back then. If I had started training back when I was a teenager, I would have had more courage and confidence to do the things that I do now. I do things now that I would never have done back then, all because I had no courage, no confidence in myself, was shy, and didn't talk that much.

Now that I have been in martial arts for quite some time, I am thankful for the teachings I have received and am still receiving, which, in return, I can share with our students. My experiences with my training, learning, and competing in tournaments are something that I share with them every class. That is what really makes me feel accomplished in what I do. I can teach what I know, and the students can gain more knowledge from a different perspective. Watching them grow in their training warms my heart because they are our future. Without new students to learn, martial arts of any style cannot have a future. Now, I am driven and motivated to be a good role model for our up-and-coming students as they train to be better, which reinforces the motto that I came up with, "Train To Be Better."

As I kick into 2024 (pun intended), I'm so excited about this year due to all of the interesting things that will be happening. I look forward to many more years of being able to be that role model for students and instructors as well.

HOW HAS MARTIAL ARTS IMPACTED YOUR LIFE?

Studying my Isshinryu Karate style has impacted my life by giving me the confidence to achieve many things that I would have never thought were even possible for me to do. Knowing that I have the training that I have gives me the confidence to go out places by myself and not worry about whether I can protect myself and others. Learning from more experienced master-level instructors is such a wonderful experience that helps out with my training as well. All of the knowledge I am gaining is helping me to help the young future of martial arts to be a better form of themselves and to give them the confidence and courage they need to become better karatekas.

As long as I am involved in martial arts, it will continue to grow within me, transforming me into an inspiration to all. My goal for the future is to be able to impact others' growth in martial arts and their personal lives.

TRAINING INFORMATION

- Belt Ranks & Martial Arts Styles: Isshinryu Karate — San-Dan
- Instructors/Influencers: Master Kyle Forrest
- Birthplace/Growing Up: High Point, NC / Harrison, TN
- Yrs. In the Martial Arts: 12 years
- Yrs. Instructing: 1 years

PROFESSIONAL ORGANIZATIONS

- United States Isshinryu Karate Association (U.S.I.K.A.)

PERSONAL ACHIEVEMENTS

- 4th place for Kata (Forms) & 4th Place for Kumite (Sparring) Beginner Adult M/F Age 30+ - 2013
- Contribution to K.I.A. Award — 2013, 2014
- K.I.A. Adult Female Kata of the Year — 2016, 2018
- K.I.A. Adult Competitor of the Year — 2015 - 2019, 2022 - 2023
- Sempai's Award — 2022
- 1st place Weapons/Division and 2nd place Kata at Autumn in the Mountains Tournament — Hendersonville, NC, September 23, 2023
- K.I.A. Female Competitor of the Year Award — 2023
- K.I.A. Female Kata of the Year Award - 2023

MAJOR ACHIEVEMENTS

- 1st and 2nd place, Weapons/Kata Martial Arts Women's Champion, Valentine's Classic- 2014/2015.
- 1st place in the division, 1st place in Kata, 2nd place in Weapons and Forms (Kata) Grand Champion at the Hazelhurst, GA, Tournament - 2017.
- Gold/Silver medals - NC State Champ in Weapons and Kata at the Powerade State Games, Underbelts Division - 2019
- Sho-Dan (1st Degree Black Belt) March 16, 2019
- K.I.A. Hall of Fame Award — December 7, 2019
- Gold/Silver medals - NC State Champ in Weapons and Kata at the BODYARMOR State Games, Black Belt Division -2021
- Ni-Dan (2nd Degree Black Belt) December 22, 2022
- San-Dan (3rd Degree Black Belt) May 27, 2023
- Female Forms Competitor of the Year Award — Isshinryu Karate, 2023 (This award is recognized worldwide. Received at the World Head of Family Sokeship Council Awards Banquet May 27, 2023, Orlando, Florida)

JON FRASER

"
I have proven that your honest-to-God belief in Jesus Christ, our Lord and Savior, can change a person's life beyond belief!

lost both legs. After nearly a year in the hospital and six months in a wheelchair, Jon was told he may never walk again. But his stubborn Scotch-Irish descent took hold, and he worked his way to crutches. Jon, who had a medical disability, retired from the Air Force shortly thereafter.

Being a construction worker by trade, and due to the extent of his injuries, Jon knew he needed to further his education and attend college. He would be the first college graduate in his family to graduate with an Associate's Degree in General Education.

Jon married his high school sweetheart, and they had one child. They relocated to New Hampshire where he earned his New Hampshire Real Estate License. He practiced real estate from 1976 to 1978 at Smith and Dearborn Real Estate Company in Manchester, New Hampshire, where he was recognized and awarded for his salesmanship. In 1979, Jon obtained his Broker's License. He then went on to open his own company (Tanglewood), where he employed a nice-sized sales team. He bought and sold investment properties. He also purchased large parcels of land and then divided them into house lots.

His injuries were still quite bothersome to him; Jon was inspired when he read an article about a

WHY THE MARTIAL ARTS?

Master Fraser's interest in Oriental Martial Arts began in 1969 while stationed at Kadena Air Force Base in Okinawa. He had always had a fascination with oriental culture and philosophy. His love of the culture grew, and he volunteered for assigned to U-Tapae Air Force Base in Thailand where he loaded bombs on and flew aboard B-52 bombers to Vietnam. Thailand was beautiful, and he was impressed by the reverence of the monastery monks.

In 1971, while home on leave from Thailand, he was a passenger in a very serious auto accident and almost

TRAINING INFORMATION

- Belt Ranks & Martial Arts Styles: Tae Kwon Do - 5th Degree Black Belt, Seibu-Do - 9th Degree Black Belt, Dim-Mak - Certificate of Instructor for the USA

- Instructors/Influencers: Master Richard Higgins, Grand Master Donald Swansey, Master Steven Burton, George Dillman, Rick Moneymaker, Art Mason, Mantak Chia, and others

- Birthplace/Growing Up: Arlington, MA / Londonderry, NH

- Yrs. In the Martial Arts: 43 years

- Yrs. Instructing: 20+ years

PROFESSIONAL ORGANIZATIONS

- American Oriental Bodywork Therapy Assoc.

- Associated Bodywork & Massage Professionals

- Martial Arts of China Historical Society

- Who's Who in the Martial Arts Elite

- World Martial Arts Hall of Fame

- World Martial Arts Alliance

- World Head of Family Sokeship Council

- United States Kido Federation

- United States Martial Arts Association

- National Assoc. of Holistic Health Practitioners

- National Qi Gong Association

- International Assoc. Martial Arts & Oriental Medicine

- Action Martial Arts Magazine & Hall of Honors

- #2 Presidential Recognition: Donald Trump and Bill Clinton

PERSONAL ACHIEVEMENTS

- Master Fraser greatly overcame his doctor's verbiage of being unable to walk again

MAJOR ACHIEVEMENTS

- Master Fraser has proved that your honest-to-God belief in Jesus Christ, our Lord and Savior, can change a person's life beyond belief!

gentleman with one leg who pursued and obtained his black belt in karate. Jon's first class in martial arts was Tae Kwon Do at the local YMCA, where he worked relentlessly up to 5 days a week, attended tournaments, did demos for charity, and broke boards and cement blocks. Jon accomplished his first black belt in 1985. He delved into every martial arts book he could. Despite his medical condition, he placed first in forms, breaking, and black belt fighting at many New England Invitational Championship Tournaments.

In 1985, Jon began teaching martial arts in the evening in Londonderry, New Hampshire. He opened other locations in Bedford and Hooksett, New Hampshire. He studied meditation under Master Mantak Chia of Thailand and Sifu John Loupos of Massachusetts. Jon's insatiable desire to pursue more, and in 1987, he received his 2nd degree black belt in Tae Kwon Do.

Jon left the YMCA to further his studies. He studied Tai Chi Chuan under Dr. Yang Jwing Ming of Massachusetts. Traveling often to and from California, he studied Jin Shin Do with Iona Teeguarden and to Indiana and Florida to study Tuite under 9th Degree George Dillman and 9th Degree Sigh Kufferath, then back to Massachusetts to study Jin Shin Jyutsu under Master Mary Burmeister. Jon educated himself in several courses, including Acupressure, Pressure Points, Natural Healing, and Dim Mak. In 1989, he received his 3rd degree in black belt in Tae Kwon Do.

In 2003, Jon was blessed by becoming a grandfather and now approaches life more slowly. Jon wants to pass his knowledge on to his black belts, his only daughter, who is a 2nd-degree black belt, and his grandson once he is old enough.

In 2005, Jon was double promoted to 7th Degree Master in Seibu-do by his current instructor. Also, on Thanksgiving Day of that year, he had a spiritual revelation he will never forget. After a 10-year sabbatical/hiatus, he reopened his school in Manchester, New Hampshire.

In 1985, Jon began teaching martial arts in the evening in Londonderry, New Hampshire. He opened other locations in Bedford and Hooksett, New Hampshire. He studied meditation under Master Mantak Chia of Thailand and Sifu John Loupos of Massachusetts. Jon's insatiable desire to pursue more, and in 1987, he received his 2nd degree black belt in Tae Kwon Do.

Jon left the YMCA to further his studies. He studied Tai Chi Chuan under Dr. Yang Jwing Ming of Massachusetts. Traveling often to and from California, he studied Jin Shin Do with Iona Teeguarden and to Indiana and Florida to study Tuite under 9th Degree George Dillman and 9th Degree Sigh Kufferath, then back to Massachusetts to study Jin Shin Jyutsu under Master Mary Burmeister. Jon educated himself in several courses, including Acupressure, Pressure Points, Natural Healing, and Dim Mak. In 1989, he received his 3rd degree in black belt in Tae Kwon Do.

In 2003, Jon was blessed by becoming a grandfather and now approaches life more slowly. Jon wants to pass his knowledge on to his black belts, his only daughter, who is a 2nd-degree black belt, and his grandson once he is old enough.

In 2005, Jon was double promoted to 7th Degree Master in Seibu-do by his current instructor. Also, on

Thanksgiving Day of that year, he had a spiritual revelation he will never forget. After a 10-year sabbatical/hiatus, he reopened his school in Manchester, New Hampshire.

Master Jon Fraser currently teaches black belts only. They, in turn, teach many students. Master Fraser's goals for his black belts are:

- Exercise regularly
- Improve their self-defense skills
- Specialize in an area of their choice
- Get educated (Associates, Bachelors, Master, etc.)
- Constantly improve our character
- Prepare them to be excellent Masters

He continues to study under his teacher, Grand Master Donald Swansey, 10th Dan in Seibu-do, and travels less, choosing to devote his time to his black belts.

Become an
AMAA
MEMBER!

TERRY MARK FRASER

"

My role as a martial arts instructor was inevitable, as I was destined to teach...

Montreal. This was truly a blessing as I went on to achieve black belt status and kept climbing the ranks. This catapulted me to venture into other martial arts such as kickboxing, Muay Thai, JuJitsu, wrestling, and a few more.

Although my journey was also to feed the mind, body, and soul, I always remained true to my Taekwondo roots as an instructor; my connection to the T.K.D. program was priceless and very humbling as I was able to give back to the community and continue to encourage and provide an outlet through a "Broken Spirits" program, very humbling to say the least.

I have taught three generations of this awesome community, "Kahnawake," and will continue doing what I love and enjoy. As we all know, there are many elements and learning experiences to martial arts. This journey led me to the combatant scene as a fighter, coach, M.M.A. organization, and sponsorships to many fighters across Canada, Quebec, and the U.S.A.

Martial arts have given me the tools necessary to succeed in life from the beginning. I continue to share the knowledge with those who enter the do-jang and with future generations. Wholeheartedly, this was and still is my destiny!

A s a young man from Georgetown, Guyana, I was fascinated with martial arts and inspired primarily by Bruce Lee. I saw him in every movie he ever made four or five times; I couldn't get enough! I practiced and practiced.

In 1988, I moved to Canada (LaSalle, Quebec), found employment, and saved to join a martial arts school. In 1990, I met my soulmate, Diana, and her family from Kahnawake, Mohawk Territory. Her brother, Mike, was in the process of opening the first "Okwehonwe" Taekwondo School in Kahnawake. He would eventually become my master in Taekwondo. During that time, I enrolled at the Oh Jang T.K.D. school in

HOW HAS MARTIAL ARTS IMPACTED YOUR LIFE?

Martial Arts have impacted my life on a multitude of levels, from discipline and perseverance to improved cognition, flexibility, and physical health. The discipline, training, and skills I've learned from martial arts have given me the tools needed to succeed and become a better version of myself.

My martial arts journey has taught me that everything in life is a process and how to set smaller goals as I worked towards bigger ones successfully. With that being said, my role as a martial arts instructor was inevitable, as I was destined to teach and provide guidance, knowledge, and support to whoever walked through the dojang.

Although it is not the belt that makes a leader, it was my commitment to help our students evolve beyond what I was teaching them. We cannot change a person's

TRAINING INFORMATION

- Belt Ranks & Martial Arts Styles: W.T.F. - 4th Dan, 1st Nations Taekwondo - 5th Dan, Muay Thai/Vale Tudo/Full Contact Kickboxing - Sr. Instructor, Thai-Ju-Jitsu - Brown Belt, International Budo JuJitsu - 3rd Dan, Muay-Thai -Thai-Boxing-B Level, Egyptian Shidokan-Cert. Expert Instructor M.M.A., Gracie Barra - Brown Belt
- Instructors/Influencers: Grandmaster Oh Jang Yoon, Master Mike Thomas, Vic Theriault, Guivi Sissaouri, Sai Sisomphou, Bruno Fernandez, Jonathan Chambers, Angelo, Nigel Scantlebury
- Birthplace/Growing Up: Georgetown, Guyana, South America
- Yrs. In the Martial Arts: 33 years
- Yrs. Instructing: 30 years
- School owner & Instructor at Fraser Core Fit Training & Wellness Center, Fighter

PROFESSIONAL ORGANIZATIONS

- First Nations T.K.D. Association
- Muay-Thai Bond Nederland
- Thai-Ju-Jitsu Academy
- Raul Soria Academy
- Egyptian Shidokan Federation
- International Budo JuJitsu Federation
- Kukkiwon - World Taekwondo Headquarters
- Mohawk Council of Kahnawake-NAIG
- International Fighting Championships (IFC)
- Pan-Am Games - California
- Olympic Carding - Montreal
- Razorwear M.M.A.
- Summum M.M.A.
- WCA Fighters Series

PERSONAL ACHIEVEMENTS

- Training Center/Business (Owner)
- Razor Wear M.M.A. Training Center
- Razor Wear M.M.A. Fight League
- Summum M.M.A. Fight League
- Razor Wear M.M.A. - M.M.A. Gear & Clothing Line
- FCF Equipment/Pro Wear - M.M.A./ Kickboxing

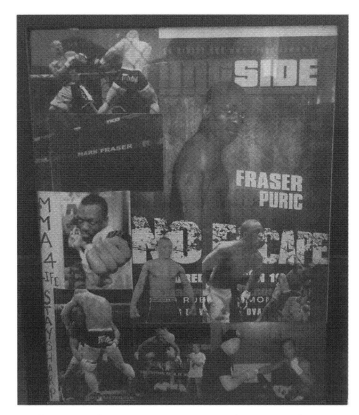

HOW HAS MARTIAL ARTS IMPACTED YOUR LIFE? (CONTINUED)

personality; we can only instill empowerment to make better choices. When teaching, we must remember that it is about the student and not the instructor. A great instructor leads their students to the paths of life, providing them with the tools of knowledge and confidence to stand and walk on their own. We do not always know the positive impacts that we have on individuals, as sometimes students can have a revolving door with commitments. Still, later on in life, when our paths cross again, we meet an adult who is well-structured and in tune with life; this is where we learn that our teachings were carried with us through life's difficult times.

We seldom know the hardships that impact a student and their family; sometimes, it is years later, we learn that as martial arts instructors, the positive impact of cultivating the values attached to life and practice of martial arts has had on ourselves and our students to become productive human beings. This is my way of life and how martial arts has impacted my life, and I am forever grateful to my Master, Mike Thomas, and Grand Master, Oh Yoon, for helping mold me into the man and martial arts instructor I am today!

PERSONAL ACHIEVEMENTS (CONTINUED)

- Fraser Core Fit Training & Wellness Center
- "Broken Spirits" Youth Program

MAJOR ACHIEVEMENTS

Amateur Fight Stats:

- Quebec Muay-Thai - Feather Weight Champ
- Taekwondo - Numerous Colored Belt Tournaments

Pro Fighter Stats:

- Canadian Olympic T.K.D. Carding - 4th Place
- Pan-Am Games - California - Silver & Bronze
- Canadian T.K.D. Nationals - 4th
- Quebec Cup - Silver
- Ontario T.K.D. Classics - 3rd
- IFC Light Weight Champion - Belt
- Night of the Warriors "Super Brawl '95" Champion
- Ringside MMA - Fighter
- TKO MMA - Fighter
- W.C.A. Pro Fighters Series - Fighter

Coach/Trainer/Instructor Stats:

- Sr. Instructor & Coach - 1st Nations TKD Academy
- Head Coach T.K.D. - NAIG 1997 - British Columbia
- Head Coach T.K.D. - NAIG 2002 - Winnipeg
- Head Coach T.K.D. - Canadian Jr. Nationals
- Head Coach T.K.D. - Canadian Sr. Nationals
- Trainer/ Coach - Summum MMA
- Trainer/ Coach - Fight Quest
- Trainer/ Coach - Razorwear M.M.A.
- Trainer/ Coach - W.C.A. Fighters Series
- Trainer - Sports Specific Core Conditioning

Sponsorships - M.M.A. Fighters & Orgs.

- Ringside M.M.A. - Fighters & Organization Sponsor
- U.S.A. Fighters - M.M.A. Sponsorships
- Quebec Fighters - M.M.A. Sponsorships
- Canadian Fighters - M.M.A. Sponsorships

GLENDYMAR
GELVEZ-MARIN

"

Everything about me, every step I take, bears Martial Arts names and teachings.

I can say why I am still here: I believe in this. I believe that what we do may not change the world, but it can change how the people who come to us see the world. Maybe we can save lives. I am not speaking about self -defense; I am talking about the imagination of a child, a teenager looking for an escape, and an adult becoming a child again. I am still here for them, and I am still here to save lives like martial arts saved me one day.

HOW HAS MARTIAL ARTS IMPACTED YOUR LIFE?

I grew up in the world of martial arts, so I could say that at each stage, I had a different impact. This shaped my personality; it gave me discipline, which I apply to my daily life today. Martial arts also gave me dreams and taught me how to lose and the correct way to win.

I can't see martial arts as something external in my life. Everything about me, every step I take, bears martial arts names and teachings.

How did martial arts impact my life? Would you understand me if I told you that he taught me to breathe?

WHY THE MARTIAL ARTS?

I am sure that my destiny was to train in martial arts; I knew it as soon as I became aware of it. I just didn't understand very well which one would be the right one for me. So, one day, I took my mom's hand and showed her a bunch of happy people kicking a sack. I told her I wanted that. I started my practice when I was eight years old. I didn't understand the differences, and I didn't understand that there were thousands of uniforms in the world.

Hapkido chose me with a clear purpose. I discovered that purpose as I grew up and understood that I wanted to travel around the world, teaching and making thousands of children point at me and tell me they wanted to practice martial arts because I inspired them.

What I started is very different from what I dreamed, and what I dreamed is very different from my present. I don't know why I chose to train in martial arts; maybe it was just my instinct.

PROFESSIONAL EXPERIENCE

- International Referee Certification Colombia - 2016
- Bodytech Gym Personal Trainer Instructor and Physical Trainer
- Assistant professor in Hodori Kwan Hapkido GHA Academy - 2007
- Hapkido Directors Koryo Kwan GHA - 2008
- Instructor in martial arts seminar at the National Guard School of Venezuela
- Teacher in physical education and sports at the Ministry of Venezuela
- Teacher in physical education and sports in the Lyceum las Flores Colon Tachira State, Venezuela. Martial arts instructor in Hapkido Yu Kwon Sul Kwan
- Director of the demo team and combat group in Hapkido YKSK
- Assistant Professor at Gold Medal Academy

TRAINING INFORMATION

- Martial Arts Styles & Rank: Hapkido Yu Kwon Sul - 4th Dan, WHU (Hapkidounion) 4th Dan, 3rd Dan in Hapkido GHA, International Taekwondo Gold Medal Academy - 1st Dan, World Taekwondo Federation - 1st Dan
- Instructors/Influencers: Master Jae Mun, Master Victor Osio, Master Emilio Gomez Ariza, Master Zhyramit Junco Gonzalez
- Birthplace/Growing Up: Maracaibo & Tachira, Venezuela
- Yrs. In the Martial Arts: 21 years
- Yrs. Instructing: 15 years
- Instructor

PROFESSIONAL ORGANIZATIONS

- Yu Kwon Sul Kwan
- HWU - World Hapkido Union
- The World Taekwondo Federation - US Oakdo Kwan Association
- Taekwondo Gold Medal Academy

PERSONAL ACHIEVEMENTS

- Degree in Sports Science Education (National University de los Llanos Occidentales Ezequiel Zamora
- Specialization in physical prescription (Bodytech Colombia Gym)
- Specialization in strength and conditioning (University Gran Politécnico Colombiano)

MAJOR ACHIEVEMENTS

- Recognition from part of the major of Michellena Fernando Andrade. Tachira, Venezuela.
- Journal Report El falconiano Deportivo
- Radio Interview on the station radio Full Colonense.
- Interview on the channel TRT TV featuring Glendymar Gelvez Marin
- Online Report for Glendymar Gelvez Marin on April 14, 2020, on the Hapkido World Championship
- Athlete of the Year, Táchira Venezuela
- Recognition to the athlete Glendymar Gelvez Marin by the National Guard as Athlete of the Year - 2014
- Glendymar Gelvez Marin was certificated as an international referee - GHA - 2016
- Outstanding Instructor HKD - USKF Black Belt Hall of Fame

CHAMPIONSHIP PARTICIPATIONS

- Latin American Championship - Colombia 2011
- Panamerican Championship - Brasil 2012
- Worldgames Championship - 2013
- World Championship - 2017
- World Championship - Colombia - 2022
- Knuckle Up Championship - Orlando, Florida - 2023

CHAMPIONSHIP ACHIEVEMENTS

- Pan American Championship, Cali Colombia - 2011
    1. 1st Place in combat
    2. 1st Place in forms
- Latin American Championship, Brazil - 2012
    1. 1st Place in combat
    2. 1st place self-defense
    3. 2nd Place in forms
    4. 3rd Place in weapon forms
- World Games Championship - 2013
    1. 1st Place in combat
    2. 1st Place in self-defense
- World Hapkido Championship - Monterrey, Mexico - 2017
    1. 1st Place in combat
    2. 1st Place in self-defense
    3. 2nd Place in forms
- Hapkido World Championship, Bogota, Colombia - 2022
    1. 1st Place in forms
    2. 2nd Place in self-defense
- Knuckle up Championship, Orlando, Florida, USA - 2023
    1. 1st Place in super fights combat

DR. ROBERT GOLDMAN

Founder and International President Emeritus of the National Academy of Sports Medicine (NASM)

founded the International Sports Hall of Fame, recognizing the world's greatest sports legends, with ceremonies held annually at the Arnold Schwarzenegger Sports Festival-the largest sports festival in the world, with over 200,000 participants, 70+ sports represented, and over 20,000 competing athletes, making it double the size of the Olympic Games and now being held annually at the Olympia Fitness Weekend.

Dr. Goldman holds two Physician & Surgeon Medical Degrees and two Medical Doctorates and has served as a Senior Fellow at the Lincoln Filene Center, Tufts University, and as an Affiliate at the Philosophy of Education Research Center, Graduate School of Education, Harvard University. He also holds Visiting Professorships at numerous medical universities around the world. He co-founded and served as Chairman of the Board of Life Science Holdings and Organ Inc., biomedical research & development companies with over 150 medical patents under development in the areas of brain resuscitation, trauma and emergency medicine, organ transplant, and blood preservation technologies. These led to the formation of Organ Recovery Systems Inc. and then LifeLine Scientific Inc., a Public Company that became a world leader in organ preservation and transport.

D r. Robert Goldman is a 6th-degree Black Belt in Karate, a Chinese weapons expert, and a world champion athlete with over 20 world strength records and has been listed in the Guinness Book of World Records. Some of his past performance records include 13,500 consecutive straight leg sit-ups and 321 consecutive handstand pushups. Dr. Goldman was an All-College athlete in four sports, a three-time winner of the John F. Kennedy (JFK) Physical Fitness Award, was voted Athlete of the Year, was the recipient of the Champions Award, and was inducted into the World Hall of Fame of Physical Fitness, as well as inducted into numerous Martial Arts Halls of Fame in North America, Europe, South America, and Asia. He

He has overseen cooperative research agreement development programs in conjunction with the American National Red Cross, NASA, the Department of Defense, and the FDA's Center for Devices & Radiological Health.

Dr. Goldman received the Gold Medal for Science, the Grand Prize for Medicine, the Humanitarian Award, and the Business Development Award. Dr. Goldman has also been honored by Ministers of Sports and Health officials from numerous nations. The President of the International Olympic Committee awarded Dr. Goldman the International Olympic Committee Tribute Diploma for contributions to the development of Sport & Olympism. Dr. Goldman was also awarded the 2012 Life Time Achievement Award in Medicine & Science. He was among the few recipients of the Healthy America Fitness Leader Award, presented by the United States Chamber of Commerce and President's Council.

Dr. Goldman served as Chairman of the International Medical Commission for over 30 years, overseeing Sports Medicine Committees in over 194 nations, and Chairman of the IFBB and NPC Medical Commissions. Dr. Goldman also served as Chairman of the AAU/ USA Sports Medicine Council, which oversaw several million amateur athletes. He founded NASM (National Academy of Sports Medicine), the premier fitness certification organization, coined the term CPT (Certified Personal Trainer), and wrote the first certification exam ever done for that profession.

He has served as a Special Advisor to the President's Council on Physical Fitness & Sports and is the only American in history to serve under four different Presidential administrations. He is the founder and international President Emeritus of the National Academy of Sports Medicine (NASM), Board Member Emeritus for the US Sports Academy, and Chairman of their Board of Visitors. The US Sports Academy is the #1 sports academy worldwide. Dr. Goldman is also the Co-Founder and Chairman of the American Academy of Anti-Aging Medicine (A4M), with outreach to over 120 nations. A4M is the world's largest preventative medicine and medical conference/ exposition organization that has trained over 150,000 medical

specialists since 1992. Dr. Goldman co-developed the American Board of Anti-Aging & Regenerative Medicine (ABAARM) and American Board of Anti-Aging Health Practitioners (ABAAHP) Board Certifications, as well as the American College of Sports Medicine Professionals (ACASP) certificate exams and such, has overseen Post Doctoral Medical Education programs the last 30 years. He is a co-founder of the Tarsus Medical Group, which comprises a family of medical conferences and exposition divisions.

Dr. Goldman donates 80% of his time to charitable pursuits worldwide, supporting sports, fitness, and medical education for the sports and medical communities worldwide, visiting dozens of nations focusing on youth mentorship.

Darrell Henegan

DARRELL
HENEGAN

"

His relentless pursuit of excellence and his unyielding spirit propelled him to the forefront of the martial arts world.

under the direct supervision of Grand Master Lee.

Darrell has been a practitioner of Taekwondo for 50 years. Even today's greats must give way to yesterday's heroes and legends.

From the earliest days of his training, Darrell demonstrated a natural aptitude for martial arts, mastering its intricate forms with grace and precision. Yet, it was not just his physical prowess that set him apart; his relentless pursuit of excellence and his unyielding spirit propelled him to the forefront of the martial arts world.

Through years of dedicated practice and unwavering determination, Darrell carved out a legacy that would stand as a testament to his indomitable spirit. From the rings of competition to the halls of academia, his influence knew no bounds, inspiring countless practitioners to reach for their own heights of greatness. Surely, his perseverance inspires whole generations.

As the annals of martial arts history unfold, Darrell Henegan's name remains etched in stone, a beacon of inspiration for generations to come. For he is not just a master of the martial arts; he is a true embodiment of its timeless principles, a living testament to the power of perseverance, passion, and the unyielding pursuit of excellence.

"Today did not just happen."

WHY THE MARTIAL ARTS?

In the realm of martial arts, there exist luminaries whose influence transcends mere skill and technique, weaving a tapestry of dedication, passion, and unwavering commitment to the craft. Among these legends, one name shines brightly: Darrell Henegan.

Born into a world where discipline and determination were the currencies of success, Darrell's journey began humbly, guided by the steady hand of mentors who saw in him a spark of potential destined to ignite greatness.

Darrell Henegan started Taekwondo in 1974. Ray Nikiel was his Master under Grand Master Chong Soo Lee. After passing his black belt test in 1978, he was

CANADIAN NATIONALS

- 1981 - Canadian National Championships Gold Named Top Competitor of The Year
- 1982 - Canadian National Championships Silver
- 1982 - Canadian National Championships Gold, Named most Impressive Black Belt
- 1983 - Canadian National Championships Gold (no medals were given)
- 1984 - Canadian National Championships Bronze
- 1996 - Canadian National Championships Silver (back on Canadian Team)

CANADIAN NATIONAL CHAMPIONSHIPS (GOLD)

- 1998 - Olympic Division National Championship Gold
- 1999 - Canadian National Championships Gold
- 1999 - 2000 - Olympic Division National Championship Gold
- 2000 - Canadian National Championships Gold,
- 2001 - Olympic Division National Championship Gold
- 12 Times Official and Unofficial National Champion from years 70's to 2000's

NORTH AMERICAN CHAMPIONSHIP

- 1980 - North American Championship Gold Hosted by
- 1982 - Invitational North American Championship Gold

WORLD GAMES, WORLD CUP, WORLD CHAMPIONSHIPS

- 1981 - World Games 1 Gold Medalist Canada vs. Korea North America's 1st World Champion Title Holder.
- 1983 - Canada's First World Champion
- 1998 - World championship Copenhagen, Denmark, 5th in World
- 1998 - World Cup Germany, 4th in World
- 1999 - World Championship Edmonton, Alta 4th World
- 2000 - World Cup, Lyon France, 8th World
- 2001 - World Cup, Ho Chi Minh City 16th World
- 2001 - World Championship, Jeju, Korea 8th World

OPEN TOURNAMENTS

- 1995 - Pan Am Open Gold
- 1996 - Pan Am Open Silver
- 1997 - U.S. Open Silver Medal
- U.S. Open Tournaments are considered International Competitions; as well as all competitors are High Performance Athletes from all over the World.

OLYMPIC PAN AM QUALIFYING

- 1999 - Olympic Games Qualification World, Porec, Croatia 8th World
- 1999 - Regional Pan Am Olympic Qualifying, Miami Bronze

PAN AM GAMES, PAN AMERICAN CHAMPIONSHIP

- 1999 - Pan Am Games Winnipeg, Canada Bronze
- 2000 - Pan American Championship, Aruba, finished 4th

HONORS OF DARRELL HENEGAN

- 2003 — 2019 - Head Taekwondo Instructor at:
- Royal Military College, St-Jean Sur Richelieu
- 2003 - Passed 7th Dan with Grand Master Chong Soo Lee
- 2007 - Inducted into Taekwondo Hall of Fame
- North American Competitor of the Year
- 2017 - Canadian Black Belt Hall of Fame
- Darrell Henegan Continued to Promote

TAEKWONDO

- Internationally and nationally promoting through Seminars in Taekwondo, starting in 1996 to present day. Examples: Lebanon, Greece, Brussels, Nationally, with World Kobudo Federation, Capital Conquest Organizations.
- Also Master Instructor with the Royal Military College, St-Jean sur Richelieu. From 2003 to 2019
- After 4 Decades, 1974 — 2004 Competing, and is still teaching and coaching Taekwondo.
- Darrell Henegan started his Kickboxing Career after a very successful Taekwondo Career, as World Taekwondo Champion.

FIGHTS IN KICKBOXING

- 1984 - Hvy Wht Provincial Championship, André Beneche (WIN)
- 1984 - Curtis Cowboy Crandal vs. Darrell Henegan, Decision Darrell (WIN)
- 1984 - Darrell Henegan vs. Bruno Vezzutti, Decision Darrell (WIN - K.O.)
- 1985 - Robert Overton vs. Darrell Henegan, Decision Darrell (WIN - TKO)
- 1985 - Super Hvy Wht Provincial Championship, Andre Beneche vs. Darrell Henegan, Decision Darrell Henegan (WIN)
- 1986 - James Waring vs. Darrell Henegan, Decision Darrell
- 1987 - Lowell Flash Nash vs. Darrell Henegan, Decision Darrell Henegan (WIN - K.O)

F.F.K.A WORLD TITLE

- 1987 - North American F.F.K.A. Championship Dennis Downey vs. Darrell Henegan, Decision Darrell (WIN - K.O.)
- 1988 - Paul Bonner Vs. Darrell Henegan, Canadian Title, Decision Darrell Henegan

F.F.K.A WORLD TITLE (CONTINUED)

- (WIN - K.O.)
- 1986 - Darrell Henegan vs. Jerry Rhome North American PKA Title, Decision Jerry Rhome (LOSS)
- 1988 - World Heavyweight Championship F.F.K.A. Jerry Rhome vs. Darrell Henegan, Decision Darrell Henegan (WIN)
- 1990 - Darrell Henegan vs. Dennis Alexio, Decision Alexio (LOSS)
- For His I.S.K.A heavyweight title.

I.S.K.A. WORLD TITLE

- 1993 - World I.S.K.A. , F.F.K.A Cruiserweight Championship, Premyslev Saletta vs. Darrell Henegan, Decision Darrell Henegan (WIN)

TITLE DEFENSES

- 1989 - Larry Thunderfoot Cureton vs. Darrell Henegan, Decision Darrell Henegan Title Defense (WIN - K.O.)
- 1989 - Neil Singleton vs. Darrell Henegan Decision Darrell Henegan Title Defense F.F.K.A. (WIN - K.O.)
- 1991 - Dennis Schotte vs. Darrell Henegan Decision Darrell Henegan, Title Defense F.F.K.A. (WIN - K.O.)
- 1992 - Sergio Baterreli vs. Darrell Henegan, Decision Darrell Henegan Title Defense F.F.K.A. (WIN)
- 1994 - Gary Depresco vs. Darrell Henegan , Decision Darrell Henegan F.F.K.A., I.S.K.A. Title Defense (WIN - K.O.)
- 1994 - Glen Pools Vs. Darrell Henegan, Decision Darrell Henegan Title Defense F.F.K.A. , I.S.K.A. (WIN -TKO)
- 1995 - Mohamed Jamal Vs. Darrell Henegan, Decision Darrell Henegan No World Title On Line (WIN- TKO)
- 1996 - Horace Craft vs. Darrell Henegan Decision Darrell Henegan, Title Defense F.F.K.A. , I.S.K.A. (WIN - TKO)

CAREER HONORS

- 15 Time World Kickboxing Champion
- 2003 — 2019 - Head Taekwondo Instructor at the Royal Military College, St-Jean Sur Richelieu
- 2003 - Passed 7th Dan with Grand Master Chong Soo Lee
- 2007 - Inducted into Taekwondo Hall of Fame
- North American Competitor of the year.
- 2016 - Recipient of the Joe Lewis Eternal Warrior Award P.K.A.
- 2016 - Who's Who in the Martial Arts Hall of Fame Legends Champion Award
- 2017 - Action Martial Arts Magazine Hall Of Honors Award
- 2017 - Who's Who in The Martial Arts Hall Fame Legends Award
- 2017 - Canadian Black Belt Hall of Fame. Proud Member of the World Kobudo Federation.
- 2018 - Honorary Native Texan Black Belt
- 2018 - The World Taekwondo Jidokwan Federation: 8th Dan Grand Master Darrell Henegan
- 2019 - World Wide P.K.A. Member
- 2019 - Veteren Warrior Award, World Kobudo Federation.
- 2020 - AMAAF Who's Who Legends Awards Recipient.
- 2021 - Lifetime Achievement Award President Joseph R. Biden
- 2023 - The World Taekwondo Jidokwan Federation: Grand Master Darrell Henegan 9th Dan
- 2024 - 50 Years of Taekwondo Development in Canada, Grand Master Darrell Henegan
- 2024 - International Extraordinary Peoples Awards: Leadership Award
- 2024 - International Community Service Award
- 2024 - Hall of Honor Williams Elite Award
- 2024 - The UK Martial Arts Hall of Fame Award

KAREN EDEN
HERDMAN

"
Karen was the first writer in martial arts magazines to become known as the 'author of inspiration.'

WHY THE MARTIAL ARTS?

Karen Eden Herdman is a 7th-degree black belt originally from Roanoke, Virginia. With over 30 years of teaching and training, she is a rare female "Grand Master" in the art of Tang Soo Do.

In 1989, Karen began training under C.S. Kim of Pittsburgh, Pa., who is considered to be a founding father of the art of Tang Soo Do in the U.S. She later went on to own her own successful karate school under C.S. Kim at the tender rank of just "red belt." Karen also competed nationally in major cities across the country, winning in forms, sparring, and in both open and closed tournaments. She competed internationally at the World Tang Soo Do Championships in 1995, ranking 4th in Women's Black Belt Sparring.

A writer and broadcast journalist by trade, Karen was

the first writer in martial arts magazines to become known as the "author of inspiration." Under the guidance of martial arts journalist John Corcoran, Karen went on to obtain three karate magazine columns ("Inside Tae Kwon Do," "Tae Kwon Do Times," and "MASuccess") and has been featured in every major martial arts magazine in the world.

Karen has also authored five books ("The Complete Idiot's Guide to Tae Kwon Do" / Simon & Shuster MacMillan, "I Am a Martial Artist" / Century Martial Arts, "They Call Me Master" / Century Martial Arts and a self-help book "Will I Ever Feel Happy Again"/ Amazon.com, Barnesandnoble.com.) Two of her book publishing's spun off product lines available through Century Martial Arts ("I Am a Martial Artist and "They Call Me Master.")

Her product line called "Dojo Darling" was purchased by The Karate Depot and became her first fundraising product line to help students who can't afford a karate uniform.

TRAINING INFORMATION

- Belt Ranks & Martial Arts Styles: 7th Degree Grandmaster of Tang Soo Do
- Instructors/Influencers: C.S. Kim, Joe Bruno, A.J. Perry
- Birthplace/Growing Up: Vinton, VA
- Yrs. In the Martial Arts: 34 years
- Yrs. Instructing: 31 years
- Instructor, Martial Arts Writer & Columnist

PROFESSIONAL ORGANIZATIONS

- The Blood and Fire Federation

MAJOR ACHIEVEMENTS

- 7th Degree Grandmaster of Martial Arts
- Major Market TV Newscaster
- Published Book Author
- Recipient of the Congressional Medal of Volunteerism

Become an
AMAA MEMBER!

Karen has also been in two major Hollywood Productions, a feature role in "Sworn to Justice" and stunt work in Van Damme's "Sudden Death."

Grand Master Karen has been inducted into eight martial arts Hall of Fames, including being the only female master to be inducted into the "Korean Martial Arts Masters Hall of Fame." She was inducted into the Sport Karate Museum in 2018 and is a 2-time inductee in "Who's Who in Martial Arts."

Karen is also a rare female professor to teach at the notorious "Karate College" of Radford University in its' 35-year inception. Growing up in poverty from a broken home, GM Karen, who is of both Asian and Native American descent, began an inner-city martial arts program through The Salvation Army. The program under her "The Blood and Fire Federation" recruited martial arts instructors from around the world to start teaching on a volunteer basis to help the less fortunate. Today Karen contributes to the Missing and Murdered Indigenous Women issues by going into tribal areas and teaching Native women self-defense. She is also an ordained Chaplain.

PETR
HLAVAC

WHY THE MARTIAL ARTS?

"

When I was seven years old, I started in the martial arts with Shotokan Karate, and I believed in this path.

I would like to introduce myself and my martial arts journey. Since I was a little boy, I have been interested in martial arts and started practicing Karate at age seven. I continued with Kung Fu and Jujitsu, and when I turned 15, I started training to become an instructor; I am teaching and still training to the present day.

Over the years, I started in the Krav Maga, and I met Master Raffael Saar Liven. This meeting was fateful, and I began to train hard in this new style. After completing many training sessions, seminars, and special commando training, I achieved the first degree

masters black belt. Over time, and after many visits to Israel, Denmark, Slovakia, Romania, and other countries, I received my higher masters' degrees.

Meeting living martial arts legends like Dr. Dennis Hanover—Dennis Survival Ju-Jitsu; GM Haim Gidon—I.K.M.A Israeli Krav Maga Association Gidon System; GM Moshe Buchnik—President Israel Karate Federation; GM Mati Elyashiv—Israeli Ju-Jitsu; and many other masters with whom I had the honor to train I was able to create the Krav Maga System. During 14 years of Krav Maga training and adding Jiu Jutsu, Karate and Judo techniques, I was able to teach this system with my instructors worldwide under the name Krav Maga Seal System. I established martial arts academies in several locations throughout the Czech Republic and organized international seminars worldwide, including the Czech Republic, the Bahamas, the UK, and the USA.

Our KMSS instructors take demanding courses and attend special seminars four times a year; they improve beyond the scope of the results achieved, start teaching children, and gradually start training adult students as well.

Our basic division of classes is as follows:

- KMMK is Krav Maga Mini Kids - 5-year-old to 8-year-old students.

- KMK is Krav Maga Kids - 8-year-old to 14-year-old students.

- KM - 15-year-old to 99-year-old students.

- KM30+ - 30-year-old and older students.

Our organisation sets up many seminars during the year, some of which have a long history. Practical seminars are held several times a year, and some exceptional seminars are held only once a year. Students from many countries meet and train at our yearly international bootcamp. This seminar is eight hours long and includes a Bootcamp for Kids, Telescopic Baton Seminar, Self Defense for Women and Girls, Carjacking and Kidnapping prevention Seminar, Attacks in a Bar/Nightclub, Attacks when on Public Transportation, Airplane Jacking and Attack, and Kubotan & Torai Seminar. Before Christmas time, we host our Kids Seminar with a minimum of 250 participating students!

Our students train according to the exam schedule I

TRAINING INFORMATION

- Belt Ranks & Martial Arts Styles: 9th Dan Krav Maga, 9th Dan Sho Shin Do Karate, 9th Dan Self-Defense, 6th Dan Lochama Ze-Ira, 2th Dan Shotokan Karate, 2nd Dan Jiu Jitsu, Certified Instructor - Czech Police, Shooting Instructor - Firearms Instructor, Executive Bodyguard, Fitness Instructor

- Instructors/Influencers: Kaicho Raffael Saar Liven, GM Bohuslav Vinopal MG, GM Professor Dennis Hanover

- Birthplace/Growing Up: Vyskov and the Czech Republic

- Yrs. In the Martial Arts: 41 years

- Yrs. Instructing: 33 years

- School owner, Manager & Instructor at Academy of Martial Arts - ABU and Krav Maga Seal System, Founder of Krav Maga Seal System

PROFESSIONAL ORGANIZATIONS

- Academy of Martial Arts - ABU in the Czech Republic

- Krav Maga Seal System

PERSONAL ACHIEVEMENTS

- Gold - Kumite in Denmark

- Gold - Kumite Karate Shotokan in Czech

- Silver - Kumite and Kata Shotokan in Czech

- Gold - Tao Lu - Nangquan - Prague in Czech

- Bronze - Tao Lu - Changquan - Prague in Czech

MAJOR ACHIEVEMENTS

- Title: Kancho

- Coach of the Year 2023 - Czech Republic

- Hall of Fame Budo Bushi in Poland

- Hall of Fame Award Professor Pierre in Orlando

created for white belts to master black belt levels. They use the Krav Maga Seal System student guides and curriculum which I published to help them prepare for their exams.

We have highly qualified professional instructors. Two of them have been training and teaching our KMSS for many years, and they have proven themselves to have a great future in training our students. They lead by example and have shown that the Krav Maga Seal System is not just a hobby but a way of life. The first is Sensei Kristýna Hlavacova; she trains over a hundred children a week and is also my wife. Second is Sensei Petr Trubak, who trains children's classes as well as adult students. I'd also like to thank all the instructors who train KMSS students in the Czech Republic, the USA, the Bahamas, England, and worldwide with regular training sessions and seminars.

Many years ago, I met my student, Argelio A. Curbelo. We started training online, and every time I visited the U.S., he did special private training and belt tests. He still trains and, a few years ago, introduced me to Sensei Nick Braaksma from Kime Ryu Dojo at Fitness CF in Orlando, Florida. One minute was enough for us to become friends, and Sensei Nick became part of our team. He started learning the Krav Maga Seal System and organizes many Krav Maga Seal System seminars and tournaments a year, and belt tests are according to the examination regulations of KMSS.

One very important meeting for me was with Sensei Elrick Mckinney from the Bahamas. Now, we have an official KMSS training center in Nassau where two times per year Sensei Elrick and I organize seminars for his students.

I love working with people of different ages and levels, and my satisfaction is reflected in the great results I have seen in my students over the years.

My life motto is: if you get attacked, you have only one chance to protect yourself, and you should use it!

HOW HAS MARTIAL ARTS IMPACTED YOUR LIFE?

All my life I have met people with good hearts; for them, martial arts is not just a hobby but like for me it is a way of life.

Thanks to persistent work and diligence, today we have more than 700 students in the Czech Republic, many students in the USA with two schools, and many students in Nassau the Bahamas.

I have never smoked in my life, and I have never tasted any alcohol in my life. When I was seven years old, I started in the martial arts with Shotokan Karate, and I believed in this path.

KEVIN
HOOKER

> "
> *My journey has been wrought with challenges with interesting twists and turns...*

WHY THE MARTIAL ARTS?

I originally started martial arts while in college. Shotokan Karate was my first experience. After graduating college with an engineering degree and moving to my new hometown of Omaha, Nebraska, I found Kenpo. From being a collegiate athlete and loving sports all my life, I wanted to maintain the physicality and hard workouts of being active. After college, I was missing that concept and the trials of being an avid sports enthusiast. So, I began training in Kenpo Karate to fill that void. In the beginning, it was exciting and invigorating. The euphoric feeling of being back in action was intoxicating. For me, karate was a way to challenge myself - working to be better at every aspect, like

learning new forms, self-defense techniques, and weapons. I wanted to improve not only my skills, like high kicks, traditional karate stances, and transitions but also my character. I wanted the courage to stand up to bullies and protect those who needed protection when the time came.

After over 25 years, it's just become a part of me — like having a third arm (if that makes sense). It's instilled in me. My training took over much of my life, and I was in the dojo every chance I could get. Yet, the school I attended shifted directions several times - but my instructor stayed humbled and maintained a course of true character - finding deeper roots in the Kenpo lineage.

As the school settled into a more organized atmosphere, I found peace and tranquility in my training. However, life got very busy with three kids and a business taking off. As time progressed, my teacher retired. I bought his school and took on the role of ownership in a karate business (alongside my current business, which was now highly successful).

My perspective changed, and my "why" about becoming a martial artist became about giving back. I settled into an already accomplished school with instructors and students. Time passed, and many chapters in my journey left me with fun stories to tell.

As the karate business sometimes does - change happened again, and I had to start over very recently. This reinvigorated me once again - even after 25 years in my art - I found a deeper love once again in creating something that I can not only give back to my community but challenge my "older" body even further. My "why" now is not just about me learning new skills, honing my art, or maybe adding a form or technique to my repertoire; it's even deeper than just giving back.

I teach life lessons like discipline, honor, humility, character, integrity, and confidence, just to name a few, although my new passion has become something I have found along the way. God has a way of putting incredible opportunities in front of you if you only step up to them. Now, I'm focused on sharing my experience with others, creating relationships, and building a better community one student at a time.

HOW HAS MARTIAL ARTS IMPACTED YOUR LIFE?

Without martial arts, I know I would not have accomplished many life-changing opportunities. I've visited both coasts several times for seminars and testing and south through Texas. I continue to gain and maintain confidence in my skills as a martial artist and my professional and business leadership skills. I've learned how to de-escalate confrontations, and I've also learned how to control my emotional responses to outside influences. Martial arts have given me

TRAINING INFORMATION

- Belt Ranks & Martial Arts Styles: Shotokan Karate — Purple (5th Kyu), Kenpo Karate - 6th Degree Black Belt, Gracie Jiu Jitsu — Black Belt
- Instructors/Influencers: Professor Nick Chamberlain, Master Greg James, Sensei Tom Scott, Professor Richard Schmidt
- Birthplace/Growing Up: Grand Island, NE
- Yrs. In the Martial Arts: 30+ years
- Yrs. Instructing: 16 years
- School owner & Instructor at Elite Academy of Martial Arts

PROFESSIONAL ORGANIZATIONS

- Member United States Kiddo Federation
- Member Kenpo Arts
- Member American Martial Arts Alliance Foundation

PERSONAL ACHIEVEMENTS

- Competed at our state games for several years, earning gold and silver medals each year
- Competed in the BJJ Tournament, earning the silver medal
- 2017 Awarded Master Rank and title of Shihan (Godan)

MAJOR ACHIEVEMENTS

- 2024 International Best-selling Co-Author in Elite Publications' Elite Martial Artists in America: Secrets to Life, Leadership, and Business, Volume II
- 2023 Inductee AAMA Who's Who in Martial Arts Legends Award
- 2023 USKF Black Belt Hall of Fame Excellence Award Outstanding Small School
- 2023 International Best-selling Co-Author in Elite Publications' Elite Martial Artists in America: Secrets to Life, Leadership, and Business, Volume I
- 2019 Keepers of the Flame Instructor
- 2018 Keepers of the Flame Instructor

HOW HAS MARTIAL ARTS IMPACTED YOUR LIFE? (CONTINUED)

confidence in my physical ability to handle many situations and my mental ability to think through scenarios and find proper outcomes. My journey has been wrought with challenges with interesting twists and turns. Suffice it to say — that overcoming each obstacle has been rewarding and inspiring.

I have had the blessing of teaching my wife and son, an amazing experience we will always cherish. As my passion takes up many hours away from my family, it also allows us to follow our dreams and gives us time for self-reflection and growth. The relationships I've built over the past 25 years have truly and pleasantly shaped me. I look forward to many more and creating new ones moving forward. I also know that those who come and go on this journey are always welcome with friendship and respect.

Another area that truly has been amazing is the ability to teach and share my vision and knowledge with so many others across the United States and, at the same time, learn from them as well. There are so many incredibly talented people from all over this astounding country. Working with people, training them, learning from them, and sharing positive life lessons of growth has been extremely fulfilling.

Become an
AMAA MEMBER!

MICHAEL
HORNSBY

"
Studying martial arts has not only impacted my life but also ultimately shaped it.

Do, and Soo Bak Kee, as well as formalized training in Ju Jitsu and Filipino Martial Arts.

The skills and achievements I have in the martial arts would never have been possible without the incredible guidance of Grandmaster Mike Fillmore, Grandmaster Able Villarreal, Grandmaster Rodney Kauffman, Grandmaster Johnny Thompson, Grandmaster Dan Roberts, and numerous other martial artists and instructors who have significantly impacted my journey in martial arts. With several rank promotions, such as my 4th dan in 2002, 5th dan in 2009, 6th dan in 2010, and 7th dan in 2017, I was honored with the promotion to 8th dan in 2018. Being promoted to the rank of Grandmaster was a true blessing by the Lord.

I am grateful and humbled by the trust and support of my fellow martial artists. I am especially thankful for the unwavering belief and encouragement from my wife, Diana, and our children: Denise, Dennis, William, Victoria, and Anthony, as well as our six grandchildren. I deeply love each and every one of you.

WHY THE MARTIAL ARTS?

My father took me to a Bruce Lee movie as a small child. After watching that movie, I dreamed of being just like Bruce Lee. My father then took me to a karate demonstration, and I was hooked. Thinking I wouldn't stick with it, my father casually enrolled me in a martial arts school around the corner from our house.

I became more serious about martial arts and martial arts training in my preteens. I began my lifelong journey in martial arts, resulting in over 45 years of training with black belts in Tae Kwon Do, Tang Soo

HOW HAS MARTIAL ARTS IMPACTED YOUR LIFE?

Studying martial arts has not only impacted my life but also ultimately shaped it. Martial arts align with the same ideals and values that my parents instilled in me. Being a forever martial arts student has taught me how to be a productive citizen, caring father, loving husband, and servant leader. There is nothing like being able to serve others.

In addition, studying martial arts has allowed me to formulate and build the foundation for my students. The foundation of Courtesy, Integrity, Perseverance, Self-control, and Indomitable Spirit will enable my students to pursue and achieve their dreams and become the great men and women they are destined to be.

If it weren't for practicing and studying martial arts, I would not have been placed in front of the right men and women in the arts. It wasn't that these martial artists were the best kickers, punchers, or world title holders, but they had the right character, values, and belief systems.

The impact of martial arts on my life has reached beyond my personal life and has impacted my professional life. It has given me the skills to not only own and run a school but also work in the managerial arena in different career fields.

TRAINING INFORMATION

- Belt Ranks & Martial Arts Styles: Tae Kwon Do - 8th degree, Tang Soo Do - 8th degree, Soo Bak Kee - 8th degree
- Instructors/Influencers: Grandmaster Mike Fillmore, Grandmaster Abel Villerrreal, Grandmaster Rodney Kauffman, Grandmaster Johnny Thompson, Grandmaster Dan Roberts
- Birthplace/Growing Up: Alaska
- Yrs. In the Martial Arts: 45+ years
- Yrs. Instructing: 25 years
- School owner & Instructor at True Force Tae Kwon Do

PROFESSIONAL ORGANIZATIONS

- Founder/President of True Force International Martial Arts Alliance
- President of World Moo Duk Kwan Tae Kwon Do Alliance 2024
- World Moo Duk Kwan Alliance Grandmaster Council
- American Martial Arts Alliance
- Vice President of the Federation of International Martial Arts
- NE-DU-U-KON -Tae Karate Kung Fu Federation
- Tang Soo Do Karate Association
- Black Knight Karate Association
- Texas Tae Kwon Do Association
- International Martial Council of America
- Ultimate Force Kali Association

PERSONAL ACHIEVEMENTS

- Internation Best-selling Author of Elite Black Belts Who Cook Cookbook
- Co-author of the Who's Who in the Martial Arts Cynthia Rothrock's Biography Book 2023 Edition
- International Champion
- World Champion
- National Champion
- State Champion
- Promoter of the True Force Global Internationals Martial Arts Championship

MAJOR ACHIEVEMENTS

- 2024 United States Martial Arts Hall of Fame Inductee: Golden Life Award

- 2023 World Moo Duk Kwan International Martial Arts Hall of Fame Inductee: Promoter of the Decade

- 2023 America Martial Arts Alliance Inductee: Who's Who in the Martial Arts

- 2021 Universal Martial Arts Hall of Fame Inductee: Distinguished Grandmaster of the Year

- 2021 United States Martial Arts Hall of Fame Inductee: Executive Competitor of the Year

- 2020 The United Kingdom Blackbelt Hall of Fame: Devoted Award

- 2020 International Martial Arts Hall of Fame: Platinum Life Award

- 2018 United States Martial Arts Hall of Fame Inductee: Outstanding Grandmaster

- 2017 United States Martial Arts Hall of Fame Inductee: Silver Life Award

- 2016 United States Martial Arts Hall of Fame Inductee: Distinguished Master

MAJOR ACHIEVEMENTS (CONTINUED)

- 2010 NE- DU-U-KON TAE Karate Kung Fu Federation Hall of Fame Award: Outstanding Contributions to the Martial Arts

- 2009 World Organization of Martial Arts Athletes Hall of Fame Inductee: USA Coach of the Year

- 2009 USA International Black Belt Hall of Fame Inductee: Master Black Belt of the Year

- 2006 USA International Black Belt Hall of Fame Inductee: School of the Year Award

- 2004 World Karate Union Hall of Fame Inductee: Master Instructor of the Year

- 2004 World Wide Martial Arts Hall of Fame Inductee: Outstanding Contributions to the Martial Arts

- 2003 USA International Black Belt Hall of Fame Inductee: Pinnacle of Success Award

- 2002 North American Black Belt Hall of Fame Inductee: Master Instructor of the Year

- 2002 US Team/Alliance Hall of Fame Inductee: Competitor of the Year

- 2002 USA International Black Belt Hall of Fame Inductee: Master Instructor of the Year

- 2002 United States Martial Arts Hall of Fame Inductee: Outstanding Martial Artist of the Year

- 2002 Universal Martial Arts Hall of Fame Inductee: Black Belt of the Year — Tae Kwon Do

- 2002 World Wide Martial Arts Hall of Fame Inductee: Male Competitor of the Year - Tae Kwon Do

Become an
AMAA MEMBER!

GILBERT
HOUSEAUX

"

Martial arts formed me. I was a shy kid who was bullied, not like nowadays; the old times were tough.

HOW HAS MARTIAL ARTS IMPACTED YOUR LIFE?

Martial arts formed me. I was a shy kid who was bullied, not like nowadays; the old times were tough. My father signed me up for a Judo school to toughen me up. That is how it all started. After I obtained my first black belt, I traveled the world, some for the military some for my own. The martial arts brought me confidence, strength, and mindset.

As I aged, I realized that the saying " as you get older, you'll get better " did not work so well until I met George Dillman and DKI. After the first seminar I attended, I knew that I had been missing something despite having a couple of black belts. I found the unsatiable power of knowledge that keeps on growing with time. I also found that martial artists dedicated to their art have a discipline that transfers to another part of life (for most of them). Now, I have concluded that I have a duty to share my knowledge and help people who need it.

WHY THE MARTIAL ARTS?

I started martial arts when I was 14 in 1960. Being in a small town then, the only martial art available was Judo, the style in which I obtained my first black belt. From there, I went to a military academy and then traveled to many places in Europe, Africa, etc.

Wherever I was, I joined the local cubs. Whatever style they were, I studied them. I did not have choices in those times and places I was in, so it allowed me to study different arts. I believe I have been one of the first ones to cross-train and mix styles, which nowadays seem to be the norm.

TRAINING INFORMATION

- Belt Ranks & Martial Arts Styles: 9th Dan-DKI, studied Judo, Jiu Jitsu, Small Circle Jiu Jitsu, Karate Tang Soo Do, Arnis, Wing Chun, Rukyu Kempo, Weapons, Kyusho Jitsu

- Instructors/Influencers: Gibeau, Jay Andis, Daryl Khalid, Bill Burch, Leon Jay, George Dillman

- Birthplace/Growing Up: France

- Yrs. In the Martial Arts: 64 years

- Yrs. Instructing: 20 years

- Instructor at Dillman Karate International, Seminar conductor in US & Europe

PROFESSIONAL ORGANIZATIONS

- NAAR

- SAG

- CERT (Community Emergency Response Team)

- Kyusho-France

- DKI

PERSONAL ACHIEVEMENTS

- I have reached many goals in my life. Starting in this country and living on the street, I became a respected and successful person. I have helped quite a few people on my journey. I have a room full of awards and trophies earned through my multiple activities. But mostly, I am proud to have survived difficult situations in many parts of the globe and to have grown into someone many turn to for advice and help when needed.

MAJOR ACHIEVEMENTS

- MA in math

- International Karate and Kicking Hall of Fame

- Becoming an American Citizen

- Getting Married

- Reaching the top of my profession

- Who's Who in America

DAVID
HUGHES

"
I take great joy in instructing new students now and seeing them become better than myself. There is no greater joy.

HOW HAS MARTIAL ARTS IMPACTED YOUR LIFE?

Since I started martial arts, I have changed in many ways. It has made me a better person, more self-reliant, and more self-confident. I'm more of an introvert than a social butterfly. As a teenager, I made the trip to Japan without my parents and stayed for six weeks, navigating a foreign country without being able to understand the language or customs.

I traveled across the US to the Pan Am games in 2014 with two students and my brother, something I would not have been able to do before.

I learned patience in teaching others and have now become comfortable with teaching one-on-one with confidence.

Martial arts has boosted the leadership training from ROTC in high school and has helped me develop into a better person.

I take great joy in instructing new students now and seeing them become better than myself. There is no greater joy.

WHY THE MARTIAL ARTS?

I have been interested in martial arts since I was a kid. My brother and I grew up watching Teenage Mutant Ninja Turtles, Power Rangers, and Dragonball Z. A couple times a week, our parents would rent Kung Fu movies, and we'd watch those at night before bed. I most admired Bruce Lee and would have welcomed the chance to meet him. Our area had no schools, so I couldn't take any lessons as a kid. In 2004, after we moved to North Carolina, my mom came home one day and told us she had signed us up for a Taekwondo school. At first, I wasn't interested in Taekwondo, thinking it wasn't that great of a martial art. But after a few weeks, I grew to love it and went to class 5-6 days a week. I had no idea that I would still be practicing 20 years later. I enjoy digging into real-world self-defense techniques and their applications and uses.

PROFESSIONAL ORGANIZATIONS
- United States Kido Federation Hall of Fame
- International Jun Tong Taekwondo Federation (2011-2022)
- Shadowriders of America SC (AMA charter)
- Upward Bound Alumni (2000 and 2001)

PERSONAL ACHIEVEMENTS
- ROTC Award - Military Order of The Purple Heart, for cadets in a 4-year program who show demonstrated leadership abilities
- JROTC award - Reserve Officers Association Award - for strong academic performance and Leadership ability. Top 10% of class
- Studied Blacksmithing, I create Damascus steel blades on my forge
- CNC operator and programmer at a granite fabrication shop
- After high school, my brother and I flew to Japan, where we lived for almost two months. We traveled by bus and train to numerous famous historical sites such as Kyoto, Osaka, Edo Castles, and Mt. Fuji, and we did a whitewater rafting tour in central Japan. We also visited a number of temples and parks. One of the most interesting things we did was to visit the old samurai houses where famous samurai such as Iayesu Tokugawa, Totoyomi Hideyoshi, and Oda Nobunaga lived and were buried.

MAJOR ACHIEVEMENTS
- Published author of two thesis papers on aquatic water quality of the rivers in the WNC region and a field study on amphibians' populations, habitat, and lifetime movements in WNC aquatic habitats
- 2014: Coached a team to Gold and Silver medals and two additional top 5 finishes at the Pan Am Games
- As a teenager, I was invited to live at Lake George in upstate NY one summer and apprenticed to a wood carver. He specialized in Tlingit totem poles from the Pacific Northwest. I learned how to fabricate my own tools and then spent several weeks working on my own project, a 4-foot-tall Tlingit-style totem pole

TRAINING INFORMATION
- Belt Ranks & Martial Arts Styles: 4th Dan Master - Jun Tong Taekwon-Do Federation, American Taekwondo, Oh Do Kwan Taekwondo, Chung Do Kwan Taekwondo, Small Circle Jujitsu, Hapkido
- Instructors/Influencers: James Craeton, Robert Dunn, Wayne Kirby, Louis Raddicione, Chuck Blackburn
- Birthplace/Growing Up: Homestead, FL / NC
- Yrs. In the Martial Arts: 20 years
- Yrs. Instructing: 14 years
- School owner & Instructor at Jung Kwon Martial Arts Academy and Asheville Self Defense

MALINEE
HUGHES

"

I have learned not to be afraid to try anything, even flying a stunt biplane for half an hour for my 50th birthday!

Luckily, years later, my husband enjoyed those movies too, and so all through the 1980s and '90s, we rented every one we could find and watched them with our sons instead of regular TV. It was good, but I still badly wanted to practice for real, but our area had no schools.

We later moved to North Carolina, and in 2004, I was sitting at a red light and saw a tiny sign across the street for a Taekwondo school. I didn't know what Taekwondo was, but I parked and went in. Master Craeton, the school owner, offered to set me up for an introductory class, but I said, "No, I want to join right now!" That night, I went home and informed my family that we were taking Taekwondo!

WHY THE MARTIAL ARTS?

When I was little, I used to walk past the city park on the way to school, where a Tai Chi master taught classes on the grass in the mornings. I was late to school sometimes because I liked to stop and watch the Tai Chi class doing their moves. I often asked my mother if I could join the class, but she said it was a waste of time and money.

My brothers and sisters and I liked to watch Kung Fu movies every night on TV (the old movies with flying masters with giant white mustaches and lots of magical techniques), and that was my only outlet.

HOW HAS MARTIAL ARTS IMPACTED YOUR LIFE?

Having wanted to practice since I was a kid, joining a school was slightly different than I imagined. But I never looked back. I frequently attended class four times per week for many years. And from 2008-2012, I drove 40 miles to Asheville, NC, for a morning class, then drove 75 miles back past my house to work at the Cherokee Casino. It was the only way I could maintain four weekly classes, so I didn't care. No effort was too far, and at 4'11", I was still ready to hit the mat in sparring against any opponent, anywhere, at any time.

My husband and I supported our schoolmaster, accompanying him and his wife to every school they visited, every belt test they attended, and every special class put on by the Grandmaster. We were there when they needed people for a public demo; when they were doing a show at a school, we went too. I guess I was making up for all the years my mother kept me from practicing as a kid and teenager. I learned a lot during this period and gained many skills that I use now in our current school. I have learned not to be afraid to try anything, even flying a stunt biplane for half an hour for my 50th birthday!

TRAINING INFORMATION

- Belt Ranks & Martial Arts Styles: 4th Dan Master - Jun Tong Taekwon-Do Federation, American Taekwondo, Oh Do Kwan Taekwondo, Chung Do Kwan Taekwondo, Small Circle Jujitsu, Hapkido
- Instructors/Influencers: James Craeton, K. A. Morris, Robert Dunn, Wayne Kirby, Louis Raddicione, Chuck Blackburn, Anthony Casapao
- Birthplace/Growing Up: Bangkok, Thailand
- Yrs. In the Martial Arts: 20 years
- Yrs. Instructing: 10 years
- School owner & Instructor at Jung Kwon Martial Arts Academy Asheville

PROFESSIONAL ORGANIZATIONS

- United States Kido Federation Hall Of Fame Alumni
- (Previously) International Jun Tong Taekwondo Federation 2009-2022

PERSONAL ACHIEVEMENTS

- I speak four languages (Thai, English, Cantonese, and French) and read/write in three (Thai, English, and Cantonese).
- I graduated from the summer studies program in Shiatsu Massage at SUNY New Paltz, New York.
- I graduated from a 6-month course, top of class, at the Cherokee Reservation/SCORE Business Center Indianpreneurship Program.
- I study international cuisines, their indigenous herbs and spices, and localized ingredients. I'm a semi-pro chef in Classic European, Mediterranean, North African, Southeast Asian, and Central Asian dishes.
- I am a successful commercial artist in historical recreations of Native American museum pieces (mentored and advised by Mohawk carving artist Henry Two Bears and Apache Elder Shanadii Crosbie (great-granddaughter of Geronimo). I have sold over 100 leatherwork and/or beadwork items that are of museum quality (most people are unaware that 90% of what they see in museums are actually perfectly detailed reproductions of the original). My area of specialty is Apache/Commanche/Lakota Northern/Central Plains, 1830-1870 era.

MAJOR ACHIEVEMENTS

- Certified Home Care Nurse (NY, 1990-1996) - specializing in homebound, terminal cases
- United States Kido Federation Black Belt Hall Of Fame, 2020 Outstanding Senior Instructor of the Year

MICHAEL
HUGHES

" *Since I started martial arts, I have changed in many ways. There are obvious things, like better strength, speed, and endurance, but it has also made me far more self-confident and independent.*

WHY THE MARTIAL ARTS?

I always had a passing interest in martial arts as a kid. My brother and I grew up watching Teenage Mutant Ninja Turtles, Power Rangers, and Dragonball Z. A couple times a week, our parents would rent Kung Fu movies, and we'd watch those at night before bed. I liked many of them, but Bruce Lee was my favorite. Our area had no schools, so practicing for real wasn't possible.

In 2004, after we moved to North Carolina, my mom came home one day and told us she had signed us up for a Taekwondo school and that she was taking us the next day, whether we wanted to or not! That's how I got started; I had no idea that I would still be practicing 20 years later.

HOW HAS MARTIAL ARTS IMPACTED YOUR LIFE?

Since I started martial arts, I have changed in many ways. There are obvious things, like better strength, speed, and endurance, but it has also made me far more self-confident and independent. I made the trip to Japan as a teenager with no parents a year and a half after we began practicing, and later, I traveled across the US to coach a team in the Pan Am Games in 2014, something I would never have done before. I teach classes regularly and work one-on-one with students every day, and I'm comfortable doing it, which was not part of my mental makeup before I started TKD.

TRAINING INFORMATION

- Belt Ranks & Martial Arts Styles: 4th Dan - Jun Tong Taekwon-Do Federation, American Taekwondo, Oh Do Kwan Taekwondo, Chung Do Kwan Taekwondo, Small Circle Jujitsu, Hapkido
- Instructors/Influencers: James Craeton, Robert Dunn, Wayne Kirby, Louis Raddicione, Chuck Blackburn, Anthony Casapao
- Birthplace/Growing Up: Homestead AFB, FL / Central & Southern NY
- Yrs. In the Martial Arts: 20 years
- Yrs. Instructing: 10 years
- School owner & Instructor at Jung Kwon Martial Arts Academy Asheville

PROFESSIONAL ORGANIZATIONS

- United States Kido Federation Black Belt Hall Of Fame Alumni
- (Previously) International Jun Tong Taekwondo Federation 2011-2022

PERSONAL ACHIEVEMENTS

- After high school, my brother and I flew to Japan and lived there for almost two months. We traveled by bus and train to numerous famous historical sites such as Kyoto, Osaka, Edo Castles, and Mt. Fuji and did a whitewater rafting tour in central Japan. We also visited several temples and parks and spent much time sampling Japanese restaurants. One of the most exciting things we did was to see the old samurai houses where famous samurai such as Iayesu Tokugawa, Totoyomi Hideyoshi, and Oda Nobunaga lived and were buried.
- I completed three courses in metallurgy and blacksmithing, learned to build a forge, and fabricated several steel-bladed knives.
- I completed several courses in filmmaking, focusing on lighting and sound, but could not complete the diploma as the state of North Carolina stopped all filmmaking tax credits and advantages, and the industry died out.
- I have been studying the various fine art techniques of various Japanese sword-drawing styles for several years and own a number of swords and armor pieces

PERSONAL ACHIEVEMENTS

- United States Kido Federation Black Belt Hall Of Fame - Outstanding Senior Instructor of The Year 2020
- JROTC Award - Veterans of Foreign Wars WW1 Award - for 4-year cadets who possess leadership capabilities and maintain academic standards.
- JROTC Award - Scottish Rites Award - for outstanding underclassmen in a 4-year program who demonstrate leadership abilities and maintain high academic standards.
- As a teenager, I was invited to live at Lake George in upstate NY one summer and apprenticed to a wood carver. He specialized in Tlingit totem poles from the Pacific Northwest. I learned how to fabricate my own tools and then spent several weeks working on my own project, a 4-foot-tall Tlingit-style totem pole.

PORTER HUGHES

> "
> *I was always an introspective person,*
> *but I learned to hone that into a useful*
> *skill as a martial artist.*

WHY THE MARTIAL ARTS?

For most of my early childhood, I lived in various deep south towns and lived on a farm in the mountains of Western North Carolina. By the age of eight, I was a decent rider and owned a horse. I regularly drove the family tractor and a small bulldozer. My father taught me to work on cars, shoot guns, and handle a chainsaw. He was a heavy equipment operator who traveled a lot, and we lived at the far end of a long dirt road with only two neighbors (no kids), so I spent most of my time alone, playing in the mountains with my dog, Blackie.

When I was nine, my parents divorced, and my mother took my two baby brothers and me back to New York. Imagine walking into a rough and rowdy suburban NY elementary school with a heavy farm boy accent, stories about guns and bulldozers, and a name like "Porter." Within months, the number of fights I was in outnumbered the number of kids in my class.

I found a karate school one day while riding my bike, but we couldn't afford it, so I started borrowing books from the local library and reading about karate and Jujitsu. Shortly after that, my mother began dating a friend of my uncles from the Marine Corps. He had just been accepted into the police academy and was learning Small Circle Jujitsu (it was a pretty progressive police department for those days). During his time in the academy, I was his training dummy, being twisted into corkscrew positions, having my arms and wrists bent in unnatural directions, and being dumped on the floor in various directions. He had no interest in teaching me the moves, but I learned them anyway, in reverse. I began using it at school with some success. I had never worked with a partner, so my moves didn't always work properly.

When he found out I could fight, he set the rule - you can never start a fight, but if someone starts one, you finish it. That got me through middle school. By high school, things were calm and quiet, and I forgot about martial arts. I joined the US Navy in 1977, went through various schools and training stations, and was assigned to a top-secret intelligence unit stationed in the coastal swamps of Southern Florida.

In 1979, I was assigned collateral duty on the base's Emergency Reaction Force and trained on various weapons, and a pleasant surprise, Small Circle Jujitsu; I was happy! Once I left the service and re-entered civilian life with a family, studying martial arts as a hobby was out of the question; all our money went into the fixer-upper house we bought and worked on.

It wasn't until 2004, when I was living in North Carolina again when my wife came home one day and announced she had found a Taekwondo school and signed us up, that I got back into it. That was 20 years ago, and we and our two sons are still active, running our own school—something I had never imagined.

HOW HAS MARTIAL ARTS IMPACTED YOUR LIFE?

I left the Navy with various long-term injuries from a helo crash that left me unable to stand up straight after sitting, sleeping, or after car travel. Surgery on my spine was out of the question, and the pinched nerves in my

TRAINING INFORMATION

- Belt Ranks & Martial Arts Styles: 5th Dan - Jun Tong Taekwon-Do Federation, American Taekwondo, Oh Do Kwan Taekwondo, Chung Do Kwan Taekwondo, Small Circle Jujitsu, Hapkido
- Instructors/Influencers: James Craeton, K. A. Morris, Robert Dunn, Wayne Kirby, Louis Raddicione, Chuck Blackburn, Anthony Casapao
- Birthplace/Growing Up: Nyack, NY
- Yrs. In the Martial Arts: 20+ years
- Yrs. Instructing: 14 years
- School owner & Instructor at Jung Kwon Martial Arts Academy Asheville

PROFESSIONAL ORGANIZATIONS

- United States Kido Federation Hall Of Fame
- (Previously) International Jun Tong Taekwondo Federation
- (Previously) Boy Scouts of America (Scout Master)

PERSONAL ACHIEVEMENTS

- Published author: (two large trade paperback editions) with USN ONI, on military training and tactics for localized naval warfare and signals intelligence operations in the Caribbean and South America. Publicly cited in writing by CinC Atlantic Fleet as the best warfare training editions ever submitted for the Navy's TSOR (Technical Standards of Readiness) program (1984)
- Graduated from the Air Force School of Applied Cryptographic with a full diploma
- Graduated 2nd in class from Defense Language Institute, Presidio, Monterey
- 1989 - Trainer of the Year, and promoted to District Manager for the Hudson Valley, NY, and Eastern Connecticut, for CPP Pinkertons Security and Detective Services
- 2011 - Founded a family-operated martial arts school with my wife and sons. Since 2011, our program has produced a steady string of highly qualified black belts, some of whom have been offered paid positions at other schools. Our school competes in 10 different styles of Korean, Japanese, and Chinese martial arts, and since 2013 (except the COVID years), our small teams have taken over 490 1st, 2nd, and 3rd place wins

MAJOR ACHIEVEMENTS

- 1977-1985 Tactical Combat Intelligence Analyst; US Naval Expeditionary Forces Medal, US Armed Forces Expeditionary Medal, 2 Meritorious Unit Citations, and 19 various commendations for spec-ops/combat deployments, including 57 combat missions as an uncertified volunteer member of shipboard helo air detachments HSL 32 and HSL 33.

- 1978-1984 I was team leader on various deployed air/land/sea teams based on 9 different USN ships (carriers, destroyers and frigates).

- 1984-1985 I was promoted to senior NCO in charge of a 32-person team doing short-notice deployments all over the Western Hemisphere and Africa. During this time I was collaterally assigned to the Admiral, CinC, Atlantic Fleet training team, and was invited to write for the US Navy's Office of Naval Intelligence training program.

- 2016-2022 Regional SE USA Director, International Jun Tong Taekwondo Federation

- 2016 USKF Black Belt Hall of Fame - Contributions to the Martial Arts (for my research program on original Chung Do Kwan/Oh Do Kwan Taekwondo practice methodology in the 1940s and 1950s).

- 2020 - USKF Black Belt Hall of Fame - Master of the Year

HOW HAS MARTIAL ARTS IMPACTED YOUR LIFE? (CONTINUED)

hands and legs became a background thing that I had just dealt with. Within three years of beginning practice in 2004, 75% of my issues had been resolved.

Due to my solitary childhood, I was always an introspective person, but I learned to hone that into a useful skill as a martial artist. I try to always review and revise my initial reactions and opinions before I speak or act—or react—when confronted with a problem or a conflict.

This approach has placed me in a position where I rarely lose my temper and almost always am able to decipher a problem and fix it before it develops (whether it be a functional anatomical problem with a new student or an intrapersonal issue between students or instructors). I run our school with nearly zero drama, possibly our greatest strength.

Become an
AMAA MEMBER!

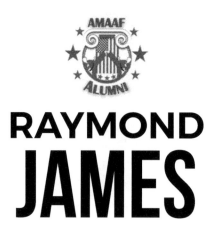

RAYMOND
JAMES

"

Martial arts have allowed me to diffuse violence, inspire, uplift, and transform minds, bodies, and spirits.

a very young age. I learned early on that even in the worst surroundings, one can still grow in a very different and positive way.

HOW HAS MARTIAL ARTS IMPACTED YOUR LIFE?

Studying martial arts has profoundly shaped my life in numerous ways. It has helped me organize my ideas, thoughts, and visions as an artist, allowing me to slow down the hectic pace of the world and discover how to achieve balance within myself and with others. Through martial arts, I have met people from all walks of life, forming deep friendships and even family-like bonds. It has given me the opportunity to travel, experience diverse cultures, compete with some of the most talented individuals in sports and art, and appreciate the beauty of the world. Moreover, it has enabled me to teach others to do the same. Martial arts have allowed me to diffuse violence, inspire, uplift, and transform minds, bodies, and spirits. They make a significant difference and promote overall well-being. Through martial arts, I have learned to persevere through adversity, become aware of the energies around and within me, master my thoughts, and improve in various roles such as producer, cinematographer, writer, actor, stuntman,

WHY THE MARTIAL ARTS?

I initially joined martial arts classes as a way to channel my energy constructively. At the time, I was frequently getting into trouble at school and lacked control and discipline. My mother was worried that without a proper outlet for my energetic and curious nature, my personal growth might be hindered. We lived in a very impoverished area of Rockland County called Spring Valley, specifically in one of its most dangerous parts known as "THE HILL"—a far cry from Beverly Hills. It was common to witness drug dealers, violence, and random acts of ignorance. My mom truly saved me from this environment by placing me in a cultured setting from

HOW HAS MARTIAL ARTS IMPACTED YOUR LIFE? (CONTINUED)

choreographer, director, athlete, and human being. Martial arts have given me purpose, helped me overcome challenges, allowed me to give back to my community, and truly understand the profound impact they can have on the development of any individual.

TRAINING INFORMATION

- Belt Ranks & Martial Arts Styles: Tang Soo Do (4th Degree), WTF Tae Kwon Do (3rd Degree), ITF Tae Kwon Do (3rd Degree), Western Boxing (Since age 15), Wrestling (Since1996), Muay Thai (Since 2000), Tai Chi (Since 1995), Kung Fu (Since 1995), Judo (since 2000), BJJ (since 2000), MMA

- Instructors/Influencers: Grand Master Anthony Richards, Grand Master Charles Lundi, Grand Master B.M Kim, Grand Master Jung Chu Lee, Master Kru Phil Nurse, Grand Master Guerredo, Sifu Karl Romain, Master Ish Perez, Sword Master Sir Richard Ryan, Sifu Samuel Kwok, Grand Master Robert Goldman

- Birthplace/Growing Up: Jamaica West Indies / Rockland County, NY

- Yrs. In the Martial Arts: 36 years

- Yrs. Instructing: 25 years

- School owner, Manger, Instructor & Coach

PROFESSIONAL ORGANIZATIONS

- Kukkiwon
- AMAA Award Recipient
- Masters Hall of Fame Recipient
- Action Martial Arts Hall of Honors Recipient
- World Martial Arts Masters Association Recipient

PERSONAL ACHIEVEMENTS

- Jamaican Tae Kwon Do National Team Member
- Action Martial Arts Hall of Honors Inductee
- 4x Good Will Games Champion
- Cover & Tear Sheets featuring Martial Arts
- Men's Health
- Details
- Muscle & Fitness
- Muscular Development
- Flex
- GQ
- Getty Images Editorial & Creative Contributor
- 10th Year Series Producer for NYC TV: Shows scope featuring Art, Culture & Travel
- Business Owner
- Mixed Media Professional
- Actor - Stage & Screen
- Model - Print & Runway
- Writer, Author & Editor
- Creative Director - For several companies
- Photographed the AMAA Who's Who in the Martial Arts Legacy Weekend (2022)
- Awarded Who's Who in the Martial Arts Bill "Superfoot" Wallace Legacy Award (2022) — Top Martial Artist chosen from the State of New York

MAJOR ACHIEVEMENTS

- New York State Champ (several times)
- US OPEN Champ (several times)
- Global Campaign for Isopure Company
- Jamaican National Team Member since 2016
- In January 2024, I had the incredible honor of becoming one of the first foreigners allowed to learn and teach High-Level Meditation (Anāpānasati) under the guidance of Grand Master Acharavadee Wongsakon. *A heartfelt thank you to Dr. Robert Goldman for this life-changing opportunity.*

DONALD JETT

"
Martial arts gave the external and internal foundation of life and sharing culture to make a difference.

WHY THE MARTIAL ARTS?

It was in 1968 that I discovered Chinese martial arts. Playful as I was while watching Kung Fu movies, my father put me in the care of a Taiwanese soldier, who gave me my first introduction. As a precocious child, as recalled by older siblings, people saw me as shy and self-preserved but energetic. If there is any disturbance, I would disappear into a room and listen to Asian music. Being the youngest, if I was being picked on, my older brother told me that he would beat me and the other person if I were beaten up. That fear alone turned me into a fighter.

For over 50 years, I've studied various Northern and Southern Chinese martial arts, with a stint in Kenpo Karate and one year of Shotokan Karate. In addition, I sought out other Kung Fu instruction during my father's military travel. I continued Chinese styles Long Xing Pai (Long Hsing Dragon), Pai Lum (White Dragon), Yong Chun (Wing Chun), and Ca Li Fu (Choy Li Fut) as my proficient study. Internal Chinese arts majorly balanced Chen Wu style Tai-Chi and

Baguazhang's "eight trigram palm." This was when I was introduced to Grandmaster Wang Jurong, the daughter of Wang Ziping. This time, I began the Kung Fu circuit and joined the USAWKF. While in Houston, I attended the Institute of Chinese Martial Arts and Medicine. I became a licensed acupuncturist to gain more extensive knowledge, with martial arts expertise, to coincide equally with the mind and body. The internal system has helped me lay a foundation of health and fitness to maximize my martial arts performance and help others. To keep it simple, a body maintaining proper nutrition and good blood circulation creates a strong heart. Martial arts is more than a rank or title; it is a way of life!

I would like to give honor and respect to other great pioneers who laid this foundation for me and other martial artists.

HOW HAS MARTIAL ARTS IMPACTED YOUR LIFE?

A martial artist is a human being first. Just as nationalities have nothing to do with one's humanity, they have nothing to do with martial arts. Life is a constant process of relating. So, this formed some major achievements in my life. In America, many

students are taught to defend themselves from school bullies or feel more confident while out at night. Others belong to karate or dojo clubs and follow the tournament circuit, collecting as many trophies as their talents can win.

I wanted to learn the seemingly complex philosophical concepts or constraints with ethical notoriety from past warrior societies. The martial way taught me technical proficiency and the external reward of athletic success. It opened the door to a rich heritage of ethical principles, training approaches, and esoteric capabilities that enriched my martial arts experience. It sharpened my ability to defend myself or succeed in competition, but most importantly, it is a way of living. It's a holistic discipline aimed at pursuing excellence in the training hall and life. I strived to apply the way in every vocation to achieve every field of my endeavor.

Martial arts gave the external and internal foundation of life and sharing culture to make a difference.

TRAINING INFORMATION

- Belt Ranks & Martial Arts Styles: Kenpo Karate, Shotokan Karate, Long Xing Pai (Long Hsing Dragon), Pai Lum (White Dragon), Yong Chun (Wing Chun), Ca Li Fu (Choy Li Fut), and Kung Fu

- Instructors/Influencers: Grandmaster Anthony Goh, Grandmaster Wang Jurong, Grandmaster Johnny Lee, Master Charles Dixon, Grandmaster Alex, Tat Mau Wong, and Grandmaster Shawn Liu

- Birthplace/Growing Up: El Paso, TX / Worldwide

TRAINING INFORMATION (CONTINUED)

- Yrs. In the Martial Arts: 56 years
- Yrs. Instructing: 41 years
- Department of Justice Instructor

PROFESSIONAL ORGANIZATIONS

- A.C.E. certificate
- National Organization Black Law Enforcement Executive Justice By Action
- Kung Fu Federation

PERSONAL ACHIEVEMENTS

- We are all loved first. To be positive is to know yourself and the creator. A good leader is acquired when you realize yourself no matter what you do in life. If you don't know yourself, you will never appreciate anything.

- Today's work of a great human being is to know yourself and assist others. I have discovered this self-help through personal experience and dedicated learning. It's the greatest help to a given task. It seems there is no end to this ongoing process. Remember to stay positive, which means enjoying yourself, planning, and accomplishing things with gratitude. Staying positive is the greatest personal achievement for me and others.

MAJOR ACHIEVEMENTS

- Working with the Department of Justice, Big Brothers Mentoring Program, Eastern Band of Cherokee Youth programs, and many martial arts awards. I owned and operated a health and wellness center and a fitness center. I organized the Art of War and China Comes to Atlanta (China Cultural Arts Festival and Expo 2003), bringing various cultures and masters from around the globe. I've officiated many tournaments for many years, including the Battle of Atlanta and the International Chinese Martial Arts Championships. I thought a career in corporate law was my answer, but I became an Instructor with D.O.J., which opened doors to give back to society and bring cultures together; it was an outstanding achievement.

- International Hall of Fame 2023, Master of Martial Arts Hall of Fame 2021, Actions Hall of Honors 2022, Who's Who Legend Award 2021

- Lastly, I am honored to hold the title of Police Tactical Instructors of America International and a Global Forum Leader for Future Development.

JEROME JOHNSON

"

To whom much is given, much is required.

WHY THE MARTIAL ARTS?

Senior Grandmaster Johnson is a 10th Degree Black Belt with more than 50 years of Martial Arts experience, a Martial Arts Hall of Famer, winner of the Sport Karate Museum Dragon Image Fighting Award, the Dojo Organization, United Karate Federation, American Martial Arts Association, and many others.

Mr. Johnson has been awarded multiple competitor of the year awards and fighting championships in light, middle, and light heavyweight divisions. Additionally, he is the National arbitrator for the National Black Belt League and several other sport karate competition circuits.

Mr. Johnson has also received Businessman of the Year, Martial Artist of the Year, Instructor of the Year, Promoter of the Year, and Man of the Year. He has been listed with Who's Who of the Martial Arts and the prestigious Lifetime Achievement Award.

Magic, as he is affectionately known, is a successful businessman, CEO, and president of W&J sales, President of CPG Technology, and former President of T-soft Software, and President of Polaris International. He is currently serving as president of The RRV Corvette Car Club. He has many other business and social titles.

Magic truly enjoys working with young fighters helping them to accomplish their dreams. His first love is being a mentor for young people and a life coach, helping them reach their dreams and goals, and more importantly, being better people. Magic is passionately involved with his church, and if you know Magic, his family is first, and he loves them dearly; also, those who know him know he works hard at being a good friend; he always says everyone counts.

Magic's favorite quotes are: "To whom much is given much is required," "Life is Karate, Karate is Life," and "Honor and Respect Always."

HOW HAS MARTIAL ARTS IMPACTED YOUR LIFE?

I am a 10th Degree Black Belt and began my martial arts training in 1968. My biggest influences in the arts are Ron Wilson, Bill Wallace and Jan Wellendorf. Martial arts has influenced me most in the areas of discipline, focus and work ethics. Being a teacher, mentor and champion are what I'm most proud of in my martial arts career.

WILLARD
JOHNSON

"

Martial Arts has taught me much self-control and improved my overall health and mental status.

WHY THE MARTIAL ARTS?

I started the practice of martial arts as a way to improve my health. I was born with heart disease and have struggled all my life with physical activity due to a disease that took one of my parents and a sister. I was born one of eleven children to a sharecropper family in the Foothills of the Appalachian Mountains. Growing up in poverty, there was little chance to take martial arts classes.

I grew up watching Bruce Lee and Chuck Norris, dreaming of a day I could practice martial arts. I always wanted more out of life, so I became the first in my family to graduate high school and attend college. I graduated from the University of Colorado School of Banking and have been a successful banker for 29 years. I presently hold the office of President/SEO of one of the most successful banks in KY.

I met my instructor when he was performing a martial arts demonstration at our elementary school. My love for martial arts began that day. Grandmaster Timmy Pickens has been my idol. He has taught hundreds of students, many of whom have been my close friends. In January of 2013, my heart condition got worse, and I went through a quadruple bypass surgery. The months post-surgery were very difficult, trying to get back into physical condition and lead an active lifestyle. I reconnected with Grandmaster Pickens and finally got my break as he agreed to teach me martial arts.

Today, I'm stronger physically and mentally than at any time in my life. Martial arts are a part of my daily lifestyle, and I will always be grateful for the opportunity to serve the martial arts community.

HOW HAS MARTIAL ARTS IMPACTED YOUR LIFE?

Martial arts has taught me that you don't have to settle for less when it comes to your health. I have suffered from heart disease since childhood, and martial arts has helped me live a better active lifestyle. I can now enjoy spending time with family and friends in the outdoor lifestyle. Martial arts has taught me much self-control and improved my overall health and mental status.

My wife and I have been married for 27 years, and martial arts have given me the courage to be a good husband. Martial arts have shown me that I can be confident that I can defend my family in a world full of hate. My teacher has taught me more than any classroom in my 16 years of education.

TRAINING INFORMATION

- Martial Arts Styles & Rank: Wing Chun, Snake, 2nd Degree Black Belt
- Instructors/Influencers: Grandmaster Timmy Pickens
- Birthplace/Growing Up: Albany, NY
- Yrs. In the Martial Arts: 7 years
- Yrs. Instructing: 1 year
- Instructor

PROFESSIONAL ORGANIZATIONS

- KY Bankers Association
- KY State Republican Party
- Appalachian Regional Foundation

PERSONAL ACHIEVEMENTS

- Professional Banker
- Financial Literacy Coach
- Elected County Commissioner
- Graduated Colorado School of Finance
- Life and Health Insurance License Holder
- Certified Welder
- Holds a 2nd-degree Black Belt in Wing Chun and Snake style.

MAJOR ACHIEVEMENTS

- I came from poverty to build a better life for myself and my family. Through martial arts, I have learned so many things about respect for others and myself.

Become an
AMAA MEMBER!

KEVIN L. JONES

"

Martial arts have taught me to be an introspective thinker before I speak or take action.

WHY THE MARTIAL ARTS?

Born on March 3, 1972, my journey as a servant leader began in Paterson, New Jersey. Growing up in this vibrant urban environment, I was exposed to the competitive nature of city life and the diverse behaviors that came with it. Navigating the challenges of urban life during the '70s and '80s taught me resilience and adaptability. After moving around the East Coast for several years, my family settled in Detroit, Michigan, where I faced the challenge of adapting to a new urban landscape. Martial arts, introduced to me through community outreach programs, became my sanctuary, offering mental, physical, and spiritual defense against the challenges I faced.

In Detroit, my educational journey continued at John J. Pershing High School. There, I gained invaluable knowledge and skills. The vocational program I attended exposed me to professional environments and career opportunities. As a member of the football and track and field teams, I learned the importance of teamwork and commitment in achieving common goals. Under the mentorship of my principal and teachers, I excelled academically, graduated, and enrolled in an Emergency Medical Technician (EMT) program. That summer, I began working as an Emergency Room Technician (ERT) at Hutzel Women's Hospital in the Detroit Medical Center.

Simultaneously, my principal, Mr. Woodhouse, introduced me to the art of Taekwondo, sparking my competitive martial arts journey. Competing locally, regionally, and in Canada, I was introduced to Ji Do Kwan Taekwondo by Grand Master Oh Yung Chung of Tiger Chung's Taekwondo. Master Chung, a former military martial arts instructor in Korea, became my mentor, teaching me the scientific aspects of martial arts and inspiring me to pursue a leadership role in the military.

I grew to appreciate the idea that martial arts training helps to grow individual abilities and how martial arts consciousness helps to grow communities. This belief led me to join the United States Air Force, seeking to hone my leadership skills. While serving in the United States Air Force, community involvement became a cornerstone of my personal development. I trained as

TRAINING INFORMATION

- Martial Arts Styles & Rank: 6th Degree Black Belt-Jidokwan, 7th Degree-ChangMooKwan Taekwondo
- Instructors/Influencers: Oh Yung Chung
- Birthplace/Growing Up: Paterson, NJ / Detroit, MI
- Yrs. In the Martial Arts: 34 years
- Yrs. Instructing: 34 year
- School owner, Manager & Instructor, Defense Health Agency, Contract Specialist

PROFESSIONAL ORGANIZATIONS

- United States Military Veterans
- United States Armed Forces Taekwondo Alumni
- United States Taekwondo Grand Masters Society
- United States National Taekwondo Federation
- The Defense Health Agency
- United States Veterans Affairs

PERSONAL ACHIEVEMENTS

- All Air Force Featherweight 1997-2002
- All Armed Forces Team member 1998-2001
- 10th CISM World Championship Bronze Medal

MAJOR ACHIEVEMENTS

- Air Force Community College, Associate of Surgical Technology
- University of Maryland Global Campus Bachelor of Health Services Management
- University of Maryland Global Campus Masters of Acquisitions and Contract Management
- Defense Acquisition University Contracting Certification

a Surgical Services Specialist (4N1x1) in the Surgical Operations Squadron. I then specialized as an Orthopedic Surgical Technician. Over the years, I gained expertise, rose through the ranks, and assumed more responsibilities, coaching, mentoring, and teaching fellow military personnel in the U.S. and Europe.

My educational pursuits continued at the U.S. Air Force Community College, where I earned an Associate's Degree in Surgical Technology. I later graduated from the University of Maryland Global Campus with a Bachelor's in Health Services Management and a Master's in Acquisitions and Contract Management.

While serving in the Air Force, I was selected to represent my country in the All-Air Force, All-Armed Forces Sports Programs, and the Conseil International du Sport Militaire (CISM) program as a Taekwondo athlete. In 1997, I earned a gold medal as a featherweight on the All-Air Force Taekwondo Team. In 1998, I won another gold medal as a featherweight on the All-Armed Forces Taekwondo Team and represented the U.S. at the 10th World CISM Games, winning a bronze medal. From 1999 to 2002, I continued to compete and contribute as an administrator/athlete, joining fellow military martial arts veterans in the Chang Moo Kwan martial arts association.

Over my 20 years of service, I had the privilege of learning from the world's best leaders and mentors. Those experiences made me a better husband, father, and businessperson. My journey in martial arts was shared with my family, who witnessed and supported my growth along the way. I am deeply grateful for my development, which has benefited my family, friends, and the international martial arts community.

HOW HAS MARTIAL ARTS IMPACTED YOUR LIFE?

Martial arts have taught me to be an introspective thinker before I speak or take action. They have helped develop my mind, body, and soul to support my ideas, attitudes, and actions. I am responsible for my own righteousness, which I use to improve the lives of those around me. This is how martial arts have impacted my life.

Become an
AMAA
MEMBER!

LAURIE
JULIAN

" Studying Kuntaw taught me various life-long qualities, such as patience, perseverance, understanding, loyalty, and discipline.

WHY THE MARTIAL ARTS?

My sister introduced me to Kuntaw as she was curious about Filipino martial arts. As I started to attend more classes, I fell in love with the art. We were greeted with open arms, and as we stood attention, the first thing my instructor had the class do was introduce themselves. They explained that we call each other "Kyud," meaning brother, and "Kyudai," meaning sister. I instantly knew at that moment that Kuntaw treated everyone like family and wanted every member to succeed.

HOW HAS MARTIAL ARTS IMPACTED YOUR LIFE?

Studying Kuntaw taught me various life-long qualities, such as patience, perseverance, understanding, loyalty, and discipline. I also have a higher respect for the people around me, especially my elders. Kuntaw has also taught me to always be alert to my surroundings, no matter the circumstance.

TRAINING INFORMATION

- Martial Arts Styles & Rank: Kuntaw-1st Degree Black Belt
- Instructors/Influencers: Great Grand Master Carlito Lanada Sr., Grand Master Cyrus Lagumen, Sr., Master Rusty Udan, Kyud Cyrus Lagumen, Jr.
- Birthplace/Growing Up: Virginia Beach, VA
- Yrs. In the Martial Arts: 9 years
- Yrs. Instructing: 4 years
- Instructor

PROFESSIONAL ORGANIZATIONS

- American Dental Hygiene Association - Student Chapter

PERSONAL ACHIEVEMENTS

- Yellow Belt Promotion: 11/6/16
- Green Belt Promotion: 5/6/17
- Blue Belt Promotion: 11/3/18
- Brown Belt Promotion: 11/2/19
- 1st Degree Black Belt Promotion: 5/20/23
- Kombat Klassic Grand Champion, VA, 2017
- Old School Fall Classic Junior Grand Champion, VA, 2017
- Grandmaster Preston E. Rodgers Superstars Karate Championships Grand Champion, VA, 2018
- Jack Dark Battle of the Seven Cities Grand Champion, VA, 2018
- Kombat Klassic Grand Champion Waldorf, Maryland, 2019
- Old School Fall Class Grand Champion, VA, 2019
- Battle of the Warriors Kuntaw Martial Arts Tournament Grand Champion, VA, 2019
- Wayne Dean Classic Grand Champion 18 & Older, VA, 2023
- Leader of Kuntaw Demo Team, 2021-2023

MAJOR ACHIEVEMENTS

- American Freestyle Kaizen Association (AFKA) Hall of Fame Inductee (Assistant Instructor): October 2022
- American Freestyle Kaizen Association (AFKA) Hall of Fame Inductee (Outstanding Martial Artist): 2023
- Phi Theta Kappa Honors Society Tidewater Community College Virginia Beach Chapter: 2022-present
- National Honor's Society of Leadership and Success Old Dominion University: 2024-present
- Leaders Candidate Silver Distinction Old Dominion University: 2024-present
- Bachelor of Science in Dental Hygiene, Cum Laude, Old Dominion University: 2024

RICHARD M.
KAHN

> *I developed a reputation for putting my Kenpo training to good use outside the judged arena on many occasions...*

impeccable. It dates back to AD 1235 with Zenko Yoshida, the 10th Grandmaster of Kenpo, followed by Jiroku Yoshida (1818 — 1890), the 19th Grandmaster, Sukuhei Yosida (1890 — 1943), the 20th Grandmaster, James Mitosi (1916-1981), the 21st Grandmaster, William Chow (1914 — 1982) Founder of Kenpo Karate, Ed Parker (1931 — 1990) Founder of American Kenpo Karate, and finally Great Grandmaster Al Tracy, Founder of Tracy's Kenpo Karate.

Great Grandmaster Al Tracy trained and promoted some 113 first-generation black belts, including those directly identified on Kahn's Hanshi diploma lineage: Grandmaster J.T. Will, Grandmaster Dick Willet, and Grandmaster Orned "Chicken" Gabriel. Richard Kahn has been etched into the Tracy Family Tree of Kenpo Black Belts in this line. GM "Sifu Jack" Shamburger is the second generation, and Hanshi Richard Kahn is the 3rd generation of GGM Al Tracy black belts.

Richard was introduced by GM Sifu Jack initially to GGM Al Tracy in the late 1980's. GM Sifu Jack was awarded his own Kenpo system by the Tracy organization in 1990, called Shamburger's Chinese Hawaiian Kenpo. Richard started long-distance training with GGM Al Tracy in 1994. Richard also trained for some years with GM Bart Vale back in the 1990s. GM "Sifu Bart" is the second generation

WHY THE MARTIAL ARTS?

Richard Kahn is an 8th Dan Hachidan Hanshi Black Belt, with four decades of martial arts training and experience, 38 years of which include Kenpo. Richard was awarded Hanshi rank in 2021 by his instructor, Sifu Jack F.C. Shamburger, who was awarded 10th Dan Grand Master ("GM") by GGM Al Tracy in 2015. Richard's Hachidan diploma includes a marque of photos and names reflecting iconic lineage in the Tracy system.

Lineage is the defining pedigree of recognized martial arts, and Richard's lineage above his entry in the Tracy Kenpo Family Tree of Black Belts is ancient and

Richard Kahn fought competitively for seven years: two years full contact and five years sport karate. He had over 220 amateur judged fight rounds on the official records, competing regionally in the Northeast, Nationally, and Internationally, and enjoying top regional, national, and international rankings. Richard's won over 70 trophies, awards, plaques and medals.

Due to the times and things he was into, Richard developed a reputation for putting his Kenpo training to good use outside the judged arena on many occasions. Delivery from which he remains grateful and carries many memories and reminders.

In 2020, Richard was honored by inclusion in the Martial Arts History book. In 2019, Richard was honored with a photo layout inclusion as one of the World's Greatest Martial Artists, Vol. 12. In 2017, Richard was recognized by the Gathering of Eagles Kenpo Yudanshakai for his contribution to the Martial Arts in Dallas, TX. Richard had the honor of escorting Steve "Nasty" Anderson to the prestigious banquet. In 2015, Richard was honored with inclusion in Tracy's Kenpo Family Tree of Black Belts at Gathering of Eagles, Chicago. In 2013, Richard was inducted into the Action Martial Arts Magazine Hall of Honors.

In August 2024, Richard is nominated for induction into the world-renowned, super prestigious Kenpo Hall of Fame Masters Division. Honored and humbled to be in the company of an exclusive membership that numbers just over 100.

In August 2024, Richard was nominated for inclusion in the 2024 AMAA Legacy Book 10th Anniversary Biography Edition and recipient of the AMAA Who's Who Legacy Award. It is an event recognizing such legends as Chuck Norris, Joe Corley, Jhoon Ree, Bill "Superfoot" Wallace, Cynthia Rothrock, and other martial arts legends.

under GM Tom Dunne. Richard and GM Sifu Bart have remained in contact for decades. GM Bart Vale is the founder of shootfighting and one of the early fighters who led up to the popular MMA and combo standup and grappling sports.

Richard began studying Kenpo Karate with GM Jack Shamburger in the mid-1980s. Prior to this, Richard had trained and competed in full-contact kickboxing for two years, a veteran of more than a few dozen full-contact fights in that time. World Champion Soke GM Steve "Nasty" Anderson, promoted to 9th Dan Kudan Hanshi by GM Sifu Jack Shamburger, gave excellent instruction in sport karate. This augmented GM Sifu Jack's US Marine Corps competitive experience in fighting and forms during the 1970s that he taught his students.

MICHAEL KAISER

"
After studying martial arts for a while, you learn you have two families: your home life family and your martial arts family...

I have the ability to meet new people and train with them. As I continued my martial arts training and did some traveling, I learned how lucky I was to have the teacher I had. Out-of-state students had mentioned to me how lucky I was to be able to train with Grandmaster Dana Miller regularly. After visiting several other schools, I realized my out-of-state friends were right. It was indeed very lucky to be training with the best.

After 39 years of training, I couldn't think of a better way to spend my time. Because of my time in martial arts, I believe I am a better family man; I also think it made me a better coach and a better foreman at work. Nowadays, I play a game called pickleball, and it certainly has helped me to be a better pickleball player.

WHY THE MARTIAL ARTS?

I started studying martial arts in 1985 and thought I would take martial arts for several reasons. My wife and I have been talking. She mentioned that I needed a hobby, and we both agreed I was a high-strung and nervous type of person and that maybe Tai Chi would help. Also, about this time, I thought I was not a large person; I felt I needed boxing, wrestling, or martial arts to defend myself. In my mind was the fact that I had three children, a home, and a wife that needed protection. I couldn't think of a better fit. It gave me a hobby that had a calming effect on me, and the bonus was it was fun and produced confidence. I felt good. It certainly is a healthy activity, and knowing you can protect your family and yourself is a nice feeling.

HOW HAS MARTIAL ARTS IMPACTED YOUR LIFE?

When I started martial arts, I wasn't very comfortable talking in front of groups. One of the rituals we had was after class, students were asked what they had learned or liked at that particular class and explained it to the class. Over time, it helped me overcome my fear of talking in front of groups in my professional career.

I eventually achieved the position of foreman. Of course, I needed to be comfortable talking in front of a group. Discipline is important in martial arts and also in raising children, of which I have three. I also coached baseball, softball, soccer, and basketball. As a person moves up through the ranks in martial arts, you need discipline, leadership skills, and speaking skills, all of which you need in life.

When you are training with other people, you need to be careful not to harm one another. In life, you might have to control someone without hurting them. Martial arts also teach humility, an important asset in one's personality. Confidence is helpful when coaching, as a foreman, and when handling yourself in stressful situations. Lastly, after studying martial arts for a while, you learn you have two families: your home life family and your martial arts family, which are both very important.

TRAINING INFORMATION

- Martial Arts Styles & Rank: 1st Degree-Shaolin, 2nd-Degree Kenpo, Extensive Training in US Chuan Fa Joint Locks, US Chuan Fa Boxing, US Chuan Fa Ground Fighting, US Chuan Fa Weapons, 6th Degree-Zu Wei Shu
- Instructors/Influencers: Grand Master Dana Miller
- Birthplace/Growing Up: MN / St. Paul, MN
- Yrs. In the Martial Arts: 39 years
- Yrs. Instructing: 20 years
- Instructor

PROFESSIONAL ORGANIZATIONS

- Journeyman Electrician
- Master Electrician
- Member of US Chuan
- Master Zu Wei Shu

PERSONAL ACHIEVEMENTS

- Raising three children who have positively impacted society
- Being a coach of all three children's sports
- Having past players come to me and say how much they learned and how much they enjoyed playing for me

MAJOR ACHIEVEMENTS

- Award from US Secret Service
- Award from the City of St. Paul Fire Department
- Achieved 6th Degree in Zu Wei Shu
- In 2007, I was inducted into the USA Martial Arts Hall of Fame

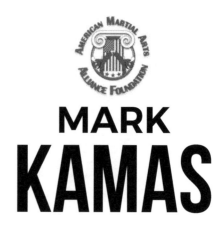

MARK
KAMAS

"
Witnessing the impact of martial arts on my students' lives has been profoundly rewarding.

WHY THE MARTIAL ARTS?

My family moved to Stillwater, MN, when I was in junior high school. I faced the classic challenge of fitting in. Like many kids, I tried my hand at different sports, hoping to find my niche. It wasn't until I stumbled upon a karate flyer at school that things started to click.

The flyer was simple: "Learn Karate on Thursday Night at 7:00 p.m." It caught my eye, and after some convincing, my parents agreed to drive me 30 miles for those first lessons. Karate became a big part of my life throughout high school, even though my part-time job made it tough to keep up with regular practice.

Fresh out of high school, I joined the US Army Nation Guard. While in AIT training, I discovered boxing and my passion for combat sports. I found myself drawn to long hours of training, and the change of competition in boxing, and the intensity of it reignited my love for martial arts. When I came

back home, I stumbled upon Chuan Lu Kung Fu, and it felt like a perfect fit. Through dedicated training and perseverance, I learned to be a good student and a good instructor.

Training in this style introduced me to incredible mentors and peers, leading to the establishment of my first school, Dragons Kung Fu, in 1994. Though it faced initial challenges, the school thrived, expanding from a humble 900-square-foot basement to a spacious storefront on Main Street.

Martial arts have profoundly shaped my life, instilling discipline, honor, focus, and respect from an early age. These values guided me not only in opening my own school but also in advancing my professional career and pursuing education later in life. Respect for the arts and its teachings continues to enrich my journey as an instructor and a student.

HOW HAS MARTIAL ARTS IMPACTED YOUR LIFE?

Studying martial arts left a profound impact on my life over the course of 43 years, becoming a cornerstone that has shaped both my personal and professional journey. Through this journey, I've encountered remarkable individuals, forged lifelong friendships, and honed invaluable skills that extend far beyond the confines of the school.

One of the most substantial impacts of my martial arts journey has been its role in maintaining balance and focus in my life. Amidst life's challenges, the discipline instilled by martial arts has served to keep me grounded, guiding me through both good times and bad. This sense of centering has not only enriched my personal well-being but has also contributed directly to the success of my other two businesses. The principles of discipline, resilience, and perseverance learned in martial arts have transformed effortlessly in every decision and action with a sense of purpose and determination.

Perhaps the most fulfilling aspect of my martial arts journey has been the opportunity to pass on the wisdom and knowledge from years of training to a new generation of students. As an instructor, I have found immense fulfillment in mentoring and guiding students, not only in perfecting their physical techniques but also in nurturing their personal growth and development. Witnessing the impact of martial arts

TRAINING INFORMATION

- Martial Arts Styles & Rank: Gojo Ryu/ American Kenpo-6th Ryu, American Boxing/United States Army, Chuan Lu Kung Fu-3rd Degree Black Belt, Tae Kwon Do-6th GUP, Studying Eskrima, Hardened Target Certified Instructor, U.S. Chaun Fa Association-8th Degree Black Sash

- Instructors/Influencers: Robert Nelson, Bob Tollefson, Nilo Barron, Tom Sipin, Dana Miller

- Birthplace/Growing Up: Stillwater, MN

- Yrs. In the Martial Arts: 43 years

- Yrs. Instructing: 33 years

- School owner & Instructor at Dragons Kung Fu, Certified Firearms Trainer

PROFESSIONAL ORGANIZATIONS

- United States Martial Arts Hall of Fame
- United States Martial Arts Alliance

PERSONAL ACHIEVEMENTS

- Owner of Guardian Tactical Solutions
- Owner of The Patriot's Den Gun Shop and Training Center
- Guardian Tactical Solutions Head Firearms Instructor
- NRA certified instructor

MAJOR ACHIEVEMENTS

Fight Choreographer - Circus Juventas Shows
- Yulong the Jade Dragon - 2009
- Sawdust - 2010
- Showdown - 2012

Cosmopolitan Brotherhood Hall of Fame
• Inducted into the Cosmopolitan Brotherhood Hall of Fame 2007
• Named International Master of the Year 2007

World Head of Family Sokeship Council
• Named Kung Fu Master of the Year 2008

United States Martial Arts Hall of Fame
• Inducted into the United States Martial Arts Hall of Fame 2004
• Named Kung Fu Master of the Year 2012
• Selected for the USA National Martial Arts Team 2006
• Lifetime Member of the US Martial Arts Hall of Fame Alumni

The study of martial arts has been more than just a hobby or a profession—it has been a lifelong journey of self-discovery, personal growth, and service to others. It has enriched my life in ways I could never have imagined and continues to inspire me to strive for excellence both inside and outside the school.

HOW HAS MARTIAL ARTS IMPACTED YOUR LIFE? (CONTINUED)

on my students' lives has been profoundly rewarding. From improving their self-confidence to instilling a sense of discipline and respect, the martial arts have empowered them to navigate life's challenges with resilience and grace.

The ripple effects of our teachings extend far beyond the confines of the school. Hearing from parents years later, expressing gratitude for the positive influence martial arts has had on their children's lives serves as a positive reminder of the impact we can have on others. Knowing that our teachings have helped steer young individuals away from potentially detrimental paths and towards a life of purpose and integrity is both humbling and deeply gratifying. It underscores the transformative power of martial arts not only as a means of self-defense but as a vehicle for personal growth, community building, and positive social change.

CHRIS
KESTERSON

"

My life, base, and core values are heavily influenced and shaped by my 40-plus years in Martial Arts.

WHY THE MARTIAL ARTS?

My father got my brother and I started at an early age. I was fortunate to grow up in an era of popular martial arts movies. As many youths at the time did, I watched actors/artists like Bruce Lee and Chuck Norris perform amazing performances on the screen. I was in awe!

I began my journey as many did with the available arts at the time in my location. Isshinryu was my first discipline, followed several years later by Taekwondo. I enjoyed the athletic qualities of both arts. As I aged, I could travel more, and other arts became available. I was hungry to try each I encountered, and over the past 40-plus years, it has been an amazing journey.

HOW HAS MARTIAL ARTS IMPACTED YOUR LIFE?

I have learned that no matter how many years you dedicate to your art, the degrees you earn, and how many disciplines you study to improve your craft and art, we should all hunger for more knowledge. We should be that anxious, eager, and hungry white belt we began as. Knowledge is the true power in martial arts, and the ability to constantly learn is crucial. My life, base, and core values are heavily influenced and shaped by my 40-plus years in martial arts.

Become an
AMAA MEMBER!

TRAINING INFORMATION (CONTINUED)

- Martial Arts Styles & Rank: Kestese 8th Dan, Karate 2nd Dan, TKD, Judo, BJJ, Ketsugo, Krav Maga, Boxing
- Instructors/Influencers: Howard Pittenger
- Birthplace/Growing Up: Knoxville, TN
- Yrs. In the Martial Arts: 48 years
- Yrs. Instructing: 34 years
- Instructor

PROFESSIONAL ORGANIZATIONS

- AMAFF (Who's Who Inductee & Ambassador)
- USMA
- USMAA
- WBBB
- MAMWF
- IBJJF
- CAC Leadership
- Shekinah Masonic Lodge
- Moose Lodge
- Tennessee Sheriff's Asso.
- ICMAF
- SKKA
- American Legion
- AZA
- POI
- Kentucky Colonels

PERSONAL ACHIEVEMENTS

- IMDB listed actor
- Tennessee Firearms and Defense Instructor
- HOF entries for martial arts
- Ambassador for AMAA
- SPF World Record holder

MAJOR ACHIEVEMENTS

- I am recognized for my contributions to martial arts by several organizations.

BONGSEOK
KIM

"

My values, ethics, and morals were all cultivated and strengthened through Martial Arts training.

WHY THE MARTIAL ARTS?

I started Taekwondo as part of normal physical education in public schools in South Korea. Once my family moved to the U.S., my parents enrolled me in a local Taekwondo school so I could maintain my Korean heritage, learn self-defense, and stay physically fit. Once I became serious about Taekwondo training, the U.S. Army World Class Athlete Program recruited me as a full-time competitive athlete in the U.S. Army.

HOW HAS MARTIAL ARTS IMPACTED YOUR LIFE?

My values, ethics, and morals were all cultivated and strengthened through martial arts training. The personal and moral courage required of soldiers was already instilled in me from my early martial arts training. The most valuable lesson I learned from the martial arts is that I must overcome my own obstacles to meet whatever goals are set.

TRAINING INFORMATION

- Martial Arts Styles & Rank: Taekwondo, Kukkiwon-7th Dan, Moo Duk Kwan-7th Dan

- Instructors/Influencers: Grandmaster Aquiles Won Kun Yang, Grandmaster Rodrigo Bohorquez, Grandmaster Byung Ho Choi, Grandmaster Bruce Harris, and Grandmaster Bobby Clayton

- Birthplace/Growing Up: Seoul, S. Korea / Miami, FL

- Yrs. In the Martial Arts: 44 years

- Yrs. Instructing: 26 years

- Organizational Leader, Current Board of Directors, USA Taekwondo (national governing body under the U.S. Olympic Committee)

PROFESSIONAL ORGANIZATIONS

- USA Taekwondo, the sole national governing body for the sport of Taekwondo under the U.S. Olympic & Paralympic Committee

- Conseil International du Sport Militaire (CISM) Taekwondo, the second-largest multi-sport organization in the world

- Taekwondo Hall of Fame

PERSONAL ACHIEVEMENTS

- 1991 International Cup, Queretaro, Mexico - Gold Medal

- 1994 World Military Taekwondo Championship, Lima, Peru - Bronze Medal

- 1994, 1997 North American CISM Friendship Exchange, Ottawa, Canada - Gold Medals

- 1993-1997, 2001- U.S. All Army and U.S. Armed Forces Taekwondo Championships - Gold Medal

- 1998-2000, Assistant Coach, U.S. Armed Forces Taekwondo Team

- 2001-2003, 2005, 2010 - Head Coach, U.S. All Army & U.S. Armed Forces Taekwondo Teams

- 2008-2014 Technical Committee Member, CISM Taekwondo Committee

- 2011, 2013 Acting President, CISM Taekwondo Committee

- 2012-2014 Secretary General, CISM Taekwondo Committee

- 2013 Inductee, Taekwondo Hall of Fame, Las Vegas, NV

- 2014-2022 President, CISM Taekwondo Committee

- 2019-Present Board of Directors, USA Taekwondo, U.S. Olympic & Paralympic Committee

MAJOR ACHIEVEMENTS

- 29 years of service in the U.S. Army

- Combat veteran (two-time Bronze Star Medal recipient)

- Served two terms as the President of the Conseil International du Sport Militaire (CISM) Taekwondo, the second-largest international multi-sport organization

- Currently serving second term on the Board of Directors for the national governing body under the U.S. Olympic & Paralympic Committee- USA Taekwondo

- Inductee in Taekwondo Hall of Fame

- "Grand Officer" in the CISM Order of Merit

STEVE KUBIK

"

As a result of being a Martial Artist, I have met some pretty interesting people and made some amazing lifelong friends.

WHY THE MARTIAL ARTS?

I started Martial Arts training in 1967 at an Okinawan Goju Ryu Club at the Marine Corps Recruit Depot in San Diego, CA. I realized that I had to do something to maintain the level of physical fitness I had achieved as a high school wrestler and from going through USMC boot camp and infantry training. I also felt that martial arts would enhance the hand-to-hand combat training I had gone through. My training was interrupted by my deployment to Vietnam from Feb. 1968 to Jan. 1970.

After discharge from the USMC, I started boxing with friends at Golden Gloves and other friends who were interested in boxing. I even got to train with Scott LeDoux a few times after he turned pro. During this time, I worked in a small neighborhood bar as a bartender and sometimes bouncer in Northeast Minneapolis, MN. This boxing training came in handy a few times. However, I found out that my reputation as a US Marine and a boxer settled disputes before they became physical.

I started Training in American Kenpo in 1980 at the Crimson Dragon School in Mora, MN. In 1982, Crimson Dragon closed, and I searched for another Kenpo school. The owner of The Karate Chop, a martial arts equipment and bookstore in Minneapolis, MN, gave me Grand Master Dana Miller's phone number. At that time, his school was teaching Chinese —Hawaiian Kenpo. Sijo Miller set me up with Bob Tollefson (3rd degree black belt at that time) early in 1983. I trained with Mr. Tollefson until Sijo Miller moved to Hinckley, MN, in 1984 (where I was residing at the time). Mr. Tollefson graciously allowed me to start training with Sijo Miller.

In 2005, I moved to Sentinel Butte, ND, and opened a school in nearby Beach, ND, from 2006 to 2012. I also taught self-defense at Home on the Range near Sentinel Butte, ND (a detention facility for delinquent boys and girls), specifically to young girls with "low self-esteem" from time to time, and conducted clinics for an organization called Women in Self Defense from time to time.

I also conducted community education martial arts training in Medora, ND, over the winter of 2012/2013.

I am currently the SW North Dakota Regional Representative for the United States Chuan Fa Association.

HOW HAS MARTIAL ARTS IMPACTED YOUR LIFE?

Studying martial arts has given me the confidence to make it through life. It has given me the confidence to properly interact in social situations and the confidence to choose not to interact in some situations. Studying martial arts has taught me to be constantly aware of and recognize surrounding situations that may be detrimental and dangerous to myself and others around me.

Studying martial arts has also exposed me to the practice of Medical Qigong. I became certified in Medical Qigong (Spring Forest Qigong) and Traditional Chinese Medicine through the Turtle Island Health Center, formerly of St. Paul, MN, back in the late 1990s. The practice of the Spring Forest Qigong form has eliminated my nightmares about Vietnam and greatly helped me deal with PTSD from my experience in Vietnam. Qigong practice (Ping Shuai Gong) has also given me relief from arthritis pain.

In addition, I have used my martial arts training a few times during my employment with the City of Minneapolis Fire Department to protect my crew from

TRAINING INFORMATION

- Martial Arts Styles & Rank: Zu Wei Shu Kung Fu-6th Black Sash
- Instructors/Influencers: Grand Master Dana Miller
- Birthplace/Growing Up: Minneapolis, MN
- Yrs. In the Martial Arts: 57 years
- Yrs. Instructing: 36 years
- Former school owner at Beach Martial Arts, Beach, ND

PROFESSIONAL ORGANIZATIONS

- United States Chuan Fa Association—SW North Dakota Regional Representative

PERSONAL ACHIEVEMENTS

- Awarded 1st Degree Black belt in September 1988, 6 months after my 40th birthday (6 months after my goal to achieve it by my 40th birthday)

MAJOR ACHIEVEMENTS

- Instructor of the Year Award, Zu Wei Shu Kung Fu, awarded by the World Head of Family Sokeship Council, May 29, 2010
- Achieved 6th Level Black Sash February 25, 2023

HOW HAS MARTIAL ARTS IMPACTED YOUR LIFE? (CONTINUED)

being attacked during medical emergencies and to restrain those who would become violent as a result of medical conditions and/or trauma.

Also, as a result of being a martial artist, I have met some pretty interesting people and made some amazing lifelong friends.

CLAUDE
LAWSON

❝

Living a martial artist lifestyle is a journey of constant self-exploration, acceptance, and growth.

HOW HAS MARTIAL ARTS IMPACTED YOUR LIFE?

Living a martial artist lifestyle is a journey of constant self-exploration, acceptance, and growth. Through the martial arts, I've accepted myself for who I am. I've explored different aspects of my character through teaching, instructing, and mentoring, which has forced me to grow as a human being. I'm not the person I was 30 years ago; hopefully, I'm a better version of that person, and there is still work to be done.

TRAINING INFORMATION

- Martial Arts Styles & Rank: Kajukembo - 9th Degree, Ki do Kai Kempo - 5th Degree, Brazilian Jiu jitsu - Black Belt, Kickboxing Coach
- Instructors/Influencers: GM James Cox, SGM Joseph Davis, SGM Patrick Mcdaniel, Prof Courtney Westley
- Birthplace/Growing Up: Royston, GA / Military Brat
- Yrs. In the Martial Arts: 49 years
- Yrs. Instructing: 30 years
- Manager & Instructor

WHY THE MARTIAL ARTS?

I started martial arts in Florida in 1975 at MacDill AFB with the study of Shorin-Ryu. My father was military and studied Shotokan. When he was deployed, my mother signed both her and me up to take classes at the recreation center. My father got me interested in martial arts, first with Bruce Lee and then with Jim Kelly and Ron Van Clief. Martial arts have been part of my life for as long as I can remember.

PROFESSIONAL ORGANIZATIONS

- American Kajukembo Association

PERSONAL ACHIEVEMENTS

- Taught Sexual Assault & Rape Prevention at Travis AFB, Incirlik Air Base Turkey, Cannon AFB, The Pentagon, Walmart employees in Fairfield, CA, and Gilbert Community College Self-Defense Class/Seminar, Gilbert, Arizona

- Taught Kajukembo/jiujitsu at the Gathering of Eagle

- Taught kickboxing and self-defense for the ILuvKickboxing franchise in Washington, DC

- Taught self-defense in Mexico City at the Association Internacional Annual Seminar

- The Travis AFB Security Forces (Phoenix Raven) special unit asked me to teach their team self-defense. At their request, I developed a Lethal and less-than-lethal combat course, trained them for over a year, and received letters of commendation

- I was the sparring partner for the West & North Texas Heavyweight and Middleweight Kickboxing Champions and a Lightweight Contender

MAJOR ACHIEVEMENTS

- Retired Senior Master Sergeant, USAF, 26 years of faithful service.

- Father of six kids - three boys and three girls (two engineers, one interior designer, one nurse/mother of one boy, one entrepreneur, and one amazing mother of two boys)

Become an
AMAA MEMBER!

PROFESSOR
GARY LEE

"
The Sport Karate Museum: Protecting the history one warrior at a time...

TRAINING INFORMATION
- Belt Ranks & Martial Arts Styles: 9th Degree Black Belt, Okinawa Karate
- Birthplace/Growing Up: Honolulu, HI

MAJOR ACHIEVEMENTS
- Gran, Hawaiian Kosho Ryu Kenpo Jiu-Jitsu
- International Black Belt Hall of Fame
- Top Weapons in Texas, 1980
- Top Ten Fighters in Texas, 1979-1999
- Rated by Karate Illustrated Magazine, rated National
- Who's Who in Karate, 1982
- 3rd Degree Black Belt Test, 1982, Lama Nationals, Chicago IL
- Creator Six Flags Amusement Park Shows, Gary Lee's Texas Karate All-Stars,
- 1984-1994, {5,000 shows}
- Texas State B.A.S.S Federation Champion, 1987
- Filmed SIDEKICKS the movie, 1990
- Gold Medalist USAKF Nationals, Dallas, Texas, 1992
- Won five {5} National NBL TITLES, Atlantic City, NJ, 1992
- Sabaki Ryu Challenge 3rd Place Kumite, Honolulu, Hawaii, 1992

MAJOR ACHIEVEMENTS (CONTINUED)
- National Black Belt League World Champion, Breaking, New Orleans, USA, 1993
- Man, of the Year, Bushshiban 1993
- BIG BASS TOURNAMENT, Sam Rayburn, Jasper, Texas, 2nd Place, 3,200.00 winnings, earned a 3rd round seed into the Classic Championship 1993, Yeah Baby!!!!
- Texas NBL Arbitrator
- Star of Hollywood Stunt Show, Astroworld, Six Flags, Houston, Texas, USA, 1993
- Creator 'KIDS EXPO" Astrodome, Houston Texas.1993-1996
- Golden Greek Top Texas Overall Winner, AOK RATINGS, 1997, 1998
- Nominated Black Belt Magazine "Player of the Year", 1997
- Texas Sport Karate Player, MVP

MAJOR ACHIEVEMENTS (CONTINUED)

- Opened World Championship Karate Studios, 1998

- Created the Living Legends Celebrity Roast; 1999 - present.

- To date Professor Lee has celebrated 15 American Pioneers in Sport Karate.

- Staff Writer for WORLD BLACKBELT, 1999

- Created Tales OF the Old Sensei for World Black Belt, monthly column

- Master of Ceremonies, Martial Art History Museum, Las Vegas, Nevada, 1999

- Director Michael Matsuda says 'Gary Lee is the voice of Karate, Black Belt Magazine

- Director of Junior World Black Belt Kids Club

- Produced and Directed Living Legends, 'the Tim Kirby Celebrity Roast, Houston, Texas, USA, 2000

- Kumite International Black Belt Hall of Fame Award and Scholarship given in Professor Gary Lee's name for $1,000.00, Pittsburg, Pa, 2000

- Creator of BLACK BELT TV, A online network for Martial Artist and Martial arts Exclusive personal interviews with the stars of martial arts.

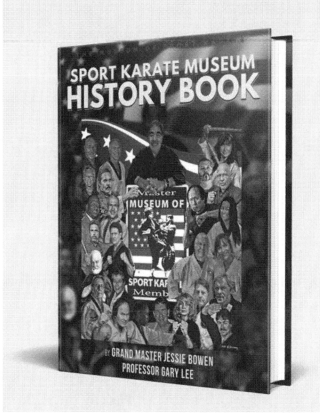

CHRIS LYLE

"
Martial arts has helped me with my physical and mental well-being and find balance in my daily life.

WHY THE MARTIAL ARTS?

Chris Lyle is an exemplary figure in the world of martial arts, whose journey is marked by dedication, humility, and a profound sense of responsibility towards those in need. A 4th Duan Sifu in Emperor's Long Fist and Five Family Fist Kung Fu, his martial arts career is distinguished not only by his mastery of techniques but also by his unwavering commitment to using his skills for the betterment of others. Chris's path, from a former Marine to a revered martial artist, reflects a life dedicated to discipline, service, and the pursuit of excellence.

Born into a modest background, Chris's early life was shaped by the values of hard work, respect, and the importance of giving back to the community. These principles guided him as he embarked on a distinguished tenure in the military, where he served with his personal code of honor and distinction; even

when faced with difficult ethical issues, Sifu Chris Lyle remained unchanged and kept to his core beliefs, marking him, even more, an unwavering soul of self-discipline. The discipline and resilience he developed as a Marine became the bedrock of his martial arts philosophy. After his service, Chris continued to contribute to his community, becoming a soccer coach for the Special Olympics. His dedication to empowering individuals with disabilities through sports showcased his belief in the transformative power of encouragement and teamwork.

Chris's martial arts journey began with an intense curiosity and a deep respect for the ancient traditions of Kung Fu. His dedication saw him achieve a 4th Duan in "Mantis Yong Chun" and a 3rd Duan in Full Circle Gung Fu, making him a formidable practitioner and a respected teacher. However, it is his role as a Red Sash instructor in Running Fist and his position as the 2nd in command in Full Circle Gung Fu that truly highlight his contributions to martial arts. Under his guidance, the curriculum was adapted to become more accessible to children and families, reflecting his belief in the inclusivity and community-building aspects of martial arts training.

Chris's training under renowned masters such as Sifu David Kash, Sijo James Robinson, and Casey Martin

TRAINING INFORMATION

- Martial Arts Styles & Rank: 4th Duan-Mantis Yong Chun, 3rd Duan-Full Circle Gung Fu
- Instructors/Influencers: Shifu David Kash, Sijo James Robinson, Sifu Casey Martin
- Birthplace/Growing Up: Charlotte, NC
- Yrs. In the Martial Arts: 18 years
- Yrs. Instructing: 14 years
- Instructor

PROFESSIONAL ORGANIZATIONS

- Cloud Forest Chin Woo Martial Arts Association
- Running Fist Kung Fu
- Full Circle Gung Fu

PERSONAL ACHIEVEMENTS

- Competed in a variety of martial arts tournaments, including Lei Tai.

MAJOR ACHIEVEMENTS

- Former Marine
- Former Soccer Coach for Special Olympics
- 2nd in command of Full Circle Gung Fu

further enriched his understanding and skill set, allowing him to synthesize a broad spectrum of techniques and philosophies. This eclectic training has enabled him to approach martial arts not just as a means of physical combat but as a holistic discipline that encompasses mental strength, emotional resilience, and ethical conduct.

Despite his many accomplishments, including competing in Lei Tai and being affectionately nicknamed the "Red Devil" of Full Circle Gung Fu for his prowess and intensity, Chris remains a figure of humility and discretion. He chooses to focus on the essence of martial arts as a tool for personal growth, self-defense, and, most importantly, for protecting and uplifting those who are vulnerable.

Chris Lyle's approach to teaching is a reflection of his character: patient and understanding, yet demanding respect and dedication. He believes in challenging his students, not only physically but also intellectually, encouraging them to question, reason, and prove the effectiveness of each technique they learn. This method fosters an environment of continuous learning and mutual respect, qualities that are evident in the diverse community of students he has built over the years.

Chris Lyle's martial arts journey is deeply connected to various groups, particularly Full Circle Gung Fu and Running Fist Kung Fu. His path in martial arts started

with Cloud Forest Chin Woo, which played a crucial role in his early training. After years away, Chris has recently reconnected with the group, now thriving under the leadership of Michael Johnson Shifu, or Wei Lei Ma, who holds an 8th Duan and is the Chief Lineage inheritor passed down by Grandmaster David Kash (Wei Jung Dao). This reunion has been positive for Chris. He appreciates the new direction the community has taken, focusing more on practical teaching and building a stronger sense of community. This change aligns well with Chris's own beliefs in the importance of practicality in martial arts and the value of a supportive and engaged community.

Chris Lyle's life and career embody the true spirit of martial arts: a journey of self-discovery, discipline, and a deep-seated commitment to the welfare of others. As a former Marine, coach, and martial artist, Chris has demonstrated time and again that the greatest strength lies in the power of giving back, making him not only a master of Kung Fu but also a beacon of inspiration for those fortunate enough to cross his path.

HOW HAS MARTIAL ARTS IMPACTED YOUR LIFE?

Martial arts have impacted Chris in many ways. It has helped him with his physical and mental well-being and find balance in his daily life. Chris is able to stay disciplined in his daily grind. Whether at his job as a chef or teaching martial arts in the evening, he can remain humble and level-headed throughout the day.

Become an
**AMAA
MEMBER!**

PETER
MALIK

"
Martial arts has given me the greatest gift: the chance to impact and empower the lives of our current students and future leaders.

better they become. When they see that progress, it fuels their motivation.

HOW HAS MARTIAL ARTS IMPACTED YOUR LIFE?

When I first started training in Martial Arts, I only thought I would learn physical skills and nothing more. As a matter of fact, for the first couple of years of training, the only thing I truly cared about was getting better at sparring and my application. I was not a gifted martial artist. To excel, I needed to put countless extra hours of training on and off the mat. Martial arts was the first thing in my life that made me willing to do the work to get the reward. Martial arts taught me how to set and strive for goals. That "good enough" was never going to be enough.

It was through martial arts that I found my second family. A family filled with people of different races, backgrounds, and religions who were all bonded with a similar mindset. These people would be there for me in both happy and sad times. Over the years, many of my teammates have stopped their training in martial arts, but it didn't matter. They were the groomsman at my wedding; I was the godfather to their children, and

WHY THE MARTIAL ARTS?

Truthfully speaking, I never wanted to practice martial arts. My best friend then was looking for a summer hobby, and they asked if he wanted to bring a friend to the lessons; I was that friend. After the first class, I was hooked. It felt like martial arts was something I didn't know was missing from my life. When I became an advanced belt, I started assisting on the floor. I felt the mental, spiritual, and physical benefits of martial arts training and wanted to help other people get that feeling. Martial arts was the truth, and there were no shortcuts involved. The beauty of it is you have 100% control of your destiny. The harder a person trains, the

HOW HAS MARTIAL ARTS IMPACTED YOUR LIFE? (CONTINUED)

and they were the ones who knew how to comfort me in the loss of my father.

My master instructors offer their knowledge as my coaches in training and life. They offered me so many lessons, both physically and mentally. As I grew in the ranks, our relationship also grew. I would go to them for advice on major life decisions. I trusted and respected their advice and took it to heart. This would only bring us closer. When I call Great Grandmaster Tony B. Thomson, he always answers the phone by saying, "How is it going, my son?" I know he means it, as I truly look at him as my second father.

Great Grandmaster Ernie Reyes, Sr. has a different relationship with me. He believed in me so much I was placed on his world-famous demonstration team. This was the next part of my evolution, as I was now performing my martial arts in front of and alongside other world-renowned martial artists. Masters like Tadashi Yamashita, Jean Claude Van Damme, Royce Gracie, Bill "SuperFoot" Wallace, Frank Shamrock, Javier Mendez, and the list continues. I was able to demonstrate my skill in front of sold-out arenas in other countries like France and Turkey.

Through martial arts, I was able to work alongside Scott Coker. Scott was one of Great Grandmaster Ernie Reyes' first black belts. He was running a small kickboxing organization called Strikeforce. I had no idea just how much of an impact this would have on

TRAINING INFORMATION

- Martial Arts Styles & Rank: 7th degree - Ernie Reyes World West Coast Martial Arts, Muy Thai, Gi BJJ
- Instructors/Influencers: Great Grandmaster Ernie Reyes, Great Grandmaster Tony B Thomson, Professor Erik Benaquisto, and multiple instructors at the American Kickboxing Association (AKA)
- Birthplace/Growing Up: Fremont, CA / San Jose area
- Yrs. In the Martial Arts: 32 years
- Yrs. Instructing: 28 years
- School owner & Instructor at World Martial Arts

PROFESSIONAL ORGANIZATIONS

- Ernie Reyes West Coast World Martial Arts Association

PERSONAL ACHIEVEMENTS

- Best Tester 1st Degree
- Best Tester 2nd Degree
- Best Tester 3rd Degree
- Best Tester 5th Degree
- Member of the Ernie Reyes Next Generation Demonstration team and the World Action Team
- Best of Mountain View Award in the martial arts school category for years 2019 - 2024
- Best Martial Arts School in the Bay Area Peninsula Award in 2023

MAJOR ACHIEVEMENTS

- I was an assistant to Scott Coker in Strikeforce MMA and K-1
- I was a Talent Scout, Assistant Director of Fighter Relations, Director of Promotions, Head of Cage Construction, and had a major role in holding MMA events across the nation including the first ever MMA event in California and the first ever MMA event at the Playboy Mansion
- Performed in sold-out arenas around the world as a member of the Ernie Reyes Demonstration Team

HOW HAS MARTIAL ARTS IMPACTED YOUR LIFE? (CONTINUED)

my life. When I first started, I simply did promotions and ticket sales. Quickly, my position would change in ways I couldn't imagine. One day, Scott Coker, Javier Mendez, Frank Shamrock, Crazy Bob Cook, and I were discussing the upcoming fight card at a table. As they talked, I offered my input, and they all agreed.

Furthermore, I would go into detail about why certain fights needed to take place and my opinion on what fighters from other organizations we should look to bring to our roster. This was the moment I became Scott Coker's assistant. On March 10, 2006, Strikeforce made history by becoming the first to hold a mixed martial arts event in California. The attendance set a record, selling out 18,265 seats. After this, my role in the company was solidified. I was not only his assistant; I became a Talent Scout, the Assistant Director of Fighter Relations, the Director of Promotions, the lead in Cage Transport and Construction, and, of course, was still selling tickets.

HOW HAS MARTIAL ARTS IMPACTED YOUR LIFE?

Over the years, Scott Coker and I have gotten closer and closer. He was an instructor who became my boss, only to become a brother. It was because of martial arts that I can say I had a historic role in the history of mixed martial arts. I contributed to the growth and popularity of the sport and made lasting friendships with some of the greatest mixed martial arts champions of the sport.

When I decided to return to teaching martial arts, I did it because I truly missed it. Helping others was my true calling. I have received so much from martial arts over the years. It taught me how to have self-discipline, honor, the importance of family, how to be brave in facing your fears, and, of course, gave me a second family.

I wanted to share this with as many people as I can. Over the years, I have realized that as a martial arts instructor, we do so much more than teach fighting techniques. We help adults maintain their confidence and fitness. We help families have a stronger bond with each other. We create a community for people to bond and become friends. We help our local community with outreach programs. But what is the biggest thing we do as martial arts teachers? We help mold the minds of our young students. Parents trust us with their number one asset in life: their children. Every day, we assist in raising the children of hundreds of families. We teach essential life skills like self-reliance, self-discipline, and goal setting.

It is through martial arts training that a child learns true confidence. One that comes from overcoming the challenges they face. We stress the importance of higher education, a strong family, and having good character. We are there when a student needs advice or a shoulder to cry on. On a daily basis, martial arts has given me the greatest gift: the chance to impact and empower the lives of our current students and future leaders.

CASEY MARTIN

>**"**
>
>*Martial arts has improved my life in many respects; it has given me the tools I need to achieve any goal that is set in front of me.*

WHY THE MARTIAL ARTS?

Casey Martin might not be a name that echoes through the halls of every martial arts dojo across the globe, but within the circles that know him, his reputation is nothing short of legendary. His story isn't draped in ancient martial arts lore or the kind of fantastical elements you might find in a novel. Instead, Casey's journey is one of genuine passion, dedication, and a profound commitment to sharing his knowledge with others, particularly those who might not believe such a world is accessible to them.

Casey's martial arts journey began the year he turned 20, a relatively late start by many standards. Yet, what he might have lacked in his early years of training, he more than made up for with an unwavering dedication and an insatiable desire to learn. By 2012, Casey was not just a student but a teacher, sharing his growing expertise with others. His teaching wasn't confined to those who could easily step into a dojo and mimic his moves. Casey saw a gap in the martial arts world, a place where those with disabilities were often sidelined, not because of a lack of interest or ability but because of a lack of accessible programs tailored to their needs.

In response, Casey created the Confident Warrior Program, a pioneering initiative designed to bring martial arts to people with disabilities. This program wasn't just about teaching martial arts; it was about instilling confidence, fostering a sense of community, and proving that martial arts could be adapted to meet the needs of anyone eager to learn.

Casey's influence and dedication didn't stop at his program. He became a sought-after instructor at the World Warrior Alliance gatherings in Virginia, where he taught seminars that were as much about philosophy and mental fortitude as they were about physical technique. His ability to connect with people, to draw them into the world of martial arts, and to show them the depth and breadth of what it could offer was unparalleled. In 2022, Casey was accepted as the director and head instructor for the Kid's Kung Fu program at Cloud Forest Chin Woo Martial Arts in Greensboro, NC. As his skills were proven over time, he was also elected as the Sports Jujitsu Coach for their upcoming Competition Team.

Competitively, Casey was no slouch either. He successfully competed in a variety of sparring and grappling events, showcasing his skills against a wide range of opponents. But for Casey, the competition was never about the accolades or the victories. It was another platform to learn, to grow, and to share the beauty of martial arts with a broader audience.

Casey's martial arts lineage is a testament to his dedication and passion for the craft. He was a student of notable figures such as Sijo James Robinson, Professor Tony Maynard, Sijo Shaan Davis, and Sifu Michael Johnson. Under their tutelage, Casey achieved a 4th-degree black belt in Full Circle Gung Fu and Wing Chun, became a full instructor in JKD Concepts, a red sash instructor in Running Fist, and earned a black belt in American Combat Jujitsu. More recently, in December 2023, Casey was invited and accepted into the Wei Family Kung Fu Lineage as a Disciple.

Michael Johnson Shi Fu says, "We have no doubt that Martin Shifu will bring even higher skills to our lineage, bring up a strong future generation, and be a Shi Fu that our students' students will tell stories about."

These achievements are not just a reflection of Casey's skill but of his deep respect for the traditions and disciplines of martial arts.

In 2014, Casey founded Full Circle Gung Fu, an embodiment of his belief in the cyclical nature of learning and teaching. He has always maintained that the true essence of martial arts is not just in mastering techniques but in sharing knowledge, learning from others, and teaching anyone with a desire to learn. This philosophy has guided his every step, turning Full Circle Gung Fu into more than just a martial arts school—it's a community where everyone, regardless of their background or abilities, is welcomed and valued.

TRAINING INFORMATION

- Martial Arts Styles & Rank: 4th Dan-Full Circle Gung Fu, 1st Dan-American Combat Jujitsu, Full Instructor-Jeet Kune Do Concepts, Red Sash Instructor-Running Fist Kung Fu
- Instructors/Influencers: Sijo James Robinson, Sijo Shaan Davis, Professor Tony Maynard, Shifu Michael Johnson
- Birthplace/Growing Up: Kernersville, NC
- Yrs. In the Martial Arts: 16 years
- Yrs. Instructing: 12 years
- Instructor

PROFESSIONAL ORGANIZATIONS

- Cloud Forest Chin Woo Martial Arts Association
- Shaan Davis Combative Science
- World Warrior Alliance
- American Combat Jujitsu
- Jujitsu America

PERSONAL ACHIEVEMENTS

- Has competed in a variety of competitions as well as coached many others to top 3 finishes

MAJOR ACHIEVEMENTS

- Founded Full Circle Gung Fu
- Founded Confident Warrior Martial Arts A program dedicated to teaching people with disabilities

HOW HAS MARTIAL ARTS IMPACTED YOUR LIFE?

Martial arts has improved Casey's life in many respects; it has given him the tools he needs to achieve any goal that is set in front of him. His level of understanding of how the human body works and moves has allowed him to adapt or deal with some of the burdens that life throws at us as we age. The confidence Casey has in his ability to defend himself and his loved ones has made it easier for them to enjoy their time out of the house; the peace of mind that it provides is invaluable. These are the same gifts Casey tries to pass on to his students.

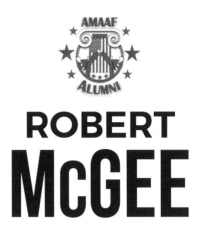

ROBERT McGEE

"
Psychologically, martial arts training has improved my self-confidence. It is now nearly impossible to bully me.

HOW HAS MARTIAL ARTS IMPACTED YOUR LIFE?

Studying martial arts has impacted my life in several ways. Intellectually, it has exposed me to Asian history and philosophy. I have studied Chinese, Japanese, and Korean versions of this art and have trained in Thailand. I have also met with the Grandmaster and his senior students who train at the historically famous Snake Hill in Wuhan, China.

My knowledge of biology and body mechanics has improved. I now have more awareness of how the body functions and how certain exercises affect health. Physically, the martial arts have improved my health. I am more flexible now than I would have been in the absence of martial arts training. My blood pressure is in the normal range. Psychologically, martial arts training has improved my self-confidence. It is now nearly impossible to bully me. Socially, I have made many friends I would never have otherwise met. I also met some famous martial artists and even acted in movies with them.

As a university professor, I know that publishing is important. Because of my martial arts background, I can now publish articles about Tai Chi and Qigong in medical journals and other outlets.

WHY THE MARTIAL ARTS?

I started practicing martial arts because I wanted to defend myself from bullies. I was small, and there were several bullies in my neighborhood.

TRAINING INFORMATION

- Martial Arts Styles & Rank: 8th Dan, U.S. Guntai-Shu; 7th Duan, Wushu KungFu; 7th Duan, Daoshu; 7th Duan, Tai Chi; 6th Dan, Kang Shi Do; 5th Duan, Qigong; 3rd Dan, Songahm Taekwondo; 3rd Dan, Moo Duk Kwan; 3rd Dan, UTA Taekwondo; 1st Dan, Shimsan Taekwondo; 1st Dan, Kukkiwon; 1st Dan, Kwon-Ki-Do; 4th Kyu, Shukokai

- Instructors/Influencers: Joseph Adames, Richard Adelman, Mac Albus, Michael & Kimberly Brown, Meghan Bryant, H.Y. Chung, S. Henry Cho, John Cook, Jaci Gran, Yulie Heaton, Gib Karnchanahari, Shigeru Kimora, Anthony Korahais, Mei Jin, Liu, Roxanne Louise, Richard Martin, Michael Pistorio, Martin Rapp, Tito Velez, Anthony ZambrowskiYrs. Instructing: 11 years

TRAINING INFORMATION (CONTINUED)

- Birthplace/Growing Up: Erie, PA
- Yrs. In the Martial Arts: 63 years
- Yrs. Instructing: 11 years
- Instructor

PROFESSIONAL ORGANIZATIONS

American Karate Association, American Martial Arts Alliance, Association of Martial Artists Worldwide, ATA Martial Arts, International Martial Arts Hall of Fame, Rou Long Ma School of Chinese Martial Arts, Taekwon-do Hall of Fame United States Martial Arts Hall of Fame, USA National Tai Chi Chuan Federation, USA Wushu Kungfu Federation, Who's Who in the Martial Arts Hall of Fame, World Organization of Martial Arts Athletes, Wushu Kungfu Federation of India

PERSONAL ACHIEVEMENTS

- Earned 23 academic degrees, including 13 doctorates from universities in the United States and four European countries

- Earned a certificate in Tai Chi from the Harvard Medical School

- Earned a certificate in Chinese Medicine from the Chinese University of Hong Kong

- Passed the CPA exam and the bar exam

- Published more than 60 books and more than 1000 scholarly papers

- Assisted Armenia and Bosnia's Finance Ministries in converting their countries to International Financial Reporting Standards

- Drafted the accounting law for Armenia and Bosnia and reviewed the accounting law for Mozambique

- Lived, lectured, or worked in more than 30 countries in North, South, and Central America, the Caribbean, Eastern and Western Europe, Asia, Africa, and Oceania

MAJOR ACHIEVEMENTS

- Won 80+ gold medals in national championship tournaments (USA)
- Won 15 gold medals in Canadian national championship tournaments
- Won 7 gold medals in Pan American

FREDDIE
McNEIL

"

Martial arts has taught me to lead by example and to guide and inspire others through my actions and words.

My goal has always been to let our youth know that they have the power to shape their futures. By applying themselves and staying committed to their goals, there is no limit to what they can accomplish. I believe in the potential of every young person and strive to provide them with the tools and guidance they need to succeed.

Join me on this journey of empowerment and inspiration as we work together to uplift and support the youth in our community. Together, we can show the youth that they can achieve their dreams with determination and a positive mindset. Let's empower the next generation to believe in themselves and unlock their full potential!

WHY THE MARTIAL ARTS?

It all began with a simple yet powerful desire to mentor and positively influence the Durham, North Carolina, Community youth. I recognized the need for strong, positive images that could guide and inspire young individuals to reach their full potential.

Through martial arts, I found a platform to teach martial arts skills and essential life lessons like leadership, discipline, respect, self-control, self-confidence, and perseverance. I wanted to show the youth that they can achieve anything they set their minds to with dedication and hard work.

HOW HAS MARTIAL ARTS IMPACTED YOUR LIFE?

Martial arts has been a transformative journey that has positively influenced various aspects of my life, instilling valuable qualities that have shaped me into the person I am today. In terms of leadership, martial arts has taught me to lead by example and to guide and inspire others through my actions and words. Family values have been reinforced through the emphasis on respect, loyalty, and support within the martial arts community, mirroring the importance of family bonds and unity.

Humility is a key virtue that martial arts has cultivated in me, reminding me to stay grounded, open-minded, and always willing to learn and improve. The rigorous training and demanding nature of martial arts have honed my work ethic, teaching me the value of hard work, dedication, and persistence in achieving my goals. Respect for others is paramount in martial arts, fostering a culture of mutual respect, understanding, and appreciation for differences among individuals.

Overall, martial arts has not only enhanced my physical strength and mental fortitude but has also enriched my character, helping me develop into a well-rounded individual with a strong sense of self-discipline, resilience, and empathy towards others.

TRAINING INFORMATION

- Martial Arts Styles & Rank: WTF Taekwondo-9th Dan, Karate-7th Dan, Korean (Moo Duk Kwan)-5th Dan, Japanese Goju-Ryu-6th Dan, Korean Hapkido 3rd-Dan
- Instructors/Influencers: Grandmaster Jessie Bowen, Grandmaster Anthony Wykia, Grandmaster James Frazier, Kyoshi Kurt Woodlan, Grandmaster Sherman Fogg, Grandmaster Jun Lee
- Birthplace/Growing Up: Durham, NC
- Yrs. In the Martial Arts: 46 years
- Yrs. Instructing: 30 years
- School owner, Manager & Instructor at Taekwondo Academy of Champions

PROFESSIONAL ORGANIZATIONS

- AMAA Member
- Kukkiwon Association
- World Taekwondo Federation
- Taekwondo Association
- International Combat Taekwondo Union (ICMAUA)

PERSONAL ACHIEVEMENTS

- Owner and Operator of Taekwondo Academy of Champions.
- Organized over 30 successful martial arts tournaments (Battle of The Bull City).
- Co-authored a book, *Elite Martial Artists in America, Vol I: Secrets To Life Leadership & Business*
- Master of Ceremony at the Global Kukkiwon Taekwondo Championships, September 30, 2023
- Recipient of The Presidential Volunteer Service Award 2023
- Awarded the Development of Kukkiwon Taekwondo Leadership from the President of the Kukkiwon President Grandmaster, Dr. Lee Dong Sup. 2023
- Founder/CEO of Sidekicks Academy Inc.

MAJOR ACHIEVEMENTS

- Retired Executive Director of Human Resources of Durham Public Schools
- Founder and Executive Director of SIDEKICKS Academy Inc. Currently serving in 5 Public Schools in Durham, North Carolina.

MAJOR ACHIEVEMENTS (CONTINUED)

- Received Prestigious Endorsement from Governor Roy Cooper, North Carolina State Senators, and Kukkiwon President Dr. Lee Dong Sup.
- Endorsing SIDEKICKS Academy Inc.

HOW HAS MARTIAL ARTS IMPACTED YOUR LIFE? (CONTINUED)

The supportive community of fellow martial artists has provided me with a sense of belonging and camaraderie, forming lifelong friendships and a network of like-minded individuals with similar values and aspirations. In essence, martial arts has been a guiding force in my life, offering invaluable lessons and experiences that continue to shape me for the better.

Become an
AMAA MEMBER!

GEORGE "GEORDIE" McTAGGART

" Martial Arts have been a major part of my life, and I strongly follow the five Tenets of Taekwon-Do.

Cynthia Rothrock, Guro Dan Inosanto, Simo Cookie Vassiliou, Guro Joel Clarke, Sifu Francis Fong, Master Jean-Jacques Machado, Hanshi Tino Ceberano, Master Richard Norton, Master Jeff Speakman, Master Michael Muleta, Grand Master Jamie Moore, Grand Master Steven Cheah, Sensei Benny "The Jet" Urquidez, Don "The Dragon" Wilson, Mohammed "Tong-Po" Qissi among many others.

WHY THE MARTIAL ARTS?

Geordie McTaggart, a 5th-degree black belt with the International Taekwondo Federation (ITF), is a highly accomplished martial arts instructor and personal trainer. He embarked on his martial arts journey at the age of six, driven by his fascination with Bruce Lee movies. With a father with a background in professional wrestling and various martial arts, Geordie's early training encompassed disciplines like Wrestling, Judo, and Karate.

Throughout his remarkable 44-year martial arts journey, Geordie has extensively studied and attained rankings in various disciplines. These include Karate, Tai Chi, Ninjitsu, Krav Maga, Wing Chun Kung Fu, Jun Fan Jeet Kune Do, Filipino Kali, Muay Thai, Machado Brazilian Jiu-Jitsu, Goju Kalis, Kenpo 5.0, and even fight choreography for movies. Geordie has had the privilege of training alongside esteemed martial arts figures such as Grand Master Chong Chul Rhee, Chief Instructor John Ragonessi, Grand Master

HOW HAS MARTIAL ARTS IMPACTED YOUR LIFE?

Since starting his journey at such a young age, martial arts have been a major part of Geordie's life, and he strongly follows the five Tenets of Taekwon-Do: Courtesy, Integrity, Perseverance, Self-Control, and an Indomitable Spirit.

Martial arts have not only given him the knowledge and physical skills but also helped him gain the confidence to speak in front of large crowds and lead or teach them.

With a nearly 15-year career as a private security contractor for the Department of Defence, Geordie worked his way up to Area Security Supervisor. During this time, while working closely with the

TRAINING INFORMATION

- Martial Arts Styles & Rank: I.T.F Taekwon-Do - 5th Dan Black Belt, Progressive Martial Arts Academy International - 8th Grade

- Instructors/Influencers: Master Michael Muleta, Simo Cookie Vasilliou

- Birthplace/Growing Up: Glasgow, Scotland / Toowoomba, Australia

- Yrs. In the Martial Arts: 44 years

- Yrs. Instructing: 35+ years

- School owner and Instructor at Denrai Freestyle Tae Kwon-Do

PROFESSIONAL ORGANIZATIONS

- United I.T.F Taekwon-Do Australia

- I.T.F International Taekwon-Do Federation

- Golden Dragons International Martial Arts Federation

PERSONAL ACHIEVEMENTS

- The founding of my own martial arts school "Denrai Freestyle Tae Kwon-Do" in 2005.

- I.T.F Taekwon-Do 5th Dan Black Belt

- Progressive Martial Arts Academy International-8th grade

MAJOR ACHIEVEMENTS

- Multiple world champion and gold medalist in Tae Kwon-Do, excelling in events like Self-defense, Power and Special Technique Breaking, Single and Team Patterns, Weaponry, and Model Sparring.

- Induction into the "2019 ITF Pioneer Awards" for Excellence

- Induction into the "2020 General Choi Hong Hi Hall of Honours" for Outstanding International Instructor

- 2020 Action Martial Arts Magazine Hall of Honours "World Award."

- 2021 Volume 33 of Grandmaster Ted Gambordella's The World's Greatest Martial Artists

- 2022 Action Martial Arts Magazine Hall of Honours

- 2022 International Martial Arts Hall of Fame "Best Master of the Year Tae Kwon-Do Award"

- 2023 International Martial Arts Hall of Fame "Golden Lifetime Achievement Award" for his 40+ years of dedication to the martial arts

- Serves as the Australian Representative and Director of the Action Martial Arts Mega Weekend.

HOW HAS MARTIAL ARTS IMPACTED YOUR LIFE? (CONTINUED)

military, he met and trained with many soldiers who were masters of various martial arts. He was eager to learn and trade knowledge and techniques with them. A willingness to learn from anyone is a trait that he has applied his entire life.

Martial arts also influenced his decision to become a qualified personal trainer as he saw it as a way to learn the right way to physically improve not only for himself but more importantly for his students.

Due to his passion for martial arts, Geordie continues to work in the martial arts and fitness as well as the security industries.

RAFAEL MEDINA-CASTRO

" Learn and teach the values of others. Respect life because it is only one; being humble costs nothing.

WHY THE MARTIAL ARTS?

I am from Candelero Arriba, Humacao, Puerto Rico. My inspiration for martial arts was watching Green Hornet episodes, the main star of which was the legendary Bruce Lee. I retired as a Sergeant First Class (SFC) with 22 years of service in the Army.

I was smaller than my peers and an easy mark for the bullies in my tough, rural Puerto Rican neighborhood. To shift the balance, I had to learn karate. I was tired of being the loser or feeling the agony of defeat. I wanted something different in my life.

My first instructors were Luis Díaz, a green belt in Okinawa-Te Karate, and the late Juan Ruiz, a green belt in Judo. My first years learning karate were difficult because my father didn't want me to learn this new way of life. He didn't believe in violence, so I trained in secret without him knowing.

On February 2, 1972, I moved in with my mother. In the meantime, I started learning and practicing karate through books and magazines until I found a Shotokan dojo at the University of Humacao with Sensei Michael. From February 15, 1973, to 1975, I started training Kyokushinkai with Sensei Miguel

Acevedo and Sensei Fernando Caraballo. As a brown belt in Kyokushinkai, he opened his first karate dojo in Humacao, Puerto Rico, the first dojo ever in his town.

In 1977, I trained with the late GM Giovanni Rosario, International Taekwondo Federation (ITF-Young Brother Association). Around June or July 1978, Sensei Caraballo and Sensei Acevedo tested me for black belt in Kyokushinkai. In August, I got married, and in October, I was into basic training (Fort Jackson, SC).

Since joining the military, I have accomplished many things. In 1985, I was among the first members of the newly formed Army Taekwondo Team, which represented Fort Bragg in the 1984 and 1985 North Carolina and South Carolina state championships.

I established the motto "One Team, One Fight," unifying the sport of Taekwondo for all the armed forces. Now, my motto is "One Team, One Fight, One Family, Stay Strong."

In May 2019, GM William Sanchez Cardona recognized me as a Grandmaster of Taekwondo by the government of Puerto Rico and certified me by the House of Representatives of Puerto Rico.

In September 2019, the International Military Sports Council (CISM) selected me as the first military and the only person in the United States to represent the nation in the World Military Taekwondo Championship as an athlete, coach, international referee, and the first Latino soldier among 140 member-nations of CISM.

After I retired from the service, I began working with children as a coach for the Liberty County Recreation Department's (LCRD) Sport Taekwondo Team. I advise kids to stay away from guns and violence at home and school, no drugs, no bullying, and to listen to the teachers and parents. Kids who train in Taekwondo become combat-capable and better human beings by learning discipline and respect.

However, my greatest accomplishment came as a complete surprise when I received the news that I was nominated for the Taekwondo Hall of Fame as The Outstanding Pioneer Armed Forces Player Award. I feel honored that our Armed Forces Technical Advisor (SGT Louis Davis) nominated me.

I was also worthy of recognition twice by the U.S. Taekwondo Champions as the Pioneer Award of the Year recipient for my performance as an athlete, coach, and referee for organizing the Armed Forces Taekwondo reunion and for being tournament coordinator. Our senior, GM Bobby Clayton, was recognized as well. Thanks to GM Jojo Stage and GM Ron Berry for this awesome award.

In 2015, I was selected as the President of the United States Military Taekwondo Foundation. The foundation's goal is to assist veterans and active military athletes. As a nonprofit organization, our foundation does not receive government funding. We rely solely on individual donations and corporate sponsorships.

I have produced many qualified athletes for the Armed Forces Taekwondo teams, many of whom have gone on to become All Army, Armed Forces, CISM, and U.S. National medalists. As a coach and even President of the CISM Taekwondo committee, I will continue to guide future military athletes and civilians to the Army Taekwondo Team to continue with the discipline and tradition of the martial arts.

TRAINING INFORMATION

- Martial Arts Styles & Rank: 9th Dan Chang Moo Kwon, 9th Dan Chang Hon Kwan, 9th Dan World Taekwon-Choodo Federation, 9th Dan Sport Taekwondo Center Associates, 7th Dan Kukkiwon, 7th Dan United States National (USA-TKD), 7th Dan ITF-America International TKD Federation Black Belt, 1st Dan Kyokushinkai-kan, 1st Dan Kuk Sool Won
- Instructors/Influencers: Master Luis Díaz, The Late Master Juan Ruiz, Sensei Michael, Sensei Miguel Acevedo, Sensei Fernando Caraballo, The Late GrandMaster Giovanni Rosario, Master Pedro Laboy, Grand Master Bobby Clayton
- Birthplace/Growing Up: Candelero Arriba / Residencial Padre Rivera, Humacao, Puerto Rico
- Yrs. In the Martial Arts: 55 years
- Yrs. Instructing: 32+ years
- School owner, Manager & Instructor at Sport Taekwondo ChangMooKwan Center

PROFESSIONAL ORGANIZATIONS

- United States Armed Forces
- United States Military Taekwondo Foundation
- Federación de Taekwondo de Puerto Rico
- World Taekwondo Federation (WT)
- Kukkiwon
- World Taekwondo Chang Moo Kwan
- The World TaekwonMoodo Federation
- United States America Taekwondo (USAT)
- Amateur Athletic Union (AAU)
- Taekwondo Hall of Fame
- U.S. Taekwondo Champions (SR. Gyoroogi)
- U.S. Armed Forces TKD Alumni
- The Pan American Taekwondo Union (PATU)
- Sport Taekwondo Center Associates

PERSONAL ACHIEVEMENTS

- Twenty-two years of Military Service
- International Master Instructor License with Kukkiwon
- Chang Moo Kwan International Instructor License
- Cable Technician/Installer Certified

Around 1986, the Department of Sport/MWR paid all competition expenses for the first time. We were literally the first soldiers (Pedro Laboy, Mark Green, Leo Oledan, and Rafael Medina) to represent the Army and Armed Forces in a Taekwondo competition.

SFC Bennett and I opened a Taekwondo dojang on base (Fort Bliss). I was getting SFC Bennett ready for the All-Army Taekwondo team trial during this time. In 1995, Coach Grandmaster Bobby Clayton asked me if I would like to be his assistant coach.

My achievements have been thanks to the support of the people around me because I would never have gotten good results without them. My support team includes my wife Nilsa, Luis Diaz, Miguel Acevedo, Fernando Caraballo, Giovanni Rosario, Pedro Laboy, Bruce Harris, Paul Boltz, Michael Bennett, Bobby Clayton, Bongseok Kim, Jessie Bowen, the Puerto Rico Taekwondo Federation, The United States America Taekwondo (USAT), Amateur Athletic Union (AAU) and many more.

HOW HAS MARTIAL ARTS IMPACTED YOUR LIFE?

Because of having an agitated, fearful, mistrustful, and disoriented youth life, we should never lose our self-confidence. Loneliness must be avoided.

Martial discipline (military or martial arts) leads to physical, mental, and emotional benefits that can improve the quality of your life in different ways. Obstacles will always be in our paths, but our quality of life must be better. Don't judge yourself by society;

PERSONAL ACHIEVEMENTS

- A happy husband, father, and grandfather
- Ambassador of the 1st - 4er Armed Forces Taekwondo Reunion
- Selected as the best referee in 4 different Taekwondo events
- Established the motto "One Team, One Fight." Unifying the sport of Taekwondo for all the armed forces.
- First president of the United States Taekwondo Foundation
- World Taekwondo Federation Poomsae and Kyorugi International
- Referee License

MAJOR ACHIEVEMENTS

- 1996-2000 All Army and Armed Forces Coach
- 1995-1998 Fort Stewart Head Coach
- 1987-1994 All Army Taekwondo Bantamweight medalist
- 1987—1998 Armed Forces Taekwondo Bantamweight medalist
- 1987 World CISM Military International Bantamweight medalist
- 1987 First Latino and Puerto Rican representing the United States armed forces in an International Military Sports Council (CISM) Taekwondo event.
- Taekwondo Hall of Fame's Technical Advisor.
- 2019 International Kyorugi Referee — level 2
- May 2019 - recognized as a Grandmaster of Taekwondo by the government of Puerto Rico and by The House of Representatives of Puerto Rico. Thanks to GM William Sanchez Cardona.
- September 2019—The Taekwondo International Military Sports Council (CISM) committee selected me as the first military and the only person in the United States to represent the nation as an athlete, coach, and International Referee in the World Military Taekwondo Championship.
- Nominated by the Taekwondo Hall of Fame for the Outstanding Pioneering Player Award for the Armed Forces.
- First President of Chang Moo Kwan in Puerto Rico.
- First President of the U.S. Armed Forces, Chang Moo Kwan.

MAJOR ACHIEVEMENTS

- 2024 - The Mayor of Humacao, Puerto Rico, delivered a Letter of Proclamation recognizing me as a leader in the sport of Taekwondo and my contribution to the U.S. Armed Forces

- 2024 - Together, with Master Louis Davis and Doctor Michael Bennett, we wrote the book "One Team One Fight One Family," which is a #1 Amazon Best-seller.

- 2024 International Poomsae Referee — level 3

HOW HAS MARTIAL ARTS IMPACTED YOUR LIFE? (CONTINUED)

seek help. We are not alone. Prepare for a better future for yourself and your family. A friend always helps us when we need it most.

When I was young and smaller than my peers, I was an easy target for bullies in my tough neighborhood. To change the balance, I had to learn how to defend myself. I was tired of being the loser or feeling the agony of defeat. I wanted something different in my life. My first training was hard, and I even cried. At that moment, I learned the best lesson of my life. Nothing is easy; we have to fight for what we want to achieve our goals. Discipline and humility go hand in hand. Learn and teach the values of others. Respect life because it is only one; being humble costs nothing. Remember, your future is in your hands.

Twenty-two years in the military, I learned to value life and thank God for each day.

Become an
AMAA MEMBER!

DANA
MILLER

"

Through the years, I've helped change the lives, I hope, for the good of hundreds of students from all over the country.

WHY THE MARTIAL ARTS?

My friend's semi-pro boxer dad taught us basic boxing fundamentals. Also, a relative of mine who had some experience with the techniques and training of the British Commandos of WWII told stories, sharing their exploits and techniques that they were taught. When JFK started the Green Beret Program, I decided that was what I wanted to do with my life. At the time, in the 1960s, there weren't any martial arts schools in my area, but there were a couple of clubs where people could get together and share training methods. I soon added Judo to my practice. A neighbor at the time was practicing Karate, so we worked out together, too. In high school, I was a gymnast. The flexibility and strength gained helped with the high kicking needed for that art. And the practice of Katas was similar to the sets or routines in gymnastics, which appealed to me.

HOW HAS MARTIAL ARTS IMPACTED YOUR LIFE?

From an early age, martial arts has been my life's major focus and purpose. The arts have given me meaning and a mission. Through these years, I have learned many lessons from my martial practices: integrity, honesty, commitment, personal responsibility, discipline, self-knowledge, and passing on that knowledge. Through teaching and sharing with others since the age of twenty, I have learned how much growth is possible for students. Through the years, I've helped change the lives, I hope, for the good of hundreds of students from all over the country. I will always be grateful for the opportunity I have had to help develop young people, leading them to become respectful and successful adults who will positively contribute to society. It has been my greatest personal achievement to watch my students Bob Berube, Peter Rudh, Steve Kubic, Mike Kaiser, Levi Wilson, Billie Brown, Gail Behr, Heide Hindsman, Kenny Patterson, Brian Bailey, Bryan Lewis, Tom Shipp, Paul Methven, and Rudy Bormann become masters.

PROFESSIONAL ORGANIZATIONS

- United States Chuan Fa Association AAU Judo President
- U.S. Chuan Fa World Martial Arts Hall of Fame - 1994
- World Head of Family Sokeship Counsel Member
- National QiGong Assn. USA, 1997
- Member QiGong Empowerment Assn. 1995
- NDEITA, Personal Trainer member

PERSONAL ACHIEVEMENTS

- President of 3M Corporation Chinese Boxing Club - 1975-1994
- 6th Dan Master level Chuan Lo Chinese Boxing Association - 1979
- Republic of Taiwan Koushu Mission Instructor Certificate - 1983
- Head of Family, U.S. Chuan Fa Assn. - 1992-present
- Grand Master of the Year, World Martial Arts Hall of Fame, WMAHF - 1995
- Member World Head of Family Sokeship Council - 1994
- Awarded Professor of Martial Arts degree, WMAHF, - 1998 Graduate
- Three Rivers Crossing Center for Qigong Traditional Chinese Healing - 1996
- Certified Medical QiGong Instructor - 1998
- Presidential Sports Award in Karate - 1993 (G.W. Bush)

MAJOR ACHIEVEMENTS

- Elected lifetime president of U.S. Chuan Fa Association - 1981
- Inducted into the World Martial Arts Hall of Fame - 1994
- Inducted into World Head of Family SokeShip Council - 1995
- Inheritor of Combat Karate System from Paul Steve Landon - 2016
- Developed and Founded Zu Wei Shu System Martial Arts - 1980
- 6th-degree promotion in Chuan Lu - 1979
- Ph.D. Professorship from the World Head of Family - 1998

TRAINING INFORMATION

- Martial Arts Styles & Rank: 10th Level Red Sash - Zu Wei Shu Gong Fu, 9th Level Black Belt - American Combat Karate, 6th Level Black Sash - Chuan Lu Kenpo, 3rd Level Black Belt - Tang Soo Do, Honorary Ranks: 3rd Dan in Tae Kwon Do, 1st Dan in Shotokan Karate, 1st Dan in Goju Kai Karate, and 1st Dan Judo
- Instructors/Influencers: Raymond McCardie, George Fibbson, Nathaniel R. Wilson, Paul S. Landon, Don B. Jones, Joe Pereira, Grand Master Chen, Jim Cravens, John Allen, Rick Faye, Larry Seiberlich, Fu Wei Zhong, Master Chunvi Lin, George Hu, Liang Sho Yu
- Birthplace/Growing Up: St. Paul, MN
- Yrs. In the Martial Arts: 64 years
- Yrs. Instructing: 56 years
- School owner, Manager and Instructor at U.S. Chuan Fa Martial Arts Center

STEPHEN MILLER

"
I try every day to walk with the confidence and discipline of a winner and with the utmost respect for everyone and everything in life.

WHY THE MARTIAL ARTS?

As a high school student, I struggled to find my footing, facing challenges in making friends, obtaining good grades in my classes, and succeeding in sports. While I feel like I got along with everyone during my first two years in high school, I never felt like I had that circle of good friends with whom you go through life. I felt like I struggled to connect with my peers and find my place in school. I often felt like an outsider, and it seemed like everyone else had their clique and friendships figured out. As a result, my self-esteem and confidence dropped, and I suffered from minor depression.

I also faced difficulties in sports, where I struggled to keep up with my teammates and felt like I did not measure up. I loved playing baseball for the City League and having my father as a coach. In high school, not having many friends and struggling with my confidence, I chose not to play the one thing I enjoyed. My parents saw this and encouraged me to try a different sport to stay active. As a result, I tried out wrestling, an individual-based sport. Never having done this before, I got to know the lights by name quickly because most of the surrounding schools had feeder programs. In fact, my final record as a freshman wrestler was 0-16. This lack of success added to my feelings of frustration and low self-esteem. I enjoyed this sport, so I began working on my own, joined a gym, and signed up for some summer clinics. While it did help some, I ended my sophomore season with a record of 3 — 12. I knew I was still missing something and was contemplating not returning for my junior year.

Feeling lost and unsure, my belief in myself was getting worse. As a result, I began to spend a lot of time at home and watching television. This is where I first discovered martial arts by watching Bruce Lee movies like *Enter the Dragon, Game of Death*, and *Fists of Fury* and Chuck Norris movies like *Forced Vengeance, An Eye For An Eye*, and *Missing in*

KORYO GUMDO

Puerto Rico
November 2023

TRAINING INFORMATION

- Martial Arts Styles & Rank: Taekwondo; 7th Dan USNTF, 5th Dan Kukkiwon, Koryo Gumdo; 1st dan WKGA
- Instructors/Influencers: Grandmaster Dae Kyu Lee, Grandmaster Young Jin Chung, Grandmaster Duk Gun Kwon, Grandmaster Stephen McArther
- Birthplace/Growing Up: New Jersey
- Yrs. In the Martial Arts: 41 years
- Yrs. Instructing: 30 years
- School owner & Instructor at CDR Taekwondo

PROFESSIONAL ORGANIZATIONS

- USNTF
- Kukkiwon
- WKGA
- Action Martial Arts Magazine Hall of Honor
- Masters of Martial Arts Hall Of Fame

PERSONAL ACHIEVEMENTS

- Starting up my TKD school, CDR Taekwondo, in July 2018
- Becoming a Director of Operations in my current career with a major DSO
- Associate Member of the Cape Atlantic Marine Corps
- Father of three amazing children
- Marrying my best friend, Robin

MAJOR ACHIEVEMENTS

- 2012 International Champion
- Inducted into Masters of Martial Arts Hall Of Fame, 2023
- Inducted into Action Martial Arts Magazine Hall of Honor, 2024
- I traveled to South Korea three times (1989, 2008, 2109) to further my training

Action, I thought that this would be neat to try because you do it on your own. With my interest sparked, I looked in the Yellow Pages, and luckily for me there, "American Tae Kwon Do," owned and instructed by Grandmaster Dae Kyu Lee, was less than one mile from my house. I asked my parents if we could go visit it and see what it was about. My mom and I talked with Grandmaster Lee and watched a class. The visit went great, and as a result, on my 16th birthday, my parents signed me up not only for a one or two-month trial but for the "Black Belt Program." They knew that I needed to commit to this and the impact that this could have on my life.

At first, it was intimidating. I was watching all the other students and all the cool things they were doing, and I struggled to do even a basic low block or get my hips straight when doing a low front stance. But as I continued training, I found a sense of purpose and

2024 Hall of Honor
Action Martial Arts Magazine
Esteemed Elite Warrior

belonging. The instructors told me that the only competitor I had to worry about was the person looking back at me in the mirror. We all have different physical abilities and/or limitations, so a technique that works for one person may not work that great for me, and vice versa. GM Lee often put me in front of that mirror and showed me a block, punch, or kick and told me to try it. He would then walk away for what seemed like hours, and I stayed there doing that technique hundreds of times. The discipline and structure that he was teaching helped me to build up my confidence and focus.

Through martial arts, I found a new path forward. I learned valuable lessons and skills and made supportive friends. I still get together with many of them forty years later. I have also developed a stronger sense of self. My journey taught me that with discipline, perseverance, and the right support, anyone can overcome adversity and find their way. I apply these principles to my life, in my relationships, in my career, and in everything.

I originally signed up for martial arts to get better at a sport and I have learned to be a better person in life. I am truly blessed to have learned such valuable life lessons, and I now have the opportunity to teach them to my own students.

HOW HAS MARTIAL ARTS IMPACTED YOUR LIFE?

When I first started my training, I did so because I was not very good at wrestling in high school and was looking for something that would help me improve and at least give a respectable performance on the mats. I was lucky enough to learn so much more. Along with learning the physical traits of endurance, flexibility, balance, and strength, I discovered the non-physical characteristics of confidence, discipline, and respect (The main reason my school is named CDR Taekwondo). While the physical traits were very beneficial, sports would end at some point in my life. Here, these other traits had impacted not only my wrestling career but also my life. I have implemented these three areas into everything. I have learned that when you want something, don't be hesitant; be confident and go get it, whether it is that new career, new home, etc.

Further, even with that confidence, you need to be disciplined to keep your focus on the result no matter what your friends may be doing that day, what show you may be missing on the television, etc. And with that, you must show and act with respect. For without that, what does it mean to get what you are after? My father always said, "You only get what you give, and that includes respect."

I try every day to walk with the confidence and discipline of a winner and with the utmost respect for everyone and everything in life. This is how martial arts have impacted my life.

TOBY MILROY

"The Martial Arts has given me a 'core' set of skills that has created an amazing life and career for me.

WHY THE MARTIAL ARTS?

The media in the late 70's was my original inspiration for studying martial arts. I first saw a snippet of Enter the Dragon in 1978. I still remember being in awe of the Super Hero like speed and skill I saw in those few stolen minutes of the film. Then I became a somewhat ravenous seeker and consumer of all things martial arts. "Kung Fu" re-runs on television, Black Belt and Karate Illustrated Magazine, and even some early Chuck Norris movies solidified my passion and resolve to study the martial arts.

I was fortunate enough that a family friend was a part time martial arts instructor at a local collage, and he agreed to work with me once a week. After a few months, my enthusiasm for training had only grown, and I was finally able to convince my Mother to enroll me in the local "real" full time Karate School.

At that time, it was NOT standard practice to accept students as young as I was, but the school made an exception and allowed me to attend classes. The 'full time' structured training at the Dubuque Karate Club, under Master David Schmidt was a LIFE changer for me.

I was already passionate about martial arts, but this experience lit a fire in me that has helped me create a level of success in the martial arts, in the martial arts business, and in my life that I never would have thought possible.

The Martial Arts has given me a "core" set of skills that has created an amazing life and career for me. It has imbued me with the sense of self-confidence and focus of will that has allowed me to accomplish goals that most people think are impossible to reach.

When I first opened a Martial Arts school, I was a good Martial Artist, and I wanted to pass on the arts that I loved so much, but I was clueless about running a successful school. I was missing a LOT of martial arts business fundamentals.

TRAINING INFORMATION

- Martial Arts Styles & Rank: TaeKwonDo (5th Dan), TangSooDo (5th Dan)
- Instructors/Influencers: Master David Schmidt, Master Jason Farnsworth, Grandmaster Jeff Smith, Grandmaster H.U. Lee, Grandmaster Stephen Oliver
- Birthplace/Growing Up: Dubuque, IA
- Yrs. In the Martial Arts: 43 years
- Yrs. Instructing: 27 years
- Executive Vice President - AMS, President and Editor in Chief - Martial Arts World News Magazine

PROFESSIONAL ORGANIZATIONS

- Successful Multi School Operator
- Author — Coaching Children to Succeed in Life
- Author — The Path to Leadership
- 2007 - Chief Operating Officer - NAPMA (National Association of Professional Martial Artists
- 2007 -Chief Operating Officer — Martial Arts Professional Magazine

PERSONAL ACHIEVEMENTS

- 2015 - Executive Vice President - AMS (Amerinational Management Services)
- 2015 - President and Editor in Chief - Martial Arts World News Magazine
- Helped Thousands of Martial Arts School Owners Create More Successful Schools

I pretty quickly realized that running successful martial arts schools requires a COMPLETELY new set of skills that I'd never really learned as a martial arts student, BUT I also realized that IF you apply the same PRINCIPLES you master while studying the martial arts, you can easily acquire the new skills you need, and implement them to create amazing businesses and make a substantial positive impact on your students and your community.

The discipline, focus and "indomitable spirit" you develop in your martial arts training are an amazingly powerful force when you apply them to ANY aspect of your life. Not only do these principles empower you to be successful in a martial arts school, but in ANY career path, profession or avocation you might want to pursue.

It's been the greatest honor of my life to help so many martial arts students and school owners reach their goals and impact more of the world with the positive values of the martial arts.

Become an
AMAA MEMBER!

JAE MUN

> "
> *Martial arts have allowed me to meet many excellent martial artists and given me the confidence to know that I can defend myself.*

I studied Tae Kwon Do during the '70s in Baltimore. Practicing self-defense was exciting. A dozen kids surrounded me with axes at a golf course and by gangs outside a memorial baseball stadium. It helped me make new friends and build my reputation at school as a karate kid. I had a smooth school life, unlike other Asian kids who got bullied at school. I did junior and senior high demonstrations, so everyone knew I did Tae Kwon Do. At the time, kids knew it as karate and gave me respect or were at least wise enough not to pick a fight.

I liked competing in tournaments. It gave me purpose, took my mind off my worries, and I wanted to make my dad proud. I also continued because I liked my instructor, Al Pigeon, who led me to Christ and socializing with members after class by visiting Friendly's Ice Cream. I chose Tae Kwon Do, even though I made the varsity soccer team in high school. I thought I would have a better chance of getting a job during my college years as an instructor. My investment in training in Tae Kwon Do paid off as a General Manager for four years in Maryland, only to heed my calling as a minister of the Gospel, pursuing a Master's of Divinity at Westminster Theological Seminary in Pennsylvania.

WHY THE MARTIAL ARTS?

I started martial arts because I was fascinated with the jump-spinning hook kick performed by my childhood friend Jong Woo, but I discovered it was Tae Kwon Do. South Korea was very poor during the '60s. I had many hobbies: fishing at Han River, hunting with a slingshot, and ice skating in the field during winter. I joined the baseball team at my elementary school, Gang Nam, but I took Tae Kwon Do lessons outside of school at the neighborhood's do jang (Tae Kwon Do School).

The self-defense aspect appealed to me since there were fights at school and neighborhood gangs. My family immigrated to the US in the Spring of 1971.

I worked full-time as a program director for many Tae Kwon Do Schools, helping them succeed in member enrollment and becoming president of All American Tae Kwon Do Academy. Now, I challenge myself as a master instructor at a Gold Medal Tae Kwon Do Academy, helping kids win AAU state and national championships. I enjoy Tae Kwon Do; I use it to minister and help develop future leaders in America.

HOW HAS MARTIAL ARTS IMPACTED YOUR LIFE?

Martial arts have helped me maintain my physical health, obtain a job, and hold the title of Founder of the All-American Tae Kwon Do Federation. Martial arts have also allowed me to meet many excellent martial artists and given me the confidence to know that I can defend myself. Tae Kwon Do has opened doors for me to be a speaker at Student for Christ Conferences in Peru and Myanmar - a tool for ministry.

Most of all, my instructor, Al Pidgeon, a Pennsylvania National Tae Kwon Do Champion, led me to Christ at Tae Kwon Do school in Baltimore, helping me to walk the straight path during my teenage years.

TRAINING INFORMATION

- Martial Arts Styles & Rank: 9th Dan - World Chunkuhn Taekwon Do Federation, 9th Dan - IJTF - International Jung Tong Tae Kwon Do, 6th Dan - Black Belt World- WTF, 6th Dan - World Combat Arts Federation, 5th Dan World Black Belt Bureau; Kukkiwon, 1st Dan - ITF International Tae Kwon Do Federation

- Instructors/Influencers: South Korea Moo Duck Kwan Masters Kong Young Il, Kong Young Bo, Al Pigeon, and Sang Ki Eun

- Birthplace/Growing Up: Seoul, Korea

- Yrs. In the Martial Arts: 56 years

- Yrs. Instructing: 25 years

- General manager, Owner & Master Instructor

PROFESSIONAL ORGANIZATIONS

- Alumni Westminster Theological Seminary

- WTS Korean Pastors

- Kentucky Colonel

- Ordained Minister of the Gospel through Kosin Presbyterian Denomination in New Jersey (2003)

PERSONAL ACHIEVEMENTS

- Master of Divinity from Westminster Theological Seminary in PA

- Youth Pastor for 20 years at numerous Korean churches (AK, WA, DC, MD, and PA)

- I prepared and led short-term missions to Mexico and Peru

- I helped organize the 1980 Worldwide Evangelization Crusade in South Korea- International affairs

- Interpreter and guide to Dr. Bill Bright, Founder of Campus Crusade for Christ

- Seminar speaker for SFC: Main speaker at Peru (2024), Myanmar, Burma (2023)

- Four-year Senator Scholarship - MD

- BS for Philosophy & Religious Studies at Towson State University

- Professor at Covenant Mission Seminary in Cambodia

MAJOR ACHIEVEMENTS

- Master of Divinity from Westminster Theological Seminary (2001)

- Ordained Minister of the Gospel (2003)

- Promoted to 9th Dan by the World Chunkuhn Tae Kwon Do Federation (2024)

- Promoted to 9th Dan by IJTF (2018)

- Hall of Fame - Grandmaster of the Year and Best School Owner of the Year by the United States Kido Federation 2X award recipient for the spreading and contribution of Tae Kwon Do by Jun Lee, President of Black Belt World (2018 and 2019)

- Hall of Fame - Evangelist/Instructor of AFKA-American Freestyle Karate Association

- Head instructor - New Life Black Belt Academy

- Inclusion into the Martial Arts Extraordinaire Biography Book: 50 Years of Martial Arts Excellence (2021)

- Award for Leadership in Spreading Tae Kwon Do by President of Kukkiwon Dong Sup Lee at Kukkiwon Presidential Cup (2023)

Become an
AMAA MEMBER!

STEVE
NEMETZ

"
It is a privilege to pass on the knowledge I have gained over the last 46 years and see how our students grow in confidence and self-esteem.

Harris also wanted to add weapons and other martial arts styles for the advanced belts, so he added Filipino Eskrima, Okinawan Kobudo, and Shorin Ryu to the curriculum training under Kyoshi Neil Stolsmark of Waukesha, Wisconsin.

Sensei Paul Harris died in January 2010, but Harris Karate Academy stayed open until January 2016. In April 2016, a group of us wanted to continue Sensei Harris' legacy and teachings through the Plumer Karate America. It is a privilege to pass on the knowledge I have gained over the last 46 years and see how our students grow in confidence and self-esteem.

WHY THE MARTIAL ARTS?

In 1978, I walked by Chay's Karate and Tae-Kwon-Do Center in Green Bay, Wisconsin, looked in the window, and saw a friend of mine there. So, I signed up and have been with the martial arts ever since. Sensei Paul Harris was the instructor and started his karate school, the Harris Karate Academy. So I went with him when he opened his school. He wanted to add more hand techniques to the curriculum we were teaching, so we started training with the Soaring Eagles Boxing Club out of Oneida, Wisconsin. Sensei

TRAINING INFORMATION

- Martial Arts Styles & Rank: American Karate 9th Degree Black Belt
- Instructors/Influencers: Sensei Paul Harris
- Birthplace/Growing Up: Rantoul, IL / Green Bay, WI
- Yrs. In the Martial Arts: 46 years
- Yrs. Instructing: 45 years

PROFESSIONAL ORGANIZATIONS

- World Tae-Kwon-Do Federation
- Superfoot International Martial Arts Federation
- IMAC
- ISKA
- NASKA
- WPKA
- AMAA

PERSONAL ACHIEVEMENTS

- Received my 9th Degree Black Belt June 23, 2023
- Wisconsin State Heavyweight Black Belt Champion in AAU Continuous Sparring in 1981 - 1983
- Wisconsin State Heavyweight Black Belt Fighting Belt Champion— 1987, 1988
- Won 50+ Black Belt Fighting Grand Championships in Midwest and National tournaments
- Fought Full Contact Karate
- Taught self-defense classes at Boys and Girls clubs helping troubled teens
- Taught self-defense classes in high schools and local Domestic Abuse and Crisis Centers
- Instructor Certified in Reactionary Knife and Pressure Point applications
- Instructor Certified in Eskrima
- Practiced Okinawan Kobudo, Shorin Ryu Karate, Boxing, Jiu Jitsu

MAJOR ACHIEVEMENTS

- Inductee, Elite Black Belt Hall of Fame
- Inductee, United States Martial Arts Hall of Fame
- Inductee, USA Martial Arts Hall of Fame
- Inductee, Legends of the Martial Arts Hall of Fame
- Inductee, Action Martial Arts Magazine Hall of Honors 3 times
- Inductee, Expo 11 Masters of the Martial Arts Hall of Fame
- Inductee, Tournament of Champions Hall of Fame
- Inductee, Who's Who in the Martial Arts Hall of Fame
- Me and my wife, Chris, have also run an adult family home for the last 25 years, where we have

BRIAN
OAKES

"

Martial arts gives me immense satisfaction watching my students change.

However, I lived in a remote small town in Northern Michigan, and no martial arts schools were available. So, I collected martial arts comics and watched films when I could. Shortly after completing my military service, I enrolled in a community college that had fitness classes in Shotokan Karate, Judo, and Aikido. I achieved a yellow belt in these systems and have been studying since.

HOW HAS MARTIAL ARTS IMPACTED YOUR LIFE?

I have become the formable street fighter and the teacher I've always wanted. However, doing my best to live up to my personal interpretation of the code of modern warrior has changed my life and, therefore, my family's. In my day job as a nurse since 1979, I've helped thousands of patients. But any licensed nurse could claim that honor. Teaching martial arts is a different story. Punching and kicking are the bait for new students; however, the changes in martial students are the best part of the arts. It gives me immense satisfaction watching my students change. They become more focused, happy, spiritual, and in touch with their families.

WHY THE MARTIAL ARTS?

Around age five, my family and I visited another family. We were taken to a mall with a Karate demonstration during the visit. Back at home, the Bruce Lee movies and Kung Fu, the greatest martial arts TV show ever, hooked me on martial arts.

TRAINING INFORMATION

- Martial Arts Styles & Rank: 9th Degree Black Belt - Kenpo/JKD Mixed Martial Arts, Brown Belt-Shotokan Karate, Yellow belts-Aikido & Judo, studied JKD
- Instructors/Influencers: Master Thomas Georgian, Sensei Koyann, Burton Richardson, Ed White, James Stacy
- Birthplace/Growing Up: Boyne City, MI
- Yrs. In the Martial Arts: 39 years
- Yrs. Instructing: 29 years
- School owner at Bigfoot Tactical Martial Arts

PROFESSIONAL ORGANIZATIONS

- American Warrior Martial Artist Alliance (Founding board member)
- The Northern and Southern Kung-Fu Association (Vice President)
- Whipping Willow Association (founding member)
- Arizona Karate Association
- World Kenpo Karate Association

PERSONAL ACHIEVEMENTS

- 1979-1993 US Navy Hospital Corpsman, rank E5 Petty Officer 2nd class
- 1982 Licensed Vocational Nurse
- 1995 US Army Reserves rank E6
- 2000 Licensed Registered Nurse specializing in Intensive Care
- 2005 Medical support for Hurricane Katrina
- 2006 County resolution from the County of San Bernardino, California, for leadership and participation during Hurricane Katrina
- 2009 Medical Support Command National Disaster Response Tennessee Brigade rank Lt. Colonel
- 2009 Certified Instructor
- 2009 Advanced Azmat Medical Life Support Instructor
- 2019 Certified Life Coach
- 2019 Certified Cognitive Therapy Technician

MAJOR ACHIEVEMENTS

- Being happily married to the love of my life, my best friend, Mina Oakes, my daughter Sierra Oakes and my son Hunter Oakes. Family is the most important thing in my life.

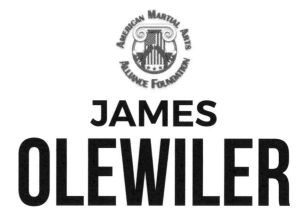

JAMES
OLEWILER

"

Anyone and everyone would benefit from martial arts as a form of self-defense, but most importantly, as a way of life.

WHY THE MARTIAL ARTS?

I grew up in an economically unstable household and a poverty-stricken neighborhood, which had crime and violence. When I was ten years old in 1972, I worked a paper route, and I would take my money and buy martial arts magazines at the local newsstand: Karate Illustrated, Official Karate, and Blackbelt Magazine, as well as others when they came out. I would study the martial arts techniques shown in the magazines and order other publications through Ohara because there were no schools I could afford close enough to my location.

I wanted to learn martial arts for my own protection and my family's protection because of the uncertainty in the world I was growing up in. The health and mental benefits intrigued me as well, especially the meditation. I have always been a spiritual person. I studied the philosophical works of many of the great masters, including the philosophies of Bruce Lee. I finally convinced my mother to enroll me in Kung Fu classes in 1974, Pai-lum Kung Fu to be exact, under Grandmaster Daniel K. Pai, who I later learned was Ed Parker's cousin.

I studied religiously at the Kwon for two years under Sifu John Weininger. I watched every Bruce Lee movie released repeatedly, trying to mimic his movements and skills to bring to my Kung Fu classes. However, there was not enough student enrollment, and the instructor suffered from marital problems, so the studio closed.

I looked for additional instruction and came across Richard Chun's Tae Kwon Do through an instructor of his, Master Bill Sprenkle. I studied there again for two years; that studio closed, too. I then found an instructor from Korea, Chung Su Kim, who is currently the founder and president of the PAN AM Tan Soo Do Federation. Master Kim had just arrived in America and spoke very broken English.

I studied and taught classes three times a week under Grandmaster Kim from 1979 until 1984; I moved above our studio and lived in an apartment adjacent to my instructor, so we trained religiously. It was like living in a Buddhist monastery and earning my first and second-degree black belts. Master Kim had a falling out with the World Tae Kwon Do Federation on a territorial dispute with another Korean master. Because he outranked my instructor, my instructor was told to close his school, so he eventually switched from Tae Kwon Do to a sister style, Tang Soo Do, with the help of Master Nam and Grandmaster Jae C. Shin (Chuck Norris's instructor), also, one of the attending masters during my black belt exams to avoid the closure of his school.

This upset me quite a bit; we're switching from Tae Kwon Do to Tang Soo; here we go...starting all over again! Another student, Thomas Sharretts, decided to continue in Tae Kwon Do by leaving Master Kim and opening a school; I decided to join him. We taught religiously for two years, but I yearned for more knowledge and was burnt out on teaching anyway. I then joined the U.S. Army 2nd Infantry Div Warriors in 1986 to serve my country, as my grandfather did during WWII. I ensured Korea was included in my contract and the Army G.I. Bill for college. I now get to further my training in Korea, the birthplace of the Korean Arts and Tae Kwon Do, at the KukKiWon and Camp Casey, Korea, for an additional two years, where I received my Master's Degree in Tae Kwon Do under Grand Master Cha, a Tae Kwon Do champion.

TRAINING INFORMATION

- Martial Arts Styles & Rank: Tae Kwon Do-7th Dan Degree Blackbelt, Brazilian Jiu Jitsu-Purple Belt, Pai-lum Kung fu- Purple Sash, U.S. Army hand-to-hand combat specialist
- Instructors/Influencers: Grandmaster Daniel K.Pai, w/ Joh Weininger, Grandmaster Jae C. Shin, Grandmaster Chung Su Kim, Grandmaster Yong Bong Cha, Grandmaster Joe Lewis, Daniel Beleza, Sifu Samuel Kwok
- Birthplace/Growing Up: York, PA
- Yrs. In the Martial Arts: 52 years
- Yrs. Instructing: 43 years
- School owner, Manager & Instructor at M.A.C.E. Martial Arts Academy, A.I.K.I.A. under Dr. Jerry Beasley, American Independent Martial Arts Instructors Association

PROFESSIONAL ORGANIZATIONS

- World Tae Kwon Do Federation
- Korea Tae Kwon Do Federation
- Western Hemisphere TaeKwonDo Association
- AIKIA- American Independent Karate Instructors Association
- World Karate Expert Association
- Team SAS Brazilian Jiu-jitsu Federation

PERSONAL & MAJOR ACHIEVEMENTS

- Becoming a Master-Level Reiki Healer
- Successful single parent
- Aspiring actor
- Community leader

PERSONAL & MAJOR ACHIEVEMENTS

- Penn State University
- 7th Degree Tae Kwon Do Black Belt
- Business owner and homeowner
- True and faithful God-fearing man

I was instrumental in 1988 while stationed in Korea to help with several Olympic activities associated with Korea being the host country and Tae Kwon Do being their national sport. I taught and trained many athletes in those days. In 1989, while stationed at Ft. Lewis, WA, and living with my girlfriend friend, Rhonda Golden, I came across Grandmaster Joo Bang Lee, the founder of Hwarang Do, and his student/instructor Eric Reyma in Oregon. I commuted from Ft. Lewis, WA, to Oregon two times a week for classes. I received the Army Commendation Medal and left the Army and Washington State.

In 1990, I moved back to Pennsylvania. I gave in-home private Korean martial arts classes, mainly Tae Kwon Do, and I ran up and down the East Coast training with martial arts legends and champions at every opportunity. All while attending Penn State University from 1990-1994 for Business Administration. A year later, in 1995, I opened my own martial arts academy, creating an eclectic system of my martial arts training: M.A.C.E. Martial Arts Academy, a martial art with combat emphasis. I learned from R.O.K. soldiers in the Korean Army and my martial arts training in the civilian world with Brazilian Jujitsu. It was taught to me by the World Champion Daniel Beleza, as well as traveling the East and West Coast attending seminars with the late great Joe "The Jaguar" Lewis, Bill "Superfoot" Wallace, Jeff Smith, Benny "The Jet" Urquidez, Billy "Tae Bo" Blanks, Don "The Dragon" Wilson, Cynthia "Lady Dragon" Rothrock, Steve "Nasty" Anderson, Renzo Gracie, Matt Serra, Mike Lee Kanarek, Grand Master George Dillman, Soke Michael DePasquale, Jr., Mark Hatmaker, GM George Alexander, and Dr. Jerry Beasley, at his Karate College in Roanoke, VA, to name a few.

I currently hold a 7th dan degree black belt in Tae Kwon Do. In 2010, when my youngest son Avery was born, I stopped chasing degrees and raised him as a single parent, a role I currently hold.

I had the opportunity to attend the USA Martial Arts Hall of Fame in 2021, where I was presented the "Living Legend Award" from Dr. Jim Thomas, and before that, I was awarded "The Man of the Year" in Tae Kwon Do in 2004 with Grandmaster Aaron Banks. In 2007, M.A.C.E Martial Arts Academy was awarded "Best School" by the Asian World of Martial Arts (AWMA).

In 2008, my gears shifted, and I got involved in mixed martial arts and cage fighting. I hired a female boxing coach, Brittany Inkrote, #3, in her weight class; I partnered with a friend who brought Daniel Beleza from Brazil and rated #3 in the world in his weight class. Then I found a Muay Thai black belt, Bobby Shah, and it was on. We had coaches. We started trying with UFC legends Renzo Gracie, Matt Serra, and Ultimate Fighter series contenders Eric "Chainsaw" Charles and Tamdan "The Barn Cat" McCrory; with this lineup, finding fighters was easy. Everyone wanted to be an MMA Cage fighter, so why not? It was on fire. So, as history has it, we went on to win the first legally sanctioned MMA Cage fighting event in Pennsylvania through the PA Athletic Commission, The Central Pennsylvania Warrior Challenge, on October 23, 2009, with ten bouts, of which our fighters took eight of the ten belts and their respective divisions. I went on to stay involved in MMA and Cage fighting, as well as traditional Korean Arts. Things went well for years, with us even having fights like "Bellator" under our belts, as well as championships.

Then Covid broke and sent businesses such as ours down to the point of failure in many cases. Still, I feel we are coming back, so with that attitude, I was recently presented with the "Esteem Elite Warrior Award" in 2024 at the Action Martial Arts Magazine Hall of Honors. I was awarded the "Lifetime Dedication to the Martial Arts" Award" at the San Francisco Golden Gate Hall of Honors in 2023. I was included in the 58th edition of the publication Martial Arts Greatest by Ted Gambordella, and I am currently learning Wing Chun from Grandmaster Samuel Kwok.

I was also privileged to appear in Cynthia" Lady Dragon" Rothrock's Black Creek movie and novel as Mr. JJ. Whiley, a gun-toting gambler and townsman. I continue to teach and spread my love and passion for martial arts and its philosophy throughout the world on a daily basis. In addition to my paid classes, I have been providing reduced and free classes at our local recreation center, Red Lion Recreation, Red Lion, PA, since 1995.

HOW HAS MARTIAL ARTS IMPACTED YOUR LIFE?

Studying martial arts has impacted my life in many ways, more than I can write about. I learned goal achieving through martial arts. I learned that once you pass the black belt test, you can pass any test in the world. Not because it magically makes you better, but it teaches you to be prepared. I learn from my students in each class as they learn from me. I have learned, and they learned, that respect is mutual. If I give it to them, they give it back to me. If they give it to me, I give it back to them; it reciprocates back and forth.

Martial arts have also impacted my life because of the changes I have made in others' lives because of my dedication and love of the arts. I can show someone where they may be now, but it is not where they have to stay, whether it's a belt or a station in life. Martial arts teaches self-growth through a trial and error learning and belt ranking process. Anyone and everyone would benefit from martial arts as a form of self-defense, but most importantly, as a way of life. The health benefits I have learned through martial arts practice have stayed with me throughout my entire life: improved flexibility, increased lung capacity, and a stronger, slower, beating, healthy heart. The meditations and philosophical works associated with training in martial arts have elevated me to a greater understanding of myself, the people around me, and the world in general. Thank you, my peers, friends, and family.

Dad loves you, Avery and Mike.

Sincerely, James Jessie Olewiler, Oss!

DAISY ORTINO

" *The dojo is our happy home. As we always say, the family that trains together stays together.*

WHY THE MARTIAL ARTS?

I was only 29 years old when I lost my first husband. He left me with three beautiful daughters. I wanted my daughters to grow up knowing how to defend themselves. My priority goal was for my daughters to grow up strong and not be bullied at school. I was bullied when I first came to Hawaii from the Philippines when I was 14 years old. I couldn't really speak English then. I saw this Thailander girl being bullied at school and she did a spinning hook kick on this bully. I was so impressed. No one bullied her again. When I met Paul Ortino, he became our Sensei in 1996. We loved karate, weapons and all the friends we were making. The other martial

arts students became family to us. The dojo became our home. We trained with Sensei Paul (now my husband) for over 12 years. We had karate in the brain. All my girls became black belts and also graduated in college with honors.

The Martial Arts has impacted my life in so many ways. Since I began training in 1996, my health has improved. I used to have severe asthma when I was growing up and heart palpitations.

Working out and training made my body stronger. My girls and I were happier and healthier. Cheryl, Sherry Anne and Shanelle were more focused in school and more confident. They always did homework first and then trained with us. All three of my daughters as well as myself became black belts and assisted teaching Sensei Paul in all of his dojos. Sensei Paul and I got married in May 1998. We had the best time of our lives while training. We developed a stronger bond together. The dojo was our happy home. As we always say, the family that trains together stays together.

TRAINING INFORMATION

- Martial Arts Styles & Rank: Sandan in Okinawa Kenpo Karate and RHKKA
- Instructors/Influencers: Hanshi Paul Ortino Jr.
- Birthplace/Growing Up: Philippines and Hawaii
- Yrs. In the Martial Arts: 27 years
- Yrs. Instructing: 14 years
- Instructor

PROFESSIONAL ORGANIZATIONS

- Okinawa Kenpo Karate Dharma-Ryu Dojo
- Ryukyu Hon Kenpo Kobujutsu Association
- Hawaii Karate Congress

PERSONAL ACHIEVEMENTS

- Achieved 3rd Degree Black Belt in Okinawa Kenpo Karate as taught by Grandmaster Seikichi Odo
- Assistant Commissioner to the Aloha State Games in Hawaii 1990 until 2003
- Assistant Instructor to the Okinawa Kenpo Karate Dojos in Hawaii 1999 until 2006
- Assistant Instructor to the Okinawa Kenpo Karate dojo in Naples FL 2006

MAJOR ACHIEVEMENTS

- A top competitor in Hawaii Karate Congress tournaments and rated in Kumite, Kata and Kobudo for many years
- Helped to run all the Aloha State Games Karate tournaments as well as all the annual tournaments put on by the Okinawa Kenpo Karate Dharma-Ryu Dojos in Hawaii
- Taught Karate for the military and their dependents in Hawaii from 1999 until 2006
- Asked to become the female representative for the Strike Back Training System

PAUL
ORTINO

"

The martial arts has been a blessing to me and I want to share the traditions with all who want to learn.

WHY THE MARTIAL ARTS?

I began my Martial Arts study when I was 13 in Judo because I wasn't that big and was getting into fights a lot with what we now call bullies. Wanting to be able to defend myself, I pleaded with my parents to let me take martial arts. I then started taking karate in Reading, PA and never stopped.

Everywhere I moved I signed up for Karate, Taekwondo or Kung Fu. The funny thing was that the better I got the less fights I was getting into. Having Senseis such as Robert Dunn (Taekwondo), Al Smith (Red Dragon), Charlie Lewchalermwong (Shotokan) and finally Richard Gonzalez and Seikichi Odo (Okinawa Kenpo) I was taught the principles of Karate as well. I realized that it was better to walk

away from a fight not because I was afraid of getting hurt but because I really didn't want to hurt someone else. The Martial Arts taught me to be humble, respectful and to refrain from violent behavior.

In the beginning I just wanted to protect myself but after I started training, I realized there was so much more to karate than meets the eye. It became a way of life. I no longer wanted to fight other people and was able to walk away feeling confident about myself. From the moment I entered the dojo of GM George Dillman back in the late 60's I wanted to become a Black Belt. Even before I became a Black Belt, I was an assistant instructor.

HOW HAS MARTIAL ARTS IMPACTED YOUR LIFE?

I wanted to help others get their self-confidence back and be able to protect themselves. I believed that every man, woman and child should learn to protect themselves and my wife Daisy, my daughters Cheryl, Sherry Anne and Shanelle all became Black Belts and helped me teach in Hawaii. My son Angelo is working his way to being a Black Belt one day. The family that trains together stays together.

TRAINING INFORMATION

- Martial Arts Styles & Rank: Hanshi,9th Degree Black Belt Okinawa Kenpo Karate Karate (GM Seikichi Odo,GM Richard Gonzalez), 9th degree black belt (GM Robert Dunn Taekwondo), 6th Dan Hawaii Karate Kodanshakai(GM Bobby Lowe,GM James Miyaji), 3rd Degree Black Belt Red Dragon Karate (GM Al Smith), 3rd Degree Black Belt Shotokan Karate, 3rd Degree Black Belt Chi lin Chuan Fa
- Instructors/Influencers: GM Seikichi Odo Okinawa Kenpo Karate (10th Dan), GM Robert Dunn Taekwondo (9th Dan), GM Al Smith Red Dragon Karate (10th Dan)
- Birthplace/Growing Up: Philadelphia PA / HI, FL, NC / Las Vegas, NV
- Yrs. In the Martial Arts: 55 years
- Yrs. Instructing: 49 years
- President and Chief Instructor (Okinawa Kenpo Karate Dharma-Ryu Dojo)

Become an
AMAA MEMBER!

PROFESSIONAL ORGANIZATIONS

- Ryu Kyu Hon Kenpo Kobujutsu Association (BOD)
- American Martial Arts Alliance
- Hawaii Karate Kondanshakai (original member)
- Hawaii Karate Congress (former President)
- Seishinkai Karate Union (former Shibucho to Hawaii- GM Robert Burgermeister, Kaicho)
- Pennsylvania Black Belt Society
- Florida Black Belt Association

PERSONAL ACHIEVEMENTS

- Won Triple Crown -1st place kata, weapons, kumite (GM James Miyaji tournament/ Waipahu HI)
- Rated in the top 10 kata, weapons and kumite in the Hawaii Karate Congress annual ratings
- Represented USA at GM Ken Funakoshi's Annual tournament San Jose CA Kumite division
- Made 4 DVDs of the Okinawa Kenpo System as taught by GM Seikichi Odo
- Martial Arts Representative for the "Strike Back Training System"
- Co-founded Florida Academy of Judo-Karate with Master Don Rosenthal 1978

MAJOR ACHIEVEMENTS

- Former President of the Hawaii Karate Congress
- Karate Commissioner for the Aloha State Games (1990-2003)
- Taught all branches of the US Military in Hawaii for 26 years
- Promoted to 9th Degree Black Belt, Hanshi June 10th 2010
- Co-founded the UNC-Greensboro Karate Club under the direction of Master Charlie Lewchalermwong 1972
- 2019- awarded " The History General Award" by Professor Gary Lee and the Sport Karate Museum

CELINE OTTO

" *It's so important to teach with love and love what you teach. Then, you become the true essence of human capacity.*

WHY THE MARTIAL ARTS?

Celine was born in 1967 on the small island of Mauritius in the South Indian Ocean. During her early childhood, they did not have electricity, running water, or a bathroom. She remembers her father serving in the British Military during WWII and working in a sugar cane factory. Her mother raised a family of seven children. When electricity came to the house, there was no television, only a radio to listen to stories at night. But despite these humble beginnings, her mother infused solid values of self-worth, respect, and ambition in all her children. Even in this third-world environment, they maintained dignity, pride, and a strong work ethic. Life became better as she grew older and completed her education. At age 20, she moved to Paris, France, where she lived for the next ten years.

In the '90s', Celine began her professional teaching career working in the private school sector in Pennsylvania, the Virgin Islands, Puerto Rico, and St. Maarten, D.W.I. After nearly fifteen years of teaching children ages three to six, she realized an essential need to teach children martial arts.

In June 2017, Celine became co-owner of the Shen Dragon Karate Dojo at the Antilles School Campus in St. Thomas, Virgin Islands, where she worked as an educator at the private preschool. She started an after-school martial arts program for children ages four and five and evening classes for older kids and adults. Celine felt compelled to teach martial arts skills and virtues, knowing this would be life-changing.

On December 1, 2018, they had the re-grand opening of the Shen Dragon in the St. Thomas business district. Over the next year, the Dojo experienced constant growth, and the future looked promising. The attendance was then nearly 100 students and growing. What could go wrong?

On February 29, 2020, the newspaper reported the first confirmed COVID-19 death. And then the unbelievable happened—the Pandemic. By April, practically every non-essential business was closed by the government. Over the next four months, the Shen Dojo was opened and closed three times, forcing the

use of Zoom live streaming to maintain continuity with their students. Many dropped off, and when the dojo reopened, some students feared contagion.

Grand Master Jerry Otto and Celine never gave up. Their passion for teaching was never stronger. Celine designed programs for the Zoom classes, which carried over to the open courses, making the students' transition back to the dojo as effortless as possible.

Celine is the program manager of St. Thomas, VI, Shen Dragon Karate Dojo. She uses her many years as an educator to create programs for all the children's classes as the primary instructor. Her experience and passion for teaching provide a safe learning environment for all children. She consistently works to develop their positive belief system, self-respect, respect toward others, and self-confidence, and she provides them with the skill sets they will use throughout their lifetime.

Celine is also instrumental to the start-up of the Virgin Islands Martial Arts Development Association, Inc. 501 (C) 3, a non-profit company whose mission is changing lives through the comprehensive practice and study of martial arts and to foster the competitive values of the U.S. National Karate Championships, World-Class Competition and the Olympic movement for men, women, and children of the U.S Virgin Islands.

At age 53, Celine achieved her Shodan first-degree black belt and is considered an inspiring and prominent female competitor in the 50 and older divisions.

She was promoted to 2nd Degree Black Belt in 2022.

TRAINING INFORMATION

- Martial Arts Styles & Rank: Okinawa Shorin-Ryu, Krav Maga
- Instructors/Influencers: Grand Master Jerry Otto
- Birthplace/Growing Up: Mauritius Island (South Indian Ocean)
- Yrs. In the Martial Arts: 7 years
- Yrs. Instructing: 6 years
- School co-owner, Program manager, Instructor at Shen Dragon Karate Dojo, Assistant Coach of the Shen Dragon Competition Team

PROFESSIONAL ORGANIZATIONS

- American Martial Arts Alliance Foundation
- VIMADA (Virgin Islands Martial Arts Development Association) 501 (C) 3

PERSONAL & MAJOR ACHIEVEMENTS

- Fifteen years as a primary school educator in the private school sector
- U.S. Capitol Classic, 2018, Women Kata Division, 50 and older, Second Place Kata
- Woman of the Year, 2019. The Students Choice Award — Shen Dragon Dojo
- Biography featured in the American Martial Arts Alliance Foundation, *Changing Lives History Book Series*, Tribute Ernie Reyes Edition, 2021
- The Martial Arts Extraordinaire Magazine featured the article: *The Art of Survival — How the Shen Dragon Survived Two Cat-5 Hurricanes and One Year of Pandemic Conditions.* Co-author
- Biography featured in the Action Martial Arts Magazine Hall of Honors, World History Book, 2022
- Biography featured in the Action Martial Arts World History Book, 2022
- Inducted into the Action Martial Arts Magazine, Hall of Honors, for Excellence in the Martial Arts Teaching, 2022
- Atlantic City, NJ: War At the Shore: 2022 Women 50 to 59 Yrs. old
  ◊ First Place Champion Kata
  ◊ Men's/Women's Second Place Weapons Champion (Competed in Master's Division)

- Atlantic City, NJ: NAFMA Valley Nationals: 2022 Women 50 to 59 Yrs. old.
  ◊ First Place Women's Kata
  ◊ First Place Women's Weapons
- Washington, DC: U.S. Capitol Classics and China Open: 2022 NASKA Women 50 to 59 Yrs. old.
  ◊ First Place in Women's Traditions Kata
  ◊ First Place Women's Traditional Weapons
  ◊ Grand Champion Women's Traditional Kata
  ◊ Grand Champion Women's Traditional Weapons
- Miami, Fl: Pan American Internationals: 2022 NASKA Women 50 to 59 Yrs. old.
  ◊ Second Place Traditional Kata
  ◊ First Place Traditional Weapons,
  ◊ First Place Creative Kata
  ◊ First Place Creative Weapons
  ◊ Grand Champion Traditional Weapons
  ◊ Grand Champion Traditions Kata
- Featured Biography in the Martial Arts Extraordinaire Magazine featuring the Powerful Women in the Martial Arts, Changing Lives.
- Inducted into GM Ron Van Clief's "Ultimate Warrior Award, Class of 2022.
- Featured as a Powerful Women in the Martial Arts in the Martial Arts Extraordinaire Mag, Feb/2022 issue
- Front Cover of the Martial Arts Extraordinaire Mag. April/2022
- Featured in MAEM, w/Michael Jai & Gillian White, Couples in the Martial Arts.
- Inducted into the NAFMA Legacy Hall of Honors Award - 2022
- Ambassador Award at the NAFMA Legacy Awards Gala, 2022
- Published co-author in the Elite *Martial Artists in America, Secrets to Life, Leadership & Business* Chapter 16 "What Makes a Great Leader," 2023

HOW HAS MARTIAL ARTS IMPACTED YOUR LIFE?

The martial arts have a lot to do with who Celine is today. Embracing the martial arts has helped her believe in herself, mind, body, and soul. Martial arts have helped her gain confidence and how to control her fears and emotions. It has taught Celine how to approach others with differences, love, and understand her interests. Finally, and most importantly, it has helped Celine identify her innermost passion for teaching children martial arts. She says, "It's so important to teach with love and love what you teach. Then, you become the true essence of human capacity."

TONY
PARKER

"
...As I started practicing Taekwondo and training with other students, I began to feel more at ease.

HOW HAS MARTIAL ARTS IMPACTED YOUR LIFE?

In my younger years, I struggled with speaking to people due to a lack of confidence and fear of saying the wrong thing. This affected my interactions in school, with my parents, and even with some friends. However, as I started practicing Taekwondo and training with other students, I began to feel more at ease. Eventually, my instructor asked me to teach my first class, which was intimidating at first, but over time, this experience helped me become a much more confident person in everything I do now.

WHY THE MARTIAL ARTS?

My interest in martial arts was sparked when I watched Bruce Lee as a kid. In 1983, I walked into my first martial arts school, led by Grand Master Y.B. Choi in New Jersey. I then joined a class with Master Crocco, whose school was fast-paced and had a large number of students, making it a comfortable environment for training. Over the years, we all became like a family. In 2001, after seventeen years, I purchased his school. Additionally, I had the honor of continuing my training with Master Malefyt for over fifteen years.

TRAINING INFORMATION

- Martial Arts Styles & Rank: ITF Taekwondo-4th Dan, Haidong Gumdo-1st Dan
- Instructors/Influencers: Grand Master Choi, Master Micheal Crocco, Alex Wilkie, Master Nicholas Malefyt, Master Park, Master Oh
- Birthplace/Growing Up: Somerset, NJ
- Yrs. In the Martial Arts: 41 years
- Yrs. Instructing: 25 years
- School owner of T-Kick Martial Arts Academy

PROFESSIONAL ORGANIZATIONS

- International Taekwondo Federation
- World Haidong Gumdo

PERSONAL ACHIEVEMENTS

- Opening my first martial arts school

MAJOR ACHIEVEMENTS

- Raising $30,000 for the March of Dimes
- Being recognized for outstanding contributions to the Franklin Township Youth Council: 2013

Become an
AMAA MEMBER!

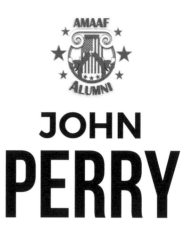

JOHN PERRY

" Studying martial arts has taken me to many places and introduced me to countless lifetime friends.

I treasure those memories forever. Although I never knew it at the time. Martial arts gave me a way to channel my anger and disappointments in life. Everything I had was put into my training. It wasn't long before it was the majority of my life.

I found that training in the forest was especially the missing element for me. Nature would bring me peace and mental clarity while training until I was completely exhausted. I would sit and meditate for hours after I finished my physical training. Fast forward the years, I developed confidence, leadership qualities, love for others, and a love for myself. The martial arts have inspired my education as well. In 2016, I received a master's degree in Acupuncture and Traditional Chinese Medicine. Studying martial arts has taken me to many places and introduced me to countless lifetime friends. It has led me to personal growth and a relationship with God through my Savior, Jesus Christ. I would like to thank the people in my life for making me who I am.

WHY THE MARTIAL ARTS?

As a child, I was intrigued by the movements of martial arts. I was always watching Kung Fu Theater and trying to mimic the techniques I saw on television. I started training in Eagle Claw Kung Fu and Hapkido in the spring of 1973. I was completely hooked and have continued a lifelong journey down the path of martial arts.

HOW HAS MARTIAL ARTS IMPACTED YOUR LIFE?

Studying martial arts has impacted my life and made me who I am. Every aspect of my life has been a part of my martial arts journey. As a child, I would spend time training with my dad. Unfortunately, he would pass away while I was young.

TRAINING INFORMATION

- Martial Arts Styles & Rank: Jidokwan Tae Kwon Do-5th Dan, Ko Sutemi Seiei Kan Karate -5th Dan, Tomiki Aikido-4th Dan, Kwok Wing Chun, Yang Tai Chi Chuan, Shaolin Five Animal Kung Fu-2nd Dan, Kenpo Karate-2nd Dan

- Instructors/Influencers: Don Madden, Samuel Kwok, Herb McGuire, Mike Stanhope

- Birthplace/Growing Up: Chillicothe, OH

- Yrs. In the Martial Arts: 50+ years

- Yrs. Instructing: 35 years

- School owner, Manager & Instructor at Tian Dao Jian Kang

PROFESSIONAL ORGANIZATIONS

- American Martial Arts Alliance Foundation

- AKJU Ko Sutemi Seiei Kan

- American Jidokwan

- Museum of Sport Karate

- Tian Dao Jian Kang / Heaven Way Health

- United States Martial Arts Black Belt Hall of Fame

- Eastern U.S.A. International Martial Arts Association

PERSONAL ACHIEVEMENTS

- Master's Degree in Acupuncture and Traditional Chinese Medicine 2016

MAJOR ACHIEVEMENTS

- Eastern U.S.A. Black Belt Hall of Fame Induction

HALL OF FAME AWARDS

- 2014 Silver Anniversary Achievement

- 2015 Martial Arts Dedication

- 2016 Master Black Belt of the Year

- 2017 Extraordinary Martial Arts Loyalty

- 2018 Continual Commitment to the Martial Arts

- 2019 Outstanding Service and Contribution to Improving Global Martial Arts

- 2020 Golden Anniversary Achievement 40+ years

- 2021 Inspirational Martial Arts Example

- 2022 Extraordinary Martial Arts Spirit

- 2023 Diamond Anniversary Achievement 50+ years

UNITED STATES MARTIAL ARTS HALL OF FAME

- 2024 Pioneer of Martial Arts

AMERICAN MARTIAL ARTS ALLIANCE FOUNDATION

- 2019 Who's Who Legends Award

- 2020 Martial Arts Ambassador of the Year

- 2021 Who's Who Legends Award

- 2022 Who's Who Legacy Alumni Award

Become an
AMAA
MEMBER!

DONALD
PLUMMER

"

Martial arts have always given me great comfort, pride, and a feeling of accomplishment that is not found in many other places.

WHY THE MARTIAL ARTS?

First and foremost, I would like to thank all of the Supreme Grand Masters, Grand Masters, Masters, and Black Belts who paved the way for me and my art.

I was born at Georgetown University Hospital in 1952 and raised in Washington, DC, until I was eighteen years old.

My first job while in elementary school was as a paperboy with the Washington News, Washington Star, and the Washington Post. I also helped a friend distribute Jet Magazines.

While sitting on a bundle of newspapers and looking through the comic strips, I saw "The Green Hornet and Kato" strip. It inspired me so much that I grabbed The Yellow Pages and found Kim Studios in Silver Springs, MD. I went to the school and talked with

Grand Master Ki Wang Kim. He was an 8th Degree Black Belt at the time, sometime between 1967 and 1969. Master Kim said I was too young to enroll and needed my parent's consent. So I took the contract home to my father, Mr. Leroy Plummer, where he signed the contract and paid the fees. I was around thirteen or fourteen years old and in the 7th grade.

I earned my yellow belt at the Kim Studio. Unfortunately, soon after earning my yellow belt, I could not continue attending the Kim Studio, but I continued practicing independently. To improve my skills, I started teaching some of my friends the techniques that I had learned: the upper block, middle block, low block, front kick, and sidekick.

The Vietnam War was raging as I turned eighteen years old at the time. One day, while at a neighborhood store with a friend, President Richard M. Nixon came on the air and said, "We need a few good men to help stop Communist aggression in Vietnam." So I told my friend, "Let's go and enlist." We got on the bus and went down to a recruiting office on Pennsylvania Avenue near The White House. It was a no-brainer for me since my brother went into the U.S. Air Force at sixteen with parental consent, so I enlisted in it at eighteen years old. OSI did their investigation, and I was inducted into the USAF in three days. My friend enlisted shortly after me. She joined the Navy following her brother's footsteps.

I can't remember how I got to Lakeland AFB in San Antonio, TX, but I did. Basic training is six weeks long. During the last week of basic training, my drill sergeant asked me, "What do I want to do in the Air Force?" I said, "I wanted to rescue people." He asked me, "Can you run a mile?" I answered, "Sir. Yes, Sir." He asked, "Can you swim a mile?" I responded, "Sir. No, Sir." Then he asked me, "Can you read?" To me, that was a piece of cake, so I gladly shouted out, "Sir. Yes, Sir." He handed me a paperback book and told me to start reading. I enjoyed reading. Being a former paperboy, I was always reading something. After I read aloud for a while, he said that I would go wherever the Air Force needed me to serve my country. I had completed my basic training with my yellow belt.

I did my textbook training at Sheppard AFB in Texas. Then, I did my PCF duty work at Castle AFB as a traffic management specialist in Merced, California. As a 10th-grade dropout, I had lots of life experience but not much formal education, but I was always eager and willing to learn. I reached the rank of Non-Commissioned Officer in less than two years. I volunteered for duty in Vietnam but was not chosen to go, so I was transferred to Clark AFB in the Philippines. I didn't want to sell my car at Castle AFB. I remember driving from the base back home to Washington, DC, in two and a half days, which was quite an accomplishment for the time. After I dropped off my car in D.C., I was flown directly to the Philippines. While at Clark AFB, I earned my GED. I passed all the GED requirements in five days. I met Master Instructor Ernie Escalante. He was a wonderful teacher who taught Indonesian stick fighting. After that, I joined the Ernie Wado School, where he trained me on "The Twenty-four Techniques of Stick Fighting." I earned my second green belt in Indonesian Stick Fighting under his watchful eyes.

Due to an on-duty injury, I was transferred from the Philippines to Andrews AFB in Maryland, where I

PERSONAL ACHIEVEMENTS

- I have traveled and trained in Alaska, Hawaii, Guam, Okinawa, Japan, Portugal, Morocco, and France.
- USAF 1971-1975
- Retired USAF 1979
- National Business School 1976-1977
- Howard University 1977-1981
- Walter Reed Hospital 1982
- University of District of Columbia 1983
- Morgan State University 1998
- Copping State AA Degree 2000

MAJOR ACHIEVEMENTS

- 1st Degree Black Belt 1976
- 2nd Degree Black Belt 1977
- Gold Medal AAU Howard University 1980
- 3rd Degree Black Belt 2014
- Bruce Lee Hall of Honor 2015
- USFL Poomse Certificate 2016
- AAU Referee for 6 years
- AMAA Who's Who Legend Award 2017
- Certified 2nd Degree Black Belt 2000
- Life Achievement Award 2020
- 4th Degree Master Instructor 2018 to the Present 2021
- Over 30 Competition Medals
- 1st and 2nd Degree Kukkiwon

Become an
AMAA MEMBER!

and worked closely with him in the 1985 Special Olympics World Games. After that, I moved to Detroit, MI, and later to Oakland, CA, where I started training again. It was no-holds-barred, full-contact fighting. As I remember, I returned to Washington, DC, minus one of my front teeth.

After living in Washington for a while, I moved to Baltimore, MA. I started training and teaching under Grand Master Se Yong Chang USTA, who certified me as a 2nd Dan with the WTF. After that, I transferred to Copping State in Baltimore and received an A.A. degree with transferable military credit.

After a seven-year absence from martial arts, I moved to Fort Lauderdale, Florida, looking forward to starting my training and lifelong dream of becoming a master. I started searching for a suitable school to join. After much searching, I found Grand Master Francisco Loureda, 9th Dan Kukkiwon. Under his strong guidance and demanding eye, I grew through the ranks to my current ranking of 4th degree Master in WTF Olympic Style Tae Kwon Do with the US Chung Do Kwan Association. I have trained with Grand Master Francisco Loureda for nearly ten years. I currently live in Pompano Beach, Florida, where I bought a home. I turned my garage into a private martial arts studio where I can train, be in the best shape possible, and continue to work on my knowledge. In the many years and miles that life has taken me, martial arts has been my constant companion. Martial arts have always given me great comfort, pride, and a feeling of accomplishment that is not found in many other places.

spent three months recovering from my injuries. I was placed on temporary military disability for five years, and in 1979, I retired from the Air Force. While on military disability, I moved back to my parent's house in D.C. My friend Viny Earl discovered I was a martial artist and asked me to train him. I refused at first, but he finally convinced me to train him. I taught in my house, and when he reached the rank of yellow belt, I told him he needed to join a certified school to rise through the ranks. He did, and the last time I saw Viny, he was a second-degree black belt. I returned to Kim Studio; by now, Grand Master Kim was a 9th Dan. I was promoted to first-degree black belt in 1976; my father was there to see the ceremony. I was again promoted, and in 1977, I was honored with my second-degree black belt under Grand Master Kim. I started Howard University in 1977 as a black belt with tournament experience. I trained under Grand Master Kim until 1982. I moved to Bridgeport, Connecticut, to live with my brother the same year. While in New Haven, CT, I studied Subak and got an orange belt. When they knew that I was a fighting black belt, I was introduced to Timothy Shiver

DR. JEANETTE "JING"
CASITAS RANA

> **"**
> *We live in a very dangerous world,*
> *especially for a woman like me; I need*
> *to be prepared. I must be*

female participant at that time. Every summer, she watched Kung Fu movies with her childhood friends. They would pretend to fight each other, copying the moves of martial arts celebrities such as Jet Li, Sammo Hung, Jackie Chan, Cynthia Luster, and Cynthia Rothrock.

When she reached college, she continued to show her love of sports. Her soccer team won several times against their rivals at the university. In 1990, before her graduation, she had learned about the most popular martial arts in Legazpi: "Kuntaw ng Pilipinas (KNP), the ancient art of Filipino hand and foot fighting." What grabbed her attention and triggered her burning desire to practice Kuntaw was the discipline, dedication, and respect among the instructors and students of Kuntaw. Kuntaw is so popular that she can frequently hear over the local radio stations announcing the tournaments to be held in Legazpi City and other cities or provinces of the Bicol region. She told herself, "One day, I will be one of those Kuntaw martial artists. I will be a black belt." She began to search for the Kuntaw martial arts school. After several months of searching, she finally found the Kuntaw gym! She immediately registered so that she could start right away. Since then, she has trained hard, not missing a class.

WHY THE MARTIAL ARTS?

A native of the land of the majestic Mt. Mayon, in Legazpi City, Philippines, Kyudai Jeanette "Jing" Chancey was born to parents Jose Rana and Dolores Casitas. She was the fourth child of four siblings. The youngest among the girls, she was very active, sociable, and constantly doing things, whether indoor or outdoor activities. Born a natural athlete, she participated in almost every sport in elementary and secondary school. She also became a member of her school's track and field team.

Aside from her love of sports, she was very creative; she even represented her school in a poster-making contest and won several times. She was the only

She has never forgotten her instructors: Senior Master Ariel Delgado, Grandmaster Nilo "Neil" Ablong, Kyud Leogildo "Dodong" Capistrano, and Kyud Joseph Abellano. She even remembered the instructors who often visited the gym: Eduardo Lancauon, the pioneer of Kuntaw martial arts in Albay province, Kyud Angel Torregoza, and Lito Mejillano, of whom they became her sparring partners/trainers.

Because of her enthusiasm and determination to learn the art, she dragged her younger brother Jonathan to go with her to the gym. In 1990, she and her brother Jonathan officially joined Kuntaw ng Pilipinas, International Kuntaw Federation (KNP-IKF), Legazpi City Chapter. This made her train tirelessly despite her busy schedule as a student. It became her weekly routine to train indefatigably with her instructors and fellow students. She embraced Kuntaw as a way of life and practiced the ancient Filipino martial arts wholeheartedly. In 1991, she and her brother received their hard-earned blackbelt. She said, "This is a big deal; this is what I hoped, dreamed, and longed for." Subsequently, Master Ariel Delgado employed her as his assistant chief training instructor. Master Jing continued teaching for almost three years. While training and teaching Kuntaw, she took it as a great learning experience. She says, "It taught me to be humbler, to have more self-control or self-discipline, helped raise my self-esteem, and more respectful to other martial arts practitioners." She added, "It was a great honor to share the knowledge I learned from my senior black belts and instructors. It was an indescribable feeling to pass along all the techniques, be a guide in molding future "Kyuds" and "Kyudais," be an instrument to develop younger martial arts practitioners with their skills and hone their potentials."

In 1995, she temporarily suspended her Kuntaw training and teaching to teach science at Pag-Asa National High School, now known as Legazpi City National High School. But her passion for Kuntaw never ceased. In October 1996, her only daughter, Janne Pearl, was born. Her daughter became a Kuntaw martial artist later when she reached high school. Her daughter is currently a Registered Nurse and works at the University of Sto. Tomas Hospital, Legazpi City, Philippines. Master Jing

TRAINING INFORMATION

- Martial Arts Styles & Rank: KLIMA International Martial Arts, Kali (Filipino Martial Arts -FMA), 8th Degree - Red, Black, and Red belt, traditional Aikido, Judo, Won Hwa Do, modern & traditional kickboxing.
- Instructors/Influencers: Senior Master Ariel B. Delgado, Grandmaster Neil C. Ablong, Dodong Capistrano, Grandmaster Alicia Kossmann, Grandmaster Bill Kossmann, Grandmaster Lhod Villaluna
- Birthplace/Growing Up: Legazpi City, Albay, Philippines
- Yrs. In the Martial Arts: 34 years
- Yrs. Instructing: 16 years
- Instructor

PROFESSIONAL ORGANIZATIONS

- KLIMA International Martial Arts

PERSONAL ACHIEVEMENTS

- First Female Kuntaw Assistant Chief Training Instructor, Legazpi City, Albay, Philippines
- Bachelor of Secondary Education in General Science Degree (1991), University of Sto. Thomas, Legazpi City, Albay, Philippines
- Master of Arts in Criminal Justice Degree (2013) from Keiser University, Tallahassee, Florida
- State Director, KLIMA International Martial Arts, Tallahassee, Florida (2020 - present)
- Doctorate of Christian Counseling Degree (2023), The New Testament Bible Church Biblical Institute, Shreveport, Louisiana
- 2023 Silver Pickle Award, Department of Revenue, Tallahassee, Florida
- 2023 Distinguished Person Humanitarian Award, Come On In Elite Inc.
- 2023 Special Congressional Recognition, California, USA
- 2024 KLIMA Lifetime Achievement Award
- 2024 Special Tribute "The Fighting Woman" ISKA Martial Arts & Combats Sports Worldwide
- Ambassador, Global Network for Peace, April 2024, Argentina

also taught Kuntaw in the summers of 2001 and 2002 at MABA Laboratory School, Legazpi City, Philippines. Master Jing became a self-defense instructor to some private citizens. The knowledge, skills, principles, and values of a Kuntaw instructor remained in her heart, mind, and spirit. She applied Kuntaw in her everyday life and at work.

In 2009, Master Jing moved to Tallahassee, Florida. She married Donald Chancey, her fiancé of five years. She began to work as a receptionist at Dr. Pat and Associates. Shortly after six months, she worked as another personal service (OPS) employee at the Florida Department of Law Enforcement (FDLE). She worked at FDLE for nine years. In 2019, she moved to the Florida Office of the Attorney General as a paralegal. After more than two years, she moved to a different position as a Medicaid fraud analyst. In 2022, she moved again to a different agency, the Department of Revenue, as a resource management specialist. She works with the Physical Security Team to provide security oversight, maintain situational awareness, and enforce the department's security and access control policy and procedures to provide for the security of state employees, contractors, and customers in the

MAJOR ACHIEVEMENTS

- Board Passer, Licensure Examination for Teachers (1992), Professional Regulations Commission, Philippines
- 1992 Champion Bicol Regional Full Contact Women's Blackbelt Division, Iriga City, Camarines Sur, Philippines
- Distinguished Team of the Year Nominee (2018), Florida Department of Law Enforcement (CJIS, Seal & Expunge), Tallahassee, Florida, USA
- 2020 Hall of Fame Inductee, KLIMA International Martial Arts, Main Headquarters, North Carolina
- Leadership Award, KLIMA International Martial Arts (2020)
- 2023 American Martial Arts Alliance (AMAA) Hall of Honors Inductee, Las Vegas, Nevada, USA
- 2023 Lifetime Achievement Award, AmeriCorps & the Office of the President of the United States
- 2023 Universal Martial Arts Hall of Fame (UMAHoF) Inductee, Alvin, Texas, USA
- 2024 Hall of Fame of Martial Artists, ASAMCO Martial Arts, Brazil
- 2024 Athena Women Warriors International Award, ASAMCO Martial Arts, Brazil
- 2024 Williams Elite Hall of Honor Inductee, Colorado, USA
- 2024 Goodwill Ambassador International Certification, Come On In Elite Global, Inc., Colorado, USA
- 2024 International Leadership Award, Extraordinary People Awards (EPA) & Come On In Elite Global (COIEG), Colorado, USA

Become an AMAA MEMBER!

department's facilities. Her busy schedule did not hinder her desire to continue teaching KLIMA.

Master Jing taught KLIMA martial arts at Lake Talquin Baptist Church. She had a few students when she first started her class there. In a matter of three months, the number of students increased. She had one potential black belt expected to graduate this year. She is serving as a Sunday school teacher at 1200 Church, where she is currently attending. She provides self-defense training classes to older women and children in her church.

Master Jing was so grateful to her former instructors; without them, she would never reach her dream of being one of them. Among the other things she was thankful for was the knowledge she acquired from her instructors; this contributed to her successful career in law enforcement and to what she is today. Master Jing stated, "Aside from God, I am also thankful to Grandmasters Alice Lanada Kossmann and Bill Kossmann for their leadership in Kuntaw Legacy (now known as KLIMA). And to all the future KLIMA martial artists: always remember, there is no such thing as perfect martial arts; constant practice makes it perfect."

HOW HAS MARTIAL ARTS IMPACTED YOUR LIFE?

Master Jing has always been an avid martial arts enthusiast. At a very young age, her curiosity began when she watched a movie and saw this short, tiny lady take down a man twice her size. She thought the lady was so impressive. So, Master Jing dreamed about being like her, a martial arts expert, a black belt, she supposed. She tried to copy some of her moves but failed miserably. Several years passed, but she still had that burning desire to learn martial arts. Then, she, a young woman who knows nothing about martial arts, wondered if she could possibly be like that lady that she watched in the movie several years back. She told herself, "There must be a way to do that!" Then, the search for scientific studies of martial arts began.

Born with an inferiority complex due to her petite stature, she needed to wrestle herself to overcome that

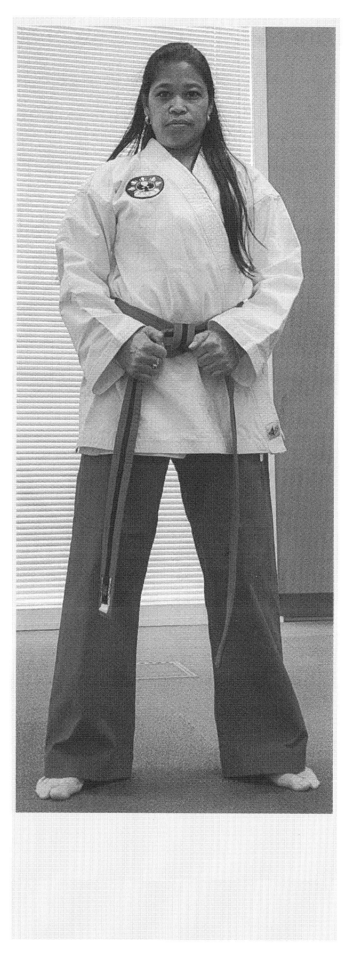

HOW HAS MARTIAL ARTS IMPACTED YOUR LIFE? (CONTINUED)

weakness and learn the art. That was her first struggle. Secondly, she had nobody to go with and was too shy to go alone alone! Thirdly, where can she find that martial arts school? Fourthly, she thought she was too old to start training (she was around seventeen or eighteen then). She struggled with those issues but had no idea how she ended up at Master Ariel Delgado's martial arts school/gym. She recalled talking to Guro Dodong Capistrano beyond her knowledge that he would be one of her instructors. Master Jing knew him as a friend and talked to him about Kuntaw and the like. Then he quietly invited her to visit the gym where he practices. When she entered the "dojo," it was a shock! Guro Kyud Dodong is the training instructor for Kuntaw martial arts at that gym! He was so humble and kind, and you could never tell he had that degree of a blackbelt.

A similar thing happened with Master Ariel Delgado; she thought Master Delgado was only the fitness/health club manager. These men appeared to be ordinary people, but she found out later that they knew how to teach martial arts. During their training, she was able to meet Grandmaster Nilo Ablong, GM Ed Lancawon, who passed away a few years back, and some of the best instructors in the province of Albay, Philippines. Master Jing learned a lot from them: to be patient, kind, humble, respectful, and tenacious. Most importantly, she was able to conquer her fears. It never left her mind what her instructors said, "Never underestimate or overestimate your opponent; respect others no matter what their age is."

Master Jing's journey as a martial artist taught her that every human being has a natural way of defending himself or herself. What martial arts does is train the brain to react or respond without even thinking about it, like an instinct. Overthinking is dangerous when it comes to a sudden attack from a perpetrator. One of her long-time instructors said, "The key to avoiding an attack is quick reaction–like a fraction of a fraction of a second." She also studied Arnis/Kali, Judo, Aikido, Won Hwa Do (a Korean Circular Martial Arts), and kickboxing. She was once coached/trained by Joe Burtoft, the trainer of MMA fighter Josh Samman, who passed away in 2016.

"We live in a very dangerous world, especially for a woman like me; I need to be prepared. I must be," she concluded.

AMAAF ALUMNUS & INDUCTEES · 2024 AMAA 10TH ANNIVERSARY LEGACY BOOK

358

LORENZO REID

"
Studying martial arts has been a transformative journey that has shaped my character, improved my physical and mental well-being...

WHY THE MARTIAL ARTS?

My journey into martial arts began with a blend of curiosity, personal challenges, and a desire for self-improvement. Growing up, I was always fascinated by martial arts movies and the discipline exhibited by practitioners on-screen. The grace, power, and philosophy behind martial arts intrigued me from a young age, but it wasn't until my teenage years that I considered it more seriously.

One of the primary reasons I decided to start martial arts was to be able to defend myself and others who were not able to do so. Like many adolescents, I struggled with bullies, but my struggle was not allowing them to pick on the little guy while also being a little hot-headed. Martial arts offered me a dynamic that combined physical fitness, mental discipline, and a holistic approach that immediately appealed to me like a yugen moment.

Starting martial arts was also influenced by my desire

for self-discipline and structure. I had always been drawn to activities that required dedication and perseverance, and martial arts provided a structured framework for achieving those goals. The belt system, where progression is earned through hard work and dedication, appealed to my goal-oriented nature. I saw it as a way to set and achieve tangible milestones while cultivating important life skills such as focus, determination, and resilience.

A pivotal moment that solidified my decision to start martial arts and learn martial science was when my grandma Yukie (Born in Kyoto, Japan) taught me Kata and the history lessons she learned from her father and mother while living in Japan. The richness of martial arts as a cultural practice fascinated me, and I wanted to immerse myself in the physical techniques and the deeper philosophical aspects that help define each discipline.

Once I began formal training, the benefits of martial arts quickly became apparent. Physically, I experienced improvements in my strength, flexibility, and overall fitness level. The structured workouts, which included a combination of cardio, strength training, and skill drills, challenged me in ways that traditional gym routines did not. The physical demands pushed me to exceed my perceived limits and strive for continuous improvement.

Martial arts helped me develop a greater sense of discipline and time management. Balancing training sessions with schoolwork and other commitments taught me the importance of prioritization and effective scheduling. The discipline instilled in me through martial arts has translated into various aspects of my life, contributing to my academic and professional success.

HOW HAS MARTIAL ARTS IMPACTED YOUR LIFE?

Studying martial arts has profoundly influenced my life in several significant ways. First and foremost, it has instilled in me a sense of discipline that permeates every aspect of my daily routine. The rigorous training schedules, adherence to technique, and constant striving for improvement have taught me the value of perseverance and dedication. This discipline has translated into my academic and professional pursuits, where I approach challenges with a structured and focused mindset.

A greatly profound impact of martial arts has been on my mental well-being. The emphasis on mindfulness, self-control, and respect in martial arts has helped me develop a calm and focused mind. Through meditation and breathing exercises incorporated into training, I have learned to manage stress effectively and maintain composure in demanding situations. This mental resilience has been invaluable in both personal and professional settings, allowing me to approach challenges with a clear and composed mindset.

Furthermore, martial arts training has fostered a strong sense of community and camaraderie. The dojo environment encourages mutual support, respect for peers, teamwork, and family. These relationships have enriched my social life and provided me with a

TRAINING INFORMATION

- Martial Arts Styles & Rank: Souseiki Ryu Sekkinsen Shigaisen (6th Dan), Marine Corps Martial Arts Program (2nd Degree), Goju-Ryu (1st Dan), Boxing, Brazilian Jiu Jitsu (Cinto Branco)

- Instructors/Influencers: Kaiso Leon D. Wright, Hanshi Larry Isaac, Hanshi Bunny Blake, Hanshi Delvon Survine, Hanshi Damon Gray, Kyoshi Ray Collins, Kyoshi Shurron D. Thompson, Kyoshi Christopher Manning, Kyoshi Charles Scarbrough, Kyoshi Trevor Tasetano, Shihan Bill Pugh, Boxing Eddie Gregg, Boxing/Vale Tudo Sylvester (Ses) Stevenson, Boxing Carlette Ewell, Faixa Preta Primeiro Grau Martin (Black Mamba) Thomas, Lt Col. Joseph C. Shusko, USMC (Ret) and Jack Hoban (Dai-Shihan)

- Birthplace/Growing Up: Indianapolis, IN / Reidsville, Sanford & Greensboro, NC

- Yrs. In the Martial Arts: 26 years

- Yrs. Instructing: 20 years

- Instructor

PROFESSIONAL ORGANIZATIONS

- Kappa Alpha Psi Fraternity, Inc.

- USMC Scout Sniper Association

- FBI InfraGard (National Capital Region Chapter)

PERSONAL ACHIEVEMENTS

- Becoming SAG-AFTRA in 2024

- Becoming a 2019 Honoree with the Leadership Center for Excellence and the InsideNoVa 6th annual class of the Top 40 Emerging Leaders under the age of 40

MAJOR ACHIEVEMENTS

- Inducted into the 25th Anniversary World Karate Union Black Belt Hall of Fame in 2023

- NC Nationals Awards Banquet Military Tactics & Combatives Instructor of the Year in 2021

HOW HAS MARTIAL ARTS IMPACTED YOUR LIFE? (CONTINUED)

network of like-minded individuals who share similar values and goals.

Overall, studying martial arts has been a transformative journey that has shaped my character, improved my physical and mental well-being, and enriched my social connections. It continues to be an integral part of my life, offering ongoing opportunities for growth and self-improvement.

Become an
AMAA MEMBER!

CARLOS RIVERA

"

Martial arts has given me the purpose of seeking new knowledge and training and educating myself.

WHY THE MARTIAL ARTS?

Carlos J. Rivera, a proud father and the head of the family of Kaizen-Do Bujutsu, was born in The Bronx on January 22, 1983. Growing up in the Bronx, Carlos faced many challenges but found his path through education and community engagement. He attended Monroe College, earning a Bachelor of Science in Criminal Justice. This academic achievement laid the foundation for his career in law enforcement.

He has dedicated over 22 years of serving as a peace officer in law enforcement. His career has been marked by commitment, bravery, and a deep sense of duty to his community. He has continued to serve, demonstrating resilience and an unwavering commitment to his role.

His journey into martial arts was profoundly influenced by his mentor and spiritual father, Dr. Geffory Smith, who encouraged him to pursue this path. Under Dr. Smith's guidance, Carlos began training in the system of American Goju. His half-brother, Kyoshi Hector "Caver" Nunez, introduced

him to Okinawan Kempo. Dr. Smith instilled in him the philosophy of Kaizen—a mindset of continuous learning and openness. On his journey in martial arts, he was blessed to train in several dojos because of unforeseen circumstances when schools in the Goju community were closing.

Significant milestones and achievements marked his martial arts training. After four years of rigorous training, he earned his first black belt in Krav Maga under Mark Massare. Social media connected him with Sijo Jamaal Studivant, who recognized Carlos's skills and awarded him his first karate black belt. He later tested in the Mushin Kail system under Kyoshi Johnny Cruz, achieving 1st Degree, Sempai. His half-brother Kyoshi Caver then awarded him his black belt in Okinawa Kempo. Carlos's journey continued under the instruction of Chief Grandmaster Anthony L. Smith, Sr., of Anthony's Worldwide Martial Arts Association.

Throughout his martial arts journey, Carlos's dedication to continuous learning and mastery led him to train in multiple styles, including American Kickboxing, Krav Maga, Brazilian Jiu-Jitsu, Kali, Goju, and Japanese Karate. This diverse training enriched his understanding and mastery of martial arts.

TRAINING INFORMATION

- Martial Arts Styles & Rank: 6th Degree & Senior Master-Anthony Worldwide Martial Arts Karate-do, Master Instructor W.E.B.B.S, 6th Degree Sash - U.K.M.A.S, Blue belt Brazilian Jiu-Jitsu, 5th Degree - Anthony Worldwide Martial Arts Karate-do, 4th Degree - Krav Maga Junior Master, 3rd Degree Niesi Goju, 3rd Degree Golden Fist Goju, 2nd degree American Sento Ryu Bujutsu, 1st Degree Mushin Kail, 1st Degree APLEA RANGERS KRAV MAGA, 1st degree American Sento Ryu Bujutsu, Black Belt Okinawa Kempo, Kickboxing instructor, Krav Maga instructor

- Instructors/Influencers: Grand Master Smith, GM Tony Ruiz, Sifu Rick Villaibus, Sifu Mark, Coach Jorge

- Birthplace/Growing Up: The Bronx, NYC

- Yrs. In the Martial Arts: 17 years

- Yrs. Instructing: 8 years

- Instructor

PROFESSIONAL ORGANIZATIONS

- Martial Arts Organization World Elite Black Belt Society

- Martial Arts Association Eastern USA

- AOBK

- International Martial Arts Association Federation Israel Martial Arts

- World Black Belt Club Society

PERSONAL ACHIEVEMENTS

- Started my martial arts program, Kaizen-Do Bujutsu Lions DEN CQC (2019)

- NYPD Letter of Commendation for World Trade Center

- Response Award of Merit Excellence on Duty - Bronx Borough

- President Community Service Award

- Local 237 President Award for Excellence

- 2x Triple Crown winner - Krane

- 2x Prime League World Championship

- Zen Combat Martial Arts Association Soke Tittle

- Soke Tittle Zen Combat Martial Arts Association

HOW HAS MARTIAL ARTS IMPACTED YOUR LIFE?

Carlos's life and career are a testament to resilience, dedication, and the pursuit of excellence. From his early days growing up in the Bronx to his distinguished career in law enforcement and his profound impact on the martial arts community, he continues to inspire and lead. As the head of the family Kaizen-Do Bujutsu, he remains humble, respects civility, and has self-control.

Studying martial arts is his medication to deal with the everyday stress of work. Martial arts has saved his life multiple times in law enforcement and has impacted him significantly with his job as a police officer inside a NYC homeless shelter. He relates to Master Ed Park's statement, "My hands and feet are my weapons."

MAJOR ACHIEVEMENTS

- B.S. in Criminal Justice Monroe College A.s. in Criminal Justice
- The World's Greatest Martial Arts, Volume 46
- 2x Action Magazine Hall of Honor
- 2x USA Martial Arts Hall of Fame Martial Arts of the Year - Martial Arts Spirit
- Martial Arts Legacy Awards
- Ambassador Master of Hall Fame Eastern USA
- International Martial Arts Dedication
- Martial Arts Sports Association Hall of Fame
- Martial Arts Hall of Fame
- Authority of India 15 years - 20 Master of the Year
- World Black Belt Hall Honor
- International Hall of Honor
- Monroe College Dean's List Winter Semester 2010
- John J. College Peace Officer completion 2009

Become an
**AMAA
MEMBER!**

HOW HAS MARTIAL ARTS IMPACTED YOUR LIFE? (CONTINUED)

Martial arts has given him the purpose of seeking new knowledge and training and educating himself. He wasn't a good reader, and he started reading more martial arts books. He believes in self-education and to train his mind and body. He believes in this Zen Philosophy. Always have an empty cup!

BERNARD
ROBINSON

"
If I had not fallen in love with the Art, I would not have become the man I am today.

Karate Tournaments, challenging me to become the best I could be. I moved up very quickly through the rankings. I received my first black belt at age 18. Then, in 1986, I began my kickboxing journey, which also promptly led to my professional kickboxing fighting career, which started in 1987. I fell in love with the challenge and the preparation for every fight. I shared the ring with some of the best during my era, and my career record is 68 wins, 8 losses, and 32 knockouts. I'm the former 3x World Kickboxing Champion and the 2x European Muay Thai Champion.

I hung up my gloves in 2009, but I'm very grateful every day for the ability to teach others this beautiful but deadly art. Life is no different, just a different arena. You can do anything if you put your mind and heart into it and focus.

"Defeat is a state of mind; no one is ever defeated until defeat has been accepted as a reality." - Bruce Lee.

WHY THE MARTIAL ARTS?

My older brother, Victor, introduced me to Karate at age nine. Just watching him and seeing how talented and passionate he was about the art and how much he enjoyed teaching me is how my martial arts journey began. From then on, I spent the next several years fine-tuning my skills with local Karate and Taekwondo schools. I was also fascinated by watching Bruce Lee movies, watching him perform, and seeing how he explained the art to others. This encouraged me to continue my journey.

I started sparring at age 13, which led to competing in

HOW HAS MARTIAL ARTS IMPACTED YOUR LIFE?

Martial arts is my life. If I had not fallen in love with the art, I would not have become the man I am today. Martial arts has impacted every part of my life. It's a lifestyle for my family and me. This beautiful but deadly art has taken me worldwide, and I have met so many amazing people, for which I am grateful.

I am a martial artist first. Fighting was just a deep passion of mine. It wasn't about the belts, money, or accolades; I loved the challenge. I love talking about martial arts and practicing martial arts every day, whether it be Karate, boxing, MMA, kickboxing, or Muay Thai — I love it all. It all has had a significant impact on my life. One of the best days I ever had was when I got a call from Grandmaster Ted Gambordella to say he was putting me in his new Super 700: The World's Greatest Martial Artist book.

TRAINING INFORMATION

- Martial Arts Styles & Rank: Texas Karate Black Belt Association (5th Dan), Dawkins Dynamic Taekwondo (2nd Dan), Okanella Kempo Karate (Black Belt), Open Hand Karate (3rd Dan Black Belt), ATA - American Taekwondo Association (Black Belt), KTF - Korean Taekwondo Association (Brown Belt), WTF - World Taekwondo Federation (Purple Belt)
- Instructors/Influencers: Grandmaster Rudy Smedley, Mr. Yang, Mr. Tanaka, Eugene Jeffrey, Mike Sanders, Victor Dawkins
- Birthplace/Growing Up: Gaffney, SC
- Yrs. In the Martial Arts: 45 years
- Yrs. Instructing: 17 years
- School owner & Instructor at Swiftkick MMA & Boxing, LLC

PROFESSIONAL ORGANIZATIONS

- Texas Karate Association
- International Sport Kickboxing Association
- World Kickboxing Association
- International Kickboxing Association
- International Muay Thai Federation

PERSONAL ACHIEVEMENTS

- 68 Professional Kickboxing wins
- Notable mention in "The World's Greatest Martial Artists" The Super 700 by Ted Gamborella
- Mentioned in Black Belt Magazine
- Featured in the "Defiance Fuel" commercial and multiple music videos
- Certified Personal Trainer/Master Trainer
- The Icon Award from Simon Promotion - 4/20/07 for a combined 110 Kickboxing/boxing bouts

MAJOR ACHIEVEMENTS

- Texas Black Belt Hall of Fame - 2016
- 3 Guinness Book of World Records
- 3 World Kickboxing Titles
- Hall of Fame Fighter

GREGORY
ROBINSON

**" **

Martial Arts has taught me how to properly communicate with individuals worldwide, and I have met amazing people.

WHY THE MARTIAL ARTS?

Being the oldest of two brothers and a sister, I was determined to protect myself and my family from the neighborhood bullies and people who would do us harm in the community. Learning martial arts techniques allow me to protect them from harm.

HOW HAS MARTIAL ARTS IMPACTED YOUR LIFE?

Martial arts have impacted my life by increasing my basic survival instincts. I will never forget what my father instilled in me to this day: "Self—preservation is the first law of nature." Another benefit I have received is that I am in reasonably good health. Martial arts has taught me how to properly communicate with individuals worldwide, and I have met amazing people.

TRAINING INFORMATION

- Martial Arts Styles & Rank: Black Dragon System of Self—Defense - (Founder) -7th Degree Black Belt, True Force Tae Kwon Do - 6th Degree Black Belt, Soo Bak Kee Tae Kwon Do - 7th Degree Black Belt, Aikibujitsu/Goshojitsukai - 6th Degree Black Belt

- Instructors/Influencers: Grandmaster Michael Hornsby, Grandmaster Dan Roberts, Soke Lee Goodridge, Shihan Muhammad Al Duha, Kyoshi Shawn McKeever, Professor Carson Hines, Guro Myron Genilla, U.S. Army Training, and Sensei George Agee Jr.

- Birthplace/Growing Up: Gaffney, SC

- Yrs. In the Martial Arts: 55+ years

- Yrs. Instructing: 42+ years

PROFESSIONAL ORGANIZATIONS

- Black Dragon System of Self—Defense International Martial Arts Alliance

- International Soo Bak Kee Federation

- International Martial Arts Council of America

- The Karate Association

- Kojukan Combat Self-Defense

- Zujitsu Self-Defense Martial Arts

- Scientific Fighting Congress of America

- Filipino Combat Congress of America

- Explosive, Speed, and Power — Jeet Kune Do

PROFESSIONAL ORGANIZATIONS (CONTINUED)

- Amerasian Filipino International Martial Arts Association
- Bushido School of Self-Defense
- World Butokukai Federation
- True Force

PERSONAL ACHIEVEMENTS

- Military Police — Basic Law Enforcement Course 029
- Military Police — Physical Security Course 7H-31D
- Institute of Criminal Justice Studies - Texas Crime Preventive Association
- Alamo Area Law Enforcement Academy — Basic Police Instructor Course
- United States Armed Forces — President and Vice President — Inauguration Recognition Letter
- Associate in Applied Sciences — Criminal Justice
- U.S. Army — Retired — Credit with 40 years of service
- House Owner for 10 years

MAJOR ACHIEVEMENTS

- 2023 International Martial Arts Hall of Fame — Outstanding Competitor of the Year Award
- 2023 United States Martial Arts Hall of Fame — Distinguished Grandmaster
- 2021 International Martial Arts Hall of Fame — Competitor of the Year
- 2020 State and World Champion
- 2019 The Karate Association — Grandmaster James Cumming Spirit Award
- 2019 The Karate Association — Black Belt Instructor of the Year
- 2019 United States Martial Arts Hall of Fame — Silver Life Award
- 2017 United States Martial Arts Hall of Fame — Distinguished Master
- 2004 United States Martial Arts Hall of Fame — Black Belt of the Year
- 2003 Universal Martial Arts Hall of Fame — Shihan of the Year
- 2002 World Head of Family Sokeship Council -International Martial Arts Hall of Fame - Outstanding Leadership of the Year
- 2002 World Head of Family Sokeship Council — International Martial Arts Hall of Fame — Achievement Award

PETER
RUDH

> "
> *Had I not committed time and effort to martial arts, I think my life may have turned out very differently, and probably not in a good way.*

WHY THE MARTIAL ARTS?

In my early teens, Kung Fu movies starring David Carradine and Bruce Lee pumped me up. A friend and I got ahold of a little Judo pamphlet and proceeded to toss each other onto the rock-hard summer sod. We were pliable kids and survived with a few bruises. High school came with a couple of incidents/scrapes, and I decided to pursue self-defense classes if I were presented the chance.

Who is so wise to pick the correct school or teacher when you begin your martial arts journey? First experiences often impress a person's direction, path, and circumstance. In 1981, at age 22, I stumbled (pun intended) into a martial arts school in St. Paul, MN. Be it fate or happenstance, I feel lucky to have engaged myself with the U.S. Chuan Fa School.

Master Miller's Chuan Fa Martial Arts School wasn't run as a business; it was run as a club with a family structure. So, I guess you could say I was adopted, and Chuan Fa became my second family. At this time, we were in a rec center (an old school building) with mats and classes in one room, but with a long hallway, we

traversed doing kicks and techniques. Uhf-da, but I felt myself gaining a degree of coordination!

Our teacher, Dana Miller, was already a sixth-degree master, and the curriculum of Chinese Hawaiian Kenpo blended aspects of Karate and Gong Fu. Stretching, posture training, energy development (Chi), and self-defense techniques filled class time, and most classes ended with non-contact sparring.

Over time, new students joined, and it became evident that I had gained some proficiency. As the months passed, I felt fortunate that I had joined this particular school. The energy felt right, and Master Miller had a knack for knowing the next little thing a student needed to correct.

Our fist forms (open hand) were the first and second sets from American Kenpo, followed by many Shaolin Forms. As we rose in rank, we were introduced to weapons forms and techniques, first staff, and later, sword.

Master Miller also schooled us in other disciplines and expanded our curriculum through the years. From western boxing to ground fighting and anti-grappling, we studied it all. Well, not everything, but I doubt

many martial artists have had the good fortune to train in such an array of systems.

Over the years, our school hosted camps with guest masters. We attended tournaments and traveled to visit other schools.

In 1987, I opened a branch school and instructed for 25 years. These were wonderful years to share and grow with students. I remain a student, living and practicing martial arts every day. It's been a good run.

HOW HAS MARTIAL ARTS IMPACTED YOUR LIFE?

The arts have and continue to keep me balanced. As a young adult, the propensity to party was ever-present. In our Gong Fu School, we were not verbally told what we could or couldn't do, but Master Miller's example of how to live and conduct oneself was clear. This had a strong influence on my decision-making. Had I not committed time and effort to martial arts, I think my life may have turned out very differently, and probably not in a good way.

I don't know if it's an atmosphere of confidence, but I haven't found myself in situations requiring a physical defense. After some years of training, I gained a sense of fearlessness. That's not saying I couldn't be harmed; it's just that I no longer feared the possibility.

TRAINING INFORMATION

- Martial Arts Styles & Rank: Third Degree Black Belt Kenpo - USChuan Fa Association. Fifth Black Sash - Master Level - Zu Wei Shu. Instructor Level various U.S. Chuan Fa Programs (Stick - Knife - Ground Fighting - Lock Flow - Boxing)
- Instructors/Influencers: Grandmaster Dana Miller, Grandmaster Paul S Landon, Grandmaster Paul Olivas, Grandmaster Don B. Jones, Master Rudy Borrmann, Master Bob Berube, Master Larry Sanders
- Birthplace/Growing Up: Fergus Falls, MN / Rothsay, MN
- Yrs. In the Martial Arts: 43 years
- Yrs. Instructing: 25 years
- Instructor

PROFESSIONAL ORGANIZATIONS

- Professional Association of Diving Instructors - PADI
- U.S. Chaun Fa Association - 1989
- World Head of Family SokeShip Council - Masters Division - 2010
- American Martial Arts Alliance - AMAA - 2024

PERSONAL ACHIEVEMENTS

- Electronic Technology Degree — 1979
- Advanced Open Water Diver — PADI - 1982
- Business Owner — Supercars — 1986 — present.
- Scout Master of the Year — BSA — 2012
- Author — Fiction Novel — Shiny in the Shade — 2022

MAJOR ACHIEVEMENTS

- Third Degree Black Belt Chuan Fa - Chinese Hawaiian Kenpo — 1994
- Instructor of the Year, U.S. Chuan Fa Association - 1999
- Master level, 5th Black Sash, Zu Wei Shu Martial Arts System — 2008
- World Head of Family SokeShip Council — Master of the Year Award - 2010

DAVID SISCOE

"

My drive, my focus, and my abilities have all been formed through the study and practice of martial arts.

WHY THE MARTIAL ARTS?

My original influence on starting martial arts was Bruce Lee; however, it was the name of TaeKwonDo (TKD) that intrigued me the most. At age 12, my older brother punched me in the mouth, giving me three stitches. I knew I could do nothing about it, as did he. But I promised him I would get him back, saying, "When I'm 21, I will be a black belt in TKD, and I will get you back for this!"

Fast-forward to age 19. I met a guy whose brother was the world middleweight champion in TKD, and it rekindled my passion to start. And where better than to start at the same school as the champ? So, I started my training at Chong Lee TKD with GM Chong Soo Lee. On day one, I had built up so much anxiety that I ended up with my head in the toilet bowl, vomiting, and PROMISING myself to NEVER return!

With my head in the toilet, a MASSIVE hand was patting my back, and a deep voice was telling me, "Everything will be okay." I looked back and saw that it was the World Heavyweight Champion Darrell

Henegan! WHY? Why would he give a crap about me, a nobody?

Well, thanks to him, I stayed, and my path in TKD began, which has since been amazing! Chong Lee TKD attracted many champions from around the world who came to train and learn the latest fighting techniques. Many of those champions would watch me training and state that I, too, would one day become a champion! It's nice to hear that from anyone, but from accomplished fighters, it was amazing to hear.

My first tournament was the US Open in NYC, and I lost; my nerves got the better of me. Notwithstanding, I kept up the training. My second tournament produced the same outcome, a loss, and I admit I was questioning my path and my choice to continue, but I did. It was my third competition, the Canadian Nationals, that everything changed, and it changed in a BIG way, earning me my first national championship.

So, by age 21, I was now a black belt, and the day before my 21st birthday, my brother called me to remind me that it was my 21st birthday, and I responded with, "I remember! But I had also since calmed down." LOL. So, he did not get the retaliation I had promised him from age 12. LOL

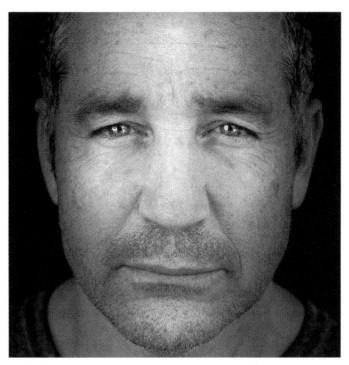

Standout moments for me have been winning at the nationals five times; training for the 88 Olympic games in Seoul, Korea; winning at the US Open three times; winning the North American Championships in Binghamton, NY; and opening two TKD schools here in Montreal: West Island TKD in 1986 and T.U.F.F The Ultimate in Fitness Fighting, six years ago in 2018.

As a Practicing Exercise Specialist, I have opened four fitness centers in Montreal. I have been the Exercise Specialist for Global Television and CJAD News-Talk Radio in Montreal for 24 years. While I thought my competition days were behind me, I was approached when I turned 50 to consider competing at the Olympic facility in Torino, Italy, for the World Masters Championship. Standing on the podium again in Torino was an amazing gift to myself for my 50th.

The second TKD training center I opened in Montreal, T.U.F.F. (The Ultimate in Fitness Fighting), is a center for the great many people who want to learn how to strike, kick, and punch like the pros but DO NOT wish to be kicked and punched like the pros!

Coming full circle in my martial arts journey, it is amazing to me that now GM Darrell Henegan, the very one who encouraged me from day one to continue, currently trains out of my fitness facility in Montreal—also the very one who has nominated me for inclusion in the American Martial Arts Alliance.

TRAINING INFORMATION

- Martial Arts Styles & Rank: 5th dan - WTF TaeKwonDo, 7th Dan - Jidokwan TaeKwonDo
- Instructors/Influencers: GM Chong Soo Lee
- Birthplace/Growing Up: Montreal, QC, Canada
- Yrs. In the Martial Arts: 42 years
- Yrs. Instructing: 37 years
- School owner & Instructor at T.U.F.F.

PROFESSIONAL ORGANIZATIONS

- Canadian Jidokwan TKD Federation

PERSONAL ACHIEVEMENTS

- Provincial / State champion Springboard Diving
- Canadian Grenadier Guards
- Five first class rifleman and seven marksman awards
- An accomplished athlete in several sports. Notably winning at the Jeux de Quebec in springboard diving
- Concordia University (Exercise Science)
- Becoming the Exercise Specialist for CJAD News-Talk Radio and Global Television
- Bench pressing 305 lbs for my 60th Birthday

MAJOR ACHIEVEMENTS

- 5x Canadian Nationals
- Training for the 88 Olympic Games
- 3x US Open (NYC)
- North American Championship (Binghamton, NY)
- World Masters (Torino, Italy)

This incredible journey continues…

HOW HAS MARTIAL ARTS IMPACTED YOUR LIFE?

Like many do, I started in TKD because I was insecure. The confidence I eventually gained with the know-how of controlling what my body and mind are capable of and the ability to control those around me is the most incredible arsenal one could hope for.

This has formed my person in sports and business. My drive, my focus, and my abilities have all been formed through the study and practice of martial arts.

Competing in tournaments is life! The score moves up and down, but the focus needs to remain if you plan to walk away ahead of the game.

Become an
AMAA MEMBER!

GM Snipes
Chief Instructor

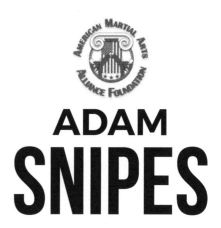

ADAM
SNIPES

"

We, as Instructors, learn just as much as the students during classes and our journey within the arts, as we all grow together.

WHY THE MARTIAL ARTS?

Adam Snipes started his martial arts training at an early age. Like most other children, he was introduced to martial arts through TV, mainly the Teenage Mutant Ninja Turtles. The first class he took was at age four. At that time, his instructor only held classes for adults until meeting him; then, he added a children's program to the Academy. This style Grand Master Snipes took was Tang Soo Do. At age 10, he started to take Tae Kwon Do. When he turned 13, he was reintroduced to Tang Soo Do in his local town. From there, GM Snipes cross-trained with Judo, Jujitsu, and Non-traditional Aikido (Aikijitsu).

Approximately a year later, GM Snipes was introduced to Manabi-Masho Jujitsu, where he cross-trained from his other combative martial arts. He then started to put together his own unique style of free-style martial arts (or what he likes to call "adaptive training")—joining stand-up styles (Tang Soo Do & Kickboxing) and combatives (Manabi-Masho, Aikijitsu, Judo, Krav Maga aspects, and Environmental Adaptation Training).

During the mid-1990s, Grand Master Snipes decided there was "no" such thing as an "ultimate or best" martial art! Every style is unique in its own way. All have something to offer (depending on what you want to achieve during your journey). The ultimate martial arts are in "life's" journey in learning (mind, body, and spirit). Therefore, Life's Ultimate Martial Arts Academy (LUMA) would be in the making.

While students earn their belts within the Tang Soo Do martial arts style, Grand Master Snipes offers the Continuous Training Aspect as an added combative course. This blend of martial arts is a great way for anyone to adapt: stand-up, ground, close-quarter combat, and environmental. On September 1st, 1998, Grand Master Snipes opened Life's Ultimate Martial Arts Academy in Flemingsburg, KY. On the Academy's 10th Anniversary, he opened his second location in Maysville in 2008. He shortly closed his Flemingsburg location (after one year) as most students transferred to his new location, keeping his centered location in Maysville, KY. LUMA remains in operation today under Head Instructor GM Snipes.

HOW HAS MARTIAL ARTS IMPACTED YOUR LIFE?

Being able to help others grow as GM Snipes still continues, and will continue to, on the martial journey. Martial arts are good, clean, fun, and a great way for kids to get a head start on life. Students and parents love the life skills one gains (confidence, patience, focus, goal setting, coordination, self-defense, and more) and being able to convey these traits of learning to others; such as the energetic, fun-filled, action-packed classes Life's Ultimate Martial Arts Academy (LUMA Academy) provides.

The Academy's classes, and martial arts, in general, keep you fit while you learn to protect yourself. LUMA Academy offers several different programs that are sure to fit everyone's training needs! LUMA's professional instructors will bring out the best in your training and experience!

Through hard work and dedication/perseverance, GM Snipes is very pleased that they were able to build a family-oriented Academy; with the vision to impact lives through the teachings of martial arts. The Academy was built on life skills; where growth, no matter how small it may seem, is a big step in the footprints of those who walk it. The Academy takes pride in knowing it's making a difference for those who believe in themselves and take the next step to accomplish their goals and dreams through martial arts.

Since 1998, the Academy has dedicated its practices and principles to the community and prides itself on the accomplishments of its students and families. When GM Snipes uses the word "we," "we" are a team, never a one-person institution, as we all grow from and with each other. GM Snipes says, "We, as Instructors, learn just as much as the students during classes and our journey within the arts, as we all grow together. This is what has and will continue to impact my life within the martial arts."

Life's Ultimate Martial Arts Academy - Serving the community since 1998.

TRAINING INFORMATION

- Martial Arts Styles & Rank: 10th Dan — A.C.T. Defense Systems (Adaptive Combat Training), 6th Dan - Tang Soo Do, 5th Dan - Aikijitsu/Manabi Masho JuJitsu (Old style), 3rd Dan — Hapkido, 1st Dan - Total Defense Combat Karate

- Instructors/Influencers: Sensei Greg Reband, Sensei Virgil Davis, Sensei Allen Wilson, GM Professor John Casarez

- Birthplace/Growing Up: Olive Hill, KY

- Yrs. In the Martial Arts: 41 years

- Yrs. Instructing: 26 years

- School owner, Manager & Instructor at Life's Ultimate Martial Arts Academy (LUMA)

PROFESSIONAL ORGANIZATIONS

- UFAF
- ISKA
- SEMAC
- WPKA
- ITKF
- ITKFG

PERSONAL ACHIEVEMENTS

- During the 1990s, Grand Master Snipes competed professionally through tournament circuits, taking numerous awards in weapons, forms, fighting, and breaking and being awarded as the overall tournament champion. GM Snipes still competes today. In his last tournament, he competed after a 2-year layoff from the tournament circuit. GM Snipes placed 1st in all divisions (weapons, forms, and fighting) and won 1st place in overall forms and fighting as Tournament Grand Champion in 2016.

MAJOR ACHIEVEMENTS

- Grand Master Snipes always says his greatest awards/achievements come from his students and in watching them grow as Martial Artists within Life Skills of everyday life.

AWARDS OF GRAND MASTER SNIPES

- WHFSC (World Head of Family Sokeship Council)
- 1998 Outstanding Asst. Instructor WHFSC International Hall of Fame
- 1999 Outstanding Instructor WHFSC International Hall of Fame
- 1999 WHFSC Hall of Fame Induction International Hall of Fame
- 2000 Martial Arts Contributor of the Year WHFSC International Hall of Fame
- 2001 Outstanding Instructor WHFSC International Hall of Fame
- 2002 Regional Instructor of the Year Manabi Masho WHFSC International Hall of Fame 2003 Mixed Martial Artist of the Year USA Hall of Fame
- 2003 WPMAC Grappling Coordinator Award
- 2004 USA Hall of Fame Induction
- 2005 Mixed Martial Artist of the Year WHFSC International Hall of Fame
- 2006 National Instructor of the Year WHFSC International Hall of Fame
- 2007 School listed within the top in the Nation United Professionals BBS International 2008 University of Asian Martial Arts Study - Title of Professor of Martial Arts
- 2008 Master Instructor WHFSC International Hall of Fame
- 2008 Mixed Martial Arts Master of the Year USA Hall of Fame

AWARDS OF GRAND MASTER SNIPES

- 2009 School of the Year (Zenith) USA Hall of Fame
- 2010 Regional Master Instructor WHFSC International Hall of Fame
- 2010 International Instructor of the Year USA Hall of Fame
- 2010 Hall of Heroes USA Hall of Fame
- 2011 Zenith Award USA Hall of Fame
- 2011 Officially Inducted as 'Member' USA Hall of Fame
- 2011 Silver Life Achievement 'Mixed Martial Arts' WHFSC (over 25 years in Martial Arts) International Hall of Fame
- 2012 Council's Master Award WHFSC International Hall of Fame
- 2012 Outstanding Contribution to the Martial Arts USA Hall of Fame
- 2014 Leading Martial Arts School of the Year USA Hall of Fame
- 2014 Ranked #1 School in the US USA Martial Arts Hall of Fame
- 2014 Black Belt Schools International (BBSI) Advanced Concept Training Certified BBSI School Instructor
- 2015 WPKA (World Professional Karate Association) - State Director (US Team)
- 2015 Martial Arts Superior Excellence USA Hall of Fame
- 2019 Hero Award Tournament Circuit
- 2022 Promoted to 10th Dan Grand Master on Feb. 12th, 2022
- 2022 Owner and Founder of A.C.T Defense Systems. Officially named on February 12th, 2022 (started its inception in the late 90s)
- 2023 Founder's Award (New Style Recognition: A.C.T. Defense Systems) WHFSC International Hall of Fame
- Along with many other awards during the years.

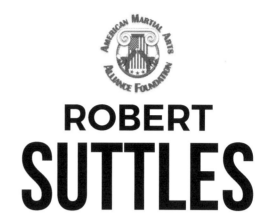

ROBERT
SUTTLES

"

I would not be where I am today, and who I am today if it were not for the influence of these men [my instructors].

WHY THE MARTIAL ARTS?

Grandmaster Robert Suttles was born in 1955 in Chattanooga, TN. He has been involved in martial arts for most of his life. He started his training as a very young boy with his stepfather, a hand-to-hand combat instructor in the USMC. Robert joined the Marine Corps in 1972 and continued to practice martial arts. He is currently an instructor, and martial arts continues to be his passion. He enjoys sharing the art and teaching the history of the art to others.

HOW HAS MARTIAL ARTS IMPACTED YOUR LIFE?

Grandmaster Robert Suttles feels very fortunate to have instructors who are friends and have trained with each other. They supported each other through the years and had a special bond. Each one of them helped GM Suttles through his journey in martial arts in a different way. GM Suttles says, " I would not be where I am today, and who I am today if it were not for the influence of these men. Some of these men are no longer with us but are not forgotten and will be in my heart and memory for the rest of my days."

TRAINING INFORMATION

- Martial Arts Styles & Rank: Kajukenbo Grand Master - 9th degree, Full Instructor Jeet Kung Do, Docs Karate - 5th Degree Black Belt, Full Instructor in Jeet Kune Do / Kali, Student of White Tiger Kung Fu

- Instructors/Influencers: GM Ron Pierce and the Emperado Family, GM Steve Golden, GM Victor A. Hughes, The Late GM Richard (Dick) Burrows, GM Miguel Garcia

- Birthplace/Growing Up: Chattanooga, TN / San Diego, CA

- Yrs. In the Martial Arts: 59 years

- Yrs. Instructing: 40 years

- School owner & Instructor at SuttleImpact Kajukenbo / JKD

Become an
AMAA
MEMBER!

PROFESSIONAL ORGANIZATIONS

- Lifetime KSDI Member
- Lifetime JKD Nucleus Member

PERSONAL ACHIEVEMENTS

- GM Suttles received the Golden Life Achievement Award and was inducted into the Masters Hall of Fame in 2009, nominated by GM Eric Lee

- GM Suttles received the Pioneer Award and was inducted into the USA Martial Arts Hall of Fame in 2019, nominated by GM Eric Lee

- GM Eric Lee is one of GM Suttles' dearest friends. He loves GM Lee like a brother, and there is nothing he wouldn't do for him. They have been friends for many years. GM would do anything for him except arm wrestle him for lunch. GM Lee will find some way to beat him; The King of Kata is also the King of lunch arm wrestling

- GM Suttles is currently teaching privately, hosting "The Gathering of Legends Events", teaching Seminars, playing music, and enjoying life

MAJOR ACHIEVEMENTS

- GM Suttles founded the annual "Gathering of Legends" martial arts event held in Branson, MO. This event highlights elite martial arts instructors from all styles and is a fun-filled family event

- GM Suttles has owned and operated his own martial arts schools, taught numerous seminars nationwide, and attended significant martial arts events such as KSDI. He has taught military, law enforcement, homeland security, and schools in seminar settings. He has also taught with the American Black Ops as a Master Instructor in Washington, D.C.

- GM Suttles was one of the Co-founders of Martial Artists Making a Miracle for the Children's Miracle Network, founded in 1997 in Eugene, Oregon.

CARL
TATE, JR.

> " *I was the very first African-American to be awarded the rank of 8th Degree Black Belt from the World General Tang Soo Do Federal.*

WHY THE MARTIAL ARTS?

Grandmaster Carl Tate Jr. began his study of Tang Soo Do at age 12 in Inkster, Michigan, 21 miles west of Detroit. He was 15 when he was awarded Cho Dan. In 1978, at age 17, GM Tate joined the U.S. Army and was stationed at Fort Sill in Lawton, Oklahoma, until December 1982. In December of 1982, he was sent to Erlanger, Germany, where, again, he was able to continue his training. Karate Illustrated Magazine named him the number two overall fighter in Europe in July 1984. GM Tate returned to the U.S. in January 1986 and opened his own school in Lawton, Oklahoma. Following his discharge from the military, he was employed by the City of Lawton. In 1988, he was named the Oklahoma Karate Association's top-ranked fighter.

In June of 1989, he moved back to Inkster, Michigan, where he continued to teach Tang Soo Do in the City of Inkster and surrounding areas. Master Tate also worked at Detroit Metropolitan Wayne County Airport as an assistant manager for Cater Air International and part-time as an auxiliary police officer for the Inkster Police Department. In the Fall of 2000, he moved to Canada and opened the only full-time traditional Tang Soo Do school in Calgary, Alberta. Later that same year, he founded Canada's first Tang Soo Do organization. He currently has four of his own branch schools that operate under the organization. In addition to serving as President of his organization, he is also President of the Canadian Tang Soo Do Association.

At 8th Dan, GM Tate holds the highest rank in traditional Tang Soo Do in Canada. He also holds a black belt rank in Tae Kwon Do, Gumdo, and Hapkido. GM Tate conducts seminars in and around Canada on the traditional teachings of Korean martial arts and breaking and sparring. He has appeared in and written articles for martial arts magazines such as Tae Kwon Do Times, Inside Tae Kwon Do, Action Martial Arts Canada, Action Martial Arts USA, Sport Karate Int'l, Dojang Magazine, World Martial Arts, and Tae Kwon Do Korean Martial Art UK.

HOW HAS MARTIAL ARTS IMPACTED YOUR LIFE?

Martial arts has opened doors for me that would never have been opened because it allowed me to meet some fantastic people worldwide. It also allowed me to open schools in Oklahoma, Germany, Michigan, Canada, and now Washington. I'm not sure if a lot of people are aware that I was the very first African-American to be awarded the rank of 8th Degree Black Belt from the World General Tang Soo Do Federal. Most of all, martial arts helped me stay focused and disciplined at work.

Become an
AMAA MEMBER!

TRAINING INFORMATION
- Martial Arts Styles & Rank: Tae Kwon Do, Tang Soo Do, Hapkido, Korea Gumdo
- Instructors/Influencers: Grandmaster Koo Kim, Grandmaster B. Moody, Grandmaster Eddie Carrillo
- Birthplace/Growing Up: Inkster, MI
- Yrs. In the Martial Arts: 45 years
- Yrs. Instructing: 42 years
- School owner at Black Belt of Karate

PROFESSIONAL ORGANIZATIONS
- World Tang Soo Do General Federation
- Korean American Tang Soo Do Martial Arts Organization

PERSONAL ACHIEVEMENTS
- 1992 World Martial Arts Hall Fame Award for Outstanding Achievement
- 1993 World Martial Arts Hall Fame Award for Instructor of the Year
- 1997 World Martial Arts Hall Fame Award for Lifetime Achievement
- 1997 WHFSC International Hall of Fame Award for Master Instructor of the Year
- 1998 International Martial Arts Council Award for Person of the Year
- 1998 International Martial Arts Council Award for School of the Year
- 2000 Michigan Karate Classic Hall of Fame Award for Person of the Year
- 2000 Great Lakes Karate Championships League of Honor Award
- 2001 Action Martial Arts Magazine USA Hall of Fame Award
- 2003 The American Tang Soo Do Association 30-years Award
- 2007 John R. Byrne Memorial Award from the American Tang Soo Do Association
- 2012 The World General Tang Soo Do Federation Citation Award

MAJOR ACHIEVEMENTS
- Achieve the rank of Sergeant in the United States Army.
- Received the following awards in the military: (2) Good Conduct Medal, Army Commendation Medal, (2) Army Achievement Medal, Army NCO - school Medal, Overseas Army Medal, and U.S. Army Services Medal

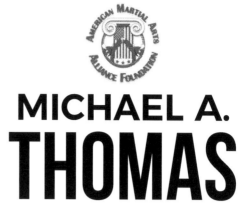

MICHAEL A. THOMAS

> "
> *If it gives me the vehicle to change one child's life, I can say I've made his world a better place when I leave this earth.*

WHY THE MARTIAL ARTS?

Mike Thomas: The Martial Artist as Carrier of Peace

"I was born in Kahnawake," Mike said. While he has lived all over, in New York, Oklahoma, Texas, and North Carolina, and was stationed overseas with the U.S. Marine Corps, close to half his life has been spent living in his birthplace and current home of Kahnawake.

When Mike was just 17, he enlisted in the U.S. Marines. "Because I'm Iroquois," he explained, "the borders under the Jay Treaty don't exist for us, so we're citizens of North America. I can go into the U.S,

and I don't need a green card." After getting out of the Marines, Mike remained in the U.S., doing ironwork, as many Mohawks did at that time. By then, he had been involved with the martial arts for many years. At age 14, he started training in Shotokan Karate, continuing until he entered the Marines.

"When I got into the Marine Corps, they were teaching self-defense. The root of that had come from Tae Kwon Do – the traditional Tae Kwon Do, not the sport." It was there that he ran into a Tae Kwon Do instructor named Scott Crotte. His instructor began to "broaden my horizon about martial arts." Crotte taught "joint manipulation, pressure points, and all the good stuff from traditional Tae Kwon Do." So significant was Crotte's influence that "I stuck with that ever since. I've been doing Tae Kwon Do for approximately 24 years." Before he left the Marines, Crotte advised him, "Mike, stick with it. You're really good at it." And Mike added, "And that's what I did."

In 1986, while working on what was to be his last ironwork job, the CIA complex in Virginia, he suffered a near-debilitating accident. Suddenly, three tons of steel came crashing down on his hand. The doctors wanted to amputate. "I absolutely refused,"

Mike recalled. So, while the doctors worked on repairing his hand, he could no longer do ironwork and returned home to Kahnawake. "There was no way I would lose my hand."

He did have to have surgery and reconstruction, but now he had to become focused to achieve recovery. "I started getting involved back with my roots here," he said, "with the traditional spirituality and the traditional government." It was time to return home, both in body and mind. "I became involved in the Warrior's Society." And he resumed his martial arts training. His recovery period was about two years. He had over 200 stitches in his hand, whose thumb joint was reconstructed, as well as numerous severely crushed bones. He also had to build back the muscles in his hand and arm.

Two years into his recovery, in 1988, Mike began training under another man who greatly influenced him, Grandmaster Oh Jang Yoon, now based in Toronto but then located in Montreal. His accomplishments included having been a world champion in Tae Kwon Do, an expert in Judo, and a Korean national boxing champion, as well as having been an instructor in the Korean Royal Marines. "We really hit it off," Mike recalled. But now, back home, Mike began to turn his attention to how to influence the next generation. Besides just training, Mike and his new teacher discussed opening a Tae Kwon Do school in Kahnawake. "He was very supportive of me in helping finance the start, giving me guidance, keeping me motivated."

Mike remembered the Grandmaster's advice, "You know, Mike, you have dreams. You have a mission that you want to do for the Native children and all children. You need to go after that dream." Simple words, complex ideas. And they hit home.

"I've been doing that ever since," Mike said, so he has.

And it all goes back to the children, the masters of the future. "These kids that are up and coming need our support. They need our guidance. They need to hear the true perspective of what this is all about from a martial arts perspective. Because if we don't give them the tools when they become young men and women, they will end up walking the path that I walked at a

TRAINING INFORMATION

- Martial Arts Styles & Rank: 9th Degree-Jidokwan Black Belt, Shotokan Karate, Taekwondo, Hapkido, Korean Martial Arts
- Instructors/Influencers: Master Scott Crotte, Grandmaster Oh Jang Yoon
- Birthplace/Growing Up: Kahnawake, QC
- Yrs. In the Martial Arts: 53 years
- Yrs. Instructing: 44 years
- School owner & Instructor at Rotiskenakete Taekwondo

PROFESSIONAL ORGANIZATIONS

- First Nations Production (Kickboxing, Taekwondo, Karate events) in Canada
- Promotor for Extreme Fighting, Battlecade on April 26, 1996, in Kahnawake pay-per-view event

PERSONAL ACHIEVEMENTS

- For ten years, Mike Thomas has supported the Kateri Memorial Foundation and Karonhiaráhstha's Winter Wonderland (KWW). He's helped by dressing up as Santa Claus or Olaf, walking in their parade, collecting money for the local food bank, donating beautiful gifts to the event, or simply lending a helpful hand
- Mike Thomas collaborated with the Playground Poker and Original Tobacco Traders and donated a life-changing Dodge Caravan to a local single mother of ten
- He made many other contributions to his community

MAJOR ACHIEVEMENTS

- In 1989, Mike opened his Tae Kwon Do school in Kahnawake, first using the Longhouse, the traditional community center, as a home for the school. The school was called Rotiskenakete Tae Kwon Do, meaning "the carriers of the peace." After that, Mike formed his own organization, the First Nations Tae Kwon Do Association.

MAJOR ACHIEVEMENTS

- In 1990, following an attempt to expand a golf course onto sacred land in the Mohawk community of Oka, a huge confrontation broke out between the Mohawk people and the Canadian and Quebec governments and military. The Mercier Bridge, connecting Montreal to the rest of the region, was occupied by Mohawks for two and a half months. At the center of this rebellion was the Warrior Society. After the Oka crisis, Mike's school sought acceptance as an independent school in the Canadian Tae Kwon Do Federation as the First Nations Tae Kwon Do Association and was accepted.

HOW HAS MARTIAL ARTS IMPACTED YOUR LIFE?

By what yardstick does one judge the life of a martial artist? By the titles, hype, and advertisements the martial artist prepares about himself? By how many tickets and videos do his movies sell? Or by what he does in the real world and how that affects the lives of real people?

To help the youth, he says, "That's been my whole motivation in all of this." Working in professional NHB groups, he insists, "Well, that's what I know. If it gives me the vehicle to change one child's life, I can say I've made his world a better place when I leave this earth."

He also views the traditional martial arts as directly related to the traditional culture of Indigenous peoples. "There are many traditional arts that are indigenous to Native people that we don't even hear about. Native Americans have been wrestling for thousands and thousands of years. The form of martial arts that they had is amazing." In this kind of wrestling, Mike observed, you see "the extension of the human body with different weapons." He emphasized, "You take a look at the world, and it's amazing how little we know about so many Indigenous peoples and their self-defense styles."

low time in my life. And maybe if I had somebody there to speak with me and tell me about these things, I might not have walked that path." And, in what should now be a surprise to no one, he adds, "I love working with kids."

For governments cutting and slashing revenues for education and other services for children, Mike advises, "If they can't invest in the greatest natural resource that we as human beings have, which is our children, then we don't have much of a future."

So, it has all come full circle. His thoughts keep returning to his roots, philosophy, community, family, and the family of us all, the youth. "If someone sticks out their hand for help, you extend that hand and help them. It doesn't matter what their color is, what their religion is, what their economic situation is." And if you didn't know that all this was what the martial arts is all about, or supposed to be about, then now, courtesy of Mike Thomas, you should.

MICK
TOMIC

"

Studying martial arts has greatly, profoundly, and positively impacted my life. It has also allowed me to meet many wonderful fellow martial artists in Australia and the United States.

WHY THE MARTIAL ARTS?

My reason for starting my journey and adventure in martial arts is rather unique. I started rather late in life. I had always wanted to start some form of martial arts training, but I could never build up the courage to take the first step and walk into a martial arts dojo. I would not have known the difference between a good instructor and dojo and a bad one. Fortunately for me, that decision was made by someone else.

My eldest daughter had just started school. She was not yet five years of age. She was somewhat shy and fidgety. At her school, martial arts was being taught in the school hall. Master Ell Gatt was the instructor there. With my daughter being so shy, Master Gatt agreed to come to our house and do some one-on-one training with my daughter. After a few lessons, she was confident enough to start in the classroom environment in the school hall. After approximately 18 months, my youngest daughter started training with Master Gatt, and shortly after that, so did my wife. Now, I was becoming nervous and fearful that the women in my life would soon be able to beat me up, so I decided to start my training in martial arts.

Unfortunately, my working hours did not allow me the luxury of being able to train with my girls. Fortunately for me, another training center had later classes available, and this was perfect for me. It was here that I began my martial arts training under Grandmaster Nick Donato in 1997, and I have not looked back since. I am so glad I decided to start my training when I did. The training under Grandmaster Donato and Master Gatt hasn't always been easy, but I would not change it for anything. As they say, anything worth having doesn't come easy, and anything that comes easy isn't worth having.

HOW HAS MARTIAL ARTS IMPACTED YOUR LIFE?

Studying martial arts has greatly, profoundly, and positively impacted my life. It has made me more confident in public settings and with groups of people. I can talk to groups of people, whether in a work setting or instructing in a martial arts class. I feel comfortable and confident, and not nervous.

The health benefits cannot be overlooked or underestimated. I now feel much fitter physically than I did in my twenties before I started training.

Martial arts has also allowed me to meet many wonderful fellow martial artists in Australia and the United States. It has allowed me to create and nurture many beautiful friendships I would have never formed. And for all the wonderful things that martial arts have taught me, the people it has exposed me to, and the places it has taken me, none of it would have ever been achieved had it not been for my instructors, Grandmaster Nick Donato and Master Ell Gatt. Without their support, guidance, teachings, and drive, I could have easily given up on this fantastic adventure. But they both believed in me and encouraged me, even when I didn't believe in myself, and for this, I cannot thank them enough.

TRAINING INFORMATION

- Martial Arts Styles & Rank: 5th Degree Blackbelt Kwon Bop Do Tae Kwon Do, 1st Grade Ben Kan Ryuha Nihon Ju Jitsu
- Instructors/Influencers: Grandmaster Nick Donato, Master Ell Gatt
- Birthplace/Growing Up: Croatia / Sydney, AUS
- Yrs. In the Martial Arts: 27 years
- Yrs. Instructing: 12 years
- Instructor & Student

PROFESSIONAL ORGANIZATIONS

- Kwon Bop Do Federation
- ITC International Tae Kwon Do Confederation

PERSONAL ACHIEVEMENTS

- Business Owner
- Husband
- Father
- Grandfather

MAJOR ACHIEVEMENTS

- Promoted to 5th Degree Blackbelt by Grandmaster Nick Donato
- World Head of Family Sokeship Council (WHFSC) Award, Outstanding Instructor, May 2023

Become an
AMAA MEMBER!

ROCCI
TWITCHELL

"

Martial Arts have been a significant source of inspiration for me during the trials, struggles, and obstacles...

WHY THE MARTIAL ARTS?

I began my martial arts journey in Portola, California, where I was bullied and picked on for many years. I was reading Black Belt Magazine and discovered if I studied and trained in martial arts, I could learn to build confidence and the ability to fight back, and that's exactly what I did. I found a martial arts instructor and began to learn fighting techniques and physical exercises that built my confidence and helped me gain physical strength and spiritual maturity. By my senior year in high school, I was no longer bullied and began my career as a martial arts instructor. I learned skills to share with others to protect and improve one's health and safety in this ever-changing world.

My greatest attributes have been gathered in the realm of martial arts.

HOW HAS MARTIAL ARTS IMPACTED YOUR LIFE?

Martial arts have been a significant source of inspiration for me during the trials, struggles, and obstacles in everyday challenges that life has given me. Martial arts taught me to be a peaceful warrior, just like Dan Millman taught me in his classic book Way of the Peaceful Warrior. Martial arts have also given me The Warriors Creed to apply for everyday applications. The Warrior Creed was created by Robert L. Humphrey, teaching me that wherever I walk, everyone is a little bit safer because I am there. Wherever I am, everyone has a friend. Whenever I return home, everyone is happy I am there.

TRAINING INFORMATION

- Martial Arts Styles & Rank: Rough & Tumble Fighting Systems-Black Belt, Jun Fan Jeet Kune Do Grappling-Senior Full Instructor, Garrison Fighting Knives-Full Instructor

- Instructors/Influencers: Guro Dan Inosanto, Carlito Bonjoc, Sifu Larry Hartsell, Guro Willie Laureano, Rita Suwanda, Olohe Solomon Kahewalu, Rocci Harry Twitchell, Clay Hughes, Caesar Gracie, Burton Richardson, Joel Champ, Craig Garrison, Daniel Docto, William De Thouras, Dionisio A. Canete

- Birthplace/Growing Up: Grass Valley, Portola, CA

- Yrs. In the Martial Arts: 42 years

- Yrs. Instructing: 41 years

- School owner & Instructor at Liahona Warrior Art—T5 Boxing

PROFESSIONAL ORGANIZATIONS

- Legacy Muay Thai Instructor

- Certified ABF Boxing Coach

- Ambassador for Jocko Willink, Jocko Fuel/ Origin Labs

- Thom Shea's Unbreakable Leadership Team

- T5 Boxing Coach

PERSONAL ACHIEVEMENTS

- 21 years at The University of California Davis Fire Prevention Department

- Former Captain, The Guardian Angels, founded by Curtis Sliwa

- 2015 Masters Hall of Fame Inductee

MAJOR ACHIEVEMENTS

- Rough & Tumble Fighting Systems - Inheritor of the System

- 1991 Utah State Golden Gloves Champion

- 1991 California Diamond Belt Champion

- Former Self-defense Instructor at the University of California Davis

- Co-author of Elite Black Belts Who Cook, a #1 International Best-seller

- Co-author of Elite Martial Artists in America, the Secrets to Life, Leadership, and Business, a #1 International Best-seller

HELEN CHUNG
VASILIADIS

"
Being involved in Martial Arts has taught me to be assertive, confident, disciplined, goal oriented, humble and kind.

WHY THE MARTIAL ARTS?

I emigrated from Korea to the United States in 1970 at the age of nine with assistance from my Uncle, Grand Master Jhoon Rhee, and I earned my Black Belt in Tae Kwon Do at the age of 16. As an immigrant, these were very humbling times and Martial Arts has been the key to my success today.

I have been blessed with a very fulfilling life in the United States. Much of my life, from the age of 9 when I first came to the US, evolved around my Martial Arts training and blossomed from my foundation as a martial artist. I spent more time at the Karate school than anywhere else. I spent hours and hours, taking classes, doing my homework, working in the office, ultimately teaching classes, and working out as often as I could. All my time and training in the Karate school affected all other aspects of my life. It taught me hard work, discipline, time management, showing respect for others, and it was the foundation for my success in other areas of my life such as school, on the karate circuit, and ultimately becoming a Mother and business owner.

HOW HAS MARTIAL ARTS IMPACTED YOUR LIFE?

Martial Arts has influenced and enhanced my life in numerous ways. Being part of the Martial Arts community, which is made up of martial artists of all races, religions, and parts of our country, who shared common values such as respect, hard work, competition, and righteousness, these values have helped mold me to become the person I am today. Through Martial Arts I have traveled around the world for countless competitions and demonstrations and I have met thousands of other martial artists who are now part of my martial arts family and who will remain friends for my entire life.

I believe that Martial Arts parallels and enhances life. All of our core values as martial artists are relevant to all aspects of life in general, from the importance of discipline and hard work, to treating others with courtesy and respect, to bravery, humility, competition and fun.

One of our mottos at the Jhoon Rhee Institute was "Lead by Example" and this had a great influence on me since I started as a white belt at the age of nine.

HOW HAS MARTIAL ARTS IMPACTED YOUR LIFE? (CONTINUED)

Beginning as a student and junior competitor, I always tried to set an example to my co-students and other competitors within the dojang, at tournaments, and in our community. For my co-students and co-competitors, during training and competition, I have attempted to demonstrate hard work as well as fierce competitiveness balanced by gracious sportsmanship. For parents of my students I have always tried to demonstrate how success within martial arts is not only compatible with but also enhances success in life. I always earned honor roll in school, I always excelled in the organization where I have worked, and I started a successful fitness business that has been in operation for 30 years. In the karate school, we are always taught that with hard work and perseverance we can achieve our goals. I believe that I spread this philosophy everywhere I go and I pride myself on being a positive and uplifting influence for my friends and family.

Being involved in Martial Arts has taught me to be assertive, confident, disciplined, goal oriented, humble and kind. My experiences throughout the world as a martial artist have helped me learn about, appreciate and respect other cultures, societies, and people.

I have had the opportunity to teach martial arts and self-defense to law enforcement groups, women's groups, in schools, on television, at professional sporting events in the US Congress, in foreign countries, and to hundreds of my individual students.

TRAINING INFORMATION

- Martial Arts Styles & Rank: Tae Kwon Do- 3rd Degree Black Belt
- Instructors/Influencers: Jhoon Rhee, Jeff Smith, John Chung, Otis Hooper, and Kwan Ro
- Yrs. In the Martial Arts: 52 years
- Yrs. Instructing: 17 years

PERSONAL ACHIEVEMENTS

- 1979 Wakefield High School, Arlington, VA
- 1984 BS Exercise Science George Mason University
- 1987-Present Owner of Six One to One Fitness Center - Personal Training Facilities in DC and VA
- 1990-1993 Graduate Studies George Mason University - MS Exercise Science
- 1990-Present Mother of Five Amazing Children
- 1984-1986 Sports Training Institute, NYC
- Personal Fitness Trainer to Movie stars Kathleen Turner of "Body Heat", Burt Young of "Rocky", Olympic Boxer Mark Breland, and Editor of Parade Magazine & Lifetime Achievement Legend in the American Martial Arts Walter Anderson
- 2015 Certified Health & Wellness Coach (CHWC) Wellcoaches
- 2017 Certified Culinary Health & Education Fundamentals (CHEF), Harvard Medical School

MAJOR ACHIEVEMENTS

- 1984-1989 Top Ten National Champion Forms/Fighting
- 1985 WAKO US Team, London, England
- 1987 WAKO US Team, Munich, Germany, World Champion Welter Weight
- 1988 Bermuda International Forms/Fighting Champion
- 1989 Centerfold and feature story "FIGHTER" Magazine
- 1990 Hall of Fame Induction- Diamond Nationals
- 2014 Masters Hall of Fame, Texas
- 2016 Joe Lewis Eternal Warrior Award, Battle of Atlanta
- 1978 Junior Miss Pageant Talent Award First Place

MAJOR TOURNAMENTS

- Battle of Atlanta
- Bermuda Internationals
- Blue Grass Nationals
- U.S. Capitol Classics
- Fort Worth Pro Am
- U.S. Open
- Top Ten Nationals
- WAKO World Championships

Become an
AMAA MEMBER!

RAUL
VASQUEZ

"Martial Arts taught me to each day live the values of Respect, Courage, Honor, Integrity, Knowledge, Leadership, and Diplomacy.

HOW HAS MARTIAL ARTS IMPACTED YOUR LIFE?

Grandmaster Robert Suttles feels very fortunate to have instructors who are friends and have trained with each other. They supported each other through the years and had a special bond. Each one of them helped GM Suttles through his journey in martial arts in a different way. GM Suttles says, " I would not be where I am today, and who I am today if it were not for the influence of these men. Some of these men are no longer with us but are not forgotten and will be in my heart and memory for the rest of my days."

WHY THE MARTIAL ARTS?

I started in martial arts to get physically fit, learn how to fight, and become proficient in numerous self-defense techniques. Of course, as I continued my training, I soon realized there was so much more involved in the participation and study of martial arts.

TRAINING INFORMATION

- Martial Arts Styles & Rank: Tae-Kwon-Do, 10th Degree Black Belt
- Instructors/Influencers: Jeff Smith, Steve Stavroff, Jhoon Rhee, J. Pat Burleson, and Allen Steen
- Birthplace/Growing Up: Corpus Christi, TX
- Yrs. In the Martial Arts: 57 years
- Yrs. Instructing: 50+ years
- Instructor, President & CEO of the South Texas Karate Black Belt Association

HOW HAS MARTIAL ARTS IMPACTED YOUR LIFE? (CONTINUED)

The study of martial arts has impacted my life very unexpectedly since the start of my training in Tae-Kwon-Do. I thought I would take lessons for six months and then quit after I learned a lot of self-defense techniques and the karate chop in order to defend myself. I had no concept of what it took to become a black belt, nor its significance. After three years of training, I acquired my black belt and realized this was not the end of my studies and training in martial arts, even though I would now be considered an expert. It was then just my personal beginning in the infinite process of learning martial arts.

I would eat, drink, sleep, and dream about martial arts. From a primary sport, it became a way of life for me. It provided me with the stamina to meet my long-term goals and the discipline to meet my personal and professional needs and responsibilities. Martial Arts taught me to each day live the values of Respect, Courage, Honor, Integrity, Knowledge, Leadership, and Diplomacy. It also taught me to lead for professionalism and quality of membership and to ensure the well-being and continued growth of the martial arts. The person I am today is because of my development through martial arts.

PROFESSIONAL ORGANIZATIONS

- South Texas Karate Black Belt Association
- American Karate Black Belt Association
- World Martial Arts Ranking Association
- International Martial Arts Council of America
- American Martial Arts Alliance Foundation
- Association of Masters
- United Martial Arts Association
- Texas Amateur Organization of Karate
- U.S. Tae-Kwon-Do Association
- Jhoon Rhee Institute
- Southwest Karate Black Belt Association

PERSONAL ACHIEVEMENTS

- A significant competition record in Kumite from 1969 to 1986 consisting of first-place wins at the Southwest Pro-Am Karate Championships (Lightweight 1972) in Austin, Texas, San Antonio Karate Championships (Lightweight 1972), National Black Belt Team Championships in Dallas, Texas (1975 National Champions - Texas Black Belt Team - David Archer, Louis Arnold, Demetrius Havanas, D.P. Hill, and Raul Vasquez coached by Pat Burleson and Skipper Mullins), Mexico Internationals in Nuevo Laredo, Mexico (Heavyweight 1977 to 1981), Universidad Regiomontana Karate Championships in Monterrey, Mexico (Heavyweight 1981), Houston Karate Olympics (Senior Division 1983, 1984, & 1985), and the Texas State Karate Championships held in Ft. Worth, Texas (Senior Division 1984, 1985, & 1986).

- Placed in numerous other major tournaments such as the U.S. Karate Championships held in Dallas, Texas, placing 3rd in the Middleweight Division in 1972 and 3rd in the Light-Heavyweight Division in 1975, 1979, 1980, and 1981. Runner-Up in the Houston Karate Olympics in 1981 (Middleweight Division), and 3rd place in the Texas State Karate Championships (Middleweight Division) held in Fort Worth, Texas in 1981.

- After a 22-year retirement from tournament competition beginning in 1986, entered each year the Texas Police Athletic Federation's Annual Texas Police Games from 2008 to 2012 and, on two occasions, won 1st place in the Kumite Division and once 2nd Place in Weapons Kata.

MAJOR ACHIEVEMENTS

- Founded and promoted the South Texas Karate Championships in Corpus Christi, Texas, for charitable purposes from 1979 to 1991.

- Promoted martial arts on many local television programs, conducted numerous Tae-Kwon-Do demonstrations throughout the Corpus Christi community, and was listed in many publications and ratings, including Professional Karate and Tae-Kwon-Do Magazine.

- Listed in and selected to provide interview data for the book entitled, Listening to the Masters: Insight, Knowledge, and Wisdom from Today's Martial Arts Masters, which was written by Master Ronnie Molina of the Sugar Land Texas Police Department and released through Amazon Publishing in 2019. His biography is included in the 2021 Edition of the Sport Karate Museum History Book Pioneers Section by Professor Gary Lee and Grandmaster Jessie Bowen.

- Founder / President & CEO of the South Texas Karate Black Belt Association (STKBBA), formed in 2014 with the sole purpose of uniting legitimate black belt martial artists from the diversified groups and disciplines of South Texas for black belt testing and validation and the continuous promotion of martial arts.

MAJOR ACHIEVEMENTS

- Founded the Annual Holiday Social/ Recognition Banquet in 2015 to bring Black Belts together during the Christmas Holidays to celebrate the holiday season and to dine with each other.

- In 2019 established the first ever South Texas Karate Black Belt Hall of Fame to each year recognize and permanently honor individuals from South Texas who have for over 40 years sacrificed and uniquely contributed to the overall development of martial arts and themselves. The STKBBA currently has a membership of 78 black belts from 18 South Texas communities. An additional six members are deceased.

- Received the following Honors and Awards due to my tournament competition record and active leadership roles in promoting martial arts: 1979 Texas AOK Award 4th Place Top Black Belt Tournament Point Fighter; Inducted into the 1981 Charter Issue of the Southwest Martial Artist; 1982 United Martial Arts Tournament Award Kumite 3rd Place Black Belt Masters; World Martial Arts Hall of Fame, Inc.; Who's Who in American Martial Arts 1984 - 1985 Edition; Who's Who in the Martial Arts Elite 1988; Inducted into the 2016 Masters Hall of Fame by the Association of Masters; Joe Lewis Dragon Image Fighting Award in 2016; Sport Karate Museum The History General Award in 2016; Certificate of Excellence in 2016 by the Alvin Francis Karate Organization ; Inducted into the 21st Annual Universal Martial Arts Hall of Fame for 2017; 116th Texas Four Seasons Fall Karate Championship Award in 2017 For Excellence and Outstanding Service to the Sport of Karate; Integrity Award by the South Texas Karate Black Belt Association in 2017; Recipient of the Memorial Fighter Award in 2019 by the Sport Karate Museum Ralph Jaschke Memorial Dragon Image Award; Certificate of Recognition by Lower Rio Grande Valley members of the South Texas Karate Black Belt Association in 2019; Awarded a Samurai Sword in 2021 by Alvin Francis for Contributions to the Martial Arts; United States Martial Arts Hall of Fame in 2022; inducted into the American Martial Arts Alliance Foundation Who's Who In the Martial Arts Hall of Honor in 2022; inducted into the South Texas Karate Black Belt Hall of Fame in 2022; and received the Elite Publications Best Seller Co-Author Award for my contributions as a writer in Elite Martial Artists of America: Secrets to Life, Leadership, and Business, Volume I compilation book on January 27, 2023.

JOSEPH
VAUTOUR
1953-2024

"
Martial arts, for me, is not just a workout but rather a way of life.

TRAINING INFORMATION

- Martial Arts Styles & Rank: Taekwondo - 7th Dan, Aristos - 7th Dan, Hapkido - 1st Dan, Wushu - 2nd Dan
- Instructors/Influencers: Grandmaster Tae E Lee, Grandmaster Brendan Wilson, Jean-Yves Theriault
- Birthplace/Growing Up: St. John, New Brunswick, Canada
- Yrs. In the Martial Arts: 45 years
- Yrs. Instructing: 40 years
- Instructor

PROFESSIONAL ORGANIZATIONS

- Jung Do Kwan International
- Kukkiwon

PERSONAL ACHIEVEMENTS

- 17 years in the Canadian Armed Forces
- 21 years as a NATO civilian employee

HIS JOURNEY

Joe started training in the Canadian military in 1979. He trained with the Canadian Taekwondo competition team and also studied Kung Fu, Tai Chi, Kickboxing, and Hapkido.

HOW MARTIAL ARTS IMPACTED HIS LIFE...

"I've been studying the martial arts since 1979. Martial arts, for me, is not just a workout but rather a way of life. It's helped me develop not only on the physical side but mentally and spiritually as well. I'm just opening an Aristos school. For my students, I just ask that you do your best, try to attend all classes, and allow the art to filter into your life as it has mine."

-Aristos Documentary, Athens, Greece, 2014

A memoir of my husband, Joseph Anthony Vautour, February 24, 1953 — May 11, 2024.

I met Joe in 1990. At the time, he was practicing Taekwondo in the military under Grandmaster Tae E. Lee, from whom he had just received his black belt. He was also training in kickboxing with Jean-Yves Theriault (23-time undefeated world kickboxing champion). Our first date was attending one of Jean-Yves's fights. He also trained in boxing at Beaver Boxing Club in Ottawa, as well as Kung Fu, Hapkido, and Tai Chi.

Joe was the youngest of 14 children, 11 girls and 3 boys. He grew up in an impoverished family in Saint John, New Brunswick, Canada. Although he was very insecure as a youth, his military service and martial arts training helped to build his character and confidence.

Joe started martial arts while in the Canadian Military. Through martial arts, he made many wonderful friends in many countries around the world. Joe pursued martial arts and music to get through many difficult and emotional times. These also provided us with an instant family wherever we went.

MAJOR ACHIEVEMENTS

- Author of In Search of a Path to World Peace: A History of the World's Major Wars.
- 7th Dan in Tae Kwon Do and in Aristos.
- He served for NATO in Afghanistan.
- He helped create a recording studio for impoverished children in Uganda.
- He taught self-defense to homeless children in Uganda.
- He was a husband, father to two children and two stepchildren, and a grandfather to seven grandchildren - all of them are wonderful.
- He created a CD titled "Tracks in the Dust: Songs from Afghanistan." It was made in Afghanistan with contributors from five countries.
- Forty-five years of recovery and mentored those in need.

Become an
AMAA MEMBER!

Joe passed away in a Filipino boxing club doing what he loved. I've had the privilege to meet a few of his friends during the process of returning him home. He made wonderful friends through martial arts up until his death. I don't think Joe would have been the person he became without his world of martial arts.

Joe helped people wherever he went. His kindness and generosity went above and beyond. He was a long-time member of a recovery program, where he mentored many young men. He helped me build a recording studio for homeless children in Uganda. He also donated a lot of martial arts equipment and taught homeless children self-defense. Joe worked with young offenders and played hockey in the Canadian prison system as part of his work with people in need.

Though he received many awards and certificates, Joe was a very humble man. From speaking with him, one would never know of his accomplishments. He volunteered to go to Afghanistan as part of a NATO force. While there, in his spare time, he started a band that produced a CD called Tracks in the Dust, Songs from Afghanistan. It was written and recorded in Afghanistan by 11 artists from five nations to promote

peace. One hundred percent of the profits went to the Wounded Warrior Project, a charitable organization to help disabled veterans through their rehabilitation and recovery. Later in life, he wrote a book urging world peace: In Search of a Path to World Peace: A History of the World's Major Wars.

It's been an interesting journey since his passing, but I have felt honored to help bring him home, prepare for his celebration of life, and then go on our final passage together to bring him home to his final resting place beside his brother in Saint John, New Brunswick.

I miss him, but I'm so happy that we shared these last years of friendship, forgiveness, and a very special spiritual kind of love.

-Joan Davidson Vautour, his loving wife.

Grandmaster Brendan Wilson's Memories of Joe Vautour

Words can't do justice to my friend of so many years, nor can they express my joy and gratitude for knowing such a wonderful person. I am sad that he has left us, but I am so very glad I had a chance to share a friendship with such a wonderful soul.

I first met Joe in 1995 while teaching an outdoor martial arts class at Supreme Headquarters Allied Powers Europe (SHAPE) near Mons, Belgium. I saw

Joe standing near where we were training. I walked over to him at the break, and he said politely, "Sir, I have a second-degree black belt in Tae Kwon Do, and I would like to join your class."

That was the start of our friendship. He trained with the class for three years until I transferred out in 1998. He was a wonderful martial artist and an inspiration to the other students. A magnificent fighter, he was also a gentle and careful practitioner. During his 3rd degree test, I had three tough Canadian soldiers, each of whom was fully protected with body armor, attack him simultaneously. Without hurting them, he sent them flying. You could see he was holding back.

Seventeen years later, we found ourselves again working at NATO in Belgium. He was back at SHAPE while I was assigned to NATO political headquarters in Brussels. Joe started school at SHAPE while I was in a class in Brussels. He would come to Brussels to train with us on weekends, and I

occasionally went to SHAPE to train with his students.

In 2014, we made a series of martial arts films in Athens, Greece. In his taped interview, he showed his gentle and sincere nature. His martial arts performance was amazing. At that time, he was over 60, and he could do a full split and break boards well over his head with his kicks.

I had planned to nominate Joe for the Who's Who in the Martial Arts Award at the Martial Arts Hall of Honor in 2024. When we learned of his passing, I contacted the event organizers, Grandmaster Jessie Bowen and his team, and they agreed to a posthumous award for Joe. On August 9th, 2004, Joe will receive this recognition at the Who's Who in the Martial Arts

Awards Banquet in Charlotte, North Carolina.

Joe was joyful, kind, thoughtful, and modest. I know that if he had lived to accept the award, he would, with all sincerity, give credit to others: his students, colleagues, and instructors.

I am sure Joe left a mark on the people in his life. I can speak for myself. I will never forget him, his smile, his sense of humor, his kindness, and his generosity.

I miss you, Joe.

MANLY VUONG

WHY THE MARTIAL ARTS?

A s a young 7-year-old full of energy, my father decided martial arts would be a terrific way to channel that energy into something practical. So, in 1995, when a new martial arts school opened at my local primary school hall, this was the perfect opportunity to let loose a bit of energy, learn some self-defense, and instill some self-discipline. Of course, growing up idolizing action heroes such as Chuck Norris, Van Damme, Schwarzenegger, Stallone, Jet Li, etc, fueled the motivational fire for training.

I grew up in an area of Sydney known to be a little rough; in fact, at one stage, it was listed as Sydney's most disadvantaged suburb. I never felt unsafe roaming the streets; I witnessed small, petty crimes, homelessness, and drug addicts on the streets were omnipresent.

My father and mother, but more so my father, endured unimaginable hardship during the Vietnam

" Martial arts have helped me overcome the darkest and most challenging times in life and given me a mindset of gratitude for what lies ahead.

War. He faced torture and slavery and came face to face with death but was stoic right to the very end. His good heart saw him get captured by the Vietcong as he attempted to guide a group of refugees through the jungle into Thailand. But it was his indomitable spirit that kept him going as he bounced between concentration camps before being released and finally making his way to Australia.

When I think about it now, in some ways, I was always destined to be in martial arts. Growing up in a disadvantaged suburb and having a father who constantly reinforced self-discipline, respect, a good attitude, and a good heart are traits that I believe are resolute in any true martial artist.

Fortunately for me, the martial arts school I joined in 1995 will be the first and last system I will be a part of. Nowadays, it is not uncommon for a practitioner to bounce between multiple martial arts schools and sometimes simultaneously. However, I will forever be grateful and in debt to the Personal Defense Studios and Grandmaster Nick Donato for all the guidance and teachings over the years. As Mum once said when relating my affiliation with the same martial arts school all these years, "as though the universe aligned itself for me to find this school."

All these 'higher' levels of thought process and the spiritual learnings and motivations that I thrive and develop week in and week out were obviously not going through my head as a 7-year-old. I merely wanted to start martial arts to learn how to kick, punch, and pull out my best Van Damme splits on the boxing ring ropes (still a work in progress, by the way).

What kept me hungry for training in those early years was the camaraderie amongst the students, the appetite to learn new techniques, and the general overall fitness benefit that I could see for myself. I was an asthmatic as a child, but through the physical training and constant pushing of my physical self, my asthma resolved.

As I entered my teenage years, an individual's most volatile years in terms of emotional and self-growth, I could begin to see the teachings of martial arts not limited to just the dojo but now apply to my daily life. Of course, I still did silly things just like any other teenage boy would, but martial arts gave me a level head, self-confidence, and the necessary tools to look after myself without the egotistical confidence to go looking for trouble.

Like many martial arts practitioners, there comes a time when they are faced with the dilemma of leaving the martial arts journey, and for me, that happened during my teenage years when my long-term training partner decided to leave. It was one of those fork-in-the-road moments, but I'm forever grateful that I chose the right path. More so now, since I am well and truly into my adulthood with little ones of my own, I hope they too can receive the life skills learnt through the arts that will guide them to a successful life, as it has done for me.

TRAINING INFORMATION

- Martial Arts Styles & Rank: Kwon Bop Do Taekwondo- 5th Dan Black Belt, Ben Kan Ryuha Kobu Jutsu- 1st Shodan, Ben Kan Ryuha Nihon Ju Jitsu- 1st Kyu
- Instructors/Influencers: Grandmaster Nick Donato, Master Ell Gatt, Master John Falvo
- Birthplace/Growing Up: Sydney, AUS
- Yrs. In the Martial Arts: 29 years
- Yrs. Instructing: 12 years
- Instructor & Student

PROFESSIONAL ORGANIZATIONS

- Kwon Bop Do Federation
- ITC-International Taekwondo Confederation

PERSONAL ACHIEVEMENTS

- Happily married and father of three
- Bachelor of Diagnostic Radiography-Sydney University
- Diploma of Medical Ultrasound- University of South Australia
- Cert III and IV personal trainer
- Super welterweight amateur kickboxing bouts
- Numerous community martial arts demonstrations

MAJOR ACHIEVEMENTS

- Kwon Bop Do Taekwondo 5th Dan- 2023
- Ben Kan Ryuha Kobu Jutsu Shodan- 2019
- WCJJO International Sport JJ World Cup, Gold Coast- 2017
- ISKA World Cup competitor, Orlando- 2007
- WHFSC World Head of Family Sokeship Council - Outstanding Student Award

SEMINARS

- Don "The Dragon" Wilson, Mark Dacascos, Richard Norton - 2023
- Arjun Surachai Chai Sirisute Thai boxing seminar — 2019
- Shihan Gordon Griffiths, Shihan Nick Donato, Sensei Joe Bracks Ju Jitsu seminar - July 2017
- Arjun Surachai Chai Sirisute Thai boxing seminar — March 2012
- Grandmaster James Keller Australian Tour - 2011
- Bill "Superfoot" Wallace Seminar — May 2008
- Grandmaster Joe Onopa seminar — September 2001

HOW HAS MARTIAL ARTS IMPACTED YOUR LIFE?

In many ways, I am fortunate to have started my martial arts journey at a relatively young age as it has been, apart from my family, the most constant and consistent aspect in my life so far.

The arts have been with me through primary and high school, from university to working life, and I am still learning and growing as I enter fatherhood, with little ones of my own about to start their own journey.

Throughout each previously stated stage in my life, so long as I got my butt to class and be consistent with training, all the external life pressures and stresses with work, studying, family, and friends will sort itself out. I trusted in the teachings and learnt how to adapt those teachings from within the dojo and applied them to my personal life in almost every facet of everyday life, from the challenges to problem-solving and interpersonal relationships, from mannerisms and how I conduct myself to family, friends, and strangers. They all stem from the learnings and teachings that have been instilled in me over the years.

Martial arts have helped me overcome the darkest and most challenging times in life and given me a mindset of gratitude for what lies ahead.

Become an
AMAA MEMBER!

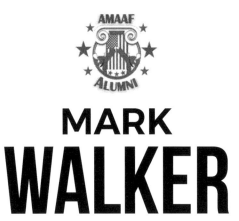

MARK
WALKER

" Martial arts have significantly impacted my life and allowed me to impact others.

WHY THE MARTIAL ARTS?

When I was nine years old, I lost my father, and I began fighting constantly. My elder brothers would come to get me and make me fight other children in the projects. When I was fighting, I liked how I felt. I didn't understand that I was upset about my father's death at the time. This anger was channeled into street fights.

One day after a fight, a two-time Golden Gloves Champion took me down to the basement in the projects where they made a makeshift boxing ring. He told me to put on the boxing gloves that were almost bigger than I was because I was very small. He put me in the ring with another kid, and I fought him.

The late Earl Morton, Jr. started teaching me the science of boxing. My father and my uncles all boxed. Two of my uncles boxed for the military: Marines

and the Army. Boxing was in my blood, but I was always attracted to martial arts. My mother was against me fighting, so she refused to sign me up for a class.

Master Sammy Adams started a class in the projects teaching the KA System founded by Grandmaster Kareem Allah. I watched the class one day, and Master Sammy saw me and invited me into the class. He told me to spar with one of his students. He was so impressed with how well I handled myself that he came to my house and asked my mother for permission for me to take his class. My mother was against it, but Master Sammy promised my mother that he would watch over me and even offered not to take any money. This was the beginning of my martial arts experience. Master Sammy was small in stature but a fierce martial artist. I equated myself to him because I was also small in stature.

HOW HAS MARTIAL ARTS IMPACTED YOUR LIFE?

Martial arts have impacted my life in many different ways. It has helped me develop my body and condition for martial arts and all the sports I played—football, basketball, hockey, and baseball. Martial arts have helped me focus my mind and spirit. It also allowed me to build personal discipline and gain confidence in my abilities. My fortitude has been formed and strengthened as a result of it. Martial arts have taught me to look at life from a different viewpoint. Martial arts shifted my perspective on life and improved my quality of life.

Through martial arts, I learned how to control and redirect my anger into a positive force of righteousness. My purpose as a teacher is to cultivate great human beings rather than good martial artists. My motto is "Train for war, but pray for peace."

TRAINING INFORMATION
- Martial Arts Styles & Rank: Licensed Hachi Dan, "Eye-to-Eye" Sanuces Ryu Jiu-Jitsu
- Instructors/Influencers: Doctor Moses Powell
- Birthplace/Growing Up: Newark, NJ
- Yrs. In the Martial Arts: 36 years
- Yrs. Instructing: 28 years
- School owner, Manager & Instructor at Schools of Moses Powell

PROFESSIONAL ORGANIZATIONS
- International Federation of Jiujitsuans
- All Japan Jiu-Jitsu International
- Academy of Masters
- World Black Belt Association
- Martial Arts Alliance
- The World Martial Arts College
- World Jiu-Jitsu Aiki-Bujutsu Federation
- Martial Arts Museum
- World Sijo Dai Soke Renmei Black Belts International Association
- Nippon Yawara Ryu Aiki Jiu-Jitsu Renmei

PERSONAL ACHIEVEMENTS
- 41 years of Law Enforcement Training
- Inducted into The Legends of The Martial Arts Hall of Fame by Cynthia Rothrock.
- 4-Time Inductee into the Martial Arts Magazine Hall of Fame, by Sifu Alan Goldberg.
- Defensive Tactics Instructor for the Department of Correctional Police Officers
- Inducted into The World Head of Family Sokeship Council
- Self Defense Instructor of The Gold Pin Project, founded by Sifu Alan Goldberg
- Inducted into The First International Federation of Jiu-Jitsu Legion of Honors by Soke Michael Depasquale
- Inducted into The USA Martial Arts Hall of Fame, Founded by Professor Marty Cal
- Inducted into the Budo Martial Arts Magazine Hall of Fame
- 3-Time Inductee into the United States Martial Arts Hall of Fame by Master Jim Thomas
- Registered Hachi Dan in The All-Japan Federation

PERSONAL ACHIEVEMENTS (CONTINUED)

- Inducted into The World Karate Union Hall of Fame by The Late Kathy Tasetano
- Samurai Award at Martial Arts University
- Martial Arts Icon Award at Martial Arts University, by Soke Michael Depasquale

MAJOR ACHIEVEMENTS

- I opened my first martial school as a Green Belt.
- Inducted into the First Grandmaster Dr. Moses Powell New York State Hall of Fame.
- Demonstrated at The First Televised Tribute to the Masters of the 20th Century, Hosted by Wesley Snipes.
- Produced two martial arts training videos.
- Book dedication written by Barry Farber.
- Grand Champion at The First Battle at the Boardwalk, Hosted by Soke Michael Depasquale.
- Featured Martial Artist on Black Belt T.V. Hosted by Soke Michael Depasquale.
- Featured in the Book The World's Greatest Martial Artist by Ted Gambordella.
- Featured in the book Changing Lives Series Vol. 6 Tribute To Ernie Reyes
- Featured in the Hall of Honors World History Book Dedicated to Soke Michael Depaquale, Jr.
- Featured in the AMAA Legacy Book 10th Anniversary Edition
- Featured martial artist on the poster for the International Martial Arts Hall of Fame for the Country of India

Become an
AMAA MEMBER!

CHRIS WETHERINGTON

"

Martial arts has impacted me so humbly that I've decided to serve others with the highest level of integrity.

I am truly grateful to my mentors who have paved the way for many martial artists, including myself: Jessie Bowen, Gary Wasniewski, Louis D. Casamassa, Chris Casamassa, Dafyd Hause, Professor John Terry, Michael Hornsby, Silverio Guerra, Lawrence Arthur, Cynthia Rothrock, Alan Goldberg, GJ Torres, Rick St. Claire, Martin Zingel, and Das Stirrat

HOW HAS MARTIAL ARTS IMPACTED YOUR LIFE?

I, Sensei Chris Wetherington, President and Chief Instructor of Balanced Warrior MMA & Karate LLC, have taken the approach to being the champion for Victim's Advocacy and Anti-bullying. Martial arts has impacted me so humbly that I've decided to serve others with the highest level of integrity.

WHY THE MARTIAL ARTS?

I got started in martial arts to help others to break the cycle of abuse and suffering. I became a victim's advocate to help and serve others, knowing one can grow up without access to support and, worst of all, hope. Through numerous top martial arts mentors guiding me through my martial arts journey, I have taken the approach to serve the martial arts community and help others with all that I do. Life is precious, and everyone needs special love and attention. It's my honor to be a champion for hope and bless all with the best quality of life I can provide through martial arts.

BOOKS, PUBLICATIONS & MEDIA FEATURES

- 2023 Co-Author Credit in the #1 International Best Seller "Who's Who In The Martial Arts Tribute to Cynthia Rothrock." Induction into the AMAA Who's Who in the Martial Arts Hall of Honors. Awarded the AMAA Who's Who in the Martial Arts Legends Award

- 2023 Co-Author Credit in the #1 International Best Seller "Elite Black Belts Who Cook" Compilation Book

- 2023 Co-Author Credit - "The Warrior's Path 2"

- 2023 "Talk About It TV" "The Master's Council" Weekly Humanitarian Educational Martial Arts Based TV Show

- 2024 Co-Author Credit - Featured in the "Action Martial Arts Magazine Hall of Honors World History Book"

- 2024 Co-Author Credit - "The Martial Arts Directory" "International Instructor's Anniversary Edition 2024"

- 2024 Co-Author Credit - "AMAA Legacy Book 10th Anniversary Edition Martial Arts Biography Book"

- 2024-05 Starring Cast Credit as Christopher A. Wetherington/Himself — "The Karate Breaker"

- Internet Movie Database (IMDb) Actor Credit for "The Karate Breaker"

TRAINING INFORMATION

- Martial Arts Styles & Rank: Tang Soo Do/ TKD - 4th Degree Black Belt, Hapkido 3rd Degree Black Belt, Brazilian Jui-Jitsu, Boxing

- Instructors/Influencers: Louis D, Casamassa, Chris Casamassa, Dafyd Andrew Haase

- Birthplace/Growing Up: Paducah, KY / Carlinville, IL

- Yrs. In the Martial Arts: 25 years

- Yrs. Instructing: 12 years

- School owner, Manager & Instructor at Balanced Warrior MMA & Karate, LLC.

PROFESSIONAL ORGANIZATIONS

- AKKF - American Karate Kung-Fu Federation

- AKA - American Karate Association

- USAWKF - United States Wushu - Kung-Fu Federation

- Traditional International Martial Arts Federation (TIMAF)

- TYGA Martial Arts International

PERSONAL ACHIEVEMENTS

- Champion for Anti-bullying & Victim's Advocate

MAJOR ACHIEVEMENTS

- 2018 United States Martial Arts Hall of Fame - Instructor of the Year

- 2019 United States Martial Arts Hall of Fame - Anti-bullying Advocate Award

- 2021 Universal Martial Arts Hall of Fame - Outstanding Achievement Award

- 2022 USA Martial Arts Hall Of Fame - Unsung Hero Award

- 2022 International Martial Arts Hall of Fame/Martial Arts Authority of India - Instructor of the Year Award

- 2023 International Martial Arts Hall of Fame/ Martial Arts Authority of India- Black Belt of the Year Award

- 2023 Universal Martial Arts Hall of Fame - Humanitarian of the Year Award

- 2023 USA Martial Arts Hall of Fame — Man of the Year Award

- 2024 Action Magazine Martial Arts Hall of Award Fame — Elite Honorable Warrior Award

- 2024 World Black Belt Club Council Hall of Honors - World Legend Award

MAJOR ACHIEVEMENTS

- 2024 GJ Torres Who's Who Night of Honors (HOF)
- 2024 Golden Gate Hall of Honors HOF/ "Outstanding Achievement in The Martial Arts" Award
- 2024 Hall of Fame Degli Artisti Marziali
- 2024 Universal Martial Arts Hall of Fame - Outstanding Contributions to the Martial Arts Award
- 2024 London International Martial Arts Hall of Fame — "Martial Arts Spirit Award"
- 2025 GJ Torres Who's Who Night of Honors (HOF)
- 2025 Kung-Fu / Karate Expo 18 Masters of the Martial Arts Hall of Fame — Award TBD
- 2026 International Martial Arts Hall of Fame Netherlands - Award TBD

Become an
AMAA MEMBER!

RUSSELL
WHITE

"
Martial arts has shown me that I can implement martial techniques within anything in life...

WHY THE MARTIAL ARTS?

My wife and I removed my oldest granddaughter (11 years old at the time) from a local martial arts school, where we thought the instructor was demeaning toward the students and failed to encourage them to excel inside and outside the dojo. That is when I found Grandmaster Brian Oakes' Chapel Hill Kenpo JKD Mixed Martial Arts. After a couple of trial classes, we enrolled her the very next week and would watch as most parents/grandparents usually do. We watched as she participated for a couple of weeks, and after observing a class one afternoon, I asked the instructor if he taught "old fat guys" too. He said he would teach anyone willing to learn. I was 42, overweight with high blood pressure, and was chained to a desk job. I started the next class with the enthusiasm of an eager teenager. I realized that I had jumped feet first into something that I wished I trained in all my life. I sunk my teeth into Progressive Kenpo and spent what seemed to be every

waking hour studying, practicing, reading, and meditating martial arts. Upon each belt promotion I earned, I noticed a different me emerging. I was finding freedom in living a healthier life by devotion to a three-word credo we used as the school class foundation: Learning, Lifestyle, and Longevity. The credo changed my life. I no longer look at those words and see just their Webster's dictionary meaning. Each word developed a deep, broad meaning that has since been burned into my heart.

Learning was not just the action to learn. Learning became the principle of continuous improvement...self-improvement... and always strive to be better than the day before. But that just does not pertain to time spent inside the dojo; it meant to be better than the day before in life, in all facets of my being, i.e., physically, mentally, and spiritually. It also meant continuing to learn and improve my communication skills, which helped me develop into the instructor I am today. It also helped me to become a better land surveyor (my career field), husband, father, grandfather (my grandkids call me Big Daddy), friend, and mentor. It helps me in every facet of life.

Lifestyle probably had the largest impact on my life. By focusing on my lifestyle and letting the martial training, meditation, Tai Chi, Qigong, and Jeet Kune Do that Grandmaster Oakes constantly drilled into me in the dojo started to spread into everything I did throughout the day. Everything I touched, moved, and interacted with, I started to see through "martial eyes." My new lifestyle totally changed my outlook on life and started to relieve stress and anxiety. The new physical lifestyle I adopted started to decrease my weight and lower my blood pressure. My wife and I have started living life as naturally as possible without chemicals and using natural remedies for things that we used to turn to pharmaceuticals to heal or give us relief. So, lifestyle has had a huge positive effect on me.

Longevity seems to be the most difficult to define when I ask my students what it means to them. Longevity is not just the healthy benefits that a martial lifestyle will give. It also increases my mentality and awareness of living in the current "now." I perceive things with mental acuteness and personal silent scrutiny, questioning everything's validity and truthfulness. It helps me see public situations, especially in crowded venues, and have a keen eye when watching over my grandchildren while they are playing, unaware of what is happening around them. Longevity has become my development of martial security.

These three words, our pillar credo foundation, are still used today in our dojo, Green Dragon Martial Arts. Grandmaster Oakes has since relocated to Salem, Oregon, and handed the school down to my senior black belt brother, Sigong Jimmy Cahill. Sigong Cahill is the school owner/administrator and financial officer and heads the youth class. I am an officer of the school and head instructor of the adult class. We have partnered to share common goals of growing our school and being an integral part of our community in Chapel Hill, Tennessee. Sigong Cahill is accredited with holding several Women's Self Defense Seminars and has developed great relationships with local businesses and community leaders. With his support, I have developed and hosted the Southern Middle Tennessee Martial Arts Seminar. We just had our second annual event in April 2024 and are poised to grow with over 100 participants next year.

TRAINING INFORMATION

- Martial Arts Styles & Rank: Progressive Kenpo - 5th Degree Black
- Instructors/Influencers: Grandmaster Brian Oakes, Professor Gino Padua, Sigong Jimmy Cahill, Sifu Kevin Gunter
- Birthplace/Growing Up: Camden, TN / Humbolt, TN
- Yrs. In the Martial Arts: 11 years
- Yrs. Instructing: 5 years
- School officer, Adult Instructor & Lifetime Member at Green Dragon Martial Arts

PROFESSIONAL ORGANIZATIONS

- American Warrior Martial Artist Alliance - Member
- North American Quan Fa Association - Secretary Officer
- Oakes Family Kenpo - Lineage Member
- Bigfoot Tactical Martial Arts - Lineage Member

PERSONAL ACHIEVEMENTS

- Founder of Southern Middle Tennessee Martial Arts Seminar (www.smtmas.com)
- Secretary Officer of North American Quan Fa Association
- Member of American Warrior Martial Artists Alliance

MAJOR ACHIEVEMENTS

- Founded the Southern Middle Tennessee Martial Arts Seminar (www.smtmas.com). We completed the 2nd Annual Event on April 19 and 20, 2024

HOW HAS MARTIAL ARTS IMPACTED YOUR LIFE?

Studying martial arts has had nothing but a positive influence on me. It has allowed me to transform my health from an overweight, stressed-out desk jockey to an energetic instructor with increased mental acuteness and spiritual growth. I have come out of my shell to embrace involvement with the local community and my martial family. Being part of Green Dragon Martial Arts has helped me on a personal level so much that my life outside of the dojo has had positive changes. I have gotten closer to my family: my parents, wife, kids, and grandkids.

Martial arts has shown me that I can implement martial techniques within anything in life, not just on the physical level but also on the mental and spiritual level. Mentally, it has pushed me to read and learn more about the history and philosophy of martial arts. Practicing Qigong, Tai Chi, and Kenpo has helped me to quiet my mind and tune in my mental focus. This has opened my heart, helped me spiritually, and brought me closer to God.

Since starting martial arts, I have joined law enforcement tactical training groups, the election commission, and the board of directors for my state land surveying association. Now, I am the treasurer for the TAPS Land Surveyors Political Action Committee Fund.

To summarize how my martial learning has impacted my life, it is a simple statement of positive evidence that has allowed me to grow personally in terms of health and fitness. This transformation has exploded my desire to learn more and more to the point of spilling over into my career as a land surveyor, a teacher, a mentor, an all-around family man, and a community leader. It pushes me to excel to greatness in all areas with a no-ego mentality of striving to improve and being aware of my surroundings, enabling me to see body language and reactions and feel "people-spheric" pressure changes. This is something that most people call tension or say, "The air was thick with tension." In addition, my martial learning has trained my mind to look at and set long-term goals while continuing to work on those small tasks and steps that, when combined, allow me to reach those far-off goals.

Does this really show that I deserve to be in the *AMAA Legacy Book 10th Anniversary Biography* edition? I am not sure I can say that I measure up to those previously published greats. However, my grandmaster, Professor Gino Padua, once told me, "It does not matter what rank you are or have been given by others. It only matters what you are doing where you are now and what you are doing to stay on your path of righteousness for tomorrow."

KAY
WILSON

"
My journey through martial arts has given me the strength, focus, and confidence to meet the challenges of my life...

WHY THE MARTIAL ARTS?

I started in the martial arts at the age of 50. I wanted to challenge myself physically, mentally, and spiritually. I did not want to be a gym rat. Instead, I wanted something to aspire to as an individual and part of a group of like-minded, dedicated people. I was inspired by the fact that other women my age were striving to set an example for me and others.

HOW HAS MARTIAL ARTS IMPACTED YOUR LIFE?

My journey through martial arts has given me the strength, focus, and confidence to meet the challenges of my life, professional, personal, and spiritual. It has also blessed me with lifelong friendships with those I met along the way.

TRAINING INFORMATION
- Martial Arts Styles & Rank: Tae Kwon Do - 1st Dan, Silkisondan Karate - Advanced Brown Belt
- Instructors/Influencers: Grandmaster Russell Burke, Grandmaster Brendan Wilson, Grandmaster Brad Fantle
- Birthplace/Growing Up: Tampa, FL / Military Family
- Yrs. In the Martial Arts: 16 years
- Yrs. Instructing: 2 years
- Instructor

PROFESSIONAL ORGANIZATIONS

- DeKalb County Board of Elections (Judge)
- Kiwanis International
- Aristos Martial Arts
- Kukkiwon
- Flying Ears Competitive Dragon Boat Team

PERSONAL ACHIEVEMENTS

- Experiencing the joys of family and friends
- Mother of two wonderful adult sons
- Grandmother to a beautiful young girl
- Married to my high school sweetheart after a long, broken path to find each other

MAJOR ACHIEVEMENTS

- Achieving a Doctorate at the age of 60
- Earning my black belt at age 63
- National Photography Award from Parade Magazine, top 100 of 120,000 entrants
- BBA in Business Marketing, James Madison University, 1980
- MS in International Relations, Florida State University, 2002
- Ed.D. Florida State University, Education Leadership Policy, 2018
- Pursuing JD at Northern Illinois University, anticipated graduation in 2026

Become an
AMAA MEMBER!

LEVI
WILSON

"

Martial arts has given me a great sense of achievement and peace in my life. I cannot imagine my life without it...

Learning fighting techniques and the use of weapons was fascinating to me as a young boy, but what really spoke to me and continued to drive me to learn more was the art contained within it: The connection of the mind and body, the graceful yet strong movements within the forms and techniques, and the inherent wisdom of generations of masters and practitioners who obviously devoted their lives to the study of it. The prospect of mastering those skills captivated me.

Looking back, I now believe that is what drew me to the martial arts and continued to interest me throughout my formative years. I consider myself very lucky to have found an amazing school and teacher at a young age. I have stayed with the same teacher and school since that first summer, and I am always honored to be able to represent it.

WHY THE MARTIAL ARTS?

I began my martial arts journey when I was eleven years old. My father was searching for a summer program for me to participate in, and through his shared interest in the arts, he found a school in a neighboring town for us to join. I had a great interest in martial arts before joining, which solidified my lifelong participation.

HOW HAS MARTIAL ARTS IMPACTED YOUR LIFE?

Martial arts has afforded me the confidence and fortitude to excel in my professional career. It has given me the strength and determination to care for my family and the challenges that we face in life. After 35 years of acquiring knowledge and experience in self-defense, qigong, and body and mind conditioning practices, I am able to help others in my community by teaching. Martial arts has given me a great sense of achievement and peace in my life. I cannot imagine my life without it, for it is at the very heart of everything I do and feel. It is my way of life.

TRAINING INFORMATION

- Martial Arts Styles & Rank: Shaolin Chuan Fa-1st Degree Black, Kong Sa-3rd Degree Black, US Chuan Fa Association Healer-4th Degree Black, Zu Wei Shu-5th Degree Black, Instructor US Chuan Fa Association Weapons Program
- Instructors/Influencers: Grandmaster Dana Miller, Chunyi Lin, Patricia Bolger, Billie Brown
- Birthplace/Growing Up: Cambridge, MN / Finlayson, MN
- Yrs. In the Martial Arts: 35 years
- Yrs. Instructing: 7 years
- Instructor, Senior Member, US Chuan Fa Association

PROFESSIONAL ORGANIZATIONS

- US Chuan Fa Association

PERSONAL ACHIEVEMENTS

- Zu Wei Shu Student of the Year 2016, 2021-2023

MAJOR ACHIEVEMENTS

- World Head of Family Sokeship Council Hall of Fame inductee-Master Instructor of the Year 2023

Become an
AMAA MEMBER!

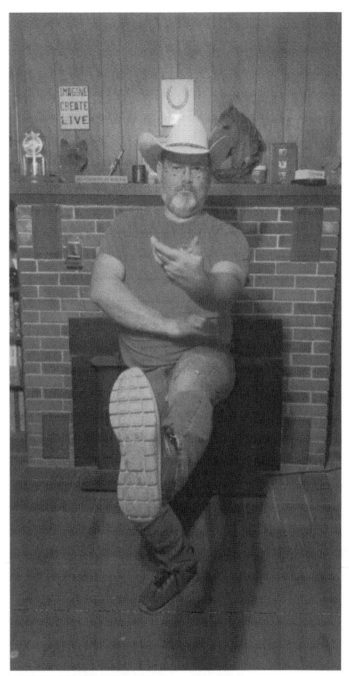

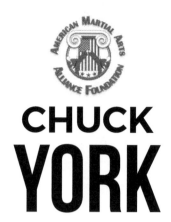

CHUCK
YORK

66

Martial arts have taught me discipline. It's taught me how to be proud of another, even if it's at a loss to me.

HOW HAS MARTIAL ARTS IMPACTED YOUR LIFE?

Martial arts have taught me discipline. It's taught me how to be proud of another, even if it's at a loss to me. It's taught me that for every ounce of pride I get, I wash it down with a bucket of humbleness. It has literally saved my life more than once, including when I had a massive heart attack. It has made me into who I am today.

TRAINING INFORMATION

- Martial Arts Styles & Rank: Shaolin Kung Fu, Five Traditional Animal Styles, Dragon Style, Eight Harmonies Drunken Style, Win Chun (direct lineage of Ip Man), Internal energy, Pa qua, 7th-Degree Black Sash

- Instructors/Influencers: Grand Master Dr. Win Lok John Ng, Grand Master Tim Pickens, Rick Pickens

- Birthplace/Growing Up: Burkesville, KY

- Yrs. In the Martial Arts: 40 years

- Yrs. Instructing: 8 years

- Instructor

WHY THE MARTIAL ARTS?

Like most kids, I was picked on growing up. My dear old dad was nowhere to be seen, so my mom signed me up for karate classes. Soon after, I learned about a different school that teaches Kung Fu. That school was run by two brothers, Masters Tim and Rick Pickens. Grand Master Dr. Win Lok John Ng oversaw the school. I was amazed and instantly hooked. I've been a student with them for 40 years, earning my 7th-degree black sash. Mom wanted me to learn how to defend myself, and boy did I ever.

PERSONAL ACHIEVEMENTS

- One of my most significant personal achievements was earning the approval of Master Pickens and gaining my black sash. This was a testament to my dedication and commitment to martial arts. I also take pride in being able to teach others not just technique but also the appropriate use of martial arts. And yes, I've even mastered the art of slap-breaking coconuts!

MAJOR ACHIEVEMENTS

- Becoming a member of the Elite Guard for the Ng family
- Graduating college and then teaching at the collegiate level
- Managing a power plant - Tva Paradise
- Starting my businesses
- Truly helping someone in need
- Becoming a genuine blacksmith

Become an
AMAA MEMBER!

CHUCK
YOUNG

"

With my attention to detail and love of knowledge, I find Martial Arts fun, fascinating, and challenging...

WHY THE MARTIAL ARTS?

Growing up in a boxing family, I thought it was normal to have your father take you to the gym and teach you how to box, fight, and protect yourself. I would sit in awe, watching my father train and witness his almost superhero-like feats that laid the foundation and set me on my path. In 1976 my parents introduced me to Bruce Lee and that sparked my interest in the kicking arts.

HOW HAS MARTIAL ARTS IMPACTED YOUR LIFE?

The type of person I am has made it easy to study the arts. With my attention to detail and love of knowledge, I find it fun, fascinating, and challenging at the same time. The results from years of dedicated training were well worth it. As I grew into adulthood, my cognitive skills and situational awareness were sharpened, my confidence and my physical strength increased, and I gained a wealth of common sense and life lessons, not to forget all of the different types of people I've had the pleasure to meet and interact with.

Become an
AMAA
MEMBER!

TRAINING INFORMATION

- Martial Arts Styles & Rank: Boxing, Tae Kwon Do-Black Belt, Kickboxing, Muay Thai Kickboxing, Hep Ki Do-Brown Belt, Hiep-Tinh-Mon-Grandmaster
- Instructors/Influencers: SFC Charles M. Young, Adrian Davis, Choi Ji Jun, Lou Chung, Sensei Randy Wozin, Grandmaster Tai Yim, Supreme Grandmaster Quoc Dung Pham
- Birthplace/Growing Up: Washington, DC
- Yrs. In the Martial Arts: 48 years
- Yrs. Instructing: 36 years
- School co-owner & Instructor at Best Martial Arts Styles

PROFESSIONAL ORGANIZATIONS

- Black Magic Filmworks, Incorporate
- Ciyoung Productions LLC
- BloodRose ind. Productions
- Scy Apparel LLC
- Friends of Old Westview Cemetery Inc.

PERSONAL ACHIEVEMENTS

- Teaching martial arts because I love empowering people with the ability to defend themselves and others.
- Becoming a stuntman in the independent film industry
- Inducted in the 2008 USA Martial Arts Hall of Fame
- Inducted into the 2013 & 2019 Legends of Martial Arts Hall of Fame

MAJOR ACHIEVEMENTS

- Raising an awesome son who has started his own company and is doing very well for himself.
- Being a single dad, I am very proud of both of my kids, and I'm proud to say that I have raised two great kids on the same values my parents raised their children on.
- Starting a film company and producing four short films

H. JAMES YOUNG

“
I have discovered that despite all the years of training I have completed... I still have much more to learn.

WHY THE MARTIAL ARTS?

I was a child, I started watching television martial arts shows. During this time frame, the actors' mouths would move, and the words would come out later.

I watched on a large black and white console TV and imitated as much of what I saw of those skillful martial artists on that TV screen. I would watch and mimic as much and as closely as I could the sounds and grunts, the moves, the weaponry, especially the sword, the katana, which I cared for and loved. As a teen, my informal journey started then, and I enjoyed what I had learned from the TV. I would imitate as much of it as possible, trying to remember the moves and maintain my balance.

But when I received information about a karate guy coming to our school, especially to the football locker room, I was thrilled to hear that. Our head coach, Mr. Spades, had invited Mr. Carter, about 5 foot two inches and maybe 130 pounds, to be decked out in this white gi (uniform) and black belt.

Mr. Carter asked who was the baddest person in this room, and before anybody else could say anything, one of the most prominent baddest people I thought, I saw, I played against, and I admit that he was one of the baddest was in the body of Merlin Johnson.

Merlin Johnson was a 285-pound solid man, about 6 feet one inch tall, who played tackle and fullback. Before the "Refrigerator," who played for the Chicago Bears, came out and ran offensive back as a lineman in his regular position. We were doing it before then and long before the Chicago Bears ever did it.

So, Merlin Johnson said he was the baddest, and I agreed. However, Mr. Carter asked Merlin to knock his block off. Merlin asks him for clarification, "Are you sure you want me to hit you, Sir?" Mr. Carter said, "Yes, take your best shot, do whatever you can. I want you to hit me." So, Merlin draws back this humongous fist, coming forth with this powerful punch at this 5-foot-two-inch man! Mr. Carter stepped forward and inside of that punch. And he took a spear hand and gently hit Merlin in his throat, which,

WHY THE MARTIAL ARTS? (CONTINUED)

of course, if he struck him harder, he probably would have killed him. Upon seeing Merlin Johnson, an all-city, meanest tackle in the district that you could ever run into, fall right at the foot of Mr. Carter.

That sold me on karate, and I've been practicing karate since that time frame!

HOW HAS MARTIAL ARTS IMPACTED YOUR LIFE?

I have discovered that despite all the years of training I have completed arriving at the point that I currently am at, I still have much more to learn. My humility and patience in all situations are above board. I learn from everyone, everything, and any level of experience they may have, whether it is as a practitioner or not.

TRAINING INFORMATION

- Martial Arts Styles & Rank: Goju Ryu - 8th Degree, Tae Kwon Do, Jujitsu, Kempo, Kung Fu/Gung Fu, Judo, Jeet Kun Do, Aikido, Aiki Jujitsu, Hapkido
- Instructors/Influencers: SGM Charles Dixon, Grandmaster Thomas Williams
- Birthplace/Growing Up: Texas
- Yrs. In the Martial Arts: 56 years
- Yrs. Instructing: 56 years
- School owner, Manager & Instructor at Youngsan Karate LLC

PROFESSIONAL ORGANIZATIONS

- Classical Martial Arts Club, Ft. Worth, TX (co-founder)
- Black Knight Karate Club
- Ft. Stewart Recreation Center, Ft. Stewart, GA
- Universal Martial Arts Association (TUMAA) Teacher, Ft. Stewart, GA
- Blackbelt Association Sam Houston (BASH), Ft. Sam Houston, TX (co-founder)

PERSONAL ACHIEVEMENTS

- Military Veteran-Retiree (Colonel-US Army)
- Master Degree-Public Administration
- Master Level-Management
- Bachelor's Degree-Psychology and Sociology

MAJOR ACHIEVEMENTS

- Published Authored
- Renshi Title
- Professor Title
- Published in The Sensational 600, Martial Arts Hall of Fame - Dr. Ted Gambordella
- US Head of Family Martial Arts Association International Hall of Honor- Hall of Champions

Made in the USA
Middletown, DE
18 March 2025

72916928R00236